Christopher Page

The Guitar in Georgian England

A Social and Musical History

Yale University Press, New Haven and London

First published by Yale University Press 2020

302 Temple Street, P. O. Box 209040, New Haven, CT 06520-9040
47 Bedford Square, London WC1B 3DP

yalebooks.com | yalebooks.co.uk

ISBN 978-0-300-212471 HB
Library of Congress Control Number: 2020932064

10 9 8 7 6 5 4 3 2 1
2024 2023 2022 2021 2020

Typeset in Garamond by M Rules
Music engraved by The Art of Music, Dunblane, Scotland

Printed and bound in Great Britain by Gomer Press Ltd

Front cover image: Louis Gauffier, portrait of Elizabeth, Lady Webster
(later Lady Holland), 1795, oil on canvas. Bridgeman Images.

Back cover image: Six-course guitar by Manuel Martínez of Málaga, 1803.
Collection of James Westbrook.

Frontispiece: *A Lady of the Petre Family Playing the Guitar*, by
(or in the manner of) Joseph Karl Stieler, 1820, oil on canvas.
Baddesley Clinton, Warwickshire (National Trust).

Published with assistance from the Annie Burr Lewis Fund

For Anne

Voici, chère Anne . . . Ce petit livre sera le messager qui vous dira le souvenir fidèle que je garde de quelques heures d'un bel été.

François Mitterrand to Anne Pingeot, 19 October 1962

Contents

Acknowledgements

My principal debt is to those who generously read the typescript in its entirety: Paul Sparks, Erik Stenstadvold and James Westbrook. Rosemary Roberts saved me from many errors and infelicities; the responsibility for any that remain lies with me. I am also indebted to the members of the Consortium for Guitar Research at Sidney Sussex College, Cambridge: Jelma van Amersfoort, Tony Bingham, Luis Briso de Montiano, Thomas Heck, Brian Jeffery, Gerhard Penn, Panagiotis Poulopoulos, Richard Savino, Kenneth Sparr, Taro Takeuchi and Ulrich Wedemeier. All of them at one time or another have answered my questions, often at length, and I have benefited immensely from hearing their research papers at our meetings and from reading their writings. I am only sorry that one of the greatest among us, Andrew Britton, did not live to see this book finished. I have very often felt the want of his advice. My thanks are due also to members of the Consortium's sister organisation, the Cohort for Guitar Research, from whom I have learned a great deal: Sarah Clarke, Nicoletta Confalone, Miles Henderson Smith, Reggie Lawrence, Luiz Mantovani, Damián Martín, Cla Mathieu, Samantha Muir and Jan van Capelle. Alexander Batov provided various kinds of help and advice. I owe a special debt to Peter Buchanan, who was always ready to help at a moment's notice, and to David Skinner for his work with some of the images.

Special mention should be made of the loyal and appreciative audiences who attended my London lecture series, 'Men, Woman and Guitars in Romantic England', given in my first year as Gresham Professor of Music at Gresham College, where some of the ideas in this book were first presented; I am grateful to the players who illustrated these lectures (Taro Takeuchi, Ulrich Wedemeier, Jelma van Amersfoort, Valerie Mignaco and Grace Davidson). Like all who work on early guitars, I owe much to Kathryn Adamson, chief librarian and guardian of the Spencer Collection at the Royal Academy of Music, but I should also like to thank the staff of the following repositories: the University Library, Cambridge; the Nederlands Muziek Instituut, The Hague; the Houghton Library, Harvard University; the library of the Dolmetsch Foundation, Haslemere; Hertfordshire Record Office, Hertford; the London Metropolitan Archives; The National Archives, Kew; the Kent Archives Office, Maidstone; Derbyshire Record Office, Matlock; Nottinghamshire Record Office, Nottingham; the Bodleian Libraries, Oxford; Lancashire Record Office, Preston; the Library of Congress, Washington; Hampshire Record Office, Winchester; the Surrey History Centre, Woking (especially Julian Pooley); and Worcestershire Record Office, Worcester. Gillian Malpass, formerly of Yale University Press, believed in this book from the beginning, and I am most grateful to Lydia Cooper for seeing it through the editing stages and production.

A friend of mine, with a lifetime's experience of playing the guitar to a professional level, recently remarked that some of the pieces I quote, in full or in part, in this book seemed rather less interesting to him than my commentary made them appear. I suspect that those guitar players, like my friend, who have had some of the most sophisticated music for the guitar under their fingers will perhaps share his impression. In this book, however, I have tried to assess the music as it might have been perceived by the average Georgian amateur with only a modest level of technical ability. I doubt if the author of a historical work has ever modelled an account quite so shamelessly upon himself.

Cambridge
Lent Term, 2020

Abbreviations

BD   P. H. Highfill *et al.*, eds, *A Biographical Dictionary of Actors, Actresses, Musicians, Dancers, Managers & other Stage Personnel in London, 1660–1800*, 16 vols (Carbondale: Southern Illinois University Press, 1973–93)

BUCEM   E. B. Schnapper, ed., *The British Union-Catalogue of Early Music Printed before the Year 1801*, 2 vols (London: Butterworth Scientific Publications, 1957)

ECCO   *Eighteenth Century Collections Online*, at www.gale.com/intl/primary-sources/eighteenth-century-collections-online

EEBO   *Early English Books Online* at https://eebo.chadwyck.com/home

ELH   *English Literary History*

EM   *Early Music*

GISE   C. Page, *The Guitar in Stuart England: A Social and Musical History* (Cambridge: Cambridge University Press, 2017)

GITE   C. Page, *The Guitar in Tudor England: A Social and Musical History* (Cambridge: Cambridge University Press, 2015)

GSJ   *Galpin Society Journal*

HMC   Historical Manuscripts Commission

JAMS	*Journal of the American Musicological Society*
LS	W. Van Lennep *et al.*, eds, *The London Stage, 1660–1800: A Calendar of Plays, Entertainments and Afterpieces, together with Casts, Box-Receipts and Contemporary Comment*, 5 parts in 11 (Carbondale: Southern Illinois University Press, 1960–68); rev. version of pt 2 online at www.personal.psu.edu/faculty/h/b/hb1/London%20Stage%202001
ODNB	*Oxford Dictionary of National Biography: From the Earliest Times to the Year 2000*, ed. H. C. G. Matthew and B. Harrison, 61 vols (Oxford: Oxford University Press, 2004); rev. and updated version online at www.oxforddnb.com
OED	*Oxford English Dictionary*, online at www.oed.com
RECM	A. Ashbee, ed., *Records of English Court Music*, 9 vols (Snodland and Aldershot: A. Ashbee, 1986–96)
RISM	*Répertoire international des sources musicales* (Munich: Henle, 1960–); online at https://opac.rism.info/metaopac/start.do?View=rism&Language=en
RMARC	*Royal Musical Association Research Chronicle*
TNA	The National Archives, Kew

Introduction

In January 1832 readers of the *Dorset County Chronicle* were advised that a London instrument-maker had sold 'upwards of *three thousand*' guitars since the preceding August (original emphasis).[1] The figure is incredible and was probably invented to enhance the business of a Dorchester guitar teacher who is mentioned in the same article; yet in a sense it was not entirely misleading. By 1832 the current of enthusiasm for playing the guitar in Georgian England was flowing rapidly, following its own channel with a vigorous independence. During a transformative period for the musical profession in general, when players were assimilating masterworks of instrumental music newly imported from Austria and Germany, the guitar remained resolutely the favourite of amateurs and supported very few professional careers. Those amateurs, repeatedly told by pundits writing for new musical journals, such as *The Harmonicon*, that they should cultivate music of more lasting value,[2] used the guitar above all for accompanying opera airs and ballads. Many of these players were young women, and they have left a very significant mark on Georgian portraiture; but the guitar was also played by men during the Napoleonic Wars and beyond, as interactions between soldiering and fashion allowed new constructions of stylish and even dandyish masculinity to form. Although the guitar was often derided by its critics for being meagre, a larger flock of literary and Romantic associations took wing when a player opened a guitar case than any other instrument of the day could release; there were memories of the lute and the abundant literature in which it was praised, and associations with the warm south, the vastness of a still pre-industrial Spain and the struggles of her people for liberty.

The great vogue for the guitar in Georgian England, which ran from approximately 1800 to the mid-1830s, is generally passed over in silence today. Even exponents of the modern 'classical' guitar rarely look beyond a few of the more significant solo works of the period. In recent years, however, there has been a marked revival of interest in the early nineteenth-century guitar, with players using reconditioned originals and replicas to recover period sonorities and playing techniques.[3] More recently still, it has become clear that the guitar vogue has a history in England that may be compared with contemporary developments in other European countries, most of which long ago found their chroniclers.[4] The premonitory signs appeared in London around 1800, in step with Vienna (though behind Paris), and the number of guitar methods printed in the British capital between 1795 and 1820 exceeds the total for any other Western European metropolis save its French counterpart. London was also the city where a guitarist of international fame, Fernando Sor, first showed his talent for a sustained period outside of his native Iberia, and numerous other established guitarists were drawn to the musical marketplace of the Georgian capital, and to the major spas and coastal resorts. Some of them settled and never left, including Giulio Regondi, Luigi Sagrini, Leonard Schulz and Madame Pratten (Catharina Pelzer).

What is more, the course of the great vogue for the guitar in England was in some respects exceptional, being broadly comparable to circumstances in Germany and Austria but not closely tracking the experience of most Romance-speaking countries. Guitars had been established for so long in Spain and Italy that they were indigenous to those countries in a sense that they never were to England, despite phases of high fashion in the Elizabethan and Stuart periods, while during the later eighteenth century the English only intermittently followed the French in regarding the guitar as a courtly and *galant* instrument. In England the guitar was regarded by its many critics as a shallow and 'fashionable' pleasure, which is one of the reasons why the modern neglect of the Georgian guitar boom may be said to have roots in the Georgian period itself.[5] The movements and diversions of the 'fashionables' who lived in the West End of London – the home of government and the royal residences – were recorded week by week in the *Morning Post* and the *Morning Chronicle*; at the very beginning of the nineteenth century these reports show that the guitar was beginning to win some elite devotees (Chapter 4). Many of the nobility and higher gentry who lived in this exclusive quarter of London led such scandalous lives of leisure, adultery and debt that it was almost impossible to use the words 'fashion' and 'fashionable' in a manner that avoided all hint of disapproval, or indeed misogyny since fashion was often associated with the expensive and volatile tastes attributed to women. Many of those who lived through the period of the great vogue for the guitar did not see it as a significant innovation in the public musical life of the day but rather as a private and ephemeral interest of wealthy or socially ambitious women.

The instrument at issue here is the one the English generally called the 'Spanish guitar' from at least the second quarter of the eighteenth century.[6] There is nothing mysterious about this usage, for it still survives in Britain, where the expression 'Spanish guitar' means, in general terms, what it meant in 1800: a plucked and fretted instrument with a figure-of-eight-shaped body, a predominantly flat back, a combined bridge and string-holder on the belly and a large round aperture there, or sound-hole. The frontispiece shows a late Georgian example played by a young woman from a noble family; it is a superior example of the imagery that insistently associates the guitar with young women, even to the point where today's Spaniards and Italians, with their traditions of exclusively male serenading and guitar-playing barbers, are taken aback to discover that an English male of the Romantic period who picked up a guitar was in danger of appearing effeminate. Almost all the concert guitarists of the great vogue period in Britain were males, but that only confirmed the questionable manliness of the guitar, for they were all foreigners.

The lady shown in the frontispiece seems so docile that one may easily forget that she is actively repudiating another kind of guitar altogether, and one that had held sway in the days of her mother and grandmother (Fig. 1). It is an oddity of the great vogue for the Spanish guitar in Britain that from approximately 1750 until at least 1800 a 'guitar' to the British was (for the most part) a different species of instrument from the one generally understood elsewhere to be a guitar – that is to say, one of the kind shown in the frontispiece. This different species is now commonly called the 'English guitar' in accordance with a rare but genuine usage of the eighteenth century.[7] Chapter 2 is devoted to this instrument, which is not the principal focus of this book but cannot be ignored, since, to Laurence Sterne, Dr Johnson and David Garrick, it was a guitar, indeed *the* guitar. The body was often shaped somewhat like a lute or mandolin, though the back was generally flat, and the strings were of wire, not of gut and overspun silk like those of a Spanish guitar. It therefore produced quite a different sound from its Spanish rival and was tuned in a fundamentally different way – namely, to an open major or minor chord.[8] During the second half of the eighteenth century, to speak of a guitar in Britain was predominantly to evoke this instrument, for it enjoyed considerable success for some three generations.

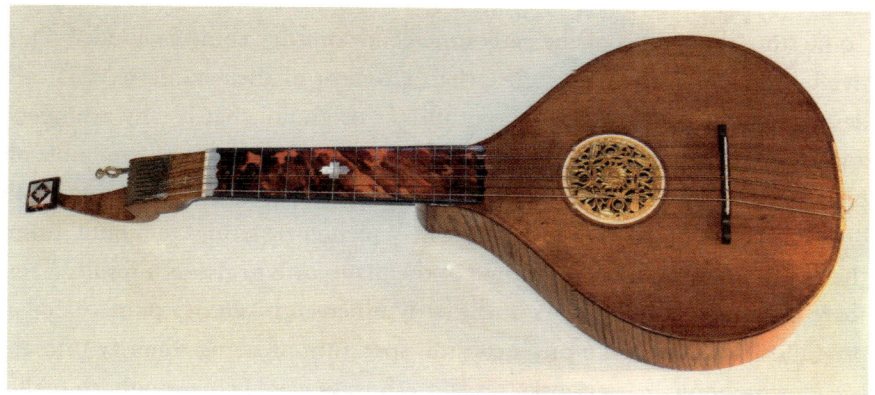

Fig. 1   English guitar, *c.*1768, with the brand-mark 'Longman & Co.'. Private collection.

Given the difference between the sound of the gut-strung Spanish guitar and its wire-mounted English competitor, contemporary observers were not necessarily well advised to interpret the ascendancy of the Spanish instrument after 1800 as a matter of *fashion* with its connotations of transience and caprice. The preference gradually given to gut as opposed to metal indicates a potentially wide-ranging change of taste in sonority that probably encompassed the rise of the harp as the salon instrument *par excellence* of the nobility during the later eighteenth century, both in England and France, and the decline of the plucked-wire harpsichord, which in 1800 was about to become 'the silent denizen of storerooms, attics, and museum galleries'.[9] Furthermore, the English guitar, thoroughly integrated into the musical life of Britain from the 1770s onwards, lost ground around 1800 to its seemingly more cosmopolitan Spanish rival during one of the most stridently xenophobic periods in British political life, inspired by war with the godless, regicidal and republican French.

This is perhaps all the more surprising since the Spanish guitar flourished, like its English counterpart, within a distinct musical ecology, which was not in every respect advantageous to the amateur.[10] Players of the violin and pianoforte could nurture ambitions in private that fed on the good example of professionals displayed in concert. For the most part, however, guitarists could not do that because the soft voice of their instrument was generally considered unsuitable for most concert spaces; a zestfully unkind commentator observed in 1836 that the Spanish guitar seemed just calculated 'for the space of a sentry box or the back room of a shopkeeper in the Burlington Arcade ... in a spacious concert room it is even worse than contemptible'.[11]

To be sure, the guitars of the early nineteenth century could be louder, relative to contemporary pianofortes, than are most of their modern 'classical' descendants relative to the modern upright or grand; that is why arrangers and composers during the great vogue period could write for an ensemble of pianoforte and guitar, a combination that became increasingly impractical once cast-iron frames allowed the tension of pianoforte strings to mount, from the 1820s onwards, and the volume of the pianoforte to rise as a result.[12] Yet there is no doubt that guitars of the early nineteenth century perpetuated a pre-industrial and even a pre-orchestral spectrum of string sonority into an age of symphonic masterworks, when fresh ways were being sought to make some mainstream instruments louder.

The sounding string length of guitars in the early nineteenth century was generally a little shorter than on modern instruments, reaching about 630 mm as compared with the 650 mm common today, and the bodies were significantly smaller.[13] The elements glued under the soundboard, for reasons of strength or sonority, could accordingly be more sparse, on the whole, and makers often disposed them as their forebears had done for some two hundred years. With due allowance made for the effects of reconditioning, which is often necessary, modern experiments with original guitars produce a drier and lighter sound than today's players would expect from their instruments; the contrast is greater still when the original is authentically strung with gut and overspun silk and plucked with the flesh of the fingertips, a common (but not the only) technique of the period.[14] With very few exceptions, attempts to make the guitar louder in the early 1800s came to little. 'Many distinguished professors of the guitar', wrote a journalist for *The Harmonicon* in 1829, have tried 'to raise the instrument from the inferior rank which it holds in the sonorous class', but 'only a thin, brief and dry sound has proceeded from the frail machine'.[15]

Although many spaces used as concert rooms were considered too large for the guitar to make much effect, this was a more complex judgement than may first appear. In part, it reflected the unfortunate circumstances in which guitarists might find themselves when they secured a spot in a concert; the programme might also include an orchestra or even a military band, hired to play an overture before each section or 'Act', which could leave an audience quite incapable of appreciating the intimate effects the guitar had to offer. In 1827, for example, Trinidad Huerta played a fantasia on a bill that also included Beethoven's C minor symphony, the Fifth, the orchestra being 'on the splendid scale of the Philharmonic Concerts'.[16] What is more, metropolitan and provincial expectations generally seem to have been different, for guitar players *do* appear on the bills of provincial concerts in theatres and the assembly rooms of inns, from the very beginning of the nineteenth century, although those who played in the provincial venues were generally singers accompanying themselves, not soloists offering sets of variations or sonatas.

The Spanish guitar nonetheless had a considerable appeal, based on some practical advantages to the amateur that no other instrument could exactly match. At a time when standards of amateur and professional performance were rising, as many contemporaries noted,[17] the guitar yielded results within six months or less if the player was not too ambitious, and might require no more than a dozen lessons or even just the purchase of a published method. The six strings offered all the harmonies commonly used in song, from Scottish ballads to Italian operatic arias. Moreover, by 1800 the guitar had undergone certain changes whose significance may be measured by the fact that they have remained in place, for the most part, ever since.[18] In effect, the guitar was renewed at the end of the eighteenth century. Figure 2 shows the guitar as it was widely played during the late 1700s in France and England before these seminal changes were made. There are five courses, all double save the highest, with low octaves or *bourdons* ('basses') on courses four and five a very common arrangement. By 1800 the gut ligatures that served as frets had commonly been replaced by strips of brass, bone or ivory, and the round aperture in the belly emptied of the decorative filling-in of parchment or fretwork. By the same date, strings of overspun silk, known to the Chinese by the eighth century but slow to make their way in the Occident,[19] had come into common use for the basses, offering a tonal response widely held to be more satisfactory than basses of plain gut. Finally, the double-course arrangement had been abandoned almost everywhere, though the Spanish held out until the 1820s.[20]

As far as English playing was concerned, the most recent change by 1800 was the addition of an E string in the bass, creating the guitar of six single strings that has remained the standard form of the instrument ever since.[21] Thus Felice Chabran's *Compleat Instructions for the Spanish Guitar* (1795) teaches the playing of a guitar of five single strings, but the Italian songs that Antonio Zaniboni dedicated to the West End socialite Lady Emily Stratford in 1802 require six. By enhancing the bass capacity, and by extending

Fig. 2 Five-course guitar and its tuning (with low octaves, or *bourdons*, on courses four and five), from B. D. C., *Méthode de guittarre par musique et tablature* (Paris, 1773), 6. Private collection.

the array of chords that could be played with the root as the lowest sounding note, the additional string altered the balance between the guitar's inherited tradition of fingerboard empiricism, as it might be called, and literate musical thinking very much in favour of the latter. With the exception of electrification, the guitar has never undergone a more potent change.

The appeal of the Spanish guitar, however, cannot be measured in practical terms alone, nor in relation to any simple model of emulation in which the members of a very narrow social elite set the fashion for their imitators. Chabran's *Compleat Instructions for the Spanish Guitar* appeared just before the first documented appearance of that instrument as a new amateur musical fashion among the West End elite, yet the player shown on the title page of Chabran's book does not represent the social class of Lady Emily Stratford, nor is she in Spanish national dress (see Fig. 18). She appears as a British serving-maid wearing a bonnet and apron, sitting with her guitar in what must be the garden of a cottage (to judge by her chair), not the drawing room of a London mansion. The image evokes contemporary depictions of country women spinning or otherwise working at their cottage door; the artist, Vincent Woodthorpe, has drawn on a sentimental, anti-Rococo fondness for the unadorned circumstances of rural life reaching far back into the eighteenth century, with *The Seasons* (1730) by James Thomson as one of its earliest monuments and the Wordsworth–Coleridge *Lyrical Ballads*, first published in 1798, as one of the century's last.[22] Nothing further from 'fashion', in any commonly accepted sense of the term, could be readily imagined. The appeal of the guitar was more complex, perhaps more conflicted, than the apparent simplicity of its means might appear to warrant, or than even the most far-reaching understanding of fashion might sustain.

The market for guitars, guitar music and lessons in Georgian England, which may be said to open with Chabran's method of 1795, was invigorated by the newspapers, and especially by their advertisements, both in the London dailies and, increasingly, in the provincial equivalents, which were generally published weekly or even, at first, occasionally. By 1800 England was the world capital of newsprint and home to an information nexus of great complexity;[23] by publishing details of grain prices, the arrival or departure of cargoes, stock values and much else, the newspapers helped to promote the manufacturing boom that took off in England between 1780 and 1800. Together with the proceeds of the French wars, which enriched many suppliers and dealers, this manufacturing ascendancy was the prime source of the surplus wealth that allowed the guitar to prosper as widely as it eventually did among those called the 'middle classes' by the 1820s. The newspapers provided a public noticeboard for instrument-makers announcing a new line, for teachers proclaiming their recent arrival in town and for players advertising a benefit concert. The scope of this material is now almost overwhelming. At the time of writing, the *British Newspaper Archive* returns more than 11,000 instances of the term 'guitar' (in both singular and plural) for a filtered search setting the datelines 1 January 1800 to 31 December 1835, of which nearly a quarter are advertisements.[24] Eighteenth-century books, journals and pamphlets, searchable through *Eighteenth Century Collections Online* and the *17th and 18th Century Burney Newspapers Collection*, add as many again; the *19th Century UK Periodicals* database and various other online sources add still more.

This abundant material must be read with abundant care. Reviews of concerts and pre-concert articles on players new in town were often shameless puffs, sometimes written by the artists themselves. Much that was praised in advertisements for being novel was not really new, and the same may be said for many of the anecdotes for which the newspapers found a surprising amount of space, recognising the need to be companionable as well as informative. These anecdotes often appear to recount some recent event, but chance discoveries occasionally reveal that they have been drawn from a stock whose materials had been passing freely for some time between encyclopedias, the miscellaneous sections in periodicals and in digests. Press reports of court cases, where guitar players appear more often than they should, involved substantial rewriting of witness testimony before typesetting as a matter of course, and while different newspapers often agree on the main facts of a case they vary greatly in the amount of detail that they include. Lists of items put up for auction when houses were cleared, because the owner had died or was selling up before moving elsewhere, often mention guitars, but often they do not for they merely reveal what caught the eye of some harassed clerk at the auction house. Accounts of high-society events in London's West End, an important source in the earliest days of the vogue for the guitar, were sometimes written at the direction of the host, the editor of the newspaper having the luxury of choosing which ones he would print from the many on offer.

Yet, when carefully filtered and collated with the reviews and articles in new musical journals such as the *Quarterly Musical Magazine and Review* or *The Harmonicon*, the newspaper material proves to be crucial. It reveals, for example, that a series of foreign virtuosi eventually convinced a section of the public, and even some music pundits, that their instrument could take its place among those with a more established professional profile. The Romantic trope of the musician who achieves a heroic triumph over his instrument is well exemplified – perhaps nowhere better – in the rhetoric that some of these converts lavished on the best guitarists, often in distantly retrospective notices that significantly reduce the risk of our being misled by biased judgements (as opposed to reports composed soon before, or soon after, a particular performance). A critic writing for the *New Monthly Magazine and Literary Journal* in 1827 was astonished by Trinidad Huerta, for the 'depth and variety of tone he can call forth are incredible, inconceivable to those who have not heard him; he gives to the puny instrument in his hand an effect like that of a band of music, heard through some diminishing medium'.[25] There was a clear sense by now that a significant development in musical life had occurred in relation to the guitar, generating newspaper reviews, advertisements and articles in the periodical press, together with published arrangements of songs, both new and long established, the occasional published showpiece for solo guitar and light chamber works enlisting flute, violin or pianoforte. The guitar had arrived. This is how it happened.

ONE

The Guitar in the Time of Anne Stuart, Princess and Queen (1665–1714)

... the fine easie Ghittar, whose
performance is soon gained ...

Edward Chamberlayne,
The Present State of England (1683)

When Britain's experiment with republican government came to an end in 1660, King Charles II returned from exile with the best of intentions and a guitar.[1] The diarist Samuel Pepys (serving his relative Edward Montagu, 1st Earl of Sandwich) was given the task of seeing the instrument safely from the wide beach at Deal to Whitehall, complaining all the way. At court, where it is always wise to respect the pastimes of a prince, Charles's enthusiasm for the guitar ensured that it was widely cultivated among those who were lodged, however briefly, in the royal palaces to attend upon him or to make their petitions. According to one who was there, the instrument enjoyed 'such a vogue' around the king 'that everybody played it, well or badly, and one was as sure to see a guitar on the dressing tables of court women' as their cosmetics. Despite the *frisson* of this glimpse into the boudoir, the same observer records that men also played, including the future James II, 'the most unguarded ogler of his time'.[2] Light, insouciant and often tricked out with surface decoration, answering well to a philosophy of life that valued the pleasures of sense, the guitar consorted well with the rakish masculinity admired at the Restoration court.

These details are recorded in the *Mémoires de la vie du comte de Grammont* by Anthony Hamilton (d. 1719), an extensive and anecdotal account of English court life in the 1660s. The book was written long after the events Hamilton describes and is essentially a historical novel, a genre just then emerging in precisely such embroidered accounts of historical personages as the *Mémoires*.[3] It nonetheless embodies the eye-witness experience of two Restoration courtiers (the Comte de Grammont and Hamilton himself), and their combined picture of the guitar in the royal entourage is largely confirmed by other sources. There were indeed players among the highest royal servants, as Hamilton maintains, probably including Sir William Waldegrave, physician to James II (Fig. 3), and Diana Bridgeman (née Vernatti), first among the waiting women of Anna, Duchess of Buccleuch and Monmouth, played the

Fig. 3 *The Guitar Player*, by Jacques van Schuppen, *c*.1700?, oil on canvas. The gentleman is thought to be Sir William Waldegrave (d. 1701), with his wife and her niece. Waldegrave was a physician to Mary of Modena, second wife of James II, and latterly to James himself. This painting was made when he resided in France at the court of his exiled master. Waldegrave made a setting of Edmund Waller's poem 'On my Lady Isabella Playing on the Lute', which takes pride of place in one of Samuel Pepys's guitar books. Walker Art Gallery, Liverpool.

guitar 'with such extraordinary skill, and dexterity, as I hardly ever heard any lute exceed for sweetenesse', according to John Evelyn.[4] This was by no means a purely court fashion, however. Samuel Pepys, a naval administrator who was never a courtier in the strict sense, began to learn the guitar in the 1670s. In the following decade an advanced manual on continuo practice for the instrument, *The False Consonances of Musick* by Nicola Matteis, was advertised in a news sheet widely read by 'harassed parish clergy, embattled magistrates, churchwardens and vestrymen'.[5] In 1666, the year of London's Great Fire, the leading musical entrepreneur of Stuart England, John Playford, even found cause to complain that women working in alehouses were sending their daughters to guitar masters who were French, or pretended to be so.[6]

Interest continued beyond the Restoration years. James II's daughter Anne, later to become queen, played essentially the variety of guitar shown in Figure 2. Her guitar book, perhaps in use as late as 1702, survives and contains over a hundred pieces copied by an unknown scribe, who was French, to judge by the way he spells the names of the various musical forms represented there.[7] In addition to the expected minuets, gavottes, gigues, sarabandes and tunes from various editions of Playford's *The Dancing Master*, the collection includes arrangements of theatre songs by Henry Purcell. Such was the patronage, and such the repertoire, that the guitar could command in England around the turn of the eighteenth century.

The guitar in the early Georgian years

By studying the guitar, Princess Anne was sharing in an education that many young gentlewomen received. A pamphlet of 1703, entitled *The Levellers: A Dialogue between Two Young Ladies, concerning Matrimony*, shows two young women debating the difficulty of making a good marriage; one had attended a boarding school where she learned 'to dance and sing, to play on the Bass-Viol, Virginals, Spinnet and Guitair. I learned to make Wax-work, japan, paint upon Glass, to raise Paste, make Sweet-meets, Sauces, and every thing that was genteel and fashionable.'[8] The very name of the guitar here suggests the instrument's 'genteel and fashionable' air in the boarding schools of the early 1700s, for the spelling 'Guitair' is not a mistake but a satirical attempt to convey the sound of French *guiterre* as imitated by the English. By the eighteenth century, *guiterre* was considered an archaic form in France; here it suggests that the lessons offered in the schools were somewhat conservative and old-fashioned in their repertoire and approach, at least when judged by contemporary French standards.

The guitar teachers who attended the boarding schools of 1700, none of whom are known by name, were probably masters of the harpsichord, violin or bass viol, who had taken up the guitar as a sideline; they also made home visits to the residences of the professional classes, whose membership is estimated to have grown by some 70 per cent between 1680 and 1730.[9] In John Vanbrugh's play *The Confederacy* of 1705 the daughter of a wealthy money scrivener receives her guitar lessons at home:

> Clarissa: Where's Corinna? Call her to me, If her Father han't lock'd her up; I want her company.
> Jessamin [*Foot-boy to Clarissa*]: Madam, her guitar master is with her.
> Clarissa: Psha, she's taken up with her impertinent guitar man.[10]

As a money scrivener, Corinna's father combined functions now shared between stockbrokers and estate agents; he would not have enjoyed the prestige of lawyers or physicians in the older profession, but Vanbrugh here reveals the kind of social ambition that such members of a new but flourishing occupation, their wealth not tied to land, might conceive for a daughter.[11]

Neither *The Levellers* nor Vanbrugh's comedy gives any indication that playing the guitar to a high standard, with the accompanying refinement of hearing and touch, might enrich the inner life of a young woman; seen through the lens of satire and homily, lessons on the guitar appeared to be an expensive indulgence, liable to retard her homely instincts by making her flighty and headstrong. According to William Darrel in 1708, the damage began as soon as a female child was old enough to leave the nursery and learned 'to plie at the Dancing-School, and to finger the Guitar, or the Virginals; and when she has master'd a *Minuet*, and an Air *A-la-mode* . . . she is now fledg'd for the World, and sets out for Company'.[12] Almost in spite of himself, Darrel reveals that such lessons prepared a young woman to take flight as she set out 'for Company', meaning her immersion in the London world of balls and card parties, where her parents trusted she would find a suitable husband and cease to be their care; it is the world vividly but contemptuously described by John Trenchard in 1722 as one where the daughters of wealthy men 'Dance, Dress, play upon the Guitar ... prate in a Visiting Room' and 'play amongst Sharpers at Cards and Dice'.[13]

An exuberant miscellany of 1710, entitled *The Ladies Cabinet Broke Open,* takes a more admiring view, though its tone is ribbing throughout and highly unstable. The preface praises the book's two female dedicatees, given the names Dorinda and Bellair, for their various accomplishments; they are noted writers of prose and verse, they have a good knowledge of French and Italian, and the reader may depend on it that a 'collection of original letters, translations & poems both serious and comical', shaped by their lively interests and tastes, as this one is, will be worth reading. Dorinda and Bellair cultivate an impressive 'air' when playing the guitar, and although the results merit no better description than 'thrumming' they perform with such grace that others must defer to them. The rhyme holds the pronunciation of the word 'Guitar' once more to an imitation of French *guiterre*:

> You Dance to a Miracle, and Sing, and Play upon the Lord k[n]ows how many Instruments,

> *And Thrumb a Guitar,*
> *With such an Air,*
> *And such a Grace;*
> *That all must give Place,*
> *When your Musick they hear.*[14]

The title *The Ladies Cabinet Broke Open* probably alludes to *The Lady's Pacquet Broke Open,* a series of letters on contemporary scandals by the female playwright, polemicist and poet Delarivier Manley, published three years earlier; if its dedicatees Dorinda and Bellair are more than a fiction standing for all the 'female wits', then, beginning to challenge the notion that authorship was a male prerogative, they may be codes for Manley and another female writer of the period, perhaps Catherine Trotter. Whatever the case may be, the guitar seems to have kept the place it enjoyed in the days of Catherine Philips and Henry Lawes as the instrument of widened, not narrowed, female minds.[15]

All the guitar players mentioned in these polemics and satires are female, a gender bias that does not accord with the legacy of the Restoration years when the guitar was also played by elite males (Fig. 3). The satires and polemics quoted above filter out the male guitarist because they are all forms of misogynistic critique. That being said, the light and insouciant guitar clearly raised questions about the pleasures and pursuits acceptable for males once libertine guitarists of the Restoration like Celadon in Dryden's tragicomedy *Secret Love* (1667) had ceased to be fashionable; by the time Queen Anne's reign began in 1702 the guitar had acquired an air, in relation to men, not of hedonistic sexual indulgence but of sexual deviance. Thomas Baker's play *Tunbridge Walks* of 1703 presents a young man, transparently named Maiden, who pretends to a great estate; he can paint upon glass, sing, dance and 'play upon the Guittar', all accomplishments taught in the boarding schools for young gentlewomen.[16] (A 'maiden name' was a sobriquet adopted by a member of the homosexual subculture, or given to him by others.) He uses a fan and pocket looking-glass to preserve his grooming, and in the tradition of the Restoration fop is terrified by the sight of a drawn sword; despising rakishness, he has no taste for the tavern, where he fears he may be raped. This is partly a class satire as well as a homophobic one, for Maiden had once been a milliner's apprentice who sold ribbons in the Exchange, and he returns to that trade at the close of the play, when his imposture is revealed and it emerges that he does not have the fine estate he claims.

The trade cards of some instrument-makers and dealers suggest that Maiden would have had no difficulty buying a guitar in Queen Anne's London, although the instruments were perhaps more often imports than London made. Figure 4 shows the trade card of Richard Meares, probably Richard Meares the younger, who died around 1743 and inherited the care of a long-established firm in St Paul's churchyard. Expansively cosmopolitan with texts in English, French and Italian, the card shows a guitar at the bottom right, plausibly drawn save that there are only seven strings where there should be nine. Such images are not a sure guide to a dealer's stock, for they draw upon an iconography nurtured in Flemish prints of the sixteenth century, in carved panels and in plasterwork festoons; yet merchants had no interest in appearing old-fashioned. Dealers like Meares, father and son, would have sold to guitar players the strings they stocked for other instruments, notably the members of the violin family, for no strings were marketed specifically for the guitar.[17] The Italian makers had a particularly high reputation; their names could travel far as a guarantee of quality, and Richard Meares senior names the string-maker Antonio Frezza of Rome in an advertisement of 1724.[18] Players in the provinces could turn to the 'Country Shop-keeper[s] and

Others' that London musical emporia such as Simpson's of Sweeting Alley undertook to supply on request. Those pursuing other, non-musical trades might also have strings to sell; examples revealed by provincial newspapers include an ironmonger in Stamford and a watchmaker in Newcastle.[19]

Some printed music for the guitar, produced in the seventeenth century and all of continental origin, was to be found in some London shops around 1700. An issue of the *London Gazette* for that year reveals a dealer offering unpublished music by Francisco Corbetta, the seventeenth-century virtuoso whose name still counted for something in London nearly two decades after his death and the end of his Westminster years. The dealer in this instance was a French immigrant, Monsieur Desert, whose shop was in the Long Acre quarter long favoured by the French; in addition to 'very fine Lessons of Francisco Corbet's, never made Publick', and other new pieces, 'some for two Guitars, or a Guitar and a Flute or Violin, in Two Parts', Monsieur Desert offered 'several

Fig. 4 Trade card of Richard Meares (probably the younger, d c.1743), instrument-maker at the Golden Viol & Hautboy in St Paul's Churchyard. Tony Bingham Collection, London.

Chapter One

extra ordinary fine and good Guitars of all Sizes and Prices to sell from 30 Guineas to 30s. a-piece, some very good for singing'.[20] In 1701 François Vaillant, bookseller in the Strand, announced that he was handling music printed by Étienne Roger in Amsterdam, including 'a great collection of Harpsicord, Luth, Guitare and Viol Books, all ingraven and printed as abovesaid' – that is to say, 'engraven on Copper Plates, and printed upon fine paper'.[21] The next year he was offering more, composed by Nicolas Derosiers, with the guitar part available separately.[22] He also sold copies of Derosiers's method, *Les principes de la guitarre* of 1689, which offers a rapid digest of the Baroque guitarist's art: the standard ornaments in the French sources, three methods for tuning, and a set of chaconnes, in different keys, using a mixed style of strumming and plucking.[23] At the very beginning of the eighteenth century anyone interested in the guitar could find several London shops stocked with all they required.

Many of the melodies played on the guitar were no doubt drawn from the theatres, balls and dancing schools, and were arranged by players or their teachers; since so little of this music survives, the work must generally have been done without recourse to either stave notation or tablature. Many theatre songs, opera airs and dance melodies famously appear in the collections issued under the title *Wit and Mirth; or Pills to Purge Melancholy*, culminating in the celebrated six-volume set of 1719–20 assembled by Jacob Tonson and containing 350 songs by Thomas Durfey. More are in the five volumes of *The Musical Miscellany* of 1729–31 published by John Watts, who was also responsible for printing numerous ballad operas, with their airs, in the wake of John Gay's *Beggar's Opera* of 1728. A melody such as 'The Duke d'Aumond's Minuet', also known as 'Let Burgundy flow', may represent the kind of piece that William Darrel associated with boarding-school guitarists in 1708: those who looked no further than a minuet or two for their repertoire (Ex. 1). It would surely have suited General Lewis Dejean, of Huguenot descent, shown playing the guitar in a group portrait of about 1733 produced by a French artist for a British country gentleman.[24]

In social terms, the guitar of Queen Anne's day was by no means an exclusively elite instrument. There were guitarists among the clowns of the *commedia dell'arte*, including Scaramouche, the comic persona that the Italian comedian Tiberio Fiorilli (1608–1694) bequeathed to a host of followers.[25] One was Joseph Sorine, who joined Thomas Betterton's theatre company at Lincoln's Inn Fields in July 1696.[26] The next year, Sorine played Pasquarel in *The Novelty* by Peter Motteux and others, a composite entertainment whose fifth act, a

Ex. 1 Upper stave: 'The Duke d'Aumond's Minuet' (or 'Let Burgundy flow'), as it appears in the published version of James Ralph's ballad opera of 1730, *The Fashionable Lady; or, Harlequin's Opera*. Lower stave: a conjectural realisation for a five-course guitar.

'farce after the Italian manner', required Sorine to tune and then play a guitar held by Pantalone. Motteux was in some doubt whether such antics suited the 'Genius of our [English] Stage', but the piece was a success and that settled the matter. Sorine and his long-standing partner Baxter, as Harlequin, caused a stir in August 1702 with a nocturnal scene, performed once more 'after the Italian manner', according to the advertisement in the *Daily Courant* for 22 August; they used a guitar, or something given that name, as the anonymous author of *A Comparison between the Two Stages* noted: 'What a rout here was with a Night piece of *Harlequin* and *Scaramouch*? with the Guittar and the Bladder! What jumping over Tables and Joint-Stools! What ridiculous Postures and Grimaces!'[27] Sorine probably used a guitar again in 1704 when he and Baxter performed interludes of Scaramouche and Harlequin at Southwark Fair with a company of rope-dancers.[28] Later, in 1716, payments for props show that 1s.

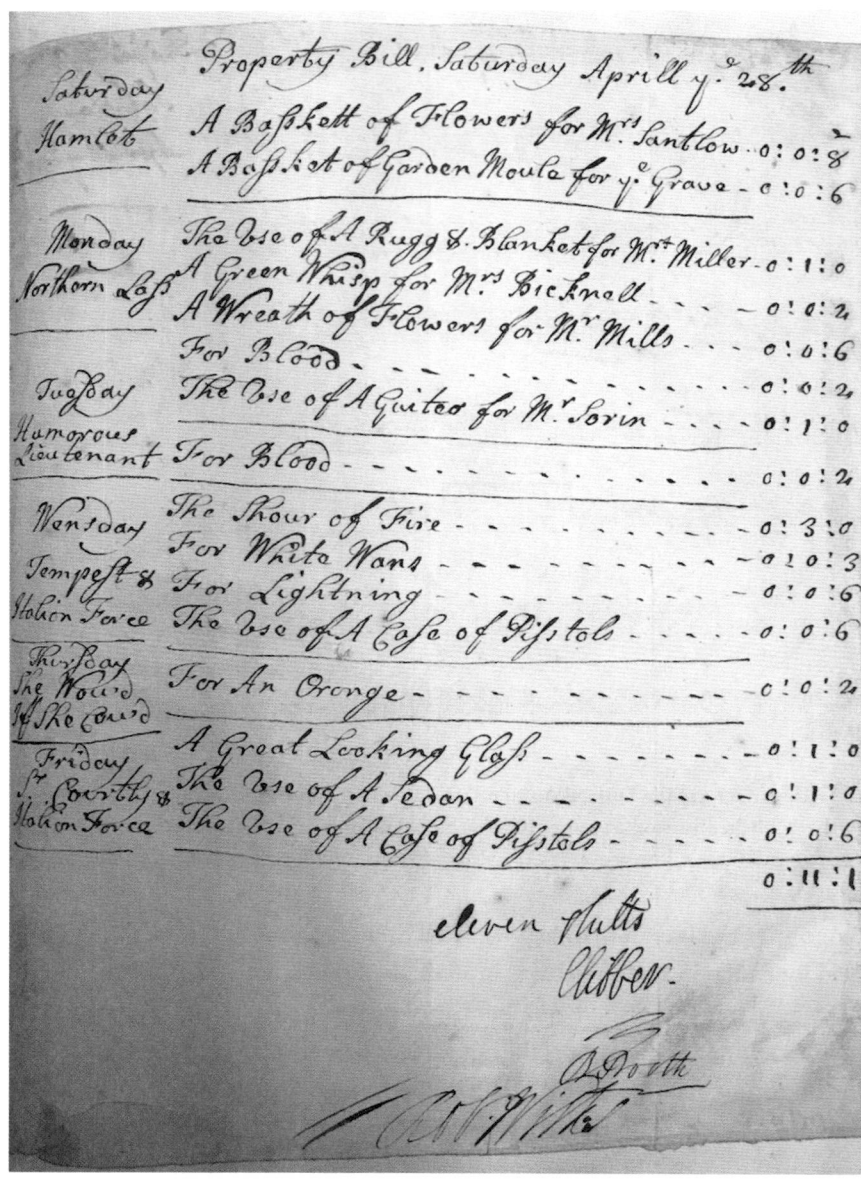

Fig. 5 List of payments for props to be used at Drury Lane theatre, dated 28 April [1716]; it shows a payment of 1s. for 'The Use of A Guitar for Mr. Sorin', a reference to the guitarist and performer Joseph Sorine. Folger Shakespeare Library, Washington, DC, MS w.b.III, fol. 45.

was spent at Drury Lane theatre to secure 'A Guitar for Mr. Sorin' to use in *The Northern Lass*, a revival of a 1629 comedy by Richard Brome (Fig. 5).

The Guitar in Georgian England

The 1720s brought the English pantomimes: the harlequinades with mimes, airs, choruses and elaborate special effects to make, as Alexander Pope put it,

> Gorgons hiss, and dragons glare,
> And ten-horned fiends and Giants rush to war.[29]

At Lincoln's Inn Fields theatre, and from 1732 onwards at Covent Garden, the actor–manager John Rich staged nearly two and a half thousand of these entertainments; a print of about 1731, entitled *The Stage's Glory*, shows the prominence that Scaramouche and his guitar could assume in the mind of a caricaturist for whom Rich's commercial success seemed a prime target for satire (Fig. 6). Scaramouche appears seated above a triumphal arch, with Punch and Columbine; within the arch, Fortune and Folly shower coins into the hat of a Harlequin who is Rich himself.

A time of rest and quietness

Both in England and on the Continent, some believed they could see the guitar falling from fashion not long after 1700.[30] In 1722 Abel Boyer published a history of Anne's reign and noted that the guitar she cultivated was 'formerly much in vogue', while two years later the composer Johann Christoph Pepusch described it as 'out of Use with us', meaning the British.[31] Much later, in 1776, Sir John Hawkins reported that an Italian guitar master who posted an advertisement for his services at the New Exchange in the Strand about 1730 'met with none that could be prevailed upon to learn of him'. [32] Despite their emphatic manner, however, these pronouncements are not easy to evaluate. When Boyer says the guitar was 'formerly much in vogue', he does not necessarily mean that it was obsolete; he may be saying only that the vogue for guitar playing, inherited from the Restoration court of the 1660s by Anne's generation, was spent by the 1720s, which it surely was. The statement by Pepusch that the guitar had fallen 'out of Use with us' by the time he published his pocket dictionary of musical terms (a genre that does not offer much scope for nuance) leaves one wondering why there is an entry for the guitar in the dictionary at all, and yet there is. Hawkins does not explain how he knows so much about an Italian guitarist who sought

Fig. 6 *The Stage's Glory*, c.1731, etching, marked 'Croquignolet Pinx.' and 'Burineaux Sculpt.'. The print is a detailed satire on the fame and financial success in the London theatre of actor–manager John Rich; the *commedia dell'arte* characters Punch, Columbine and Scaramouche (playing his guitar) recline on a triumphal arch, and to either side is a detailed key to the other figures. Victoria and Albert Museum, London, s.3926-2009.

work around 1730, when Hawkins himself was a lad of eleven. None of these critics attempts to account for the precipitate decline they observe in the guitar's fortunes, for it seems that the tradition of associating the guitar with 'fashion' is already established here. The mainspring of change seems to be that genteel taste is capricious, and that all novelties must eventually lose their appeal.

Yet however we adjust our understanding of what these commentators say, it must be admitted that the guitar's claim to attention was always open to challenge in a way no mainstream instrument of contemporary art music was required to endure. In 1683 Edward Chamberlayne shrewdly captured the inherent instability of the guitar's appeal in an edition of his great work *The Present State of England*, where he refers to 'the fine easie Ghittar'.[33] It is a particular kind of art that is both 'fine' and 'easy', if indeed such a thing is possible. For all its associations with the court that made it seem 'fine', the guitar yielded results quickly to those of modest talent or ambition and was in that sense 'easy'. That was both its strength and its weakness. If the player wished to pluck the strings in the manner of the lute – a more demanding technique than strumming – the only advantage of the guitar over its more versatile and capacious companion was that it could endow the results with a distinctive timbre, and perhaps lend the whole performance an 'easy' air – construed as a kind of courtly nonchalance or *sprezzatura*. The guitarist who combined plucking with strumming, in the mixed style of the seventeenth century and somewhat beyond, alternated between delicate finger-work and a grosser, sweeping action, with musical results that few (save guitarists themselves) have ever really relished outside the flamenco tradition, and for which few complimentary terms have ever been invented (as the history of the words 'strum' and 'thrum' reveals).[34] The observer of the Restoration court, with whom this chapter began, remembered the strumming of King Charles's courtiers as a 'raking' sound or *raclerie*;[35] that was not a compliment, and indeed the reputation of the guitar was bound to suffer when posterity turned a critical eye upon the Restoration years and the Francophilia of Charles II's court. In 1722 Daniel Defoe interpreted the plague of 1665 as a 'terrible Judgement upon the whole Nation' by a Divinity determined to punish the 'crying Vices' of the Restoration court, and by the 1730s it was quite in order to flatter the Hanoverians by lamenting the mischief done 'to the Morals of the Nation' by the example of King Charles II's entourage.[36] The virtue of that court, like the guitar, had been too easy.

The guitar was a quiet instrument, and to judge by one of the major French sources of this period – perhaps the most articulate we possess – it appeared to be getting quieter. In 1757 an entry for the guitar in a volume of the *Encyclopédie* of Diderot and d'Alembert recorded that it is 'so soft that the greatest silence is necessary to hear all the delicacies of a fine touch; in a noisy place, one can often hear nothing but the "tac" of the fingers, so that its charm is totally lost'.[37] (The 'tac' is the sound of the nails striking the strings in a downward strum, another reference to the 'raking' sound of strumming that was deemed unwelcome.) If that were all the article had to say, it would be of small account; what matters is the subsequent assurance that the guitar cannot succeed in an ensemble (*dans un concert*) because the prevailing taste in sonority has become so 'enlarged' (*étendu*). The social and artistic forces that had led, by the time of the *Encyclopédie*, to the emergence of the orchestra had raised the default level of sonority in concerted music. The guitar sounded softer in 1750 than it had done in 1650.

Perhaps the most telling indication of metropolitan opinion in England appears in John Mottley's play *The Widow Bewitch'd* of 1730, staged in the recently opened theatre at Goodman's Fields in the London suburb of Whitechapel. The cast of characters includes Old Lady Languish, described as a 'whimsical, talkative old Woman; a great Admirer of the Manners of the last Age', and it is one measure of her dated tastes that she regards the guitar as a treat worth bringing to the metropolis: 'I'm resolv'd ... to send for my Guitar to Town, on purpose that you may hear me play *Huntly's Chimes*, and the hundred and thirteenth Psalm; then there's old *Gautier's Saraband,* and *Price's Gavott*, are good pretty Things.'[38]

The part of Old Lady Languish was played by the singer Mrs Palmer, often to be seen in the comedians' booths at Bartholomew Fair; she specialised in 'mature women, pert servants and comic eccentrics', so there is doubt about the general nature of Mottley's intent.[39] The play offers a vivid comic portrait of a woman who still cultivates the guitar, and it is especially valuable for the comprehensive way it places her outdated taste for that instrument in the wider context of other eccentricities. Since she was married wearing the fashions of forty years before, her eligible years lie in the 1690s, when Princess Anne was studying the guitar and giving the royal leadership that Old Lady Languish is perhaps still following, well after that monarch's death. She is also described by a character in the play as a person of 'old-fashion'd Breeding and Country Sincerity', which invokes the familiar contrast in Restoration and later comedy between the ways of the Town (meaning fashionable London) and the culture of the landed families conventionally presented in satire as boorish but also as honest and hospitable. Old Lady Languish is of their country party, for she despises London ('this stinking Town') with its pall of smoke from thousands of coal fires, while her taste for anagrams and acrostics recalls the country-house verse of Mary, Lady Chudleigh (d. 1710).[40] In a contemptuous aside, one character in the play refers to the 'musty Morals of the last Age' by which she lives, probably meaning the stricter morality associated with the post-Restoration court of King William III (r. 1689–1702) and Queen Mary (r. 1689–94). (Old Lady Languish shudders at the mention of a masquerade, 'that Scene of Nonsense and Debauchery'.) Her reference to 'old *Gautier's Saraband*' – if it is designed to evoke any particular piece rather than the most old-fashioned variety of instrumental music John Mottley can think of – is presumably to an arrangement of a piece by Jacques Gaultier, the French lutenist who dominated solo lute music at the court of Charles I and is last heard of in England, where he thrived, in 1652.[41]

The guitar and Spain

Instruments called by some form of the name 'guitar' have been regarded as an Iberian speciality since at least the 1480s, when the Flemish music theorist Johannes Tinctoris regarded the *ghiterra* or *ghiterna* as a Catalan invention.[42] The association probably owes much to the vigour and appeal of the strummed accompaniments and dances that were played in the lands of the Spanish kingdoms and dependencies reaching from Spain across the western Mediterranean to Naples, where Tinctoris was writing. In France the term *guiterre espaignole* appears in the poetry of Mellin de Saint-Gelais (d. 1558),[43] and in Italy *chitarra spagnuola* was the name musicians gave to the guitars they used for strummed musical forms in the seventeenth century, some with Castilian names such as *passacalle* ('thoroughfare'), while others, such as the *zarabanda*, reflected some unknown Romance dialect. In England guitars had sometimes appeared on the Restoration stage in a Spanish setting, and could scarcely have failed to do so given the debt of the Restoration and later dramatists to the plots of Spanish plays,[44] but the expression 'Spanish guitar' was virtually unknown to the English language before the eighteenth century. It is found only once in the seventeenth, in a translation from Italian.[45]

The notion of a 'national instrument', like the belief in a 'national music', developed gradually in the eighteenth century, notably in Britain and Ireland, where English, Scottish, Irish and Welsh (to name only the largest affiliations) laid claims to territory, distinctive cultural traditions and separate tongues. It is no coincidence that the first English-language reference to a 'national instrument' appears in Joseph C. Walker's *Historical Memoirs of the Irish Bards* of 1786.[46] Given that Europe was a patchwork of competing and often warring states in the eighteenth century (as it was long to remain), it was inevitable that polemics against the music and musical instruments of a nation would become a weapon in the hands of its adversaries. The Spaniards' fondness for the guitar is occasionally noticed in English books of the eighteenth century that give (or pretend to give) an eye-witness report, though the view taken is often darkened by war or the immediate prospect of conflict. *A Short Account and Character of Spain* (1701), written immediately before hostilities began in the War of the Spanish Succession, sarcastically observes that 'Musick is likewise so *liberal*' among the Spanish 'that the veriest Varlet that can thrum a Ghittar, tho' it be never so vilely, will expect a Month's wages, and notwithstanding quit you before half the time is out'.[47] Even worse than the Spaniards' dishonesty, in the judgement of some, was their laziness, never more apparent than when they idled with a guitar; in 1721 Thomas Salmon thought it 'a miserable thing to see a peasant playing upon a wretched Guitar in summer', when he should be 'gathering in the Fruits of the Earth'.[48]

The War of the Spanish Succession (1701–14), greatly increased the number of Englishmen with genuine experience of Spain and its guitars by taking many servicemen to Iberia. In 1705, at an early stage of the war, an anonymous author claiming to be an officer in the navy published a tirade with the uncompromisingly vituperative title *A Trip to Spain: or, A True Description of the Comical Humours, Ridiculous Customs, and Foolish Laws, of that Lazy Improvident People the Spaniards. In a Letter to a Person of Quality by an Officer in the Royal Navy.* He inveighs against the smoky inns where guests elbow their way through a herd of mules to find a room where men and woman are playing their guitars and singing 'like so many Cats a Roasting'.[49] The author may never have visited Iberia, but the memoirs of Captain George Carleton, who served there in the war from 1705 onwards, show that servicemen did notice the guitar on campaign and were not impressed:

[The Castilians] have here as well as in most other Parts of *Spain*, *Valencia* excepted, the most wretched Musick in the Universe. Their *Guitars*, if not their *Sole*, are their darling Instruments, and what they most delight to: tho' in my Opinion our *English* Sailors are not much amiss in giving them the Title of *Strum Strums*. They are little better than our *jews-harps*, tho' hardly half so Musical. Yet are they perpetually at Nights disturbing their Women with the Noise of them, under the notion and name of Serenadoes.[50]

A satire in an issue of *Brice's Weekly Journal* for December 1725 echoes Captain Carleton (adding an allusion to *Don Quixote*) by mocking 'the abominable Strum-strum of a Spaniard's Guittar under his *Dulcinea's* window'.[51]

These two reports are even more disdainful than they may first appear, for the name 'strum strum' was sometimes given to the instruments of slaves and others regarded as primitives; an issue of the *Daily Journal* for 1728, for example, calls for news of an escaped black slave accustomed to go into the streets 'with a Strum Strum'.[52] Not surprisingly, the expression 'Spanish guitar' definitively entered the English language at about this time, the earliest example, being a political satire that can be referred to the year 1719. Entitled 'The Contents of the Sea-Chest on board the PRETENDER's Ship, bound for *Scotland*', this is directed against Cardinal Alberoni, who supported James Francis Edward Stuart, the 'Old Pretender' to the British throne in that year; and since Alberoni was serving the interests of King Philip V of Spain the satirist assigns him a 'creature' (meaning a servant or puppet) who plays a 'Spanish guittar'.[53]

The belief that the guitar was the national instrument of Spain would become the most potent single strain in the guitar's symphony of associations during the first three decades of the nineteenth century. Yet despite the longevity of the connection in Western European culture, major developments in the balance of political power, and indeed a major European war, were necessary before the English came to regard the Spanish guitar as Spanish in a positive and evocative sense. When George II came to the throne in 1727 the outlook for the Spanish guitar seemed bleak, and so it remained until mid-century, when it became decidedly worse. An elegant and companionable interloper arrived from abroad, filling the privileged position the Spanish guitar had once enjoyed and long delaying its return to favour.

TWO

'so languishing and so portable':
The English Guitar

The true pathetic is only to be found in simplicity.

Anonymous, *Euterpe* **(c.1780)**

In 1753 Samuel Foote's farce *The Englishman in Paris* was performed in London with a musical scene that was long to be remembered. One of the principal characters, Lucinda, is taking lessons from her music master in Paris. He has recently shown her an instrument previously unknown to her, and she is quite delighted with it:

Lucinda: Oh! I am quite enchanted with this new instrument; 'tis so languishing and so portable, and so soft and so silly: But come, for your last Lesson.

Gamut: D'ye like the Words?

Lucinda: O! Charming! They are so melting, and easy, and elegant. Now for a *Coup d'Essai.*

Gamut: Take care of your Expression; let your Eyes and Address accompany the Sound and Sentiment . . .

SONG

Par un matin Lisette se leva,
Et dans un bois seulette s'en alla.

Ta, la, la, [etc.] [1]

[12 more verses]

Lucinda is pleased to find that the 'new instrument' is so portable, soft and 'silly', a word to which we shall return. Samuel Foote, who had just come back from Paris when his play was staged, presents Lucinda as a keen Francophile, eager to hear the latest news from Versailles or to learn when Rameau will compose his next opera; he certainly intends this scene of a music lesson (as indeed the whole farce) to be a satire upon the English appetite for French fashions. Another purpose of the farce, however, was to offer a vehicle for the young actress, Miss Macklin, who played the part of Lucinda. In that regard, the play was a resounding success; a member of the audience who attended the first night, Francis Delaval, was so taken with her performance that he fired off a letter to his brother in praise of her when he got home.[2] He noted that she danced a minuet during the play and sang to an instrument that he calls a 'pandola', a term that does not appear in the published text of the piece. Miss Macklin accomplished all this, Delaval relates, 'with much elegance', and many others were of the same mind. Within a few months, the actor–manager West Dudley Digges found that she was winning extravagant praise in every quarter of fashionable London – 'such encomiums on her accomplishments as appear almost romantic'.[3]

A decade later the same musical scene, still remembered with admiration, is mentioned in the *Memoirs of the Bedford Coffee-House* (1763). The anonymous writer of these reminiscences certainly knew Samuel Foote, for the Covent Garden haunt he commemorates was a favourite with theatre people and Foote was a regular there. The memoirist was also in a good position to know what instrument Miss Macklin had used on stage during the farce, and now it is called a 'guittar':

Miss Macklin … drew the attention of the theatrical world; she had appeared in Mr. Foote's new piece of The Englishman in Paris to the highest perfection; she had here an opportunity of displaying her talents, or rather bringing them into one point of view. She danced, played upon the guittar, and thereby gave it the present vogue – spoke and sung French.[4]

It remains an open question whether this author was correct to claim that Miss Macklin had played a 'guittar' (of whatever kind it might be) back in 1753; we have just seen that a member of the audience used another name for the instrument altogether ('pandola'). Yet to press for an answer would be to miss the point. *The Englishman in Paris* and the 'present vogue' a decade later for something called a 'guittar' both reveal a growing current of interest in small, hand-held, plucked and fretted instruments in the wake of the 'Spanish' guitar's decline from favour (charted in Chapter 1).[5]

The pandola affair

There is only one serious candidate to be the 'guittar' that the Coffee-House memoirist mentions in 1763, and that is the instrument shown in Figures 1 and 9–12, now commonly called the 'English guitar' (a genuine eighteenth-century term, albeit rare; see Appendix 1).[6] The London newspapers begin to mention it, mostly in advertisements for lessons, in 1754, when a teacher announces it as 'a very proper instrument to be introduced in Boarding Schools, especially to such Ladies as find the Harpsichord too difficult for them, it being a pleasant melodious Musick, adapted to the Voice, and very delightful to sing with'.[7] At first, the English guitar was associated with various names, as competing teachers, players and makers tried to brand it in an appealing way; Thomas Call, who taught Miss Macklin, called it 'the Citter, otherwise Guittar, otherwise Lute or Pandola', leaving nothing to chance.[8] The variety of names also reflects the range of different designs that were used, for the body could be built in various shapes and sizes.[9] Usage eventually settled on 'guitar' (spelled various ways), but there were those who objected: it still rankled with Sir John Hawkins – never one to give his opinions mildly – as late as 1776.[10]

    Continental antecedents for the English guitar can be traced in Habsburg territory,[11] and the carriers who first brought it to Britain included members of the Moravian Brethren, an ancient protestant denomination with historic roots in eastern Europe.[12] Their community life made use of a very similar instrument. The Coffee-House memoirist, however, explicitly attributes 'the present vogue' for the guitar to the impression created by Miss Macklin. What is more, her teacher, Thomas Call, who certainly had

Moravian connections, mounted a determined newspaper campaign hoping to turn his pupil's renown to his own account.[13] From April 1755, when *The Englishman in Paris* was in repertory at Drury Lane with Miss Macklin still taking the role of Lucinda, Call announced that anyone who applied to him could now study 'the very identical' instrument used in the play by taking lessons with the very master who taught the star;[14] he even began to grace his advertisements with allusions to the scene quoted at the beginning of this chapter, as if he expected them to be recognised, which perhaps they were.[15]

The time was ripe for Call's enterprise, for the recession of the Spanish guitar in the 1720s and 1730s had left those who could afford such luxuries in need of an instrument that was not too difficult to master and was well equipped to accompany the voice. Moreover, Miss Macklin was effectively in league with royalty (whether she knew it or not) in her advocacy of such instruments. A Dublin newspaper advertisement of 1754 shows a musician named Nicolas Cloes advertising himself as teacher of the 'pandola' to Augusta, Princess of Wales.[16] This may be believed, for on 4 January 1749 the *General Advertiser* had announced the publication of Cloes's collection *One Hundred French Songs*, a volume whose title page mentions the pandola and offers the dedication to the Princess and Prince of Wales:

ONE
HUNDRED
FRENCH SONGS
Set for a Voice, German Flute, Violin, Harpsicord
and Pandola.
Dedicated to Their Royal Highnesses
THE *PRINCE* AND PRINCESS OF WALES,
By their most Obedient
Humble Servant
Nicolas Cloes

The book opens with a tally of subscribers that rivals the guest list for a royal banquet. In addition to the two royals, there are earls, countesses and major personalities from political life, such as Horace Walpole and William Pitt the Elder. (The printer, John Walsh, sold the volume with a suitably opulent binding and gilded leaves.) The songs, in the light courtly manner of French *vaudevilles*, *pastorales* and *brunettes*, are presented as melodies with figured bass (Ex. 2). [17] In the world of early Georgian fashion, an alliance, even if undeclared, between a celebrated actress such as Miss Macklin and a female member of the royal family could be very influential indeed.[18]

Ex. 2 The beginning of 'La chasse amoureuse' from Nicolas Cloes, *One Hundred French Songs Set for a Voice, German Flute, Violin, Harpsicord and Pandola* (1749?), 41.

The English guitar was intensively publicised in the London press: the *Public Advertiser* and the *London Evening Post* had already run more than a hundred advertisements placed by teachers, makers and music sellers before 1760. The means were swiftly put in place to make the instrument a viable commodity in the fullest sense, with networks of suppliers, buyers, advertisements, prices and trade lists. Panels in the *Public Advertiser* revealingly show Thomas Call and the distinguished furniture-maker turned luthier Johan Friedrich Hintz vying for custom as teachers and suppliers of English guitars in a rapidly expanding market; as early as 1754 Hintz was trying to get ahead by trading from an address 'At the Golden Guittar'. Some of those who offered lessons were organists like Thomas Call or Thomas Green of Hertford (see below): literate musicians who swiftly saw a way to enhance their income as the instrument came into fashion. George Lambert of Hull, who advertised lessons at Manchester in 1769, had studied with the organist of Beverley Minster,[19] while in 1766 Lady Cook of Wheatley Hall, near Doncaster, received lessons on the guitar from William Herschel (1738–1822), the noted astronomer, who became organist at Halifax parish church and then at Bath.[20] There were teachers from other walks of life as well, for in 1760 at Manchester, where the English guitar thrived, a teacher ready to give lessons on the violin and guitar – should he 'meet with reasonable Encouragement'

– was the servant of a military officer.[21] Many were onto a good thing in these early years, notably London music publishers such as John Walsh, John Johnson and James Oswald, who published arrangements and accompanied songs.[22]

The repertoire of the English guitar

Sometimes likened to a mandolin, whose name it occasionally usurped,[23] the English guitar was strung throughout with wire, making it a miniature belfry of sounding metal. Beginning at the treble side, there were commonly two double courses of soft iron, followed by a third course, also double, of yellow brass wire; then came a fourth course of plain or overwound yellow brass, and two single strings in the bass of yellow brass wire, overwound with silver or copper alloy.[24] The full set was tuned to a major chord that was generally notated (and no doubt tuned to a pianoforte or harpsichord) as *cegc'e'g'*, a C-major chord, though other keys were used. By sacrificing the sonority of a strum that encompassed all the strings, and other conveniences of playing in the home key, players could also render melodies in F major and G major without great difficulty; by moving a capotasto to a maximum distance – on most surviving instruments – of five frets, they could change key, but only between pieces and with a progressive thinning of the tone the higher the music went. The soft iron strings of the period could not support a high tension and required tactful playing; the consequences of an untutored touch are described by Abbé Carpentier, in a French method for similar instruments, as a *feraillement* or 'clang'.[25] Only those with an advanced technique, like Ann Ford, a professional, could venture a bold stroke, and in her guitar method of 1761 she inveighs against those who pluck the strings too timidly, producing a 'very insipid and inexpressive' result.[26]

The English guitar could nevertheless blend well with a harpsichord, at least when confidently played, and it acquired an ambitious chamber repertoire, which allowed the best amateur players to claim a place in the parlour or drawing room with exponents of the violin and the flute. There is a glimpse of such an occasion in the journals of John Marsh, who attended a musical evening in 1776; a young woman named Ann Littlejohn took part in a piece for the English guitar, joined by violin and bass:

Miss Littlejohn ... played the guitar in some of Giardini's trios ... the effect of w[hi]ch I was much pleased with, especially as Miss L. brought much more tone than was commonly done from the guitar, w[hi]ch therefore appear'd of equal consequence with the other instruments.[27]

Felice Giardini was a prominent violinist on the London scene, whose *Six Trios for the Guittar, Violin and Piano Forte, or Harp, Violin and Violoncello*, op. 18 (1775), had only recently appeared when this performance was given. Ann Littlejohn played the music so well, according to Marsh, that her instrument seemed 'of equal consequence' with the others taking part, and a player of the English guitar could scarcely ask for more. Giardini was not the only composer who encouraged the instrument's devotees to aim high. In 1758 Giovanni Battista Marella complained about the 'total Ignorance of the Power of the Instrument', and offered his *Sixty-Six Lessons for the Cetra or Guittar, in Every Key, both Flat and Sharp*, op. 3, as a remedy, while Rudolf Straube's *Three Sonatas for the Guittar, with Accompanyments for the Harpsichord or Violoncello* (1768) contains some of the most elaborate ensemble music in the instrument's repertoire (Fig. 7).

Such compositions suggest that the English guitar should be assigned a place in the history of later eighteenth-century chamber music, underwritten by the exceptional efforts of certain composers who deliberately set out to elevate it. In the Introduction to *The Art of Playing the Guitar or Cittra* (1760), Francesco Geminiani is explicit about his own efforts to 'improve' the music of the English guitar 'by adding more Harmony and Modulation to the usual manner of performing on it', and the same may certainly be said for Marella.[28] Yet although the results of such efforts have a considerable appeal for modern aficionados of the English guitar, a small but dedicated band, it may be asked whether the majority of eighteenth-century players valued them in quite the same way. Much of the published repertoire for the instrument confirms that players often sought what Charles Avison in 1752, making a general point, called music that 'might properly be calculated for those Entertainments, where the public Ear should be always consulted'.[29] Straube was careful to leaven his book of ambitious sonatas with 'a Choice Collection of the most Favourite English, Scotch and Italian Songs', and although the English guitar had indeed become 'extreamely fashionable in the polite world', as Geminiani maintains, that was not because anyone had done much by 1760 to anticipate the extended 'Harmony and Modulation' he sought to introduce. It was rather

Fig. 7 The first part of Rudolf Straube's Sonata no. 1 for English guitar, harpsichord and cello. From *Three Sonatas for the Guittar, with Accompanyments for the Harpsichord or Violoncello ... with an Addition of Two Sonatas for the Guittar Accompanyd with the Violin. Likewise a Choice Collection of the most Favourite English, Scotch and Italian Songs for One and Two Guittars, of Different Authors, properly Adapted for that Instrument, also Thirty Two Solo Lessons by Several Masters* (1768), 3. Private collection.

because 'the usual manner of performing' upon it was marked, as he concedes, by an 'obliging easiness'.[30]

We should neither speak of 'easiness' too lightly in this context nor miss what is implied by Geminiani's allusion to the 'polite world', for they are linked. Politeness, more often commended than defined in the eighteenth century, ensured easeful relations between men and women of different social classes in mixed company, as between men engaging with one another in commerce.[31] The English guitar, with a very high proportion of C-major airs and accompaniments in its repertoire, produced a sound picture of assured civility, rarely presuming upon the patience of listeners for long or uttering anything indiscreet. Its reputation was no doubt enhanced by the efforts of some composers to achieve unusually ambitious results, but the 'usual manner of performing' employed the simpler repertoire of dance music, song arrangements and accompaniments that were the foundations of its politeness. Thus, although it would be a mistake to minimise the cosmopolitanism of the English guitar's repertoire, to which foreign musicians made a signal contribution, its ethos was predominantly British and especially Anglo-Scottish.

The large corpus of song in a Scottish musical idiom of 'forcible and pathetic simplicity' was regarded by some, both in London and Edinburgh, as a prime source of whatever national music Britain could claim that was not borrowed from Handel.[32] Its 'pathetic simplicity' also has some claim to represent the truest musical value of the English guitar, with the more ambitious compositions of Straube, Geminiani, Giardini, Marella and others forming a luxuriant florescence upon the instrument's rich topsoil of Anglo-Scottish balladry with English words and beguiling melodies. The airs of Italian opera were cosmopolitan, elitist and urban, qualities mostly inimical to the spirit of balladry as eighteenth-century British antiquarians had discovered (and in part invented) it, whereas many songs in English, occasionally seasoned with Lowland Scots, were predominantly homely, popular and pastoral, as if to reflect what David Herd of Edinburgh called 'the romantic face of [Scotland] and the pastoral life of a great part of its inhabitants'.[33] As mentioned above, even Straube, ambitious for the instrument, registers this Scottish note in one of the songs that follow his sonatas (Ex. 3).

Ex. 3 Excerpt from 'Thro' the Wood Laddie', from Rudolf Straube, *Three Sonatas for the Guittar, with Accompanyments for the Harpsichord or Violoncello* (1768).

When novelists of the period set out to describe a scene of guitar playing they often chose a pastoral setting rather than a parlour or drawing room, reflecting 'the extraordinary preoccupation of the educated segment of British society of this time [the later eighteenth century] with domestic life in the country'.[34] A rural cottage provides the context in Emily Clark's *Ermina Montrose; or, The Cottage of the Vale* (1800), where Clark offers a painterly scene of moonlight on a rustic dwelling with a view through a window:

She . . . found herself near a cottage, to which she quickened her steps, and, looking through the casement whence the light came, beheld a beautiful young girl seated on a rustic bench, accompanying a guitar with her voice, while an old woman sat listening to her with great earnestness.[35]

The taste for scenes of rural life, country homesteads and cottages reveals a strain of primitivism, a dream of the pastoral, that impelled the extraordinary success, throughout the eighteenth century, of the four-book poem *The Seasons* by James Thomson (1730).[36] Pastoral verse celebrating 'Herds, flocks, and harvests, cottages, and swains',[37] in the manner that Thomson owed to John Gay's *The Shepherd's Week* (1714) and indeed to Edmund Spenser's *The Shepheardes Calender* (1579), may seem remote from the attractions of the English guitar, so emphatically broadcast by urban newspapers like the *Public Advertiser*, and seemingly so light-courtly and French in *The Englishman in Paris*. Yet the distance may not be so great. When Lucinda describes the English guitar as 'silly' in that farce, she means to praise it, so the word carries one or more of its positive senses, now obsolete, including 'artless' or 'rustic'.[38] Lucinda has no sooner enthused over her 'silly' instrument than she uses it to accompany the thirteen stanzas of 'Par un matin Lisette se leva', a song used in the highly successful French *pantomime* of rustic life by M. Favart, *La vallée de Montmorency, ou Les amours villageois* from 1752, when Foote was perhaps still in Paris.[39] By having Lucinda call her new instrument 'silly' in a positive sense, Foote almost certainly intends that it should appear to complement the cultivated artlessness of such songs, and their often rustic settings.

This had a British equivalent, though it was less courtly and more sentimental. British song of the eighteenth century is densely populated with 'silly' shepherdesses and swains as in 'Poor silly Fan' or 'Silly swain, no longer dwell', with characters such as 'Silly Damon' and 'Silly Colin', among others, guarding their sheep or playing their oaten pipes. When the English guitar was played in the home key of its tuning, by a musician who did not dampen the strings, it necessarily created an enduring resonance of the tonic chord which could be heard as a light drone, a device established in the musical tradition of the eighteenth century as a means to evoke pastoral. The effect can be emphatic in dance pieces for the English guitar, with their clearly focused tonality, as the melody lands repeatedly on open strings that spell a major chord. When added to a melody in triple time, with frequent movement in parallel thirds or sixths, the performance of some airs on the English guitar probably acquired something like the lilting, pastoral character of a *siciliana*.[40] William Jackson's 'When first this humble Roof I knew', a paean to cottage peace and self-sufficiency, is marked *pastorale* in William Wilson's *A New Selection of . . . Songs for the Guittar* (*c*.1780), though there is nothing inherently more pastoral about this piece than most others in the repertoire for the English guitar (Ex. 4). The instrument answered better than any other to the village tales, incidents of rural life and dialogues of rustic courtship that are so prominent in Scottish–English songs and others.

Ex. 4 The beginning of William Jackson's 'When first this humble Roof I knew', from his Drury Lane opera *The Lord of the Manor* (1780; text by John Burgoyne), as arranged for voice and English guitar in William Wilson, *A New Selection of the Most Admired Songs for the Guittar* (Aberdeen and Edinburgh, n.d. [*c*.1780]), Bodleian Library, Oxford, Harding Mus. E 753, 28–9.

Although chains of arpeggios were a constant resource (Ex. 5), both in accompaniments and airs, melodies were often played on the English guitar, as on the flute and violin, with little or no harmonic support. The tune was simply transposed into an appropriate key, and created a plain effect that was only in a limited sense an arrangement or indeed an accompaniment; the melody might be supplied with the first verse of a text, so that the guitar could double a voice, but often there was only an incipit. The airs in Thomas Arne's 'New English Opera' *Artaxerxes* of 1762 were arranged for the guitar in this plain manner and published the following year (Fig. 8). In 1824 a reviewer looked back on such versions and deemed them 'little adapted to the genius of the instrument' because they contained 'merely the air itself transposed into a convenient key';[41] that is a late judgement, dating from a time when the vogue for the English guitar was spent, but some players no doubt added swept chords, chains of parallel thirds or sixths and other devices found in the more elaborate written-out accompaniments by Straube and others.[42]

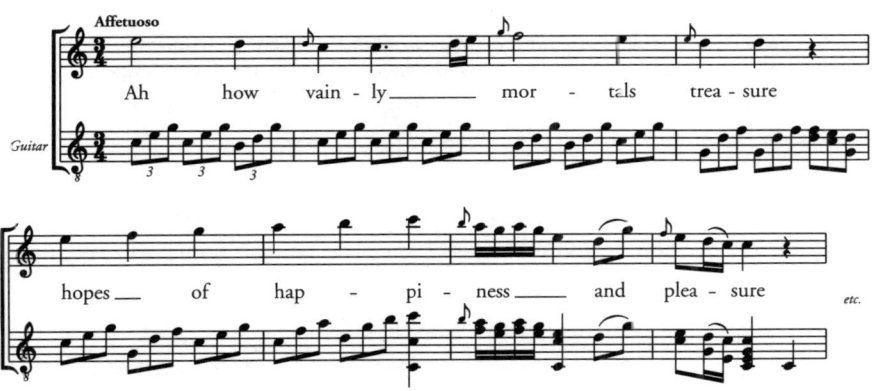

Ex. 5 The beginning of 'Ah how vainly mortals treasure', from William Wilson, *A New Selection of the Most Admired Songs for the Guittar* (Aberdeen and Edinburgh, n.d. [c.1780]), Bodleian Library, Oxford, Harding Mus. E 753, 2–3.

The London pleasure gardens were a major source of airs for the English guitar. As the light evenings of summer gave way to dusk at Vauxhall, for example, visitors could enjoy vistas with painted scenes, notoriously overpriced food, and songs or instrumental pieces performed on the second floor of a Moorish–Gothic temple in the central grove. The resident orchestra comprised the usual strings, with the addition of flutes, oboes, clarinets,

Fig. 8 A page from *The Airs with all the Symphonies in the Opera of Artaxerxes: Corrected, Transpos'd for the German Flute, Violin and Guitar* (1763), 8. The arrangements provide only the first words of the text, but follow a long-standing practice in printed songs by naming the singer who performed the air in the stage work.

bassoons, horns, trumpets and drums, all called for in surviving scores and band parts.[43] Although many of these orchestral concert songs were musical dragonflies that flitted around the lamps of the walks for a season and soon expired, they could burn brightly while they lasted; newspapers such as the *Morning Herald and Daily Advertiser* sometimes printed the words of current favourites in their poetry columns, while the blank diaries sold by stationers, especially to a female clientele, sometimes had the words of recent favourites printed on their flyleaves. The guitar versions usually appear at the ends of scores principally devoted to a single air reduced for voice and keyboard; the copies often have the appearance of a souvenir, even to the point of claiming on the title page that the song was performed 'this evening', as if the purchaser of the sheet music had been present at Vauxhall or Ranelagh to acquire it. These prints preserve, as a souvenir should, a memory of what seemed pleasing and impressive on the night, and must have seemed alluringly immediate and metropolitan when purchased from a shop in a provincial town (Ex. 6).

Ex. 6 The beginning of Jonathan Battishill's 'At eve with the woodlark I rest', sung by 'Mr. [Daniel] Arrowsmith at Vauxhall Gardens', as published in a transcription for voice and English guitar by Longman & Broderip (1784). Private collection.

The English guitar was also associated with material more conducive to reflection – indeed, to piety. In the anonymous novel *Eliza: or, The History of Miss Granville* (1766) a guitar lies on a table with some music books that prove, when inspected, to be 'chiefly of hymns', while in John Raithby's *Delineations of the Heart; or, The History of Henry Bennet* (1792) a guitar lies beside a volume of sermons by Hugh Blair, minister of the Church of Scotland and one of the most respected moralists of the age.[44] Metrical hymns and psalms in English provided a Sunday substitute for Vauxhall songs and ballads. A letter published in an issue of *St. James's Chronicle or the British Evening Post* for August 1761, supposedly written by a young woman (the author is surely male), shows the writer tuning her guitar in the hope of relieving the dullness of an English Sunday in the country; the assembly rooms are closed and there are no public breakfasts; her pious aunt, who has been getting ready for church, rushes into the room and threatens to break the instrument as a punishment for the 'abomination' of touching it on the Lord's Day. As a compromise, the young lady plays 'Psalm-Tunes'.[45] Several collections of appropriate material were published, including two with Moravian connections. Johan Friedrich Hintz, best known to music historians as a leading maker of English guitars (historians of furniture know him as a cabinet-maker), issued *A Choice Collection of Psalm and Hymn*

Tunes set for the Cetra or Guittar, probably in 1760, while the only known publication of Thomas Call is a set of melodies and hymns from the Magdalen Chapel 'Properly Set for the Organ, Harpsichord and Guittar', of much the same date.[46]

Men, women and the home

It is widely believed that the English guitar was played primarily by women, sometimes with the added nuance that it was first marketed as a pastime fit for both sexes (which was plainly the case) but became increasingly feminised as the century wore on.[47] Yet many of the literary and pictorial sources on which the received view depends are open to the charge that they repeat the same cultural trope, which might be described as 'lady dressed to be seen, with guitar, in comfortable surroundings'. To be sure, each image has its particularity, which should be respected, just as each reference to guitar playing in a novel of the period must be taken on its own terms; nonetheless, a comprehensive view suggests that the preponderance of females in both kinds of source is designed to reinforce the subordinate position of women by insistently holding them before the eye in a prettified, homebound pose, and associating them with pastimes of no account to the public life of men.

An undated watercolour after Thomas Rowlandson, however, shows an English guitar being played by a man (Fig. 9), and while it is not the only example of its kind there are few that offer so many deliberate tokens of a bluff masculinity.[48] The man is bearded, which was not the fashion for gentlemen, and wears no wig, having let his hair grow too long to accommodate one; his shirt is open at the neck, and he wears a coachman's greatcoat over plain fabrics. A bottle by his side evokes the alehouse, with its gambling and danger of disorder, but also the tavern's scope for business and financial dealings. This man gives no sign of caring for the refined politeness of the age, but has nonetheless taken up a polite instrument.[49]

The problem of how politeness could consort with masculinity was much discussed during the later eighteenth century and was liable to surface whenever a man picked up the English guitar, which had become, as Geminiani maintains, 'fashionable in the polite world'.[50] The engagement of eighteenth-century males with the instrument is in some respects as puzzling and contradictory as Rowlandson's portrait. There are several episodes

Fig. 9 *Rogero*, after Thomas Rowlandson (1756–1827), undated, watercolour on paper. The title appears to pun on the name Roger and the title of a dance melody, *Ruggiero*, known since the sixteenth century. Yale Center for British Art, New Haven, Conn., Paul Mellon Collection, B1977.14.5340.

in fiction of the later eighteenth century where a man is shown to be quite capable of tuning a guitar that a woman has handed to him because she cannot tune it herself, or because she pretends she cannot do so as a gesture of deference or flirtatiousness. In *The Feelings of the Heart; or, The History of a Country Girl* (1772), the heroine takes ship with her father and is led into the main cabin, where she finds a lady with a music book, seated at a window, while a gentleman tunes her guitar; Christopher Anstey's novel *The Mercenary Marriage* (1773) has a young woman recount how the handsome Lord Glandour, 'quite a master of musick', tuned her instrument, waited on her and expressed 'the greatest admiration' for her playing.[51] Such gestures were not confined to novels: John Marsh once accorded the instrument of a young woman at a social gathering; she eventually became his wife.[52]

Men who go further and *play* the guitar occasionally appear in eighteenth-century fiction, but there is notable resistance to the notion that they could demonstrate any real mastery. In *Hartlebourn Castle: A Descriptive English Tale* (1793), Sir William Beaumarice is asked whether he has any skill with the instrument; he seems unperturbed by the question, but admits he found the work of learning it so 'infinitely oppressive' that he abandoned the study before he could play Foote's minuet, a well-known beginner's air.[53] If the guitar is inherently unmanly here, it is only so in the sense that learning it is fastidious, indoor work liable to keep a properly sportive gentleman from his hunting dogs or horses. (So would his accounts when he had to sign them off, or his architectural plans if he contemplated renovations.) Mr Thornhill in Oliver Goldsmith's highly successful novel *The Vicar of Wakefield* (1766) plays the guitar 'very indifferently' when he joins his tenants in their garden. The vicar, who is here the narrator, regards Mr Thornhill's behaviour as improper not because it somehow compromises his masculinity but because it involves excessive familiarity towards his social inferiors.[54] Beyond the realm of fiction, the naturalist and famous macaroni Sir Joseph Banks passed his time at sea with 'a Poor innocent Guittar which Lay in the Cabbin'; he clearly believed he had descended from a more obviously fitting instrument, such as the violin.[55] This suggests one way to interpret the gendering of the English guitar that may underlie these references to male players. Banks was neither unwilling to play the guitar nor reluctant to reveal that he had done so; it was simply one option among many available to him as a male, and relative to the violin or flute it did not rank high. In this domain, at least, a male's liberty to choose, albeit with due sensitivity to his surroundings and company, could override a gendered association if he so wished.

In the narrower range of options available to women, however, the guitar (together with the harp and harpsichord) was more prominent. A woman's sense of her opportunities might be formed in infancy. John William Jolliffe's painted silhouette of the Ashburnham nursery, made about 1767, shows the earl's four children as they occupy themselves, immaculately behaved, under the watchful eyes of their parents (Fig. 10); Henrietta Theodosia plays the guitar before an open book of music, or perhaps a method, while one of her younger sisters, seated at the same table, plays with cards to practise for the many evenings of quadrille and whist that aristocratic life will

Fig. 10 The nursery of the Ashburnham family, by John William Jolliffe, painted and cut silhouette, *c.*1767. The children of the 2nd Earl of Ashburnham are shown engaged in pastimes that will stand them in good stead for the future; Henrietta Theodosia (*left*) is practising the guitar, reading from a score or perhaps an instrumental method. Private collection.

bring her once she has come out into society. To the right, her brother toys with a dog, anticipating the sporting pleasures he will enjoy when he inherits the estate as the 3rd Earl of Ashburnham. The youngest child plays with her doll as a preparation for motherhood to come. The technique of silhouette gives stark emphasis to the contrast between these gendered pursuits.

When the nursery gave way to the boarding school for young gentle-women, the English guitar retained its place in a gendered regime of education. Unlike the harpsichord, likely to be kept in the school's music room or dancing hall, a guitar was easily taken into a chamber or a garden, and with a large repertoire of amorous songs from the stage it was an easy target for lubricious satire. A hand-coloured mezzotint of 1774, entitled *The Boarding-School Hair-Dresser*, shows a handsome young barber standing very close to his young and smiling female client, positioned between her legs which hold him fast as he dresses her hair for a ball. A guitar and a book of music lie on a table nearby, issuing an unmistakable warning.[56] In addition to what schooling could provide, with all its attendant hazards, there was a social and often a familial infrastructure for teaching the guitar to young women. In her youth the novelist Catherine Hutton (1756–1846) was taken in hand by a neighbour, who acted as her chaperone to balls, plays and exhibitions; she also taught Catherine to play whist and gave her lessons on the guitar.[57]

Portraits showing women playing the English guitar make a distin-guished gallery of paintings by some of the major artists of the day, including Thomas Gainsborough, Joshua Reynolds and Angelica Kauffman, for no musical instrument of the eighteenth century has a more emphatic presence in contemporary portraiture.[58] The pervading theme seems to be reverie and depth of sensibility, the effect often decidedly pensive. A mezzotint of 1772, after a painting by Tilly Kettle and perhaps depicting the artist's daughter, shows a young woman dressed for sociability but nonetheless alone, playing a large English guitar depicted with great care (Fig. 11). Scarce emerged from girlhood, as the sapling on her right suggests, she returns the viewer's gaze with heavy-lidded eyes whose gaze is too soft to be called a stare. The effect, enhanced by the mezzotint's grisaille, is distinctly melancholic.

References to guitar playing in fiction register the same note. Some, indeed, seem almost to be descriptions of paintings, so well defined is the sense of frame and image. In Elizabeth Bonhôte's novel *Olivia; or, Deserted Bride* (1787), a peer turns a corner in a garden and espies a young woman

Fig. 11 Portrait of a woman, perhaps Miss Kettle, playing the English guitar, 1772, mezzotint, with legend 'T. Kettle pinx.' and 'Val. Green fecit'. British Library, London, 1867,0413.576.

seated in an alcove, and singing a plaintive air, which was accompanied by some of the softest tones of her guitar', while in the anonymous *Belleville Lodge* (1793), a gentleman sees Maria through a sash window 'fast asleep, her guitar by her side'.[59] In Henry Man's *The Trifler* (1775), a young woman seeks a secluded place, where she plays a 'melancholy air' on her guitar to complement her pensive spirit, while *Montrose* (1799), again anonymous, has a gentleman pass by a lattice window through which he hears his beloved 'plaintively touching her guitar'.[60] Perhaps the most elaborate of all such passages appears in *Eliza: or, The History of Miss Granville*, where the narrator tells the story of a woman who bade farewell to all her amusements, taking 'a kind of pleasure' in indulging her sadness, for she was ever of a 'romantic turn'. She turned away from everything that might divert her mind from her sorrow; only her guitar remained, on which she chose to play a 'few mournful airs ... which rather fed, than softened' her melancholy.[61]

It may seem surprising that a polite and insouciant instrument like the English guitar should so often be associated with plaintive or affecting situations; part of the explanation may lie in the solitariness of those who actually played it, from day to day, and who, wishing to live life as much as possible through literature, charged their imaginations with passages in fiction that show feeling and sentiment excited to a degree well beyond the everyday. *The Life of Mrs. Sherwood*, incorporating the letters of Mary Martha Sherwood, who was a teenager in the late 1780s, reveals a woman who believed that the 'first exercise' of her imagination had occurred when she was inspired by the sound of her mother singing to a guitar in her dressing room.[62] In her youth she had longed to be the heroine of a novel (as well she might, since she learned the guitar in the decidedly unromantic context of a boarding school at Reading during the 1790s). Later in life she wrote of a summer day in 1795 when she played the guitar in her parental home:

> I remember it was bright and beautiful weather, and after dinner ... I went up to my mother's dressing room, from one window of which I could clearly discern the high road from Kidderminster, in two distinct places, as it descended from the eminence between the Abberley and Warsgrove hills ... I had got my guitar with me, and was playing 'Henry's Cottage Maid', and musing on many things ... To this very day the air of that song, however played, whenever heard, has power to bring all the feelings of that hour back to my mind, even to a painful degree.[63]

We follow the writer's gaze through a window to a distant road as it winds between the Worcestershire hills. She sits in the chamber where, as a child, she heard her mother sing and play on what was perhaps the same guitar; then, she had perched on the stairs to listen, but now she is 20 and may be admitted to the room. Her father is mortally ill, and as she watches the road for the coach that will bring him home she opens the album of memory at a page showing her mother with a guitar, and places herself within it, 'musing on many things'. The plangent lyric that she sings, entitled 'Henry's Cottage Maid', published several times in arrangements for the English guitar, borrowed an air by Ignaz Pleyel (Ex. 7):

> Ah where can fly my soul's true-love,
> Sad I wander this lone grove,
> Sighs and tears for him I shed,
> HENRY is from LAURA fled,
> Thy love to me thou didst impart,
> Thy love soon won my Virgin heart,
> But, dearest HENRY, thou'st betray'd
> Thy love with thy poor Cottage Maid.[64]

Ex. 7 'Henry's Cottage Maid', to an air by Ignaz Pleyel, arranged for English guitar, published by Maurice Hime (Dublin, n.d. [c.1790]), Bodleian Library, Oxford, Vet. Mus. i 2.79(43).

'Henry's Cottage Maid' tells how a woman of the rustic poor wanders in a 'lone grove' as she weeps over Henry's betrayal. Many such songs of female misfortune were published with arrangements for the English guitar, including The Hopeless Maid, A Favorite Ballad' and 'The Poor Blind Girl: A Favorite

Pathetic Ballad'. The term 'ballad' was not applied to such affecting songs alone, but antiquarian interest in the traditions of British balladry during the eighteenth century had done little to lighten the associations of the term.[65] In the more sombre songs published with guitar arrangements or accompaniments, the dead appear as drowned or bloodied revenants to console or horrify those who pine for them; wronged lovers lament their betrayal; and exiles bemoan their fate. In 'Mary's Dream, or Sandy's Ghost', 'sung by Miss Chanu at Hanover Square Concerts and at the Pantheon' (1794), a sleeping woman, who believes her lover to be at sea, receives a visitation from his drowned corpse 'with pallid cheek, and hollow Eye'.[66] For all the brightness of the English guitar's tone, much of its repertoire encouraged pensiveness, even ruefulness.

Some other references to women's guitar-playing in fiction emphasise the pleasures of companionship and visits. *Eliza: or, The History of Miss Granville* describes how a group of women, caught in a storm, take shelter in a modest house, where they are offered tea and some airs on the guitar by their hostess. Such moments of hospitality, in the social round of London and county society, underlie various entries in the financial records of Thomas Green (d. 1791), who supplemented his stipend as an organist in the market town of Hertford, 30 miles from London, by tuning and refurbishing the instruments of local families. The guitar first appears in Green's records for January 1756, when Lady Sarah Cowper and Lady Mary Mordaunt paid him for tuning, stringing or mending their instruments; it is probably no coincidence that these early clients for Green's guitar-related services were persons in an exceptional position to discern the rising fashions of the metropolis on their visits to London.[67] The following year Green attended to the guitars of several ladies, as the fashion spread through county society. He tuned an instrument for Lady Mary Mordaunt, this time while she was at Hatfield visiting the rector, and another for Miss Raynolds at Thundridge Bury, the family home of the Gardiners. A third client, Miss Snell, he found at Lady Blount's. Behind many of the entries in these accounts lie scenes akin to those shown in contemporary 'conversation piece' portraits: family gatherings, formal visits and tea parties.[68]

The English guitar suited such occasions for, if its music sometimes had a pastoral air, the instrument itself had the material qualities of a card-table or some other piece of furniture not usually found in a country cottage. The stain often applied to the soundboard counterfeited the glimmer of mahogany furniture (see Fig. 1), and the fingerboard was sometimes

I'll twine fresh Garlands for my Lovers brows, *The*
And consecrate to him eternal Vows. MUSICAL
Charmer.
The Charming Youth shall my Apollo prove,
And shall adorn my Song & tune my Voice to Love.

Fig. 12 *The Musical Charmer*, hand-coloured mezzotint, with etching, 1780. A well-to-do young woman is singing a song from a manuscript book lying open on the sofa beside her, and accompanying herself on the guitar; the verses printed at the foot of the picture read: 'I'll twine fresh Garlands for my Lovers brows, / And consecrate to him eternal Vows, / The Charming Youth shall my Apollo prove, / And shall adorn my Song & tune my Voice to Love.' The Geffrye Museum of the Home, London, 81/2009.

veneered with tortoiseshell, a substance widely employed for small luxury objects, such as the lids of snuff-boxes. In contrast to the Spanish guitar of wood and gut, the English guitar made an almost triumphal display of the small metal parts that were increasingly associated, in the later eighteenth century, with the ascendancy of English manufacture.[69] These included the wire strings and inlaid metal frets, to which might be added an inset rose of metal, often gilded, silver-tipped tuning pegs, a watch-key tuning mechanism of brass, and a capotasto with a brass screw. A mezzotint of 1780, entitled *The Musical Charmer*, shows a young woman playing in a well-appointed room, with a carpet, a looking-glass in a fanciful frame made, like the balcony, of cast iron, a brass vase, a sofa and window curtains; the guitar seems quite at home among the desirable objects on show, and so does the young woman, for she is merely another such (Fig. 12). Wills and inventories confirm that guitars could be valued possessions in the home, akin to items of furniture or plate; the testament of Dame Sarah Fitzherbert of Tissington (1795) bequeaths diamond earrings, a watch and a 'guitar by Hintz', the name of the London maker specified as it might be for other goods of material and social value such as 'Wedgewood ware'.[70]

By the turn of the nineteenth century, the drawbacks of the English guitar's open-chord tuning had become as patent as its advantages. Much of the instrument's repertoire was cast in the home key of the tuning employed – very often C major, for most other keys posed a considerable challenge to all save proficient players. Even civility can become tiresome after a while if it is too unbending. What is more, the open tuning could also lead to frustration if printed or manuscript versions of an air were not available appropriately transposed; in 1795 a provincial gentleman searched the London music shops for 'The Duke of York's March', but could not find a copy 'in a proper key for the guitar' and therefore went home empty-handed.[71] The metallic sonority of the strings also began to seem old-fashioned, even distasteful, by the first decades of the nineteenth century, as contemporary comments will soon reveal with surprising explicitness. Towards 1800, players found themselves on the lookout once again for a new, hand-held instrument that was not too demanding and could provide an adequate accompaniment, above all, for their own voice. The way was open for the Spanish guitar to return.

'more harmonious and pleasing': The Spanish Guitar Returns

. . . nothing is so easy as to metamorphose this instrument, of which the harmony may be rendered so sweet, into a mere kettle.

Charles Burney in A. Rees, *The Cyclopædia*, vol. xvi (1819)

Early in the 1760s, when the English guitar was enjoying high favour, a Portuguese visitor to London named Rodrigo Antonio de Meneses played the Spanish instrument for an aristocrat and his guests.[1] Among those present, in addition to the Earl of Eglinton, were Johann Christian Bach, Carl Friedrich Abel, and Charles Burney, then a provincial music master. Burney describes de Meneses as a musician 'with the appearance of a gentleman', whom he suspected of involvement in the notorious plot of December 1758 to assassinate the Portuguese king; if Burney was right, de Meneses had somehow escaped the savage reprisals that followed this treasonable act, for he was now living in London, 'seemingly as a man of fashion'.[2] With such a discerning audience assembled to hear him play, de Meneses strove to impress. According to Burney, he used a 'large Spanish guitar', strung with gut, which was perhaps a genuinely Iberian example, mounted with six double courses in what was then the latest fashion in Spain (Fig. 13).[3] He played voluntaries 'in the same full and learned manner of a great performer on the organ', introducing subjects 'in three and four parts through all the keys of legal modulation'. Burney was astonished, and remembered the performance for forty years. Such things were not to be expected from a guitarist.

Fig. 13 Portrait of Maria Walpole, Countess of Waldegrave and later Duchess of Gloucester, by Francis Cotes, 1765, oil on canvas. The countess is shown holding a large Spanish guitar, strung with six double courses. This is one of the earliest pictorial records of such guitars, which were then of a very new design, and it remains unknown how the instrument that served as the model for this impressively detailed and accurate depiction came to Great Britain. Sold at auction, Bonhams, London, 8 December 2004, lot 59, current location unknown.

The situation that Burney describes will occur again in the English history of the guitar: an Iberian virtuoso playing before sceptical listeners and revealing the powers of an instrument they had hitherto overlooked or disparaged. The fact that we would know nothing of this particular instance had Burney not decided to recall it, many years later, suggests how imperfect our picture of the guitar in eighteenth-century England may be, despite the volume of contemporary writing that can now be searched electronically and the riches of contemporary portraiture. Furthermore, the vast majority of newspaper materials available before 1800 are metropolitan, leaving much of provincial England unrepresented, to say nothing of generally unrecorded private circumstances of the kind Burney is recalling; and textual references of all kinds, wherever they are found, usually employ the term 'guit(t)ar' without specifying whether the instrument is of the English variety, the Spanish, or something else again. Yet an important body of material in newspapers, satires and periodicals does employ the term 'Spanish guitar', and it seems reasonable to proceed on the assumption that the term is being used as we would expect unless there is some reason to suppose the contrary.[4] As far as paintings and prints are concerned, the situation is much clearer: with a few exceptions, the visual arts of eighteenth-century England show English and not Spanish guitars, though once again there are some exceptions, none more spectacular than Figure 13.

Most advocates of the Spanish guitar during the second half of the eighteenth century in England were not flamboyant performers like de Meneses, and if they were virtuosi there is no trace of their fame. They were obscure figures, mostly either Italians joining the great diaspora of musical talent from their homeland, or French, including refugees set adrift, and sometimes perhaps disinherited, by the Revolution of 1789 and after. They were drawn to the cosmopolitan areas of London west of St Giles, long favoured by their compatriots in the musical and catering trades, such as Soho and Marylebone; others settled amid the odours of Italian grocery shops, the rasp of tools at work in the Long Acre coachyards and the discarded orange peel of the Covent Garden quarter. Yet however congenial such areas might have been, there were no salaried positions there or anywhere else in England for such musicians to hold, and no professional or charitable associations for them to join, unless they also played one of the mainstream instruments such as the violin. In short, the guitar players of eighteenth-century London were not really functioning members of the musical profession at all. They were, however, foot-soldiers in a campaign to convince the British public that the Spanish guitar was much more worth cultivating than they supposed, and in the end they won the day.

The French

In France the guitar did not experience the degree of eclipse during the eight-eenth century that it did in England.[5] There was a certain decline around 1730, and three decades later François-Alexandre-Pierre de Garsault was still clear in his mind that 'the taste for this instrument, which cannot take part in any ensemble, is lost'.[6] Yet at much the same time Jean-Benjamin de La Borde described the guitar as 'born again' in France among those who used it to accompany the light songs variously known as *vaudevilles, pastorales* and *brunettes*.[7] The genres mentioned by La Borde were not new at mid-century but, allied to the guitar, it seems that they were newly in fashion. Example 8, the first section of a *brunette* from the manuscript additions by François Campion (d. 1747) to his *Nouvelles découvertes sur la guitarre* of 1705,[8] suggests the airy simplicity of what might be required from the guitar in such pieces. There was a contemporary and court response to this fashion in England, as Nicolas Cloes's *One Hundred French Songs*, advertised in 1749, reveals (see above, pp. 41–2), but that book shows the taste for diverting such French and light-courtly settings to another plucked instrument, the pandola, which was either a form of the English guitar or one of its relatives.

Ex. 8 The beginning of a *brunette* from manuscript additions made by François Campion to a copy of his *Nouvelles découvertes sur la guitarre* (1705) some time after its publication; Campion notated the song in the common shorthand form of a texted tablature. The text is taken from *Poliphème*, a tragi-comic pastoral and harlequinade in five acts, from 1722, where the song is called a *vaudeville*; in the play text this is the second stanza.

From the 1760s onwards, French advocates of the guitar advanced the cause of their instrument with a series of elegantly engraved methods (see Fig. 2). Whatever we may hope to learn about more technical aspects of the guitar in neighbouring England must principally be gathered from these handsome books, for they have no surviving British counterpart before 1795. Some players in Francophone territory were using overspun strings on courses four and five by the first quarter of the eighteenth century, though they were apparently uncommon as yet.[9] The anonymous *Methode pour aprendre e joüer de la guitarre* of 1758, published in both Paris and Madrid, reports that the lower-octave strings of courses four and five should be entirely overspun (*filé en plein*); the author – known only by the respectful title of 'Don', which he awards himself, and almost certainly a Spaniard – observes that in Spain the core is made of silk.[10] Michel Corrette's treatise *Les dons d'Apollon* (1762) commends a bourdon on the fourth course that is 'half overwound' (where the winding forms a spiral over the core) and a full winding for the fifth; he must be referring to an overspun core of gut, for as an alternative he mentions silk 'in the Chinese manner'.[11] (Western musicians like Corrette learned about Chinese practice from the writings of Jesuit missionaries.) By 1780 Pierre-Jean Baillon regarded strings with a silk core, entirely (not partially) overspun, as standard for the lower-octave strings of the fourth and fifth courses, complementing a higher octave of plain gut; he reports that this is the usage of masters such as Vidal (whom we shall soon find in London), and of Spanish and Italian masters.[12] According to Charles Burney, who is here following the account in the *Encyclopédie*, the overspun strings of the guitar had 'two inconveniences: the one is of wearing out and cutting the frets: the other, still greater, of overpowering the other strings, particularly in sweeping the chords'. He adds that the relatively strong sound of the basses could nonetheless be useful in continuo playing, but that otherwise 'the silvered strings must be touched very gently'.[13] No sooner had a means been found to give the guitar a more sonorous bass than advice was issued to contain the result.

The French methods say a good deal about the arpeggio, destined to become a major resource of the guitar but still in the 1760s a relatively new manner of creating an accompaniment, as opposed to a flourish.[14] The Alberti bass, an arpeggio in the pattern c–g–e–g, named after Domenico Alberti (d. 1740), provides an early instance in the Italian keyboard repertoire, and as the harp became an especially favoured salon instrument composers such as Joseph Deleplanque and François Petrini began to employ arpeggios extensively in their published works.[15] The mandolin was also affected, for Pietro Denis and other Parisian mandolinists produced arrangements of songs in the 1770s, often from the *opéra comique*, with arpeggio accompaniments.[16] The English guitar, with its major-chord tuning, could produce such accompaniments with great fluency (see Ex. 5).

Although the arpeggio rapidly became a core resource of guitar players, and may often have been viewed by them in pragmatic terms as a broken chord, there was also a sophisticated aspect to the technique which lent it a certain prestige. The French methods resolve the arpeggio into two elements: a bass note played by the thumb and an accompanying harmony played by the fingers, which sounded the constituent notes of the harmony one after another.[17] Arranged in long chains, arpeggios were therefore a means to play a bass line – the bass being an indispensable element of a piece's musical grammar – together with a secondary element, a harmony, which could be omitted without that grammar being disturbed, but merely thinned. In effect, therefore, the arpeggio was a simple form of continuo, which is precisely what the methods say. For François Campion it is a technique where the thumb 'stipulates in advance the harmony that the other fingers provide',[18] while for Giacomo (or perhaps Bernard) Merchi the arpeggio is a form of *basse continue*.[19] The guitar part in 'De L'Amour je bravois l'empire', from Merchi's *Raccolta d'ariette francesi ed italiane per la chitarra*, op. 4, of 1760, offers a clear instance, for while it may look like a succession of broken chords it is actually a grammatical bass line for the thumb with the fingers adding a harmonic infill (Fig. 14). The bass line appears, extracted from the chords, as the lower part in Example 9.

Fig. 14 'De L'Amour je bravois l'empire', a popular *ariette* from *Le peintre amoureux de son modèle*, an *opéra comique* in two acts by Egidio Duni with a libretto by Louis Anseaume, as arranged for voice and guitar in [Giacomo] Merchi's *Raccolta d'ariette francesi ed italiane per la chitarra*, op. 4 (Paris, 1760), 2. Private collection.

etc.

Ex. 9 The treble and bass counterpoint in 'De L'Amour je bravois l'empire', from [Giacomo] Merchi's *Raccolta d'ariette francesi ed italiane per la chitarra*, op. 4 (1760), showing the counterpoint between the melody and the first note of each broken chord in the guitar part.

A miniature by Anne Wetherill, probably dating from the 1780s and decidedly French in style (Fig. 15), serves to introduce the cross-Channel exchanges that helped to transmit a continuing French enthusiasm for the gut-strung guitar to England, where interest appears to have waned by the second quarter of the eighteenth century. Wetherill became a member of the Académie des Beaux-Arts at Lille in 1780 and was soon thereafter living in London's Cursitor Street, a tributary of Chancery Lane in the legal quarter.[20] Her finely executed miniature shows a woman, perhaps the artist herself, playing a guitar with five single strings. The newspapers reveal various guitar players from France at work in London during her lifetime, some of whom prove to be British sub-jects returning home after a period of schooling. In 1782 a young lady, 'a native of England', advertised for a situation as a companion or governess after fifteen years spent in Paris and elsewhere in France; she spoke French and English, had 'a good knowledge of music' and taught the Spanish guitar.[21] Other players were French nationals living among their compatriots in Soho and Marylebone. In 1783 there was a 'Concert Francois' involving the guitar at 40 Great Marlborough Street, the Soho house of M. Noverre junior, son of the famous French ballet master; the evening included two scenes from comic operas, *L'amoureux de quinze ans* (1771) and André Grétry's *La fausse magie* (1775), together with a 'variety of Petits Airs, accompanied upon the Spanish Guitar'.[22] Noverre had apparently recruited much of the local French talent in his quarter of London. Resident French teachers of the Spanish guitar included M. Du Bournay, whose career shows that there was a market for lessons in the London satellite city of Bath in 1788; there he offered 'the *French language, Drawing*, and *painting on silk*, in a manner peculiar to himself; likewise to *paint tables*, &c for varnishing ... also the Spanish Guittar. – Transparent Colours, and China Cement, sold as usual. – Patterns for Drawing, Painting, or Embroidery, executed to direction.'[23]

Even this did not exhaust the ways M. Du Bournay made his living, for in his capacity as a teacher of French he can be found at Bath publicly rehearsing a 'most striking and interesting scene' from Voltaire's tragedy of *Zaïre*.[24]

The following year, political events began to impel a more active diaspora of French nationals.[25] Not long before the fall of the Bastille on 14 July 1789, a musician who had been a child prodigy in France and was already established in Paris as a player of the *cistre* (closely related to the English guitar), can be found in London advertising his services as 'Professor of the Cistre, Spanish Guittar, and English Guittar', the lessons to be given at his Soho lodgings. His advertisement, somewhat mangled by a compositor unable to read elements of French in the copy he was given, records that he

Fig. 15 Portrait of a young woman playing a five-string guitar, miniature by Anne Wetherill 1780s?, gouache on ivory, in original frame. Private collection.

has a fine harp of Paris manufacture to sell or exchange for a 'Forte Piano' or for some 'Forte-Piano [i.e. keyed English] guitars'; he also has two *cistres* with 'ex[tended] marches' (*sic*, presumably for French *manches*: 'necks') and 'great bases', made by the best craftsman in Paris. Finally, M. Grumaille has 'an exceeding good Spanish Guittar' to sell.[26] This had presumably come over from Paris with the other instruments mentioned. Another Frenchman active in the capital was M. Prador, who offered lessons in the French language 'in its utmost purity and elegance', together with tuition in singing, the violin, the harp and the Spanish guitar, 'which is totally different from the English, and which is at present very much the vogue in France'. He feared a reproach for 'making a lucrative use of his talents', but hoped that his motive, when known, would be his excuse.[27] Like M. Grumaille, but more desperate, he sounds like a refugee from the Revolution trying to establish himself in London.

Such an exile is the dedicatee of the first music for the Spanish guitar printed in eighteenth-century England: M. Vidal's *Collection of Easy Pieces for the Guitar dedicated to Mrs de St Albain*, undated but probably published in 1791, was sold from the composer's London lodgings at 132 Swallow Street in St James's.[28] Vidal, possibly Spanish by birth, was well known in France, where he published several methods for the guitar and a stream of airs (many from the *opéra comique*), together with duos for the guitar and violin, *romances*, sonatas, minuets, *petits airs variés* and a guitar concerto that sustained his reputation for being 'particulièrement distingué par son rare talent'.[29] The music Vidal offers to 'Mrs de St Albain' includes minuets, an allemande, an *air varié* (the well-known song 'Ah! vous dirai-je, maman') and sonatas for guitar with violin; all are set for a guitar of five strings or courses.[30]

To pursue the dedicatee, 'Mrs de St Albain', is to uncover a scandal in English high life that also shows the transplanting to London from France of a level of interest in the guitar well in excess of anything found in England during the late eighteenth century. On 26 August 1789, two weeks after the Assemblée Nationale in Paris voted to abolish the privileges and feudal rights of the nobility, a 'Madame St. Aubin', who is almost certainly Vidal's dedicatee, is mentioned in *Oracle: Bell's New World* as one of the French voluntary exiles hospitably received by the British nobility. She is a guest of the Marquis of Cholmondeley, and a fine player of the Spanish guitar:

But, above all, the welcome afforded by Lord Cholmondeley is to be extolled . . . marked for that *spirit* which is the true characteristic of the *English nobility*. – For the order and system of his Lordship's establishment, much is due to Madame St. Aubin. Every proof of courtesy and politeness distinguishes her behaviour; – and to these domestic attentions she unites very striking musical accomplishments: – On the *Spanish guitar* in particular she excels.[31]

This 'Madame St. Aubin' who excels on the Spanish guitar is Marie-Françoise Henriette Laché, the mistress of the French financier and politician Charles-Pierre Maximilien Radix de Sainte-Foy, whom she accompanied to London at various times from 1783 onwards, including the period in 1789 to which the above passage refers.[32] While in England that year, she became the lover of George James Cholmondeley; by the time the *Oracle* published its account of their association in August 1789 she was heavily pregnant with his child – whence the journalist's ironic reference to the way she maintains 'the order and system' of his establishment.[33] Thus the only French patron of guitar music traceable in English high society during the last quarter of the eighteenth century comes to light through an attack on the sexual peccadilloes of the idle rich. The journalist clearly knew something about Madame de St Aubin's association with the Spanish guitar; even if he is not making a direct allusion to Vidal and the collection he dedicated to her, the abundant reports about her in the English press provide rich material for reconstructing the milieus in which Vidal was moving by virtue of his association with her. They included gatherings at the Cholmondeley house in Piccadilly, evenings at her lodgings in Golden Square and the *petits soupers* she hosted.

A stipple etching of 1789 by Charles Ansell RA, entitled *Dressing Room a la Francaise*, suggests how easily the guitar, by association with a range of French visitors, from fashionables like Madame de Saint Aubin to impecunious music masters, could become entangled with both the prejudice and the admiration that characterised British attitudes to France (Fig. 16). Two gentlemen converse with a lady as she completes her morning routine in the boudoir; a Spanish guitar, indifferently drawn, with a tailpiece like a viol, lies on top of an ornate cabinet. The image expresses the common English belief that 'Frenchmen wear court dress when inappropriate, spend more time with ladies than the English normally do, and preside over feminine spaces and practices such as the *toilette*'.[34] The guitar, ready to be drawn into a display of polite accomplishment, or perhaps a seduction, contributes to a sense that these persons are at ease, in a very un-English way, with the intimacy and latent sexuality of their situation.

The Italians

According to Hester Lynch Piozzi, friend of Dr Johnson, the Italians are inclined to neglect their shops and are 'easily disposed to loiter under their mistress's window with a guitar'.[35] Considered as a judgement about the Italian shopkeepers of London, this could not be more mistaken, as any eighteenth-century visitor to the Haymarket quarter, with its Italian warehouses selling imported spices and Mediterranean delicacies, would soon have discovered. Viewed as an expression of the Italian's great fondness for the guitar, however, Piozzi's remark is well grounded.[36] The eighteenth-century diaspora of musical talent from Italy brought to London numerous advocates of the gut-strung guitar. One of the earliest was the violinist Giuseppe Passerini of Bologna, who announced in 1760 that he was opening an academy 'in the great Parlour of his House, being the front of that which is generally called the Concert Room in Dean-Street, Soho'; there he proposed to 'Lecture and Instruct young Ladies and Gentlemen' on numerous musical instruments including 'the English and the Spanish Guittar'.[37] Passerini had been promoting various subscription series of concerts and oratorios in London since at least February 1753, the concerts mixing works by Handel and others with songs in Italian or English.[38] Even by the standards of the later eighteenth century, Passerini struggled hard, throughout his London career, against the competing attractions of other entertainments, musical and non-musical, including the Italian Opera and the Newmarket races; the purpose of the academy, convened in the front parlour of his house, was to sustain his income during the summer season, when much of his concert clientele left London. The location was a good one, for it stood very close to the Great Concert Room in Dean Street, one of London's general-purpose halls for dances, music and auctions, which Passerini regularly engaged for his concerts.

An Italian who moved into the Haymarket quarter, less than a mile from Passerini, was by far the most active advocate of the Spanish guitar in later eighteenth-century London. Giacomo Merchi of Brescia spent some

Dressing Room a la Francaise.

Fig. 16 *Dressing Room a la Francaise*, by Charles Ansell, 1789, stipple etching. A Spanish guitar, suggesting the pleasures of music and perhaps of courtship, lies on a cabinet in a lady's chamber, where she dresses in the company of two gentlemen. A companion picture, *Dressing Room a l'Anglaise*, shows only women (one with a child), and no guitar. Private collection.

years in the Netherlands and Paris, then came to London in (or soon before) 1766.[39] In that year he announced many of his Parisian publications in the *Public Advertiser*, showing that he had brought much of his stock with him to England.[40] The English elites, no longer constrained by the Seven Years War, were reputed to be spending as much as £1 million a year in Paris on various French 'trifles', and Merchi probably hoped that his Parisian wares, now brought to London, might find a ready market. He soon realised, however, that he would need to teach the English guitar as well as the Spanish during his English sojourn, for the former was in greater demand; in February 1769 he accordingly advertised lessons on 'the English and Spanish Guittar, and Singing, on the newest Principles'.[41] Some years later, 'being just come from the West Indies' (where he had gone in circumstances that remain unexplained, but were presumably connected with trading in sugar or slaves), Merchi offered lessons in singing and the art of accompaniment on both kinds of guitar, but expressed a clear preference for the Spanish variety. It is 'a more difficult Instrument than the English Guitar', he observed, 'yet it is more harmonious and pleasing; nay, it proves as proper for Accompanyment as the Harpsichord'.[42] This is one of several hints that some immigrant teachers were discreetly agitating against the English guitar in the cause of the Spanish, and Merchi may have intended some of the London music he published for the English guitar under the name *chitarra* to suit both instruments. His *Scelta d'ariette francesi italiane ed inglesi con accompagnamento di chitarra*, op. 15 (1766), is designed with the English guitar in mind, but some of the accompaniments can be played upon the five-course Spanish instrument of the day without difficulty.

Devotees of the Spanish guitar could also purchase a method by Merchi, for in 1766 he announced his 'Opera 7th, The easiest Method of learning the Spanish Guittar'; this was presumably *Le guide des écoliers de guitarre*, op. 7, published at Paris in 1761, and not a version of that book translated into English or a new work altogether.[43] Merchi explains there how to tune the strings, insists on the need to abandon tablature in favour of staff notation (Fig. 14 shows him using both), gives major and minor chords in all the principal keys, and illustrates a wide range of arpeggio patterns with thirty variations on the chord sequence 'Folia di Spagna'. The book does not lack pieces that could be played as effective solos, even if they never quite escape the character of an exercise (Ex. 10).

Ex. 10 Excerpt from a minuet, from [Giacomo] Merchi, *Le guide des écoliers de guitarre*, op. 7 (Paris, 1761), 12.

It may have been during the last years of his English sojourn that Merchi considered removing the double courses on his Spanish guitar and playing on single strings. The advantages of making the change are clearly explained in the *Traité des agrémens de la musique* of 1777, which may be the work either of Giacomo or (perhaps more likely) of his brother Bernard:

> Il est plus aisé de trouver 5 cordes justes qu'un plus grand nombre; les cordes simples sont plus faciles à mettre d'accord et à pincer nettement; enfin, elles rendent des sons purs, forts et moëlleux, et qui approchent de ceux de la Harpe; surtout si l'on se sert de cordes un peu grosses.[44]

> (It is easier to find five true strings than a greater number; single strings are easier to put in tune and to pluck cleanly; finally, they give sounds that are pure, loud and velvety, and which approach those of the harp, especially if one uses strings that are somewhat thick.)

This is a careful account of a crucial step in the evolution of the guitar's musical resources by one who either pioneered the initiative or was close to the guitarist who did. During the last third of the eighteenth century the guitar was slowly moving towards single strings everywhere in Western Europe save Spain, though the change was by no means rapidly consolidated. (French makers were still building guitars with ten pegs, to accommodate a full total of five double courses, until at least the 1790s.)[45] As described by Merchi, the purpose of the modification is to achieve a more convenient array of strings that can be tuned and plucked more easily; if the strings chosen are 'somewhat thick', Merchi adds, their sound will better reproduce the quality of the harp, the instrument that set the tonal ideal for the Spanish guitar for much of the later eighteenth century and indeed the nineteenth. There is a prevailing sense here of an instrument that has acquired a more focused response in the bass (since any high octave strings hitherto used on courses four and five have gone) and which has thereby acquired a darker timbre. That quality was reinforced by plucking the strings with the flesh of the fingers (as opposed to the fingernails), the technique on which Merchi insists, for otherwise the sound will be 'dry and unobliging'.[46]

It is uncertain what degree of success Merchi achieved in England, but he probably made a significant contribution to the revival of interest in the Spanish guitar that was taking place, albeit very slowly. Around 1760, before Merchi arrived in London, Thomas Gainsborough sketched Ann Ford with a Spanish guitar, but in the final portrait showed her with an English instrument;[47] yet just a year after the appearance of Merchi's *Scelta d'ariette francesi italiane ed inglesi*, Laurence Sterne asked a friend, by letter, to obtain a five-course guitar from Paris for his daughter.[48] In December 1768 the *Bath Chronicle and Weekly Gazette* announced that the well-known musician Thomas Linley would take part in a concert to be given by one of his daughters at Bath; the programme was to include 'some favourite French and Italian Airs', sung between the acts, which Linley would accompany 'upon the Spanish Guittar'.[49] A few years later, Thomas Gainsborough painted his well-known portrait of the two Linley sisters, showing Elizabeth Ann Linley resting her arms on a guitar with five single strings.[50] The Spanish guitar was by no means mainstream, yet it was no longer a backwater.

More Italians followed where Merchi had led. M. Deramoncy from Naples played the 'Guitar de Spagniola' in numerous London entertainments during 1780, all at the Great Room, Panton Street, in the Haymarket.[51] The ostentatious (and mangled) attempt to give the instrument its old name in Italian, *chitarra spagnuola*, is clearly an attempt to capitalise on its foreign associations and to make Deramoncy (who sounds French) seem genuinely Italian. The entertainments in which he took part cannot exactly be called concerts, for the programmes included card tricks, displays of 'artificial' (that is to say, scientifically made) fireworks, and performances by a one-man band, as well as Deramoncy, who accompanied a female violinist. This is not the only sign that the guitar had an association with the world of showmen; Signor Gonetti, who set off 'philosophical fireworks' on stage during his act, also offered lessons on the 'common and Spanish guitar', as John Marsh noted in his journal.[52] In October that year Marsh went to hear Signor and Signora Gonetti perform on the pianoforte, musical glasses and psaltery, and an instrument called 'Apollo's harp', 'with singing in Italian'. Gonetti attended schools when the number of pupils made it worthwhile; in 1785 he was working in London as a teacher of singing, harpsichord and the Spanish guitar, which he was happy to commend for having 'all the accords of the Harpsichord, and all the sweetness of the Harp, without their numerous and great difficulties'.[53]

Other Italian advocates of the guitar were singers, dancers, choreographers or violinists (sometimes all four), either in the orbit of the Italian Opera, or directly employed there, with lodgings in the Haymarket quarter or just across the river in Lambeth. One of the most prominent was Giovanni Battista Noferi, who published violin sonatas in London but was also known in Newcastle and Durham.[54] At the Italian Opera his task was to compose or arrange music for ballets; from the winter of 1778 until the spring of 1780 the London newspapers regularly advertised his *pas de deux* in a 'Grand ballet espagnol'; in this afterpiece he used the 'inimitable Spanish Guitar' he had been due to play in a 'Pastoral Dance' at the King's Theatre shortly before his demise in 1782.[55]

The Spanish connection

The London interest in the Spanish guitar, whether fostered by immigrant players and teachers, by showmen or by versatile musicians like Noferi, is all somewhat unexpected, for Catholic Spain was widely regarded with animosity in eighteenth-century Britain. The two countries had been on opposite sides in the War of the Spanish Succession (1701–14) and were almost continuously at war thereafter. The British blamed the Spanish for piracy in the West Indies, which damaged their interests in the sugar and slave trades, and Spanish repression in the New World colonies and the Inquisition were widely regarded in Britain with a self-righteous disgust. Few were prepared to admire the national instrument of the Spanish when they actually heard it in Iberia. Sir John Talbot Dillon's *Letters from an English Traveller in Spain, in 1778* decry 'the jarring sound of a dissonant guitarre' used with castanets for a fandango, while Alexander Jardine's *Letters from Barbary, France, Spain, Portugal, etc.* (1788) evoke a 'ragged Spaniard' whom the author met playing the guitar.[56] When Henry Swinburne travelled through Spain in 1775–6, he sometimes found himself assailed by 'the twanging of a wretched guitar', an instrument that he associates only with the coarser technique (as he sees it) of *rasgueado*, for the players strike the instrument 'with their nails, without any notion of air, but merely as a kind of accompaniment, sometimes high, sometimes low, but very coarse and monotonous'.[57]

Yet the true home of the Spanish guitar in the Georgian imagination was not the Spain of the Inquisition, once a major Atlantic and Mediterranean power and still to be reckoned with. Instead it was the Spain of *Don Quixote* and *Gil Blas*, of stage comedies, afterpieces and theatrical spectacles with highly miscellaneous and changing programmes that might include a fandango, or what passed for one on the Georgian stage. The fandango, sometimes with a seguidilla, is often named in London advertisements for theatrical performances in various venues ranging from the King's Theatre, Covent Garden and the Pantheon to the Royal Circus and the spectacle shows of Sadler's Wells. Madame Rossi and Monsieur Lepicq repeatedly performed their 'much admired Spanish dances', namely 'the Sequedilla and the Fandango', at the King's Theatre in a ballet entitled *Le tuteur trompé, or, The Guardian Outwitted*.[58] In 1778 *The Spanish Barber* ran for many nights at the Haymarket Theatre with 'a Fandango overture' that was prominently advertised in the press, and during the 1780s a rope-dancer with the stage name La Belle Espagnola performed a fandango repeatedly with castanets, 'after the Spanish fashion'.[59] *The Castle of Andalusia*, performed at Covent Garden in 1793, featured 'a New Dance' advertised as 'THE SPANISH FANDANGO'.[60]

By 1784 interest had reached the point where it was possible to contemplate publishing a method – the first English-language manual for the gut-strung guitar since *The False Consonances of Musick* (1682) by Nicola Matteis, issued almost exactly a century earlier. Surprisingly, this pioneering book was the work of a Briton: William Burnett of Hart Street, Covent Garden. Burnett was a versatile musician employed to play the kettledrums at the Italian Opera and a member of the ad hoc band serving the Coldstream Guards; his published works include *Summer Amusement . . . Twelve Country Dances and Three Cotillons, entirely New, for a Violin and Bass, Harpsichord or Harp* (1782) and *Twenty-Four Military Divertimentos* scored for clarinets.[61] In February 1784 Burnett advertised another work, entitled *Six Familiar Airs for the Spanish Guittar, with a Compleat Scale for that Instrument* and priced at only 1s.; he also announced that he was offering lessons.[62] By June, the work had grown to become *Eight Familiar Airs for the Spanish Guitar* and was now to include something more ambitious than a 'Compleat Scale', namely:

an explanation of the Finger Board; the Natural
and Cromatic Scales; with the Chords in the different keys,
and the manner of fingering them,
By WILLIAM BURNETT, Musician,
Belonging to the Coldstream Regiment of Foot Guards.[63]

Alas, no other trace of this method or the 'Familiar Airs' for the Spanish guitar has ever been found, and they may never have appeared; Burnett's advertisements have the air of an evolving prospectus for a work 'in hand', as Georgian advertisements for publications often say, with the plan gradually becoming more ambitious until it became too costly (Burnett was publishing the work himself). Yet there would have been a market for such a pamphlet; Burnett advertised it in the very year when John Marsh heard 'a duet on 2 Spanish guitars' at a musical gathering in London, suggesting that a polite constituency for the Spanish guitar was now emerging.[64]

Since Burnett's tutor has not come to light, the first surviving method for the Spanish guitar published in eighteenth-century England is *Compleat Instructions for the Spanish Guitar* by a violinist of Italian lineage, Felice Chabran, registered at Stationer's Hall on 9 October 1795.[65] Chabran was appointed 'Leader of the Ballets' at London's Italian Opera, upon the death of Noferi in 1782.[66] Despite the markedly Italianate frame of Chabran's musical life in London, *Compleat Instructions* records an interest in the Spanish guitar as an actively *Spanish* instrument, for it includes a lively fandango (Fig. 17), a genre not represented in the repertoire of the English guitar but often found, as we have seen, on the English stage, in a variety of no doubt anglicised forms. Its opening measures recall the 'tune to the fandango, a Favourite

Fig. 17 Fandango (the title has been cropped by the binder) and opening of a 'Sigadilia' from F. Chabran, *Compleat Instructions for the Spanish Guitar* (1795), 20.

Dance of the Spaniards' published in the Appendix to *A General History of the Science and Practice of Music* (1776) by Sir John Hawkins; the openings of both melodies share material with the fandango in Act II of Gluck's *Don Juan* and therefore with Mozart's allusion to that piece in *Le nozze di Figaro*.[67] These are all related to a melody printed with a bass by Richard Twiss in his *Travels through Portugal and Spain* (1775).[68] Whatever Chabran's fandango in *Compleat Instructions* may owe to contemporary guitar music in Spain, therefore, this probably reached him filtered through theatrical entertainments exploring a shared British and even a general northern European idea of the fandango that coalesced in a family of closely related melodies.

The title page of *Compleat Instructions* gives Chabran's address as 15 Stangate Street in Lambeth, located south of the river in a quarter that had grown considerably after the opening of Westminster Bridge in 1750; it was far too close to a working stretch of the riverside, with its wharves, detritus and scavengers, to be an elite district. Stangate Street nonetheless offered the advantage of swift access to the opposite bank of the Thames and the streets of the West End, including the Haymarket, where Chabran was employed.

J. Doane's compendium *A Musical Directory for the Year 1794* shows that Stangate Street had become so popular with rank-and-file members of the musical profession that it had become, in effect, a musicians' quarter (Table 1), though in that year Chabran is not listed as a resident, as he is on the title page of his method from 1795.

Table 1

Musicians lodging in Stangate Street, Lambeth. From J. Doane, *A Musical Directory for the Year 1794*.

Name	Instrument / Voice	House number
John Ashbridge	drums	8
Hezekiah Cantelo	trumpet	–
James Cornish	oboe	–
Cornish, Jr	oboe	–
Charles Evans	organ, violin	–
Joseph Hill	double bass	–
William Howard	violin	–
[Charles] Lockhart	composer, organ, tenor	20
Lowin	reed-maker	21
Jeremiah Parkinson,	bassoon	10
J. Sharp	double bass	16
John Sowerby	flute	11
William Turner	tenor, bass	27
William Warren	violin	7

It is tempting to suppose that Chabran could venture a method for the Spanish guitar in 1795, and advertise himself on the title page as a teacher of that instrument (among others) because he lodged in a tightly packed quarter where musicians recommended one another to their clients, as the opportunity arose, in a mutually supportive network.[69] (Chabran's house survived until the 1960s, when one of London's many planning catastrophes of that decade swept it away.) A renumbering plan for Stangate Street dated

Fig. 18 Title page of F. Chabran, *Compleat Instructions for the Spanish Guitar* (1795), engraving, by Vincent Woodthorpe. The vignette accurately depicts both the instrument – a five-string Spanish guitar – and the position of the seated player.

1881 reveals that in all cases save one where a house number is known, the musicians lived on the same side of the street – the south side – further enhancing the sense of a musicians' quarter and providing an example of the concentration of a particular trade in a specific district or street with which any visitor to Georgian London soon became familiar.[70]

The title page of *Compleat Instructions* (Fig. 18) is the work of Vincent Woodthorpe, printer and engraver of Fetter Lane. Although Woodthorpe is best known for his fanciful illustrations to George Barrington's book *An Account of a Voyage to New South Wales* (1801), many of his engravings reveal a pragmatic artist accustomed to drawing meticulous plans, shop façades and cards for tradesmen. The figure of the guitar player is minute, yet it successfully shows a guitar with five strings, the correct number for the teaching Chabran offers, supported by a strap, as the text recommends. The player rests her left foot on a small stool (a detail Chabran does not mention), and is etched with as much care as the guitar. Less ostentatiously fashionable than the young women in empire dresses who will very soon adorn the title pages of other methods, Chabran's player wears a tied bonnet, a fichu (a small kerchief worn to fill a low neckline) and an apron ruffled at the hem and not embroidered. Although the setting appears to be a garden belonging to the implied cottage that has supplied the parlour chair and stool, Woodthorpe decisively breaks with the *fête champêtre* and *comedia dell'arte* scenes of Jean-Antoine Watteau, rich in guitars, and associated in England with a large legacy of prints and porcelains.[71] His guitarist is more akin to Blouzelind, 'In Apron blue or Apron White', the country girl in John Gay's poem *The Shepherd's Week* of 1714; a mezzotint of 1781 shows her seated on a wooden chair in a cottage garden, like Chabran's musician, but occupied with her spinning wheel instead of a guitar.[72] With Chabran's *Compleat Instructions*, the Spanish guitar inherits the associations of its English predecessor with the rural and cottage picturesque (see above, p. 47).

At first, it may seem surprising that the text of Chabran's book, the primordial English method, has mostly been taken verbatim from Robert Bremner's *Instructions for the [English] Guitar* of 1758. Such borrowing was not uncommon in methods, and it would be misguided to look for signs of rupturing traditions as the Spanish guitar begins seriously to bid for the position hitherto enjoyed by its English counterpart. For the most part, indeed, there is only ease and continuity here, as one kind of guitar, the English, slowly fades into another, the Spanish. The English guitar's prevailing home key of C major is the one most often employed in the pieces Chabran provides for the novice to play, and a piece from his book such as 'The Nymph', with its triadic figures and parallel sixths, would cause no surprise if it were to be found in a collection for the English guitar, whence it may indeed have come (Ex. 11). Chabran needs no new conceptual or pedagogical tools to place the Spanish guitar before the public, and does not much anticipate the sense of a bass territory ruled by the thumb, and a treble area commanded by the fingers, to be found only a few years later in the accompaniments published

Ex. 11 The first two sections of 'The Nymph', from Felice Chabran, *Compleat Instructions for the Spanish Guitar* (1795), 18.

by Bonaventura Sperati (see Chapter 4). The newness of the Spanish guitar in 1795 seems to lie with its Spanish associations (essentially theatrical), with its versatility (it plays in many more keys than the English guitar without the use of a capotasto), and in the harp-like timbre of its strings, made of gut or overspun silk. Chabran uses the first sentence of his book, indeed, to establish that the sound of the Spanish guitar is 'much like the Harp'.

Chabran advises the novice to pluck the five strings near the bridge, where a beginner is most likely to produce a decisive result, but does not specify whether the player should use the nails or the fingertips. A brief section on trills beginning on the upper note ('the shake') or the lower ('the beat'), followed by a simple set of tuning instructions, completes the pedagogical part of the book, as the reader is plunged straight into arpeggio exercises with a 'Prelude to exercise the right hand Fingers'. The pieces that follow, in seven different keys, represent many layers of Georgian musical life: the playhouses of Covent Garden and Drury Lane, the Italian Opera and the dancing academies. The range extends to the fife and drum repertoire of the militia, for there is a close parallel to Chabran's choice of airs in James Aird's *Selection of Scotch, English, Irish and Foreign Airs Adapted for the Fife, Violin or German Flute*, probably also of 1795; six of the melodies that Chabran arranges for the guitar appear in Aird's series ('God save the king', 'Rule Britannia', 'Duke of York's Troop', 'O dear what can the matter be', 'The White Cockade' and 'Sally in our Alley'). Like Aird's collections, which show soldiers or a military drum on their title pages, *Compleat Instructions* registers the bellicose and patriotic mood of the mid-1790s, when the volunteer militias and their tunes could be heard in many English towns (the book has three marches in addition to the National Anthem and 'Rule Britannia'). Some of the other airs Chabran uses, such as 'Sally in our Alley', had become folksongs, in effect, their composers either forgotten or rarely remembered; his 'Scotch Air' (the traditional melody 'Corn riggs are bonny') belongs in the same class.[73] Other solo pieces include three allemandes, probably drawn from the repertoire of the dancing academies (the same may be said for 'Del Caro's Hornpipe'), and three airs by Ignaz Pleyel, resident in London from December 1791 until May 1792 and the only composer whom *Compleat Instructions* finds cause to name; Pleyel's pieces are all identifiable as sections from chamber works, which possibly reached Chabran through the intermediary of vocal versions, several of which appeared with arrangements for the English guitar.[74]

The final pages of *Compleat Instructions* offer six accompanied songs, most with theatrical connections, and an instrumental duet:

1. 'A shepherd lov'd a nymph so fair'. Sung by Mrs Bland in the comic opera *The Cherokee* by James Cobb and Stephen Storace at Drury Lane, 1794.

2. 'In the dead of night'. The text is a translation of Anacreon's Ode III by William Hall. From *The Wedding Day*, performed at Drury Lane, 1794; as sung by Mrs Jordan, it ranked as a 'favourite song' in 1794 (*LS*, vol. v, 1700, 1751).

3. 'Nel cor non più mi sento'. From Act II of Giovanni Paisiello's *La molinarella*, performed at the Pantheon, May 1791, with Chabran as 'Leader of the Ballets'. It was widely known in England with the English text 'Hope told a flattering tale' (*LS*, vol. v, 1352–3).

4. 'Son perfetta cacciatrice'. Set for two voices and guitar. In the 1791–2 season the song was performed by two Italian singers, Giovanni Morelli and Giovanni Garelli, at the Haymarket in an afterpiece entitled 'The Festive Board' (*Diary; or, Woodfall's Register*, 19 April 1792; cf. *LS*, vol. v, 1448).

5. 'Vous désertez notre rivage'. Unidentified.

6. 'Non vi turbate no pietosi'. From Gluck's *Alceste*; the first performance in London was given at the King's Theatre on 30 April 1795 (shortly before Chabran's *Compleat Instructions* appeared).

7. 'Vive le vin a favourite duet in the Deserter'. From Act II of Pierre-Alexandre Monsigny's *Le déserteur, drame en trois actes* (1769). Chabran uses the melody of the original (which is given to the guitar), generally follows the harmony implied by the bass, and variously adapts or simplifies Monsigny's second violin part to create a duet for violin and guitar; the piece is not a duet in the original.

This selection draws on songs for the English stage, notably Drury Lane (nos 1–2), but also shows Chabran steering for the first time in *Compleat Instructions* towards his professional domain, the Italian opera (nos 3, 6). Example 12 gives the music and the first stanza of 'Vous désertez notre rivage', a characteristically melodious instance of the contemporary French

Ex. 12 'Vous désertez notre rivage', from Felice Chabran, *Compleat Instructions for the Spanish Guitar* (1795), 32–3.

romance, with its prelude and short postlude, its scatter of inverted chords to leaven the root-position harmonies, its shifts in and out of double-speed arpeggios, and occasional doubling of the voice in thirds or sixths. Just as French in manner is the light-courtly pastoral imagery and the mannered eroticism of the poem: a seducer's blandishments to young Manette, who is leaving her village and whom he addresses as a bird about to migrate, and then in subsequent stanzas as a 'fleur nouvelle', which the sweet breeze of the west wind will open. An error of the printer, not prudery, is presumably responsible for the misprint that effaces the notorious sexual ambiguity of the verb *jouir* ('to take pleasure', but also 'to reach a sexual climax') at the close of verse 2.

Adieu les plaisirs du Village,
Vous les emmenez avec vous,
Puis quils sont de votre voiage
Ramenez les bientôt chez nous.
Retenez la leçon du sage
Prêtresse aimable du plaisir,
Quand on a la vie en partage
Le bien suprême est d'en jou[i]r. *bis.*

De vos vingt ans faites usage
Manette profitez du jour
C'est sur tout; oui c'est à votre âge
Qu'en lisiere on mene l'amour.
Vous êtes une fleur nouvelle
Qu'un doux Zephir vient entrouvrir
Soyez docile autant que belle
Et laissez souffler le Zephir. *bis.*

FOUR

The 1800 Moment

*The sounds that pleased me yesterday ... weary me
today, and will grow yet more wearisome tomorrow.*

Samuel Johnson, *Rasselas* (1759)

The nineteenth century began twice in Britain. A dispute about the method
of reckoning ensured that many dated the new age from 1 January 1801; even
then, the sense of a historic moment was diffused by a conflict with France
that seemed set to continue. Yet, as astrologers have always maintained, the
movements of the heavenly bodies may be apparent in small things as well as
great. Around 1800 the Spanish guitar passed through a brief but formative
phase of its history in England: the guitar of six single strings made its first
documented appearance, the first London collection of printed music for such
guitars appeared in the capital and the enhanced instrument began to find
influential devotees among the elite of London's West End.[1]

By 1800 the brilliant sounds of plucked metal strings, admired since
the Middle Ages and clearly adored in the Elizabethan period, had lost some
of their appeal. It is important not to overstate the distinction contemporaries perceived between the harpsichord and the pianoforte during the later
eighteenth century, when the latter could be regarded as a 'harpsichord with
hammers',[2] yet the differences in timbre were sufficiently marked for the
sound of the pianoforte to make the sonority of plucked wire appear old-
fashioned, even displeasing, as some surprisingly explicit remarks about the
wire-strung English guitar will soon reveal. At the same time, the ascent of
the harp as the aristocratic salon instrument of choice – well attested in elite

portraiture of the later eighteenth century – reflected a developing taste for the more velvety sound of gut strings. This is the taste that the gut-strung Spanish guitar had long been able to satisfy, but it was also one that numerous hand-held instruments invented during the decades around 1800, such as the 'harp-lute', were designed to exploit. As early as 1774, Giacomo Merchi was trying to persuade readers of the *Public Advertiser* that the Spanish instrument was a 'more harmonious and pleasing' instrument than its English counterpart. After a period of indifference, public taste in Britain eventually caught up with him.[3]

The six-string guitar appears

The change was a matter of comment in the summer of 1800, when the *Morning Post* suggested that the fashionable world might consider cultivating the mandolin, whose strings, 'being of catgut, instead of wire, are more harmonious than those of the [English] guitar'.[4] Charles Burney, writing soon after 1800, admired the Spanish guitar for being 'superior in tone, expression, and power' to the English instrument 'strung with wire', while in 1809 an observer deemed the Spanish variety 'very superior to the common, simple, instrument of that name' because its tones 'so perfectly resemble that of the harp'.[5] There is even a note of disdain for the English guitar in 1811, when an officer fighting in the Peninsular War in Iberia was anxious lest the guitars he mentioned in his letters home might be confounded with 'that twanging thing of wires which is often seen in England'.[6] By the 1820s the contrast between the Spanish and the English guitar could be seen in terms of a generational difference; C. B. Tayler's collection *A Fireside Book; or, The Account of a Christmas spent at Old Court* (1828), published when the English guitar was definitively out of fashion, features a young woman with a Spanish guitar she thinks 'so much better' than her aunt's English equivalent with its 'wiry' strings.[7] The whirligig of time had brought in its revenges, and now the English guitar had found its Old Lady Languish.

On the threshold of the new century the demand for Spanish guitars was already responsive to innovations, to judge by an advertisement of 1799, where Tebaldo Monzani announces a 'New Pattern Spanish Guitar which is approved by the most esteemed Masters'.[8] The precise nature of the 'New

Fig. 19 Portrait of Rosemund Mountain (née Wilkinson), by Adam Buck, 1802, medium unknown. The singer is shown playing a six-string guitar. Formerly in the possession of Mrs Eliott Wood, current location unknown; repr. in *The Connoisseur*, 48 (May–August 1917), facing 142.

Pattern' remains unknown, and yet it may be no great mystery; the seminal innovation of this date was the addition of a sixth string in the bass of the Spanish guitar, and by 1810 nobody had done more to encourage the use of six-string guitars than the flautist and musical entrepreneur Monzani.[9] A portrait by John Russell from 1799 shows the actress and singer Elizabeth Bannister playing a guitar with five single strings, and Charles Burney's essay on the guitar for Rees's *Cyclopædia*, drafted by 1805 from old notes, still assumes that five is the standard number;[10] in 1807 the Oxford humorist James Beresford is still complaining about the 'dead, lumpish, tubby tones of the fourth and fifth strings of the guittar' as if there were no sixth.[11] Yet such instruments would soon have begun to seem old-fashioned, especially in London, and a full-length portrait of the singer Rosemund Mountain, exhibited at the Royal Academy summer exhibition in 1802, shows her using a six-string guitar (Fig. 19). This may allude to her appearance in *The Gipsey Prince* the previous year, in which she played Antonia, a character said to be 'married' to her guitar, so keenly does she play.[12]

The new sixth string, which enlarged the scope of the guitar's bass response, should be viewed as one current in a long-standing play of contrary forces. On one hand there was the lure of devices peculiar to the guitar, such as the strummed chord. Here, players might follow a written bass line but did not conceive the chords they were producing as the result of contrapuntal relations; instead, a chord was a triad whose ingredients the guitar supplied in whatever inversion the choice of tuning and stringing produced when the player made the appropriate shape on the fingerboard and swept all or most of the strings. On the other hand there was a drive, apparent from the very beginning of notated guitar music in the sixteenth century, to bring the idioms of the guitar more into accord with mainstream and literate practice. One manifestation of this impulse was the demise of tablature and its replacement by staff notation – a change already championed by Giacomo Merchi in 1761 – so that literate players now began to use the common coin of all mainstream musical transactions.[13] The interplay of these opposing forces in the eighteenth century explains why Merchi, for example, uses standard harmonic progressions in his guitar compositions but does not realise them in a way that a contemporary keyboard player would have considered grammatical; the bass resources of his five-course (later five-string) instrument were not designed for such purposes and could only intermittently be made to serve them (Ex. 13). The widespread adoption of the sixth string in the bass, however, shows that many players by 1800 wanted more consistently grammatical results, not least because the new arrangement permitted more root-position chords.[14] The guitar was better able to speak the standard, literate musical language because it gradually relinquished much of its own vernacular.

Ex. 13 Excerpt from a gigue, from [Giacomo] Merchi, *Le guide des écoliers de guitarre*, op. 7 (Paris, 1761), 9. The underlying harmonic motion is a movement round the circle of fifths; yet much of what Merchi writes seems tonally unfocused: the defining bass notes E, A, D and G are only intermittently present and the harmonic function of some chords (e.g. the first sonority of bar 3, with the upbeat) is vague.

Accompanied songs using the full resources of the six-string guitar make an early appearance in print with *Three Favorite Canzonetts, Arranged with Accompaniment for the Piano Forte or Guitar* (1799), the guitar parts of which are the work of the Scotswoman Sophia Dussek (née Corri), and with Luigi Lolli's collection entitled *Six Italian Canzonetts, with Accompaniments for the Spanish Guitar* (1800?).[15] The songs arranged by Madame Dussek are presented in separate scores, one for the pianoforte and another for the guitar, each in idiomatic keys for the instrument. Example 14, from the beginning of 'Mi sento dentro al cor', shows her luxuriating in the unprecedentedly sonorous and grounded quality that the sixth string gave to the key of G major. Lolli's set of six Italian songs, another festival of arpeggios for the guitarist, with the sixth string in constant commission, bears no date but cannot be much later than Madame Dussek's anthology since Lolli died in 1805.[16]

The sixth string allowed the guitar to be taken in a more pianistic direction, in the sense that a condensed version of parlour pianoforte accompaniments could be devised, with a serviceably low bass, and could be notated on a single stave. Bonaventura Sperati's series *A Periodical Collection of Italian, French and English Songs ... for the Spanish Guitar of Six Strings*, in twelve numbers, advertised in the late spring of 1801, offers good examples of such accompaniments.[17] *A Periodical Collection*, the first attempt in England to apply the

Ex. 14 The beginning of 'Mi sento dentro al cor', arranged for Spanish guitar by Madame Dussek: Canzonetta II from *Three Favorite Canzonetts, Arranged with Accompaniment for the Piano Forte or Guitar* (1799).

established device of serial publication to the Spanish guitar, was published by the partnership of Monzani and Cimador from their Opera Music Warehouse in Pall Mall, and since the songs in the series are mostly in Italian (two are in French) the ethos of the work is predominantly Italianate and operatic, well in accord with the reputation of the company, which published 'all the music of the Operas and Ballets' performed at the Italian Opera close by.[18] The introduction to 'Si ride amore', the fifth number of Sperati's *Periodical Collection*, shows the kind of texture he created – more consistently grammatical than anything Chabran had ventured with five strings in 1795.[19] The dominant chord, E major, can now be sounded in root position with a low bass, giving the chord a handsome spread of two octaves (Ex. 15). The guitar is functioning, in effect, as a simplified and portable pianoforte.

The final number of *A Periodical Collection,* clearly intended to be the *pièce de résistance* of the series, shows the effect the sixth string could have upon an accompanying part when the addition was considered not only new but also a technical challenge that some would not care to meet. Sperati scores the piece for two voices, two flutes and one or two guitars *ad libitum*, with the option

Ex. 15 The beginning of the canzonetta 'Si ride amore' by Bonaventura Sperati: no. 5 in his series *A Periodical Collection of Italian, French and English Songs ... for the Spanish Guitar of Six Strings*, published by Monzani and Cimador (1801–2).

of a thoroughbass accompaniment on the pianoforte and a cello doubling the bass line. A note on the score distinguishes the guitar part on the penultimate stave in Example 16 as the 'Easier Accompaniment' which 'may be play'd also on the Guitar with 5 strings' and will be found to be 'sufficient occasionally'.[20] The guitar part on the lowest stave, labelled the 'Principal Accompaniment' in Sperati's score, is for a six-string guitar and is clearly more elaborate, with the root of the key, F major, sounding an octave lower than in the five-string version.

Number 1 in Sperati's series is the first manual for a six-string guitar published in England: *New and Complete Instructions for the Spanish Guitar with Six Strings*, first advertised in 1802 (it seems to have been somewhat delayed).[21] Amid the expected directions for tuning, chords and arpeggio exercises, Sperati remarks that a guitarist may wish to play while walking, perhaps for a serenade. He assumes that most players still pluck the strings using only the thumb and first two fingers of the right hand in the common eighteenth-century manner, but he makes a point of insisting that all fingers should be employed save the little finger, which is to rest on the soundboard. In a revealing aside, he observes that the guitar 'may be used in Country-dances

Ex. 16 The beginning of Bonaventura Sperati's setting of 'Già riede primavera': no. 12 in his series *A Periodical Collection of Italian, French and English Songs ... for the Spanish Guitar of Six Strings* (1801–2).

to fill up the harmony instead of the harp', thus extending the instrument's repertoire to the robust tunes published in annual collections such as *Astor's Twenty Four Country Dances for the Year 1803: with Proper Tunes and Directions to each Dance as they are Performed at Court, Bath, and all Public Assemblies* (1803). Sperati also describes the guitar's advantages in terms that will recur throughout the first four decades of the nineteenth century, evoking the genteel existence that he assumes his readers enjoy or aspire to lead:

> Besides all these and other advantages, it has that of being so light, handy, and portable that it suits all purposes of amusements either in the house or garden; it is also so convenient to travel with, so pleasing in the solitude of the Country, that it is a matter of surprise it is not so fashionable in England as it is abroad, particularly among the Ladies, to whom it adds so much grace and elegance being (the Piano-forte excepted) the Instrument the most adapted to them.

At 1*s*. per number, or 1*s*. 6*d*. if the piece were more than two pages long, Sperati's material would have seemed expensive to many, the method, priced at 3*s*. 6*d*., still more so. This was material for a wealthy clientele, though second-hand copies could be cheaper; in September 1807 the London firm of Broadwood sent his *New and Complete Instructions*, together with a square pianoforte, a Spanish guitar and a guitar case, to Miss Thomas in Parliament Street, Westminster, for transit onwards by waggon to Elizabeth Williams of Derby.[22] In this revealing instance of a woman with a metropolitan address obtaining a guitar and a method – a complete beginner's kit – for someone in a provincial town, the price of Sperati's method is given as only 2s. 6d.

Opera singers and the West End routs

Given that Italians have always understood the usefulness of the guitar, it is no surprise to find that singers from London's Italian Opera used it to accompany themselves at private gatherings. The tenor Giuseppe Viganoni 'used to accompany himself sometimes on the Spanish Guittar' at private parties, according to the eye-witness R. J. S. Stevens, professor of music at Gresham College from 1801, and on those occasions 'his fancy, taste and beautiful expression in singing were most uncommon and inexpressibly delightful'.[23] A concert hosted by the Duchess of York at Bath in 1802 featured a performance by Rovedino junior, probably a son of the Italian *buffo* bass Carlo Rovedino, who appeared regularly at the King's Theatre until at least 1811; on this occasion, Rovedino junior 'sang several airs, and accompanied himself on the Spanish guitar'.[24] In a more narrowly professional context, the tenor Diomiro Tramezzani sang and accompanied himself on the 'French guitar' at the King's Theatre in April 1810; three songs by Luigi Gianella, published around 1809, 'with an Accompaniment for the Piano Forte or Spanish Guitar Composed Expressly for Signor Tramezzani', may provide a glimpse of his wider repertoire.[25] Even 'the great, the far-famed' Angelica Catalani,[26] who first came to the King's Theatre for the 1806–7 season, accompanied herself on the guitar, to judge by Jean-Urbain Guérin's miniature of her with a converted Neapolitan instrument having ten pegs but six single strings (Fig. 20).

The occasions when these musicians performed included the densely crowded parties or 'routs' that drew 'the Brahmins of the ton', in Byron's phrase: the most elite aristocratic families with London residences.[27] Hannah More, the religious writer and philanthropist, believed that those who attended such routs went only in order to say 'fond and flattering things at

Fig. 20 Jean-Urbain Guérin, portrait of Angelica Catalani playing the guitar, early nine-teenth century, miniature on ivory. The famous Italian opera singer is shown playing a six-string guitar, presumably to accompany her own singing, as she did at performances in London and the provinces, starting in 1806. Département des Arts Graphiques, Musée du Louvre, Paris.

random to a circle of five hundred people every night', but there was much else to enjoy (or endure) besides.[28] In addition to performances by professional singers and instrumentalists engaged for the night, there were amateurs hardy enough to hazard their reputation by performing, or unable to refuse because they were a daughter of the hostess. There were various reasons why such elite amateurs might choose the Spanish guitar for such a purpose, not least because the instrument was associated with the pleasures and prizes of the Grand Tour. Had not the venturesome Lady Webster commissioned a

Fig. 21 Louis Gauffier, portrait of Elizabeth, Lady Webster (later Lady Holland), 1795, oil on canvas. Lady Webster is seated at her ease at home in Florence, having laid aside her guitar on the chaise-longue beside her. Sold at auction, Sotheby's, New York, 26 May 2016, lot 83, current location unknown.

portrait of herself at Florence in 1795, sharing the sofa with a five-string guitar that closely resembles the work of the Fabricatore atelier in Naples? It would be hard to find a more elite image of the guitar at this date than this portrait, with its suggestion of balmy air, and a cool marble floor, in a southern city (Fig. 21).

Fig. 22 Life-size dummy board of a female street guitarist and ballad seller, English, *c.*1780, oil on wood. A companion board shows a man with a barrel organ. Both were probably made for a tea garden or an inn. Victoria and Albert Museum, London, CIRC.107-1938.

Chapter Four

The fashion for the guitar in the beau monde of London's West End also drew upon a curious musical fashion that has rarely received its due.[29] An early trace of it appears at the close of Chabran's *Compleat Instructions* of 1795, where Joseph Dale, 'Importer and Publisher of Music, and Manufacturer of Musical Instruments', placed a general advertisement. One might suppose, from the context, that Dale was a seller of Spanish guitars, but that is not how he appears in his other publicity; in 1799 he informed 'the Nobility and the Public in general' that he had made major improvements in the *tambourine*, removing certain metal elements from the frame so that it may be thrown 'round with more grace . . . more effectively to accompany any piece of music'.[30] The fashion for playing the tambourine while dancing, or striking 'attitudes', was one of the ways in which elite musical fashion around 1800 registered the taste for statuary and decorated vases brought back from the Grand Tour, or newly excavated from classical sites such as Herculaneum. Various society ladies, including Emma Hamilton, had themselves painted or drawn as a 'tambarina'.[31]

The tambourine was also a favoured instrument of the street musicians commonly called 'Savoyards', after the duchy of Savoy, regardless of their actual country of origin. There developed a fashion for women of the beau monde to garb themselves as Savoyards and play appropriate instruments, first perhaps as a form of disguise at masquerades; 'a brace of beautiful Savoyards' appeared with barrel organ and tambourine at a West End masquerade in May 1792.[32] The fashion is ridiculed in a satirical print of 1799, by George Woodward, entitled *Savoyards of Fashion: or, The Musical Mania*; five elite women appear with barrel organ, horn, cymbals, tambourine and triangle – all, except the horn, being established street instruments (though the horn was often heard in the streets when played by coach boys).[33] By the 1780s, and perhaps well before, some street musicians had begun to combine the barrel organ with the Spanish guitar, to judge by an English dummy board produced in that decade (Fig. 22). Such dummy boards, painted in oils on wood, were commonly used to mask a cold hearth or embellish an empty corner, and could be made life-size: this one is somewhat more than 165 cm high. A woman dressed in a cotton or linen printed gown with the sleeves rolled up, a spotted neckerchief and a large coarse apron – working clothes of the period – strums a guitar, clearly singing, and carrying what is probably a sheaf of ballads in her apron pocket. A companion board shows a male associate playing a barrel organ, so there is little doubt that both boards depict Savoyards. A stipple engraving of 1799 by Adam Buck RA, entitled *Savoyards*, shows a woman playing a guitar (it is too shallow to be a hurdy-gurdy, bearing in mind that over half the wheel would be within the body of the instrument) while her two female companions sound the tambourine and triangle (Fig. 23). Hiding their faces partly or entirely, as if to emphasise the theme of disguise, they all wear elegant empire-style dresses and offer a striking visual counterpart to the alliance of street music and elite parlour fashion that contributed to the vogue for Spanish guitars around 1800.

Reports in the 'Fashionable World' column of the *Morning Post* reveal several guitar players in the elite circles of London's West End soon after 1800. These are unlikely to be the disinterested pieces of society news they purport to be, for such notices were often drafted at the behest of the hosts; yet the Spanish guitar clearly was returning to London's high life. One of these beau monde players, Emily Stratford, played before some two hundred people at a mansion, on the edge of Hyde Park during a rout in 1801. The other performers on the same occasion, hosted by her mother, the Countess of Aldborough, included the celebrated beauty Emma Hamilton, who was related by marriage to the countess; Emma, recently caricatured by James Gillray as an overweight Dido lamenting the departure of her Aeneas, Horatio Nelson, sang two duets with Viganoni from the Italian Opera; when they had finished, the 'beautiful Lady Emily Stratford played and sung several select pieces on the Spanish guitar, with much judgment and fine effect'.[34] Some of the 'select pieces' she played are perhaps among the songs with accompaniment for six-string guitar and basso dedicated to her by Antonio Zaniboni, traceable in Bath during 1798 but later living in London's Haymarket, according to the title page of his *Six Italian Canzonetts and Eight Divertimentos principally for Spanish Guitar and Bass Accompaniments or any other Instruments, Composed and Dedicated with Permission to the Right Noble Lady Emily Stratford* (1802?).[35] The texts of the songs are in Italian, as suited a social circle keener to be known as aficionados of Italian opera in the Haymarket than of the English stage, and the collection was issued again by Monzani and Cimador from their Opera Music Warehouse in Pall Mall (Ex. 17).

The Spanish guitar appeared again a few weeks later in the West End, when Mrs Morton Pitt of Arlington Street arranged a masquerade to mark 'the *debut* of her beautiful and accomplished daughter in the *beau monde*'. The Prince of Wales was present to see some of the guests cause a great stir with their disguises. The outstanding musical performance was given by Miss Vaughan, of Manchester Square, who danced and then 'displayed her vocal talents in Signora Vinci's favourite Pollacia, accompanying herself with great taste on the guitar'.[36] The 'favourite Pollacia' was 'Già un dolce raggio', an air that Marianna Vinci was just then performing at the King's Theatre in *La principessa filosofa*, the work in which she made her debut at London's Italian

Fig. 23 Adam Buck, *Savoyards*, 1799, coloured stipple and aquatint. The women play guitar, tambourine and triangle, in line with the fashion among elite women for imitating street musicians (the Savoyards of the title). Victoria and Albert Museum, London, E2620-1930.

Ex. 17 The second section of the canzonetta 'Della cara mia biondina', from Antonio Zaniboni, *Six Italian Canzonetts and Eight Divertimentos principally for Spanish Guitar and Bass Accompaniments or any other Instruments, Composed and Dedicated with Permission to the Right Noble Lady Emily Stratford* (1802?).

Opera.[37] In February 1802 the *Morning Post* reported a musical evening, at the residence of Lady Milner in Portland Place, showing that Emily Stratford was not the only guitarist in her family; this time her sister Louisa 'played on the Spanish guitar with the most ravishing sweetness'. Later that same evening, she sang a duet with a gentleman, which was accompanied on the Spanish guitar and was 'very much admired'.[38]

Within a few days these indefatigable socialites soon gathered again. The hostess was again the Countess of Aldborough and the professionals present included the tenor John Braham and the soprano Nancy Storace, two of the most celebrated singers of the day. There was 'much fine singing and playing', runs the newspaper report, 'but what seemed most to charm', says the account, paying the necessary compliment to the daughter of the hostess, 'was a duet, sweetly sung by Lady Louisa Stratford, and a Gentleman amateur, accompanied by the Spanish guitar'.[39] On the same occasion, several Italian and Spanish airs were played 'with fine execution' by 'Mr. Zanoni', probably a compositor's mistake for Zaniboni, the guitar master who dedicated to Emily Stratford the collection of Italian songs mentioned above. The notice of the occasion observes that the Spanish guitar 'seems to be daily gaining ground on the public, and is now to be met with in most of the circles of fashion; it is undoubtedly a sweet accompaniment to the voice'.

The Savoyard craze continued throughout the first decade of the nineteenth century. In 1808 a little-known musician named Thomas Bolton published scores for a remarkable domestic ensemble, combining the Savoyard's tambourine with the Spanish guitar, castanets and several other instruments, as revealed by the fulsome title, which is worth quoting at length: *A Collection of Airs, Marches, Dances (with Figures), Waltzes, Pollacas, and Quick Steps . . . The Whole Adapted for the Piano Forte, with Accompaniments and Directions ad libitum for the following Fashionable Instruments: Lyre or Lute, Spanish Guitar, Harp, Tambourine, Castanets, Flute or Violin.* The collection contains dance pieces for small ensembles with the 'figures' for the dancers specified, and while there is no separate part for the tambourine or castanets these are to be used 'at pleasure with the whole of the Music', together with the triangle, another Savoyard instrument welcomed indoors. Example 18 shows the beginning of an untitled piece scored from Bolton's parts, using the Spanish guitar with the pianoforte, flageolet and lyre or lute. The lyre is perhaps Edward Light's 'Apollo lyre', first offered to the public in

Ex. 18 The opening section of the second piece from Thomas Bolton, *A Collection of Airs, Marches, Dances (with Figures), Waltzes, Pollacas, and Quick Steps . . . The Whole Adapted for the Piano Forte, with Accompaniments and Directions ad libitum for the following Fashionable Instruments: Lyre or Lute, Spanish Guitar, Harp, Tambourine, Castanets, Flute or Violin* (1808).

1807, while the lute required is presumably the long-necked 'Regency lute' that has recently been brought to light.[40] As the example shows, Bolton uses the Spanish guitar and the lyre in a very similar manner, and the same may be said for the Spanish guitar and the Regency lute; the only clue to what will soon give the guitar the edge over its rivals lies in its compass, for at the very end of the piece Bolton takes the guitar down to low *G* on the sixth string (still with a minor third to spare, as the string is tuned to *E*) but asks the lyre and lute to descend no further than *c* a fourth above.

Periodical Amusements (1807–)

By 1807 the Italian mandolinist Bartolomeo Bortolazzi had begun publishing a large collection of music for the six-string guitar, in monthly parts, under the general title *Periodical Amusements for the Spanish Guitar*. Once again, the *éminence grise* is Tebaldo Monzani, who published the parts with his new business partner, the instrument-maker Henry Hill. Bortolazzi had issued an earlier series in Vienna, which was so well received that the *Wiener Zeitung* announced a reprint in October 1804.[41] Three years later he was in London to publish and promote the twenty-four parts of its successor, dedicated to Frederica, Duchess of York.[42] Each number offered ten pages of music, which might include a guitar solo, a theme and set of variations, an accompanied song or duet (often with a choice of guitar or pianoforte accompaniment) and a small chamber work. The series attracted some distinguished subscribers, including two foreign counts, eight titled ladies, two lords and a penumbra of notable commoners;[43] the royal family was represented by the Yorks and by Augustus Frederick Hanover, 1st Duke of Sussex, who played the guitar and was not abashed to sing English and Irish songs to the instrument at his London soirées.[44]

Bortolazzi's first number is a succinct guitar method for the six-string instrument, while the remaining twenty-three issues combine to form a substantial collection of vocal and instrumental pieces, some derived from material recently performed at the Italian Opera in the Haymarket. There are eighty-seven pieces in total (counting sets of variations and sets of waltzes as single items), using a wide variety of scorings (Table 2).

Table 2

Scorings used in Bartolomeo Bortolazzi, *Periodical Amusements for the Spanish Guitar* (1807–)

Accompanied vocal	No. of pieces
Single voice with guitar	23
Single voice with guitar *or* pianoforte	15
Two voices with guitar	5
Two voices with guitar *or* pianoforte	7
Three voices with guitar *or* pianoforte	1

Instrumental	No. of pieces
Solo guitar	21
One *or* two guitars	1
Guitar and flute	1
Guitar and pianoforte	2
Guitar and violin	7
Guitar, flute and violin	1
Guitar and flute *or* violin	1
Guitar and violin *or* mandolin	1
Guitar and cello	1

The chamber pieces in *Periodical Amusements* include little, perhaps, that modern players might wish to revive, and in the pieces for an ensemble of guitar and pianoforte Bortolazzi is prone to make both instruments lapse into garrulous arpeggios. In the music for solo guitar he is sometimes clearly working to order, ensuring that each number of the publication will be neatly filled by the simple expedient of composing whatever is needed to take up empty space, especially on the last page. (The waltz squeezed in at the close of no. 20 is an egregious case.) Yet something might be made of his 'Notturno', a very early instance of a nocturne for any instrument in England; the melodic minor scale is eloquent in the moonlit, but not necessarily tranquil, context of the Romantic nocturne, and the stilling yet also somehow tensing effect

Ex. 19 'Notturno' (first section), from Bartolomeo Bortolazzi, *Periodical Amusements for the Spanish Guitar*, no. 13 (n.d.), 10.

of the upper pedal note in the third stave of Example 19 could be expressive in the hands of an engaged player.

The songs in *Periodical Amusements* show Bortolazzi at his best. With the exception of two French *romances*, they are all Italian and borrowed from a wide selection of established opera composers such as Simon Mayr, Niccolò Antonio Zingarelli, Marco Portogallo, Antonio Bianchi and Giovanni Paisiello. Some are drawn from recent Haymarket productions including *I due nozze ed un sol marito* of 1806, *Semiramide* and *Il ritorno di Serse,* both of the 1806–7 season. Portogallo's *Semiramide* was the work in which the celebrated Madame Catalani made her London debut, and Bortolazzi duly names her at the head of his arrangement of 'La pena ch'io sento' in his second number.[45] His arrangements may capture something of the accompaniments that Catalani, Viganoni and others could provide for themselves at private events; 'La pena ch'io sento' even has virtuosic graces in the vocal part that are presumably based on Catalani's own, both on and off the operatic stage.[46]

With just under fifty arrangements of Italian airs in total, Bortolazzi's series provides eloquent witness to the important place of the Spanish guitar in the domestic performance of Italian operatic airs and duets (Ex. 20). The links between some of his pieces and recent productions at the Italian Opera might suggest that *Periodical Amusements* is a somewhat elite affair, given the Opera's dependence upon the patronage of the nobility, for whom performances offered a favourite *lieu de rencontre*. To some extent, indeed, the opening of guitar repertoire to airs from current Italian opera (as opposed to Italian song in general), complete with their original Italian texts, does seem broadly to distinguish the repertoire of the Spanish guitar from its English predecessor, and among music masters it was notorious that the tradesmen who employed them were likely to be impatient with Italian music and ask instead that their offspring should learn popular airs like *Robin Adair*.[47] Yet we should not be misled by that – one of the many satirical stereotypes ready to distort our sense of the aspiration and enterprise to be found within a vitally

Ex. 20. Excerpt from 'Dolce dell'anima', duet from Act II of *Sargino*, by Ferdinando Paer (d. 1839), arranged by Bartolomeo Bortolazzi in *Periodical Amusements*, no. 6 (n.d.), 8–9.

important social class. Lessons in the Italian language were readily available in almost every educational context that late Georgian England could offer, from grammar schools and clergymen giving private lessons to governesses and ladies 'of a small independency' seeking extra income.

FIVE

Mixing Memory and Desire: The Peninsular War

But hark, his country calls — the hand
That, trembling, struck the light guitar,
Now firmly grasps a soldier's brand
And love resigns his heart to war.

Cheltenham Chronicle, 13 August 1812

The most important event in the history of the guitar in Georgian England was a European military conflict. Known in Britain as the Peninsular War, the conflict began when Napoleon invaded Lisbon in November 1807, hoping to damage the maritime interests of his resolutely counter-Revolutionary enemy, Great Britain, whose ships were still permitted to refit and resupply there. (Portugal had so far refused to comply with Napoleon's embargo on British trade.) At first, the Spanish supported the emperor in his move, but by the summer of 1808 there was widespread Spanish and Portuguese resistance to the French regime in Iberia. The effect upon Anglo-Spanish relations was immediate and far-reaching, for the agents of this insurgency were loyalist juntas, whom the British immediately interpreted and accepted as allies in their own struggle against French tyranny.[1] According to 'A Spanish Lady' (presumably an enterprising British journalist) writing for the *Morning Post* in late July, 'the whole kingdom, justly indignant at the outrages committed by the emperor of the French against our King and our nation, is preparing by arming its provinces to resist and destroy the enemy that seeks to enslave us'.[2] During the resulting conflict, which lasted until 1814, many thousands of British and Irish soldiers were shipped to Spain and Portugal as combatants and support staff. Tramping the roads of Iberia, they bivouacked in the open country, lodged in private houses, saw fandangos danced by peasants in the fields and at fiestas, heard the daughters of their hosts sing to guitars and sometimes attempted to learn the guitar themselves.

The Peninsular War: The home front

On the home front, the Peninsular conflict inspired what has been aptly called a 'pleasure culture of war'.[3] A contributor to the *British Review* observed in 1813 that anything related to Spain had become an object of interest, including Spanish buttons, chocolate, mantles, fans, feathers and boleros.[4] Civilians could tour the barracks built to house the soldiers before they set sail for Iberia, and enjoy exhibitions of painted panoramas showing scenes of recent battles. There were comic operas set in Spain, such as such as *The Castle of Andalusia*, originally performed in 1782 and revived,[5] while theatres specialising in equestrian and other spectacles staged re-enactments of battles. Songs with titles like 'The Maid of Tagus' became well known, and at balls the bands played tunes called 'The Salamanca Castanets' and 'The Vittoria Waltz', named after allied victories.[6] From 1809 onwards the term 'bolero', virtually unrecorded in English before the Peninsular War, appears in a succession of advertisements for entertainments such as the ballet of *Don Quichotte* given at the King's Theatre and incorporating 'the favourite Spanish dance of il bolero'.[7] In 1810 'a new Spanish Divertissement' was performed there with the 'much admired bolero', while the Theatre Royal at Chester in 1812 offered 'The Original Spanish Bolero' danced by two sisters with castanets.[8]

Something more authentically Spanish appeared around 1810 with *Three Favorite Spanish Boleros as Sung by Madame Vaccari, Arranged with an Accompaniment for Spanish Guitar or Piano Forte*. The compiler, Francesco Vaccari, was an Italian, who had formerly been first violin in the court orchestra of the King of Spain; he went into exile when Napoleon invaded and his royal master abdicated in favour of Napoleon's brother, Joseph. The collection shows what many in Vaccari's adopted country expected from the national music of Spain when it was not permeated by the famous Spanish melancholy. 'No consiste el ser hombre', for example, the last in the set, combines ebullient rhythms and exhilaratingly repetitive tonic–dominant harmonies (Ex. 21). Vaccari took this kind of material on the road, for in March 1812 he was in Bath for a concert where Madame Vaccari sang 'an original SPANISH BOLEROS [sic]', which he accompanied on the guitar.[9]

Ex. 21 The beginning of 'No consiste el ser hombre', from Francesco Vaccari's *Three Favorite Spanish Boleros as Sung by Madame Vaccari, Arranged with an Accompaniment for Spanish Guitar or Piano Forte* (n.d. [c.1810]).

The guitar was well known to be the national instrument of Spain, for travelogues had often noted the Spaniards' fondness for it during the eighteenth century. At no time, however, had the guitar been associated by the British with Spanish courts and courtiers; long regarded as an instrument of Iberian streets and taverns, it swiftly became, during the war years, an emblem of the Spanish as a brave but captive people fighting to recover their freedom with the aid of British and Irish arms.[10] In 1810 readers of the northern *Manchester Mercury* and the southern *Kentish Gazette and Canterbury Journal* learned how a leader of the Spanish guerillas had stood at the gates of Salamanca, brandishing his guitar as if it were a banner and challenging the French to come forth.[11] In the literary sensation of the age, *Childe Harold's Pilgrimage*, Byron evokes the Maid of Saragossa, who famously worked a gun during the French siege of her city, and he imagines her hanging 'her unstrung guitar' on a willow (Canto I, stanza 54). Deprived of its strings, that guitar is as surely an emblem of the Spanish people bereft of liberty as the tree is of the willow where the captive Israelites hang their harps in Psalm 137.[12] The Battle of Vitoria, an allied victory of 1813, was immediately celebrated in poetry, printed in various newspapers and journals, which envisaged the Spanish combatants as guitar players adapting their serenades to sing the praises of the supreme allied commander, the Marquis (later the Duke) of Wellington:

> The youthful hero, resting from the war,
> Shall to thy glories tune his light guitar;
> And 'mid the watchings of the serenade,
> Sing thy lov'd triumphs to his list'ning maid.[13]

One of the most prominent Spanish expatriates in London, Pablo Rosquellas, exploited the political and emblematic quality of the guitar as the Spanish people's instrument in *A Complete Tutor for the Spanish Guitar*, probably published in 1813.[14] The book was a significant contribution to the Iberian cause on the British home front and to the pleasure culture of war, with its 'interweaving of fashion, sociability and militarism'.[15] Like Vaccari, Rosquellas had been a violinist at the Spanish royal court, who went into exile and made his way to London after the French invasion. He succeeded in making a name for himself there as a composer, for in 1812 *The Times* praised his violin concerto for revealing the true nature of Spanish music, so 'eminently *romantic*', marked by 'rapid transitions to exuberance and fantastic gaiety' and expressing 'the natural talent of the people'.[16] In the same year, Rosquellas was among the distinguished guests in London invited to celebrate the Spanish constitution promulgated on 18 March 1812 by the Cortes of Cádiz; he sang in the Spanish ambassador's chapel for a festal liturgy, which incorporated his own patriotic march, 'Vive siempre Yberia', played again later in the day, by a military band, during a grand dinner. *The Times* reported the occasion in detail and the account was widely reprinted.[17]

In the Introduction to *A Complete Tutor*, Rosquellas explicitly takes his place among Iberian expatriates and political exiles in London, expressing the fond hope that his method will contribute to 'the social pleasures and rational amusements of this hospitable Nation'. The accompanied songs he provides for the novice to study include an otherwise unknown setting of Robert Burns's poem 'From thee Eliza I must go', a soldier's song of parting as he sets sail, facing death in what a contemporary, disposed to find a topical meaning, might well have identified as the Peninsular War. There is also an arrangement of the well-known 'Yo que soy contrabandista', for such songs had become familiar in the drawing rooms of London; the Italian physician Augustus Granville, who settled in London in the same year that Rosquellas published his method, used to sing this one to the guitar at the salons of the West End society hostess

Ex. 22 The beginning of 'Vive siempre Yberia' by Pablo Rosquellas, arranged by him for three voices and guitar in his *Complete Tutor for the Spanish Guitar* (1813?), 25–7; the song was also sold separately.

Lady Charleville in Piccadilly Terrace.[18] The method also contains a version of Rosquellas's own 'Vive siempre Yberia', arranged for three voices and guitar, in which the guitar part tries to evoke, within its means, the rousing effect of the military band that played the piece at the constitution ceremony of 1812 (Ex. 22).

Rosquellas dedicated his *Complete Tutor* to Princess Charlotte of Wales, for she 'sang and performed on the piano, the harp, and the guitar, with more than usual skill', according to the official obituary of 1817, printed in newspapers the length and breadth of England when she died in childbirth that year.[19] One of Charlotte's letters from September 1813 reveals that she was '*decidedly very much attracted*' to Spanish songs (her emphasis), which she found 'so expressive and so very melancholy'.[20] Her first guitar teacher was Angelo Benedetto Ventura, followed by Francesco Vaccari, composer of the *Three Favorite Spanish Boleros as Sung by Madame Vaccari*, discussed above; the two Vaccaris served Charlotte at Windsor and elsewhere. The memoirs of Charlotte's lady companion, Cornelia Knight, recount how the princess took her lessons during 1813–14 at her residence, Warwick House, 'an old moderate-sized dwelling . . . situated at the extremity of a narrow lane' in St James's, and in the Lodge at Windsor Great Park:

> [the princess] had instructions on the guitar, first from Ventura, a Venetian, who sang prettily, and had practical facility, and afterwards from Francesco Vaccari, a scientific professor of music, and an excellent player on the violin, who had left the band of the King of Spain, and whose wife was a Spaniard, and taught Princess Charlotte the wild Spanish manner of playing, which the Miss Fitzroys also imitated very happily.[21]

The 'wild Spanish manner of playing' that Charlotte learned, according to Cornelia Knight, would have involved strumming full chords, sometimes with a degree of syncopation quite beyond the range of English drawing-room songs. A bolero for two voices and guitar by Philippe Verini, perhaps of the early 1820s, conveys some sense of the effect; a rubric calls for the guitar accompaniment to be 'play'd in the Spanish style' (Ex. 23). As for other music that Charlotte played, 'Vive siempre Yberia' would have suited anyone 'decidedly very much attracted' to Spanish songs in the last years of the Peninsular War, while the first part of *Vaccari's Miscellaneous Selection for the Spanish Guitar* (c.1813) offers seven works for guitar with flute or violin *ad libitum* in a collection that is

Ex. 23 The beginning of Philippe Verini's bolero 'Ten piedad vida mia', from *Bolero Arranged as a Duet for Two Voices with an Accompaniment for the Spanish Guitar* (n.d. [c.1820]).

not only dedicated to Charlotte but also carries an engraving on the title page that is almost certainly intended to represent her, perhaps in the gardens at Frogmore (Fig. 24).[22] Her features are known from various contemporary or posthumous portraits and the resemblance is close. This collection would have given Charlotte the opportunity to play the guitar in duets with Vaccari on the violin, including a 'Spanish dance, minuet and fandango' (Ex. 24).

Ex. 24 Excerpt from 'Spanish dance, minuet and fandango', for guitar and violin or flute *ad libitum*, from *Vaccari's Miscellaneous Selection for the Spanish Guitar Humbly Dedicated to H.R.H. the Princess Charlotte* (n.d. [c.1813]).

Fig. 24 Detail of the title page of *Vaccari's Miscellaneous Selection for the Spanish Guitar Humbly Dedicated to H.R.H. the Princess Charlotte* (*c.*1813), lithograph. The player strongly resembles Charlotte, Princess of Wales. Private collection.

The Peninsular War: The battle-front

Princess Charlotte was much concerned by what she called 'the *Spain affair*', and in 1813 she made a resolution, no doubt hard to keep, to think no more about it.[23] Wars are easily forgotten, however, once they are over, as those who suffered in them quickly discover. Many who served in the Peninsular conflict, determined that the war should be remembered, wrote memoirs or assembled their letters from the campaign and found publishers for them.[24] A conspectus of the material recording their encounters with Spanish guitars and guitarists, extracted from about seventy-five memoirs, appears in Table 3. Soldiers in Spain must frequently have seen guitars strung with six double courses in the Spanish manner, as in Louis-François Lejeune's painting of 1828, which shows the artist, a serving military officer, among British counterparts attending to his needs in their camp at Mérida in 1811; the picture includes a guitar with six visible pegs, which is clearly intended to be a standard Spanish instrument of the period with six double courses (Fig. 25). Soldiers in Portugal may have seen *bandurrias*, *violas* or other forms of regional guitar.

Table 3

References to the guitar in a corpus of Peninsular War memoirs and letters written by British and Irish combatants or support staff; the list is ordered by the years to which the references relate, while the date within each entry is that of publication (for full citations see 'Other Printed Primary Material' in the bibliography, pp. 274–9).

1808

Robert Ker Porter	1809	painter, writer, and diplomat

1808–9

James-Wilmot Ormsby	1809	chaplain
Henry Crabb Robinson	1869	'war correspondent'

1809

Peter Hawker	1810	officer
William Stothert	1812	captain

1809–10

Moyle Sherer	1823	officer

1811

George Bell	1867	ensign
Walter Henry	1839	physician

1812

John Cooke	2000	lieutenant
Edward Costello	1841	non-commissioned officer
Joseph Donaldson	1845	sergeant
William Grattan	1847	lieutenant
John Patterson	1837	captain

1812–13

E. W. Buckham	1827	commissary

1813

Thomas Henry Browne	1987	captain
Charles Crowe	2011	lieutenant
Francis Seymour Larpent	1853	judge-advocate general

These memoirs, mostly written by officers, often show members of the military negotiating between the Iberia they encountered, sometimes in arduous or brutal circumstances, and a romantic Spain of picaresque adventure, fandangos and guitars that some knew from novels, serialised stories and plays. There were probably many – at least among the better read – who felt with Walter Scott that it was extraordinary to find places mentioned in *Don Quixote* and *Gil Blas* suddenly becoming 'the scenes of real and important events' during the Peninsular conflict.[25] If all wars necessarily have their ironies, the incongruity of this one was that the fight was not purely political or a matter of right and wrong, but – at least on the part of those soldiers of a Romantic turn of mind – a struggle to save the imaginary Spain of fiction and drama. As the British and Irish military moved about the Peninsula from one battle or billet to the next, stock characters from fiction and the stage appeared before them. Muleteers wend their slow way through many pages of *Gil Blas* and whistle 'the merry *seguidille*' in Walter Scott's *The Vision of Don Roderick* (1811; stanza 34). Ensign George Bell was delighted to encounter them, playing guitars as they rode:

pleasant music it was to us many a starry night on the lonely march to hear the muleteers coming along through the cork woods, singing plaintive strains, accompanied by the light guitar. The muleteer is a fine, honest, independent fellow, well made, quaintly dressed, always gay, strong and active, and very fond of music and dancing when time admits; but he never neglects his work, carries his guitar, sits between two bags of biscuit, both legs on one side, singing a serenade, and twitching his own heart with something plaintive, or perhaps with a fandango, the Castilian Maid, or a bolero.[26]

Plays and serialised romances also shaped the way some soldiers worked up their experiences for a memoir. When Moyle Sherer of the 34th (Cumberland) Regiment of Foot was invited to celebrate the festival of San Domingo with some Portuguese villagers, he compared the scene to plays he had enjoyed in London. The 'novelty of the picture', he wrote, 'the dresses, the singing, the guitars, the cork-trees, and the chapel, produced a very pleasing effect', and if the curtain of the Drury Lane playhouse were to 'rise and discover such a scene and such a group, the applause would know no bounds'.[27] In another episode, Sherer describes leaving Lisbon by water at midnight in 1809; all was silent save for bells, the gentle plashing of the oars and a beautiful female voice, accompanied by a guitar, emerging from a waterside mansion, where candles still blazed at that late hour.[28] The scene is so much the stuff of tales serialised in magazines such as *La Belle Assemblée* that it is difficult to separate Sherer's reading of his experience from his experience of reading.

If any soldiers on campaign went to a *tertulia*, or domestic soirée, expecting to hear guitars matching the Spanish decor of comic operas such as *The Gipsey Prince*, they were not disappointed. When Captain John Patterson lodged in the town of Don Benito (Extremadura), the daughter of his host sang 'a few pleasant songs on the guitar' at a *tertulia*, accompanied by one of her sisters; the Spaniards, Patterson noted, 'seem, at all times, to have a soul for music'.[29] At Badajoz, Captain William Stothert was invited to a *tertulia* where a widow sang 'in a pleasing style, and with much taste' accompanied on the guitar by Señor Fuentes, whom we shall meet again. Her singing was followed by a bolero with castanets and then a fandango, both probably danced to one or more guitars.[30] Some of the military were not pleased by what they saw and heard: a few remembered the fandango, commonly danced to the guitar, as a thoroughly

Fig. 25 *Réception aux cantonnements anglais à Mérida en Estramadure le 1er mai 1811*, by Louis-François Lejeune, 1828, oil on canvas. The seated figure in the foreground (*left*) is playing a Spanish guitar with six double courses. Private collection.

indecent exhibition, and Robert Ker Porter was persuaded that this 'lewd dance of south American origin' revealed the 'wanton taste' of the Iberian nobility.[31] This is the voice of the eighteenth-century travelogue. Yet in general the soldiers' responses reflect occasions when the music of the guitar might be combined with a memorable or even an affecting experience at a time of respite from the march or from combat. Victory festivities naturally made a strong impression on soldiers exhilarated by the twin blessings of their triumph and their survival; Lieutenant John Cooke reports the triumphal British entry into Madrid of 1812 when 'all the beauty of the place' welcomed the soldiers, 'striking guitars, tambourines, and castanets, with eyes beaming love and admiration'.[32] According to Thomas Henry Browne, a captain in the adjutant-general's office, 'Spanish Guitars were gaily sounding in the English Camp' shortly after the Battle of Vitoria in 1813, with girls singing 'extempore praises of the immortal Wellington'.[33] Some five hundred Spanish women followed the armies in the hope of booty, and they 'had almost all guitars, which they accompanied with pretty voices'.[34] Passing through a village between Toro and Zamora, E. W. Buckham found groups of dancers singing to the 'mellow and sweet accompaniment' of the guitar in the square.[35] Men such as Buckham, accustomed to lands whose climate made nightlife in the streets very chill for much of the year, were taken with the warm Spanish evenings; the stroll, or *paseo*, in Madrid, where 'groups of singers with guitars slung across their shoulders' might appear, delighted William Grattan, while Moyle Sherer sometimes listened to the villagers with their 'pleasing ditties, the pauses and cadences of which they mark so feelingly, yet so simply, with the light guitar'.[36]

Occasionally, the veterans encountered a performance that impressed them as more than simply pleasing or picturesque. Peter Hawker, billeted in a convent at Tomar (central Portugal), heard a guitarist, of high repute among the Spanish, deliver one of the finest solos he had ever heard.[37] There was also a guitarist, a Spanish commissary, who particularly impressed the officers in the entourage of Wellington, the supreme commander of the allied forces in the Peninsular campaign. Francis Seymour Larpent was present when this musician played so well that Larpent wished he had his cello with him so that, 'with a flute or two', they might have some music in the evenings.[38] This was at Freineda, the Portuguese headquarters where Wellington 'enjoyed the society of his young, high-spirited, mainly aristocratic aides-de-camp', for there 'were usually a number of casual visitors at his mess dinners'.[39] At this same place, Thomas Henry Browne heard 'a very amusing fellow called Fuentes' – almost certainly the same man as the Señor Fuentes mentioned by Stothert – play the guitar well and sing. According to Browne, Wellington would occasionally summon Fuentes to play at his table in the house that still stands in the village square.[40] This musician was more than he seemed, however, for he was one of Wellington's spies.[41]

Some soldiers began to learn the guitar while on campaign. In 1808 Colonel Landman of the Royal Engineers was at Gibraltar, where he tried 'to acquire the talent of playing on the Spanish guitar', but realised that he would never advance 'beyond the humblest mediocrity'.[42] At Truxillo, Walter Henry passed his evenings 'with lessons in *Don Quixote*, singing and the guitar', which suggests that he was being instructed in all three.[43] A non-commissioned officer in the Rifle Brigade, Edward Costello, claims to have spent many nights serenading with a guitar,[44] while another English officer was so proficient a guitarist that he entertained the locals at Salvatierra in the province of Salamanca. Lieutenant Charles Crowe, a draper's son from Earl Soham in Suffolk, heard him at a late stage of the war:

> A wounded English officer, a very handsome and gentlemanly fellow although a decided coxcomb, had a good quarter in the lower part of the plaza near the mall. Frequently in an evening he would stand in either balcony to his windows, a monkey on one side and a parrot on the other, touching his guitar in a scientific style to the Spanish, English, Scottish and Irish airs which he sang admirably, while the assembled crowd below, priests and peasants, listened with wonder and delight.[45]

The guitar as souvenir

Guitars were not hard to find if a soldier wished to return from the war with a trophy. Robert Southey records in the second volume of his *History of the Peninsular War* (1827) that they were to be found wherever the French bivouacked in 1809.[46] A massive auction of French booty was held after the Battle of Vitoria in 1813; there was also a market for plunder taken from private homes, where guitars were more likely to be found than in the military camp. Today, a number of genuinely Spanish guitars survive that were made between 1797 and 1816 and were brought home to Britain by returning soldiers, or were obtained shortly afterwards (Table 4). The instruments are mounted with six double courses, the arrangement found on Spanish-made guitars until approximately 1815–20, and are signed by Spanish makers, principally Josef Pagés. Some were modified soon after they reached Britain: the example of 1809 in the Royal College of Music, like the 1816 guitar in the

Horniman Museum, has a replacement head characteristic of the workshop of the instrument-maker Louis Panormo in London, reducing the number of strings from twelve to six. Conversely, a few guitars have survived with the original head and bridge intact, suggesting that they were used as souvenirs or ornaments. Even these post-war instruments have a place in this discussion, for some discharged soldiers remained in Iberia for years, and brought back their guitars to Britain well after the end of the conflict.[47]

Table 4

Surviving Spanish guitars made between 1797 and 1816, obtained during or just after the Peninsular War.

Bologna, Collection of Gabriele Lodi
Josef Pagés, 1813: Panormo head conversion (probably carried
    out in the Panormo workshop) and tuners replaced by the
    British firm Rance

Brighton, Collection of James Westbrook
Manuel Martínez of Málaga, 1803 (Fig. 26)
'Josef Pages Cadiz 1814' [label]: original head and bridge; it has
    a Panormo end-pin, suggesting that it came to London
    not long after it was made. It remained in London until
    the 1980s, when it was purchased in an estate sale.

London, Horniman Museum
Rafael Roldan, 1797 (inv. no. 15.2.60/7)
Francisco Pagés, 1815 (inv. no. 15.2.60/2)
Josef Pagés, 1816 (inv. no. 1976/272)

London, Royal Academy of Music
Josef Pagés, c.1805 (inv. no. 2006/2963)

London, Royal College of Music
Josef Pagés, Cádiz, 1809 (inv. no. 173)[48]

London, Victoria and Albert Museum
attrib. Josef Pagés, Cádiz, 1798 (inv. no. 415/1905)

University of Edinburgh, Musical Instrument Museum
Josef Pagés, 1813 (inv. no. 282)[49]

Fig. 26 Six-course guitar by Manuel Martínez of Málaga, 1803. It is possible that this guitar, by a maker whom Fernando Sor admired, was brought to England during the first third of the nineteenth century. At some stage the bridge and saddle were moved closer to the sound-hole, shortening the string length and thus requiring the neck to be refretted; frets of ivory were used, which is consistent with the work being done at that time in England. The guitar was also supplied with an end-pin to carry a strap – an accessory not found on Spanish instruments; the end-pin is of a type found only on guitars made by Louis Panormo in London. Collection of James Westbrook.

There were more such instruments in circulation. In 1859 the *Sligo Champion* listed a guitar by 'Josef Pages' among items for auction, and in 1892 the goods of Charles Stewart Parnell's widow, Catherine, then living at Hove in Sussex, included a guitar by 'Joseph Page [*sic*] in a case of Rosewood'.[50] The 'real Cadiz guitar' sold by a Wiltshire bookseller in 1837 was perhaps another example, together with the 'Guitar (Spanish, old) with 12 strings' and the 'Guitar . . . [a] genuine old Spanish Instrument' offered for sale at Birmingham in 1882 and 1891 respectively.[51] Various 'real Spanish guitars' were put up for auction during the nineteenth century; those from the earlier decades include one at Chichester in 1811, another at Cheltenham in 1817 and yet another at Manchester in 1826.[52]

Some collected guitar-accompanied Spanish songs for themselves or for family members. Between 1812 and 1814 Robert Henry Clive, who was not a combatant, obtained manuscript copies of numerous songs with

Fig. 27 Portrait of Alexander Fraser, 16th Lord Saltoun of Abernethy, by William Salter, c.1837, oil on canvas. Saltoun was an enthusiastic amateur guitarist, perhaps as a result of his service in the Peninsular War; he continued to serve under the Duke of Wellington, and in this portrait he wears the Waterloo Medal. National Portrait Gallery, London.

guitar accompaniment, including pieces by Fernando Sor and Federico Moretti, while travelling in Portugal, Spain, Sicily and Malta with George Bridgeman, afterwards Earl of Bradford.[53] Bridgeman himself commissioned scribes to copy examples of 'the Fandango, the Seguidillas Manchegas, some

Boleros, Cachuchas, and Oles, and the Zapateado'.[54] The materials in Clive's collection, comprising forty-one items with guitar accompaniment, were probably commissioned in much the same fashion; they survive as a bound set, marked with the name of Lady Harriet Clive, the collector's wife. As might be expected, given the time when they were gathered, there are patriotic and loyalist items from the war years, including widely known works by Fernando Sor such as the 'Himno de la victoria' ('Venid, vencedores') and 'Vivir en cadenas'.[55] There are also anonymous pieces of equal fervour, such as 'Españoles, la patria oprimida' and 'El gran José ninguno' (Ex. 25), the latter in mockery of Joseph Buonaparte for his entry into Madrid in July 1808 and his rapid exit only a few days later.

Ex. 25 The beginning of 'El gran José ninguno', from Lady Harriet Clive's manuscript collection of pieces with guitar accompaniment, Spencer Collection, Royal Academy of Music, London, MS 605, fols 180–81.

As far as an interest in the guitar is concerned, the best-documented of all the combat veterans is Alexander Fraser, 16th Lord Saltoun of Abernethy, who served in the Peninsular War and at the Battle of Waterloo (Fig. 27). His reputation as a guitarist crossed the Atlantic, according to an issue of the *New-York Mirror* for 1830:

> The guitar seems, at present, as favourite and fashionable an instrument with British amateur vocalists of all ranks and ages, as with the Spaniards. It is fair to presume that the Peninsular war has brought into vogue, of late years, this continental instrument, as well as the beautiful melodies adapted to it.

Many officers in the army patronize the guitar, both in their own persons and in their families; and, amongst these, Lord S— is, we understand, a distinguished performer on this instrument.[56]

The 'Lord S—' mentioned here is certainly Lord Saltoun. William Gardiner's memoir *Music and Friends: or, Pleasant Recollections of a Dilettante* (1838) recalls hearing Saltoun play the guitar in an ensemble with a pianoforte, cello, double bass and violin. The guitar, so often associated with parlour pianofortes, 'lightweight sheet music, and sentimental songs',[57] is here directly involved in domestic chamber music of some ambition:

> At Lord Saltoun's I heard parts of the new operas cleverly arranged for his lordship's parties by Mr. Ella. Lady Conyngham was at the piano-forte, Captain Montague, violoncello; the Duke of Leinster, double bass; Mr. Ella, violin; and Lord Saltoun, the guitar. This is an agreeable way of becoming acquainted with the elaborate productions performed in the Opera House, especially to these noblemen who support the theatre. It is like reading the play before you go to see it ... I could not but be pleased with the singular felicity with which Captain Montague touched the violoncello; it was very superior to the play of a professor, for its unrestricted elegance and unfettered style. When persons of rank do excel, there is a freedom in their play that few professors arrive at, or would dare to employ.[58]

When Saltoun played at his home in London's Great Cumberland Street, during the 1820s and 1830s, he often combined his guitar with other instruments in this way, only to have a lady waspishly remark that his playing was inaudible, drowned by the sounds of the other, more powerful instruments. 'I hear it myself,' he replied, 'and that's enough for my pleasure.'[59]

Saltoun's extensive collection of manuscript music for the guitar, now in the Library of Congress, contains much of the ensemble music he played, and it reaches well beyond the latest opera airs. In addition to solo works by Sor and Moretti, his repertoire included arrangements of music by Beethoven, Donizetti, Rossini and others for guitar and chamber ensemble.[60] There are manuscript parts for Beethoven's Sonata for pianoforte and cello, op. 69, for instance, arranged for a sextet of flute, violin, viola, cello, double bass and guitar by an otherwise unknown Mr Pigott.[61] An especially lively

Ex. 26 Excerpt from an arrangement of Beethoven's Sonata for pianoforte and cello, op. 69, for flute, violin, viola, cello, double bass and guitar, by Mr Pigott, prepared for Lord Saltoun, Lord Saltoun's collection of guitar music, 1810–50, Library of Congress, Washington, DC, Box Folder 1/7.

and clamorous passage appears in Example 26; with abundant *forte* markings, the texture is rich and would indeed have overwhelmed a contemporary guitar. This is what makes the arrangement a magnificent demonstration of the aristocratic insouciance that Saltoun showed on being told that he was inaudible in performance, for of all the manuscript parts for the individual instruments, required for this arrangement, only the guitar part carries the title of the work.

There is a possibility that Saltoun's commander, the Duke of Wellington, also played the guitar. William Gardiner's memoir, mentioned above, attributes an intriguing remark to the duke: 'I am never so pleased with Saltoun as when playing the guitar, or, sword in hand, playing about him in battle.'[62] Gardiner does not say how he came to hear of this comment, which could imply that Wellington also played, even that he and Saltoun played duets together. Wellington would occasionally summon Señor Fuentes to play the guitar at his table, and it is possible that he made at least a start on the guitar, like Saltoun, while in Spain. Some members of Wellington's family certainly played: the Misses Fitzroy, who learned 'the wild Spanish manner of playing' in company with Princess Charlotte of Wales, were Wellington's nieces, and Lady Georgiana Fane, the dedicatee of Verini's bolero 'Ten piedad vida mia' (see Ex. 23), was romantically linked to Wellington for several decades.[63] For his private pleasure, Wellington would have had no difficulty in securing arrangements of his favourite Rossini airs in various numbers of guitar albums such as Felix Horetzky's *L'Aurore* or Fernando Alberti's *The Apollon*. Soldierly patronage of the guitar could go no further.

SIX

Careers in the Provinces,
Fernando Sor in London

*. . . they are stimulated by every motive
that the love of fame or the necessity as
well as the desire of gain can inspire.*

Quarterly Magazine and Music Review, 1 (1818), 423

In Elizabeth Spence's novel *The Spanish Guitar: A Tale for the Use of Young Persons* (1814), a Portuguese refugee from the Peninsular War has a lucky encounter with a generous young woman. Her name is Emily Maynard and she lives with her widowed mother in 'very reduced circumstances' that have compelled the family to abandon London for a remote part of Cumberland where life is not so expensive. A lady in the neighbourhood, 'a fine performer on the Spanish guitar' in her day, offers to give Emily lessons and presents her with the instrument that gives *The Spanish Guitar* its title. When Emily finds the Portuguese refugee playing a violin in the streets, she learns that he is a fine guitarist but has no instrument, so she charitably gives him her own. Her mother immediately sends to London for a replacement, for, although she had hitherto been anxious about the time her daughter was spending with her guitar, she is impressed by her Emily's charity and the mature sense of self-denial it reveals.[1]

The heroine of *The Spanish Guitar*, an overtly moral and Christian work, stands for all young women eager to reach a high standard on the guitar and in danger of neglecting their duties, or becoming ungovernable, by too determinedly pursing their pleasures. The problem of excessive attention to the guitar was obviously not confined to London, for Emily Maynard lives in the border county of Cumberland and therefore about as far from the metropolis as it is possible to dwell while remaining in England; Spence's tale is instructive precisely because it reveals the kind of sociability that could foster an interest in the guitar but has left little trace of its operations. The principal town of Cumberland had its own newspaper by 1801, the *Carlisle Journal*, but it is almost entirely innocent of guitars and guitarists during the period evoked in Spence's novel, save for a showman who appeared at the town theatre in 1815 playing the guitar and walking on the ceiling.[2] If counterparts of the fictional Maynards were buying, learning and playing guitars in the villages and towns of late Georgian Cumberland it did not register on the public noticeboard of the county.

Going professional in the provinces

In 1814, when *The Spanish Guitar* was published, there were two principal means of earning money with a guitar in provincial towns. Players might give lessons, which is how the Portuguese refugee in Spence's novel gets back on his feet, or they might apply for a spot in a concert, where they would principally be expected to appear as a self-accompanying singer. Neither option seems to come within Elizabeth Spence's range of expectations for a young woman of good Christian family such as Emily Maynard, for they were neither respectable nor dependable as sources of income. There were some guitar players, however, who did make the transition from sitting room to stage in the provinces during the first twenty years of the century, usually as versatile entertainers who might drift from concert work to singing roles on the stage and then back again.

In some respects, it was easier to become such an entertainer far from London, for provincial towns mounted shows that offered scope for local and itinerant talents in the assembly rooms of coaching inns and theatres. The inns, soon to lose much of their trade to the railway hotels, offered public rooms for small-scale entertainments suitable for singing to the guitar, while the theatres – mostly new creations supported by local investors – were usually smaller than the more important of their metropolitan counterparts. The theatre at Manchester, for example, represented in James Winston's album *The Theatric Tourist* of 1805 (Fig. 28), shows the solid presence many of these buildings established in the townscape, but it was of modest size; Winston

Fig. 28 Manchester's Theatre Royal, from James Winston, *The Theatric Tourist* (1805), hand-coloured aquatint. Provincial theatres like this one, which measured 102 × 38 feet (31 × 11.6 metres), were often better suited to the guitar and to guitar-accompanied singing than many of the London concert rooms. Private collection.

considered it 'extremely incommodious' and quite unfitting for a major manufacturing town.[3]

The assembly rooms and theatres might accommodate many different kinds of show within a single month of the season. Although they often tracked the London venues by taking up entertainments that had done well in the metropolis, they needed to be eclectic if they were to stay open. Musical programmes could be lengthy, some including one or more theatrical pieces, and they were invariably miscellaneous. When a 'Gentleman of Hereford' sang two Venetian ballads and a song beginning 'He was famed for deeds of Arms' to the guitar in 1812 at that town's theatre, he came on immediately after *The Merchant of Venice; or, The Inexorable Jew* and was followed by 'wonderful Feats on the SLACK ROPE' by another performer, followed in turn by a musical farce, *The Children in the Wood*.[4] The English song that the Hereford gentleman performed enjoyed considerable popularity in the second decade of the century, when both the Peninsular War and the Waterloo campaign ended in victories; arranged for voice and guitar, it appears in a manuscript of the 1820s, now at Cambridge (Fig. 29).

At the Manchester Theatre Royal, a certain Mr Asker sang to the Spanish guitar at a benefit concert in April 1800; after *Speed the Plough,* a five-act comedy from 1798, he performed 'I sing of love', probably a composition of

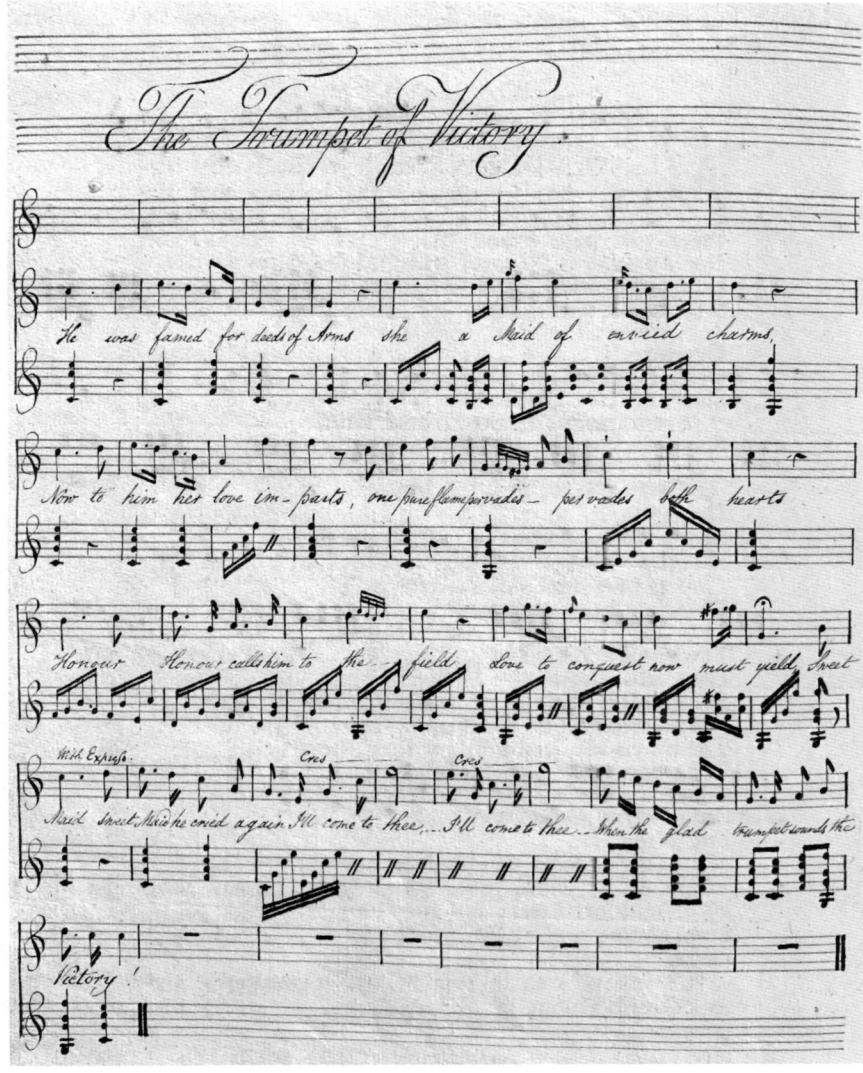

Fig. 29 'He was famed for deeds of Arms', arranged for voice and guitar. Cambridge University Library, MS Add. 9098, fol. 8v.

his own; like 'Poor Primrose Bet', which he sang the same evening, it was apparently never published.[5] Another guitar player, Miss Andrews, appeared at the assembly room of the London Inn at Plymouth in 1806; when she announced the concert in the Exeter press as her benefit night, she ensured that her guitar-accompanied songs were billed as a major attraction of the evening (Fig. 30). The opening paragraph of the panel says nothing about the inclusion of music by Mozart but it does promise 'two favorite airs on the Spanish Guitar'; the

PLYMOUTH.
LONDON INN ASSEMBLY-ROOM.
Under the Patronage of Gen. and Mrs. ENGLAND.

MISS ANDREWS most respectfully informs her friends and the public, that her benefit is fixed for Friday evening, May 2, 1806, when there will be a grand CONCERT of VOCAL and INSTRUMENTAL MUSIC, when Miss Andrews will accompany herself, (the first time in public,) in two favorite airs on the Spanish Guitar.

ACT I.

Overture, ... MOZART.
Glee, three voices, *Bragela.*
Song, MISS ANDREWS. *Venetian Air.*
(Accompanied on the Spanish Guitar.)
Song, " *Deep in the Fountain of this*
brating Heart." From the favorite opera } BRAHAM.
of " The Travellers." ....
Quartetto.
Song, MISS ANDREWS. " *Down in the*
Valley," a favorite Rondeau, in the comic
opera of " the Soldier's Return."
Glee, *A Canadian boat song.*

ACT II.

Favorite Concertante, ... PLEYEL.
Glee, three voices, " *In Liquid Notes.*"
Song, MISS ANDREWS. " *The Willow,*" }
(Accompanied on the Spanish Guitar.) } BRAHAM.
The much-admired trumpet song, from }
the opera of " The Travellers." ..... } BRAHAM.
Concerto, violin, Mr. HUTTON.
Song, MISS ANDREWS. " *Mamma Mia.*"
Full piece.

☞ To begin at half-past seven o'clock.
Tickets, 3s. each, to be had of Miss Andrews, No. 19, Frankfort-street; at the libraries; Mr. Huss, Stonehouse; and at the music shops, Plymouth and Dock.
⁎ Instructions in singing, the piano-forte, and the Spanish guitar, by Miss Andrews.

Fig. 30 Advertisement for Miss Andrews's benefit concert at the London Inn assembly room, Plymouth, on 2 May 1806, from *Trewman's Exeter Flying Post*, 24 April 1806. Miss Andrews 'will accompany herself, (the first time in public,) in two favorite airs on the Spanish Guitar'.

instrument is mentioned each time it was to appear, and the advertisement closes with the announcement that Miss Andrews is available to give lessons. The audience heard her sing an unidentified 'Venetian Air' followed by John Braham's 'Beneath the willow tree' from the comic opera *Thirty Thousand*.

Musicians such as Miss Andrews were not professional guitarists, but versatile singers and sometimes singer–actors. The public demand for song on the theatrical stage was insatiable and did not cease to mount. In *The Road to the Stage* of 1827, a manual for aspiring actors, L. T. Rede maintains that the public demand for music in the theatre has become so keen that 'first singers', able to play the principal roles of operas and other musical entertainments, are in great request.[6] An ability to sing offered the 'safest line' for male actors, according to Rede, and guaranteed them an engagement, while the best female singers had a chance to achieve 'metropolitan distinction'. Mr Asker, who sang to the guitar at Manchester's Theatre Royal, can be found four months later at Brighton Theatre, taking the singing part of Lubin in the comic opera *The Quaker*; he was presumably a peripatetic actor or singer, as the opportunity arose.[7] Miss Andrews of Plymouth may be imagined as a local version of Mrs Mountain, perhaps with ambitions to achieve the 'metropolitan distinction' enjoyed by that artist.[8]

There were other guitar players at work in the localities, almost all of whom were (or claimed to be) foreigners offering novelty acts. In 1803 Signor Romany performed 'a variety of melodious Airs on the Pandean Pipes' at the assembly room in Hull and accompanied himself on the Spanish guitar.[9] He was possibly among the five men at Northampton Town Hall the next year who played two instruments simultaneously, including the pandean pipes, and ended their act with 'Several Italian airs . . . accompanied by three Spanish guitars'.[10] In 1811 'Sieur Sanches' appeared at Mr Bailey's Great Room at Norwich, a venue for municipal dinners, touring entertainers and auctions; he accompanied himself on the Spanish guitar, played the 'Grand Harmonic Glasses' (no novelty by now) and ended his set with a rope-dancing act.[11] By the time he reached the theatre at Canterbury in 1814 he had added 'masterly imitations of the feathered songsters of the grove' to his routine, accompanied by a Spanish guitar, with results 'truly worthy of the attention of the naturalist, the harmonist and the liberal patron of refined science and TASTE'.[12] The audience was especially encouraged to admire how he walked on the ceiling head downwards, 'with a flag in each hand forming a number of attitudes'. (Elizabeth Spence's fictional family in *The Spanish Guitar*, the Maynards, could have seen him the next year at the New Theatre in Carlisle.)[13] Another of these novelty acts, the 'celebrated Italian minstrel' Signor Rivolta, appeared at Truro in 1815, where he ended his performance with 'God save the king' played on eight instruments simultaneously, including the Spanish guitar and, once more, the pandean pipes.[14] The street had come indoors.

Fernando Sor: A metropolitan career

'This young man belonged to a most respectable family, and though intended for a serious profession, wasted his opportunities of distinguishing himself in it through his passion for music . . . for he only attained the reputation and name of the first Spanish guitarist.'[15] That is how a Milanese physician, Augustus Granville, remembered and assessed one of the foremost guitarists of the nineteenth century, the Catalan Fernando Sor (1778–1839). Granville had known Sor at Málaga in 1804–5 and was his pupil there for a time; yet the account quoted above, published posthumously in 1874, is coloured by the many years Granville spent in London from 1813 onwards. The guitar was not an instrument anyone generally parted with money to hear in England at that date, save in the assembly rooms and theatres of the provinces, where it was often handled by showmen and those with little prospect of finding fame in London. Granville admired Sor's skill with a guitar, which he thought prodigious, and was impressed by his 'mellow' singing voice, but after many years in good London society, where even the best musicians were treated like tradesmen, he saw nothing admirable in Sor's decision to pursue a passion for music at the expense of a military or administrative career. The fact that Sor became famous for playing the *guitar* only made the matter worse. 'In Germany,' Granville wrote, 'with a grand piano before him, Sor might have become a Mozart, or a Wagner with grandiose ideas; but with so simple and poor an instrument as the guitar, none but light or trifling melodies could be expected.'[16]

This begins to explain why there was 'a sort of a suppressed laughter' when Sor first walked out upon the stage of London's Argyll Rooms, a major venue for serious music, in 1815.[17] In one respect, at least, Sor did not represent a complete breach with the provincial scene, for he was a noted singer (as Granville remarked), and made use of that talent on occasions – perhaps more often than is generally acknowledged. His career was, nonetheless, almost exclusively metropolitan, interrupted only by a visit to the London satellite town of Bath, for there is no trace of him in the provincial theatres or the assembly rooms of the great coaching inns and hotels. Sor must swiftly have perceived that his talent as a guitarist exceeded anything British audiences had encountered hitherto. In effect, his performances made an implicit claim for the guitar as a serious solo instrument, as if it were a flute or violin, and since the guitar had as yet no concert repertoire of agreed quality, Sor principally played his own compositions and arrangements. His activities during his London years, however, show that he aspired to much more than renown as a guitarist.[18] He composed various sets of *ariettes* for voice and pianoforte, some of which were admiringly reviewed in *Ackermann's Repository*; his three-act grand ballet *Cendrillon* was premiered at the King's Theatre in 1822, and he collaborated on an opera based on *Gil Blas*.[19] Yet it was Sor the 'artist of unrivalled excellence' on the guitar that lingered most in the memory.[20]

Sor possessed a natural talent, schooled by a training in harmony and counterpoint of a kind that few guitarists of his day had received. Between 1790 and 1795 he was a chorister at the Benedictine abbey of Santa Maria de Montserrat in Catalonia, an ancient pilgrimage site, and the education he received there was a source of great pride to him.[21] In accordance with ancient Benedictine tradition, it was designed to train children in the performance of Latin plainsong and to nurture any talent they showed for composition as a means to heighten the worship of the Catholic Church. While at Montserrat, Sor performed and studied choral works ranging from four-part hymns, set in a homophonic style, to eight-part compositions and canons enriched, in performance, by the Montserrat organ and an orchestra whose players, like Sor himself, were boy choristers. On one occasion, he heard a psalm for Compline, 'Cum invocarem', by the Catalan composer Joan Cererols of Montserrat (d. 1676), a conservative work in eight parts for double choir and continuo. Sor records how he tried to capture on his guitar the harmonic effects, many of which were sounded in four parts as the two choirs sang *alternatim* then joined in eight.[22] What mattered to him, it seems, was the composer's control of harmonic syntax from chord to chord, the grammatical relations between the parts that constituted them and the 'harmonie religieuse si grandiose' that it all created in performance. Unsurprisingly, Sor failed to reproduce on the guitar what he heard that day as a child, and yet there is a sense in which he never quite abandoned the attempt as an adult.

At an early stage of the Peninsular War, Sor opposed the French by taking a military command and writing patriotic songs; yet for some reason he could not sustain that commitment.[23] He accepted the abdication of the rightful Spanish king and swore an oath of loyalty to his successor Joseph Buonaparte, thus becoming one of the 'swearers' or *juramentados*, whom the French supplied with the means to fight but never trusted, and whom the British expected to surrender at the first sign of trouble. Sor served the French administration as commissioner of police in the Andalusian town of Jerez de la Frontera, which would have required him to supervise the imprisonment of any guerillas who came into his hands; as the course of the war turned against the French, Sor therefore had good reason to fear violent reprisals, for guerilla vengeance was brutal. Convinced that he could no longer make a career in his homeland, Sor left Iberia among a 'great number of public functionaries, persons of all classes, women and children', mentioned in a British report of the general exodus from Spain, which he had now joined as a former functionary of the French administration.[24]

Sor made his way to Paris, where he was well received. Augustus Granville was delighted and surprised to meet him, ten years after their Málaga days together, at the Paris residence of Jane Fane (née Huck-Saunders), Lady Westmorland, in 1814. As Granville entered the rooms, he found Sor singing his seguidilla 'Acuérdate, bien mío' to a circle of her distinguished guests.[25] The *Memoirs of the Life of the Rt. Hon. Sir James Mackintosh* (1835) offers a similar portrait of Sor's activities in Paris, for the 'wonderful Spaniard' whom Mackintosh heard performing 'miracles on the guitar' there during an embassy soirée in October 1814 is likely to have been Sor.[26] Since there were a great many British visitors and military officers in Paris at the time, Sor's decision to cross the Channel to England may have owed something to their encouragement; perhaps he had also communicated with prominent Spanish expatriates in London such as the ambassador, Fernan Nuñez, with whom he was soon in touch after his arrival. Contacts at this level would explain how Sor, within a month of settling in London, was invited to perform before royalty during an occasion that consolidated him as a guitar player of high renown among the members of the aristocratic and military elite, many of whom were present.

This event took place on 5 May 1815 in circumstances of the greatest prestige. The prince regent, the queen and the princesses were present, together with an assembly of gathered nobility. According to the *Morning Chronicle* for 8 May:

> On Friday evening the PRINCE REGENT had a musical party to entertain the QUEEN and the PRINCESSES, at which the professional talents of the artists lately arrived in England were exhibited; – M. KALKBRENNER on the piano-forte, the brothers BOHRER on the violin and violoncello, and M. SORR on the guitar.

The brief account in the press does not say where the event took place, but the *Morning Post* for Saturday 6 May calls the occasion a splendid party at Carlton House 'last night' to welcome the queen and the princesses back to London; so Sor played in the neoclassical palace on the south side of Pall Mall, by St James's Park.[27] The building was demolished in 1827–8, but detailed descriptions and architectural drawings exist, including coloured prints of the major state rooms, to show the opulent interiors as Sor encountered them in 1815 (Fig. 31).[28]

The Carlton House event offered Sor the most distinguished audience that he was ever to encounter in England. An article in the *Morning Post* for 8 May reveals that many of those present went on, that same evening, to a ball, which 'drew into its *vortex* all the fashion of the metropolis, with a very few exceptions'.[29] The reports of that occasion reveal the congregation of dukes, duchesses, marquises, marchionesses, viscounts and others for whom Sor had played a few hours before. The presence of many officers in their military uniforms, mentioned in the newspaper report, is a reminder that the struggle against Napoleon was soon to reach its climax at Waterloo; no doubt some of the men who heard Sor play that night were soon to depart for the conflict:

> Carriages innumerable poured into the spacious courtyard, with not less than two footmen behind each ... The company were dressed in a style of grandeur unusual – the Ladies, mostly all, attired in gold or silver lama, with plumes of white ostrich feathers, towering in the full plenitude of beauty – the Gentlemen mostly in Regimentals or court dresses. It may be asked – 'How came the invited to appear so gorgeously apparelled?' – They had previously attended a party given by the PRINCE REGENT at Carlton House, at which was present the QUEEN and the PRINCESSES.[30]

Fig. 31 The round room at Carlton House, Pall Mall, from W. H. Pyne, *The History of the Royal Residences of Windsor Castle, St. James's Palace, Carlton House, Kensington Palace, Hampton Court, Buckingham House, and Frogmore* (1819), vol. iii, facing p. 24, hand-coloured engraving. Carlton House was the residence of the prince regent, remodelled from 1783 by Henry Holland in the French style of Louis XVI.

Some London compositions and patrons

Wherever Sor was engaged to play in the capital, nobody had ever heard solo music of such finesse from a guitar within living memory. The most accomplished of Bortolazzi's solo works in *Periodical Amusements* do not approach the assurance of Sor in even his minor pieces, so an acquaintance with Bortolazzi's solo music is arguably the best preparation for understanding how Sor's compositions sounded to guitar aficionados in London at the time of Waterloo and beyond. Example 27a–c shows passages from works for guitar by Bortolazzi; in (a) the marking *Allegro maestoso* suggests something in the region of crotchet = 120, which might save the regular restatements of phrases from becoming predictable, though only just,[31] while (b) shows the kind of untutored counterpoint to which guitarists had become accustomed

Ex. 27 (a) Excerpt from a fantasia by Bartolomeo Bortolazzi, from *Periodical Amusements*, no. 7 (n.d.), 7; (b) Excerpt from a 'Sonatina for the Spanish Guitar' by Bortolazzi, from *Periodical Amusements*, no. 22 (n.d.), 8; (c) Chord sequence from the introduction to 'Introduzione e Tema with Six Variations for the Spanish Guitar', by Bortolazzi, from *Periodical Amusements*, no. 16 (n.d.), 8.

by 1807–8. Sor would never have allowed himself the parallel octaves that appear in (c).[32]

For comparison, Example 28 shows a brief extract from *Six Divertimentos for the Spanish Guitar*, op. 1 (1816), dedicated to Miss Davenport, which was one of the works Sor published during his London years. It is admittedly one of his finest from this period. Over a grammatical bass, the music iterates a rhythmic figure that occupies almost every measure, invigorated each time by a suspension across the barline. As the melody unfolds, in a series of melodic sequences, the tessitura gradually rises, lifting the texture away from the sombre C minor at the beginning of the extract to a brighter and higher harmony, enlivened by modulation. There is a clear sense here of a composer trained by a solid schooling in musical grammar, by proficiency at the keyboard, and by the experience of listening attentively to a wide range of music and studying orchestral scores.

Although Sor was well received in London, and played in some of the major concert venues, it would be misleading to suggest that he definitively

Ex. 28 The 'Minore' section of the fifth divertimento from Fernando Sor's *Six Divertimentos for the Spanish Guitar*, dedicated to Miss Davenport and published before September 1816; the work was later designated op. 1. From *Complete Works for Guitar of Fernando Sor*, edited by Erik Stenstadvold (Heidelberg, forthcoming).

established the right of the Spanish guitar to be regarded as a concert instrument of equal standing with the violin, for example, or the pianoforte. The programme for a 'Vocal Concert' at the New Rooms in Hanover Square, held on 10 May 1816, helps to establish a contemporary perspective. The 'First Act' began with the 'Grand Overture' to Gluck's *Iphigenia*, then moved on to works by Handel, Mozart, Paisiello, Pergolesi and Arne, to name only some of the more prominent composers featured. Sor played in one piece: a 'Fantasia Concertante, Composed of French, Spanish and Tyrolese Airs for the Spanish Guittar, Violin, Viola, Violoncello and Double Bass'.[33] No composer is listed (it is the only item in the programme left anonymous), so this was presumably an arrangement, perhaps by Sor himself. If so, it proved ephemeral, for there is no sure trace of it among his surviving works. The other melodies in this fantasia will only have enhanced the sense of a pleasant potpourri of 'national airs' rather than a work of real substance.

Some of Sor's most prestigious engagements, perhaps most of them, took him to private gatherings, which were usually left unrecorded. One that can be rescued from oblivion shows him performing in 1817 at the home of Elizabeth Burdett, Lady Langham, whose soirées in Portland Place were major events in the social and musical life of the London elite.[34] The occasion was a musical *divertissement* on Friday 2 May 1817; some details are recorded in the *Morning Post* for the following Monday, and taken together with other reports they reveal a soirée at which Sor was conspicuous as both a guitarist and an eminent Iberian. The guest of honour was the Spanish ambassador, Fernan Nuñez, who was about to relinquish his post and leave for Paris; Lady Langham had arranged a farewell party for him, with Sor invited as the outstanding exponent in London of the Spanish national instrument:

> The company arriving about ten o'clock, the amusements commenced half an hour after with a concert, preceded by a solo on the Spanish guitar, by Signor Sor, an artist of unrivalled excellence on that instrument, who was introduced by his Excellency Count Fernan Nuñez. The various beauties and embellishments are not easy to describe; it was enriched by singing, in which the judgment, the curiosity, the taste and feelings of the audience were completely absorbed ... Soon after midnight vocal and instrumental music again gave interest and novelty to the scene; there were only four male performers, and the songs were Spanish and Italian alternately.[35]

Sor was treated with an exceptional regard; not only did he open the concert with a solo but he was also introduced by the ambassador.

The lofty social connections that Sor sought in London are revealed by the compositions he published there. The Honourable Miss Upton, to whom he dedicated his arrangement of 'Vedrai carino' from Mozart's *Don Giovanni*, is probably Sophia Upton (1780–1853), daughter of an Irish viscount, who has left several traces of her musical ability and interests. She was one of 'the best vocal performers' at a private London concert of 1803, and later received the dedication of another work for guitar, Luigi Sagrini's *Divertissement*, op. 20. The *Six Divertimentos for the Spanish Guitar*, dedicated to Miss Davenport in 1816 (Ex. 28), and the *Second Fantasia for the Spanish Guitar*, offered to 'Miss Cornewalle' in the same year, both show Sor complimenting members of the West End elite. Miss Davenport is probably the daughter of Davies Davenport of Capesthorne Hall in Cheshire, whose family is regularly mentioned in the 'Fashionable Arrivals' section of the *Morning Post*; their addresses in London never took them more than half a mile from the pleasure gardens and fountains of Green Park.[36] In the late spring of 1823, this Miss Davenport attended a concert in Savile Row, where a Miss Cornewall was also present – probably identifiable with the second person whom we seek.[37] She is Anna Maria Cornewall (d. 1872), daughter of the baronet Sir George Amyand of Stanhope Street; Sor offers her a spacious composition that reveals his ability to be charming without being trite or sentimental. The closing coda, over a sustained pedal point, slowly spends the energy of the piece in a manner that could scarcely be more graceful, given the simplicity of its means (Ex. 29).

Ex. 29 Excerpt from Fernando Sor's *Second Fantasia for the Spanish Guitar*, op. 4 (1816), dedicated to 'Miss Cornewalle'. From *Complete Works for Guitar of Fernando Sor*, edited by Erik Stenstadvold (Heidelberg, forthcoming).

Besides his elite patrons, Sor found pupils among the professional classes in the London squares and, beyond them, in the City of London proper. This was noticed by George Capel Coningsby, Earl of Essex, in a letter of 6 August 1821 to the guardian of his daughter Harriet: 'Sors the Guitar Player has so many scholars that Both himself and his Brother have constant employment and yet I never have met or heard of a Guitar Lady Player excepting Poor Lady Worcester. All this is confined to the City, Russell and Bedford Square etc. etc.'[38] This is the first reference from nineteenth-century England to a guitar teacher being in great demand by virtue of having acquired real fame. According to the earl, Sor and his brother Carlos drew some of their pupils from the City of London (meaning essentially the area delimited by the Roman and medieval walls) and also from beyond the City in Bedford

Square and Russell Square. The City was primarily the domain of merchants, bankers, artisans and shopkeepers, while the Bedford and Russell Square developments were more consistently the home of professional and titled individuals. Planted with avenues of trees, which compensated the inhabitants for not being close to the parks further west,[39] these squares included among their residents authors, prominent Nonconformists, music lovers who organised concerts or literary salons in their homes, parliamentarians, senior judges and successful lawyers, among others. Sor and his brother were wise to seek pupils here, for there was a great deal of new money in these elegant terraces.[40]

A trace of what Sor taught in London appears in the writings of Major Algernon Langton, a veteran of the Peninsular War. While in Spain, Langton had become interested in a semi-autobiographical novel by the guitarist Vicente Espinel (d. 1624) entitled *Relaciones de la vida del escudero Marcos de Obregón*. On his return to England, Langton translated the novel and published the result in 1816, with a preface about Espinel and the guitar. At one point, he alludes to Sor (the footnote is his own):

> It has been observed by an able Spanish Professor,* who has attained great Celebrity in Europe, as well by his Execution on, and complete Mastery of this Instrument, as his artistical and philosophical Knowledge of it, that the Guitar is more adapted to Harmony than Melody; consequently, those who execute quick Movements thereon, do not succeed so well, as when they seek a Number of Positions, in order to produce the Concord of Sounds, corresponding to the Melody of their Pieces.
>
> * Don Fernando Sor, now in England.[41]

Sor's 'philosophical Knowledge' of the guitar, to which Langton refers, reaches its zenith in his *Méthode pour la guitare* of 1830, a book whose foundational concerns seem partly anticipated here by Langton in 1816.[42] Langton knows that Sor was accustomed to disparage the older school of players, whose representatives sought to astonish with the rapid passagework that Langton calls 'quick Movements' and Sor *passages d'agilité*.[43] He is also aware that Sor values the skill of the harmonist and has a low opinion of teachers who treat the guitar as a melody instrument, setting their pupils to study scales that leave them poorly prepared to play counterpoint with a proper bass line and intermediate parts.

How did Langton become so well informed? The answer may be that some form of method by Sor was already circulating in London by 1816. In 1822 the *Quarterly Musical Magazine and Review* published a substantial review essay referring to 'Mr. Sor's Instruction Book' and comparing it with Charles Sola's *Instructions for the Spanish Guitar* (1820). The comparison is not developed because the writer of the piece does not have Sor's set of instructions to hand. This 'Instruction Book', if it ever existed, was presumably in manuscript, and would have been written in Spanish, which was Sor's second language, or more likely in French, his third, for Sor never achieved any proficiency in English.[44]

By 4 October 1822 Sor had left London never to return.[45] The excellence of his playing, and the depth of his reflections upon his art, made him the greatest foreign virtuoso of the guitar to take up residence in London since Francisco Corbetta in the 1660s. He won praise to the end of his English sojourn, and beyond. The year after his departure, an English journalist noted that Sor was being compared in Paris to Jean Racine.[46] In England, that dramatist was praised for excelling 'in the delineation of the softer passions', for 'the classical correctness of his style placed him without a rival'.[47] Sor would have been content with that.

SEVEN

The Guitar and the 'Middle Ranks of Life'

And scatter'd round, by wall and sofa, lay
Emblems of thoughts that love from earth
to spring.
Upon a portrait fell the evening ray . . .
And there lay a guitar.

George Croly, 'The Artist's Chamber' (1820)

In September 1823 two young men, Alexander Ward and John Brown Bowden, were tried at the Old Bailey for stealing a guitar in London's Bond Street.[1] They had set off from the Seven Dials quarter at seven o'clock one morning, casing many different shops before they came to the premises of the instrument-maker Job Rutter. There was a guitar in the window, placed on a stand; finding Rutter's shop unattended, Ward swiftly took the guitar and tried to hide it under his coat, but it was too large to be completely concealed and he was spotted by a servant sweeping the doorway of the shop opposite. In court Ward claimed that he had accidentally knocked the guitar from its stand, but his account was rejected and he was sentenced, together with his accomplice, to transportation for seven years. The punishment may seem severe, but it was no deterrent; as the 1820s proceeded there were to be more cases before the courts of guitars being stolen from music shops, from a bookseller's stall in a quiet street and even from a noted player.[2]

Thieves steal whatever people particularly desire. There are other indications of the guitar's mounting good fortune, besides the growing incidence of theft. The stream of published guitar methods, ostensibly designed for beginners who wished to learn the basics without incurring the expense of lessons, began to flow freely in London from 1820 onwards, after a relatively quiet period in the preceding years; some twenty titles had appeared by the end of the decade.[3] It was also during the 1820s that the instrument-maker Louis Panormo, who had established himself in London, decided that the guitar would henceforth be his principal product, with results that were much sought after in his day, as they still are. In 1827 a correspondent for the *New Monthly Magazine and Literary Journal* even ventured to suggest that no 'drawing-room or boudoir is furnished without a guitar lying on the sofa or *fauteuil*',[4] and during the very month when Alexander Ward made his failed attempt to steal a guitar the first advertisement headed 'New Spanish Guitar Music' and detailing nothing else, appeared in a London newspaper.[5]

The guitar and those 'with little time to spare'

Some observers looked upon these developments with the censorious or bemused regard they brought to everything they associated with fashion. Viewed in those terms, the guitar was 'nothing more than an elegant trifle', as a correspondent for the *Bristol Mercury* wrote in the issue of 9 June 1832. More sophisticated observers, however, such as the polymath Thomas Perronet Thompson, recognised that the vogue for domestic amateur music in general, and for the guitar in particular, cut deeper because it revealed the prominence of a particular social constituency – one whose members were prospering by commercial shrewdness and sheer application. Thompson possessed an unrivalled sense of the guitar's technical failings but he nonetheless commended the *usefulness* of an instrument that brought 'an orchestra to every man's hearth for about the cost of an alderman's dinner'.[6] Since the meaning of 'every man' here is limited to those who knew what an alderman's dinner cost, Thompson is not referring to the proverbial man in the street; he means those in the middle ranks of life, who had created a nexus of commerce, investment and information as wondrous and varied in its complexity as the classified advertisements and notices on the front page of the *Morning Post*.

These 'middle ranks of life' were increasingly the subject of explicit concern in the 1820s, as observers pondered the momentous changes that had taken place in recent generations. In 1822 the Whig politician Lord John Russell, later to be an architect of parliamentary reform, observed that the London and provincial papers had never circulated more widely, and that the revenue of the state, like its expenditure, had never been higher.[7] In Russell's judgement, this revealed 'the great increase in importance of the middle ranks'; it was they, for the most part, who had overseen the surge of manufacturing, and they who were now the nation's principal source of financial and moral capital. This was the constituency from which most of the business partnerships (and therefore most of the bankrupts) came, and it was among them, in the words of another commentator, that 'generally speaking, the great stock of useful knowledge' in the land resided.[8]

The guitar proved very accommodating to those deploying their 'useful knowledge' in commerce but looking for a musical pastime that they could encompass in their limited free time. As a commentator observed in 1821, the guitar seemed 'peculiarly adapted for those amateurs who have *but little time to spare*, but who have some voice . . . and its facility must, of course, recommend it to many' (my emphasis).[9] Those 'with little time to spare' were not the members of the beau monde, notorious for their sexual intrigues and lavish entertainments; nor were they in any obvious sense the gentry, commonly understood to have landed income that freed them from the need to do remunerative work. Instead, they were the manufacturers, merchants, larger retailers, officers of the army and navy, professional men, the greater farmers, and the women who married them all, together with their offspring.

Members of those middle ranks might discover what the guitar could accomplish, notably as an accompaniment to the voice, in ways that various literary sources reveal, including the sketches written in a mildly satirical vein of social observation, requiring an eye for representative detail, that became especially popular in the late Georgian and early Victorian period. In 1834 Charles Dickens published a story of a company taking a trip down the Thames on a steamboat, in which three sisters sing to their guitars as the hired band in the stern takes a rest (see Chapter 8); in another piece, collected (like the one just mentioned) in *Sketches by Boz* (1836) and there entitled 'The Boarding-house', he describes the bustle as young women arrive in a London boarding house with 'parasols, guitar cases and parcels', ready to accompany their own singing after dinner as others read or play cards. In *Sketches of Young Ladies* (1837), written in the manner of Dickens's early vignettes, Edward Caswall evokes the kind of soirée where young ladies may be expected to arrive with their Mamas and guitars, more eager to sing than Caswall to hear.[10] Prints and portraits suggest how a guitar might be glimpsed in someone's house, perhaps laid on a sofa to create the kind of effect that gives Biedermeier painting one of its most persuasive images of middle-class domestic peace after the exertions of the Napoleonic Wars (Fig. 32), and one with literary parallels in England.[11] Placed casually in a room, a guitar could suggest a certain ease, even a quality of bohemianism, as in George Croly's description of an artist's chamber quoted at the head of this chapter. As portable as a cushion, it could be moved for comfort and visual effect, as it is in a novelette of 1833, where a young woman places her guitar in the room 'with studied negligence'.[12]

The associations of the guitar were beguilingly at odds with the reputation for industry earned by those in the middle ranks of life, and were to some extent perhaps a welcome release from it. When the contributor to the *New Monthly Magazine and Literary Journal* observed in 1827 that no drawing room or boudoir is complete without a guitar 'lying on the sofa or *fauteuil*', the French word, italicised to proclaim that it is foreign, nicely suggests the affectedness of middle-class aspiration. Yet the writer then proceeds to rhapsodise about 'moonlight nights, serenades and lovers muffled in Spanish cloaks'.[13] Soldiers returning from the Peninsular War had evidently found a hearing, just as serialised romances like *Second Love* from 1812–13, where a Spanish Don tunes his guitar while reclining on a sofa, had found readers.[14] The imagination has its own kind of capital, and the associations of the guitar could be as enticing as its practical advantages. Another commentator of 1827 was wise to assess its appeal as a combination of both: 'it is elegant, it is portable, and it is *foreign*'.[15]

The supply of instruments

Most of the guitars used in England before about 1800 were probably imports, either in the precise sense of goods legally traded in transmarine commerce or in the relaxed understanding that they were purchased abroad by private individuals for their own use at home.[16] This certainly continued, for dealers in the capital were well placed to introduce consignments such as the 'extensive assortment ... from the most esteemed Makers on the Continent' that

Metzler and Son advertised in 1826.[17] Yet the expertise of craftsmen skilled in the manufacture of English guitars and violins, supplemented by the skills of new immigrants, enabled the London manufacture of Spanish guitars to begin in earnest not long after 1800; Elizabeth Spence's novel of 1814, *The Spanish Guitar*, takes it for granted that a new instrument will be obtained in London, even if it means sending the order some 300 miles. The portrait of Mrs Mountain from 1802 (see Fig. 19) shows a guitar that is clearly London made, for the painted purfling on the ribs, established by James Westbrook as a defining feature of London work, can be clearly seen.[18]

More than twenty guitars manufactured in the capital before about 1820 are known to survive, mostly in private hands, and contemporary images provide a collateral record. Opinion was slow to acknowledge the quality of such English-made instruments even though (to judge by surviving examples) they were capably built. In 1818 a commentator for the *Literary Gazette* believed that English builders had not yet 'found the art of making good guitars ... the defect seems to be in their massiveness',[19] and as late as 1833 a contributor to *The Giulianiad* can still complain that 'the English guitar makers have as yet a vast deal to learn in the construction and finishing of their instruments'.[20] In 1825, however, readers of George Henry Derwort's *New Method of Learning the Spanish Guitar* were assured that English-made guitars had reached 'great perfection'; they would soon be as fine as the 'generality' of those brought from abroad or might even surpass them.[21]

Derwort is probably responding to the exceptional achievement of one particular firm, run by a family that adopted the name Panormo to commemorate its Sicilian origins.[22] One of their number, Joseph Panormo, built some guitars in consultation with Fernando Sor (which must have been before Sor left London for good in October 1822), presumably to improve the standard of manufacture by drawing upon the established practice of Spanish craftsmen (Fig. 33).[23] By February of the following year Louis Panormo was running his Musical Instrument Warehouse in Bloomsbury, where he became known for good work and a dependable business practice that kept him from poverty throughout his life. (His brother Joseph died in a workhouse.) In 1822, or thereabouts, Louis decided to specialise in guitars, and within six years was selling instruments with labels that proclaimed him to be 'the only maker of guitars in the Spanish style'.[24]

The cheapest guitars sold by Louis Panormo cost 2 guineas, which seems low given that the same price was being charged in 1831 for one hanging

Fig. 32 Georg Friedrich Kersting, *Woman Embroidering*, 1817, oil on canvas. The subject is the painter Louise Seidler, who has turned to her needlework from practising her guitar, which she has set aside on the sofa.

on a bookstall in the London suburb of Pentonville, where it was probably being sold second hand.[25] A guitar of unknown make stolen at Bristol in 1820, however, and the one that Alexander Ward tried to steal from Job Rutter's shop in Bond Street three years later, were valued at just 20s.[26] For the most part, London music emporia charged significantly higher prices than these,

Fig. 33 Six-string guitar in the Spanish style, by Louis Panormo, 1822. The label reads: 'Panormo. – Fecit. / London. *1822* / *26 High street. Bloomsbury*' (italic type indicates manuscript additions).

as did Louis Panormo himself, whose most expensive models in 1828 sold for 15 guineas.[27] Richardson's in Covent Garden stocked 'An original Spanish Guitar' (perhaps another legacy of the Peninsular War) for 8 guineas, among various other 'cheap musical instruments' in 1816, while two years later Shade's Depot in Soho Square offered a 'Spanish Guitar' priced at 2½ guineas but a 'real Spanish Guitar' for 3½.[28] If all these sums are referred to the year 1822 – for the sake of argument – the Bank of England's current calculations for equivalences in sterling would assign Panormo's cheapest model a price of about £250 and his most expensive a price of £1,950 at 2019 values. To be sure, such comparisons are potentially misleading, for some items competing for a person's expenditure in the 1820s (including many food items, garments and pieces of furniture) were more expensive than their industrially made equivalents have become; yet early nineteenth-century makers and dealers were clearly charging appreciable sums, which only a comfortable constituency could meet, although there were 'economy' and second-hand instruments in circulation that significantly undercut the lowest rate for new instruments.

A 'real Spanish guitar' could cost more than a merely 'Spanish' instrument in 1816 because it mattered to have the real thing in the immediate aftermath of the Peninsular War. That is one of the reasons why Louis Panormo was wise to advertise as the only maker of instruments 'in the Spanish style'. Some even believed that returning soldiers from the Peninsular War were largely responsible for the guitar vogue. In 1827 the *Quarterly Musical Magazine and Review* published a notice of two guitar publications attributing much of the guitar's success to the experiences of returning 'peninsula heroes'.[29]

Teaching and learning in the 1820s

The number of guitar players and teachers fortuitously mentioned in a criminal case, a newspaper anecdote or an advertisement begins to mount in the 1820s, as the London papers are joined by provincial counterparts. Teachers appear (not necessarily always for the first time) in spa towns such as Bath and Cheltenham, in ports such as Bristol and Liverpool, in watering places such as Brighton, in manufacturing centres including Birmingham, Leeds, Leicester, Sheffield and Manchester, and in the cathedral cities of Canterbury, Coventry, Chester, Exeter, Hereford, Norwich, Truro, Worcester and York.[30] In Birmingham, those eager to learn the guitar could study with Mr Lambley, whose *Guide to the Art of Accompanying on the Spanish Guitar* went on sale there in 1829,[31] and their town forms the backdrop for Robert Seymour's caricature *The Brummagem Conversazione* of 1832, a sharply satirical glimpse of the guitar in use among the middle ranks of life in a manufacturing centre (Fig. 34). The accompanying text identifies a wine merchant, a feather merchant (a dealer in the ornamental feathers of rare birds) and a tailor among those who are talking in bad French and enjoying 'something they [call] Italian singing'. A schoolmaster, resolutely unfashionable in his antiquated wig, frowns and stops one of his ears.

The port city of Liverpool offered one teacher of the guitar – 'a Spanish gentleman' – and perhaps others from the Hispanic world, a particular opportunity. The 'gentleman' in question was Don Celestino de Bruguera, who claimed to have been disinherited as a result of his 'high rank in the independent cause': the struggle of South American states to achieve independence. The pursuit of liberty in Iberia and the colonies, whether it was to be wrested from the absolutist King of Spain, Ferdinand VII, or from Spanish colonial rule in America (which the British had always liked to believe was particularly cruel and exploitative), reinforced the association between the guitar and political freedom. We should not underestimate the sympathy that Hispanic political exiles could arouse in Britain from at least the time of Pablo Rosquellas around 1813 to that of Charles Cochrane, alias Juan de Vega, who seems to have made good money in 1828–9 by posing as an exiled Spanish officer with only his guitar to live by. According to de Bruguera, the trading connections of Liverpool made it advisable to have teachers of the Spanish language and the guitar, now that the 'emancipation of the late colonies of Spain' offered merchants so many opportunities for extensive connections

Fig. 34 *The Brummagem Conversazione*, by Robert Seymour, 1832. The guitar easily found a place in such provincial evening gatherings for music and conversation: it was portable, well suited to providing harmonic support for an untrained voice, and was associated with a large repertoire of accompanied songs, many available in print; no doubt there are some among the items the guitarist's neighbour is showing to the unwilling schoolmaster. Private collection.

there. It will therefore be wise, de Bruguera proposes, for 'young men in commercial ports' to learn Castilian, and to take guitar lessons to make the process lighter and more pleasant.[32]

Among the towns with guitar teachers further south, the spa town of Leamington was the subject of several guidebooks by 1818, while Cheltenham, another spa, had 20,000 inhabitants by 1826 and was well served by a transport network of coaches.[33] In these places, as in the coastal resorts, the guitar became part of the leisure culture enjoyed by a transient population. The leader of the band in Cheltenham's Theatre Royal advertised lessons on the guitar in 1809 and five years later Angelo Benedetto Ventura stayed for the season, teaching and announcing himself (truthfully) as sometime guitar master to Princess Charlotte of Wales.[34] R. L. Downes, whose *Eight Esteemed*

Italian, Portuguese and Spanish Songs with an Accompaniment for the Spanish Guitar appeared around 1820, performed at the town's new ballroom in 1816, and 'real Spanish guitars' were sold by an emporium on the High Street the following year.[35] As in the case of several other centres, including Bristol and Brighton, Cheltenham's view of itself as a place of airiness and fashion is revealed by its acquisition of a quarter named Montpellier, after the city in Languedoc associated in England with 'beauty, verdure, retirement' and orange groves.[36] Perhaps no town better shows what the urban renaissance of the later eighteenth century and beyond could mean than Cheltenham in the 1820s, with its Montpellier quarter, its assembly room and its guitars.

It is rare to find a teacher claiming to be a 'professor' of the guitar *tout court*, like Signor Huyghues at Cheltenham; more numerous are those who also offered lessons in their native tongue and perhaps some other accomplishment besides. At Coventry in 1829 there was Monsieur Descroix, 'Professor of the French Language, Drawing and of the Spanish Guitar';[37] at Leicester Mr Poletti (guitar and Italian); at Worcester Signor Pedrotti (guitar and Italian); and at Leamington Señor Urraca (guitar and Spanish). Sheffield had Monsieur Theodor Wahast (guitar, French and Italian), while citizens of York could approach Signor and Signora Noel (guitar and Italian). Alexander Sosson's *Complete Instruction Book for the Spanish Guitar* of 1826 shows that the musical proficiency of such guitar-and-language masters should not be underestimated, for it is a solid manual, designed to bring the pupil to the point of singing and accompanying songs like the simple French *romances* that he provides.[38]

Although most of the teachers who advertised guitar lessons are shadowy individuals, a few step unexpectedly into the light. In July 1826 Anne Sturges Bourne of the Hampshire gentry wrote to a friend about Señor Urraca, whom we have just found at Leamington. Urraca, according to his own account, had come to England as an impoverished Iberian exile; he described himself as a former soldier, but he did not match Miss Sturges Bourne's expectations of a dashing Spaniard with such a past. She found him to be just 'a little man with black hair and moustachios'; furthermore, he had arrived in England destitute, which 'is not a romantic termination to a Spanish adventurer', she wrote, and 'the man is not romantic looking, but just like all the other language masters'.[39] Another of her letters gives a better impression, for Urraca had played 'so beautifully' she was now 'quite wild' about Spanish music.[40] In 1827 we find her reading *Recollections of the*

Peninsula, presumably Moyle Sherer's work of that title, published in 1823. Such readers of the Peninsular memoirs, admirers but not necessarily players of the Spanish guitar, probably did as much as the returning soldiers to consolidate the association of the Spanish guitar with that conflict.

Some of the teachers were noted individuals, even minor entrepreneurs, in the musical life of their towns, perhaps holding a position of some importance in the local Philharmonic Society or among the organisers of the concert series. The black violinist Joseph Antonio Emidy (*c.*1770–1835), who taught 'Guitar, and Spanish Guitar' in 1815, was 'Leader of the Band' under the auspices of the Truro Philharmonic Society.[41] A composer, leader of the quadrille ensemble for local events and a pianoforte tuner, he was a general musical animator for the citizens of his town. Another violinist, Mr Lacy, was 'Leader of the Liverpool Concerts' and offered guitar lessons in the city in 1818.[42]

MR LACY,

Leader of the Liverpool Concerts

Begs leave to acquaint the Ladies and Gentlemen of Liverpool and its vicinity, that he has taken up his residence in this town, for the purpose of teaching the VIOLIN, PIANO FORTE AND SPANISH GUITAR. A proficiency on the latter instrument, now become so fashionable, and forming a delightful accompaniment to the voice, may be acquired in *very few lessons* by a *new* and *simple* method of instruction.

7 Great George-street.[43]

In a similar manner, W. H. Hagart, who was 'Principal Violoncello of the Theatre Royal, Drury Lane', advertised at Brighton during the summer season of 1826; his offer of lessons on the cello in the same panel almost seems an afterthought:

SPANISH GUITAR TEACHING

Mr. W. H. Hagart, Principal Violoncello of the Theatre Royal, Drury Lane, respectfully announces that he proposes giving lessons on the above fashionable and much admired instrument. Mr. H. will also give lessons on the Violoncello. Cards of Address to be had at Mr. Mencke's Musical Repository, 39, East-street, and at Mr. Gutteridge's, 19, Castle Square.[44]

Some of these teachers announce in their advertisements that they have 'just arrived' in the town, perhaps because, like Mr Lacy, they have newly taken up a position, or because they were essentially itinerant musicians.[45] Many undoubtedly were. Some sought to settle and establish a business by opening a music shop in their lodgings, although they might give it a more prestigious air by advertising it as a 'repository', or even, because lessons were given there, an 'academy'. There could be instruments on sale, both new and second-hand, together with accessories, a range of the latest printed music and ancillary services such as pianoforte tuning. The core activity, however, was teaching, planned in courses to be paid for on a quarterly basis. One of the more successful of these repositories or academies was opened by Giuseppe Anelli. In 1828 he announced his new Repository of English and Foreign Music in his lodgings at Clifton, then a village and minor spa but now a suburb of Bristol, handsomely supplied with fine Georgian houses. Anelli opened this repository 'for the convenience of the Ladies and Musical Amateurs', supplying guitars 'made under his direction', which he had personally adjusted and overseen to ensure that they were of the best quality.[46] This is all being done for the convenience of visitors, not for profit: Anelli will not have his repository thought of as a *shop*.

Immigrant teachers were generally male, but women seeking employment as governesses during the 1820s increasingly listed the Spanish guitar among their attainments. A governess post was one of the few paid positions a woman might hold and remain respectable, for it was commonly regarded as an extension of her supposedly natural inclination to motherhood.[47] She would usually give instruction in a language or two, in geography ('the globes'), in history and in basic literacy, and while rates of pay were commonly low (full board was usually provided for a resident governess) there were various reasons why such a post might prove tempting. One woman who taught the guitar had 'recently lost her surviving parent', according to her advertisement, while another claims (perhaps truthfully) to be a lady 'born and educated to superior expectations' but compelled by circumstances to work.[48] One possessed a small income, so a salary was less important to her than having a comfortable home, while another hoped to go to the Continent and would gladly waive a salary if she were allowed to accompany her employers to any 'places they might think worthy of notice'.[49] Behind that modestly expressed wish to be included in the family's excursions there lies a wealth of humiliation, known to many a governess who thought herself a gentlewoman, but was used as a kind of servant.

Some sense of what these teachers and governesses taught can be gained from the guitar methods published in England during the 1820s. The impulse behind most of them came from firms that might combine publishing and the sale of music with making and dealing in instruments, and which were now on the lookout for a 'house' guitar method. The majority were printed at the cost of their publishers, not their authors, and once a firm had invested in such a book the process was rarely repeated, though there might be subsequent editions; one guitar method was much like another, unless it were a work of genius (and very few were). Such books were expensive to produce, and a title-page lithograph added to the cost; the only English method with a prefatory illustration by an artist of real note, George Hayter, is Philippe Verini's *First Rudiments for the Spanish Guitar*, published around 1825 at the expense of its author. In contrast, the firm of Chappell turned to the satirical etcher John Phillips for Alfred Bennett's *Instructions for the Spanish Guitar* in 1829, a significantly cheaper option than Verini's society portraitist.

Those unfamiliar with staff notation could usually find what they needed in the opening pages of a guitar method. They could then study, with the aid of a chart, how the notes available on the fingerboard translated into pitches on a staff. (These diagrams are sometimes impressive examples of the engraver's art, and one especially accomplished instance, a fold-out strip in *Rudiments for the Spanish Guitar* by 'Paulus Prucilli', alias Robert William Keith, was sold separately.) The student could then turn to charts of chords in the principal keys, to exercises demonstrating standard arpeggio patterns and to some beginners' pieces, perhaps including a small collection of songs. The title-page illustrations, when they were supplied, were intended to be worth a thousand words, liberating the authors from the obligation to say very much about matters of posture or the disposition of the hands. In fact, most compilers – whether aided by such an image or not – took the liberty of saying considerably less about technical matters than they might, including the crucial question of how the plucking hand should approach the strings. Bennett and Verini counsel that the strings should be pressed downwards which is good basic advice, even if the subtleties of the action are impossible to grasp from so succinct an account; yet many methods do not give any such advice at all. The equally fundamental question of whether the player should use the nails or flesh of the fingertips is commonly left unanswered, perhaps to accommodate teachers who wished to teach either method, although Nicario Jauralde insists that the 'nails of the right hand should be rather long than otherwise, as the sounds produced on the strings are much clearer than when they are short'.[50]

Often the authors do not agree in their advice. Sosson maintains that the little finger of the right hand should rest on the soundboard and never be lifted, while Jauralde and Verini, among others, prefer it to be kept free. There is general agreement that the thumb of the left hand should lie concealed behind the neck; this is the posture shown in the majority of illustrated methods, but the thumb can be clearly seen in the line drawing accompanying Sola's *Instructions* of 1820. Derwort, Duvernay and Sosson allow that it may sometimes be needed to stop the sixth course, but Jauralde says this is a 'very rare' device, and Duvernay insists that 'this expedient is never to be resorted to, except when wholly and unavoidably indispensible [*sic*]'.[51]

If the subtleties of touch are rarely discussed in these methods, there is perhaps sleight of hand of another sort. Whatever they may claim on their title pages, or in their introductions, these methods do not really provide the self-sufficient means of home instruction, or the innovative method of study, that they sometimes announce. The methods existed to be sold as a supplement to personal instruction, to promote a teacher's name (perhaps beyond the bounds of a purely local fame) and to put his pedagogical materials into a durable and remunerative form.

The results often appear staid, redolent of flower displays under glass domes in Georgian front rooms rather than moonlit Spanish gardens, yet at least one of them illustrates how closely the guitar in the 1820s remained associated with the fraught political situation of Spain and her colonies during that decade. The title page of *The Spanish Lyre* (1825) by F. V. Molina identifies the author as an 'Officer in the Spanish Army', and shows a couple in Spanish national dress.[52] The book offers parallel English and Castilian texts in the pedagogical section, which prepares the reader for five songs in Spanish, three supplied with singing texts in both languages. The author is almost certainly the Captain Molina who served under Sir William Carroll in the Peninsular War and was among the 'hundreds of other brave Spaniards now in London' mentioned in a newspaper report of 1825. These troops had fought to resist the French as they attempted to reinstate Ferdinand VII, King of Spain; the French eventually succeeded in putting Ferdinand back on the throne in 1823 and he initiated reprisals that explain the rapid departure to London and elsewhere of those who had opposed him. The newspaper account also notes that Molina and his brother 'have been frequently invited by personages of the first rank and fashion to their parties, and have given the highest gratification to the lovers of harmony'.[53] That report is confirmed by another of Molina's London publications, *Spanish Serenades . . . which have been Admired in the First Circles of London . . . for the Piano Forte and Guitar* (c.1825), whose list of subscribers is quite stellar: in addition to many titled persons, it includes Madame Catalani and various people who can be connected in some way with Fernando Sor (the Earl of Essex, Miss Davenport and Miss Cornewall), Robert Henry Clive, and Molina's commanding officer in the Peninsula, Sir William Carroll.

Who purchased such methods? Perhaps the higher gentry and nobility would look for something more personalised than a printed tutor, and few of the English methods can be described as handsome productions. We should probably therefore look to substantial tradesmen such as the coal merchants, linen drapers and cheesemongers who are addressed in an advertisement of 1834, in which a finishing school offers their daughters lessons on the guitar.[54] The new suburbanites also come into view, for advertisements in the metropolitan press by women seeking work as a governess, and naming the guitar among their accomplishments, give reply addresses in places such as Chelsea, Hampstead and Pentonville, or south of the Thames in Brixton, Camberwell and Clapham. The suburban guitarist tending a window box of flowers or kitchen-garden plants was a familiar figure by 1833, when the *New Monthly Magazine and Literary Journal* evoked one strumming at a window 'among the bean pots in some suburban street'.[55] It does not strain the imagination much to envisage a guitar method on the parlour table.

Repertoire in the 1820s

By the end of the decade there was enough good music in print or manuscript to reassure devotees that an estimable solo repertoire, mostly by masters of foreign origin such as Ferdinando Carulli, Mauro Giuliani and Fernando Sor, had been consolidated. There was also a demand for arrangements of airs taken from works by Beethoven, Meyerbeer, Mozart, Rossini and Weber, among others, for such versions offered guitarists their sole point of contact with the composers of highest esteem. These arrangements, rarely covering more than a page or two, lent themselves well to serial publication in cheap and even sixpenny numbers, which were being used 'to prise open print culture for a new lower middle class readership' in the wider world of publishing.[56]

One such series, entitled *Dolce ed utile* (1828?), was overseen by a tireless worker in this particular vineyard, George Henry Derwort.[57] The series offers pieces selected and lightly fingered 'for the Use of Amateurs', largely drawn from the simpler works of Mauro Giuliani, one of the greatest guitar virtuosi of the age but one who never came to England, where his name was clearly revered by some (as the niche magazine *The Giulianiad*, founded in 1833, bears witness). Each of the twelve sixpenny numbers of *Dolce ed utile* appeared with an engraved title page and two printed sides of music;[58] the Italian title gave the work a cosmopolitan allure, and although the allusion to Horace's *Ars poetica* (line 343) probably escaped some buyers, the commendation of the music as 'sweet and useful' made an appeal to the pragmatic values of the middling sort.

L'Aurore, ou journal de guitare of 1827, at 1*s*. per number, each with a title page showing a good deal of floridly engraved French, was a more ostentatiously elegant and ambitious affair. Compiled by Felix Horetzky and published by John Ewer and Julius Johanning – the latter 'in the forefront of Spanish guitar-making, selling and promoting in London'[59] – *L'Aurore* featured music by Aguado, Carcassi and Carulli, together with arrangements of Haydn, Méhul, Mozart, Paisiello and Rossini. (An indifferent waltz by 'I. W. Millais' in no. 4 is a real curio, since the composer is almost certainly John William Millais, the father of the Pre-Raphaelite painter John Everett Millais.)[60] Some of the pieces that make significant technical demands are abridged, reworked and retitled; the third of Sor's *Six Divertimentos*, op. 2, is briskly reduced to its first section, with the sixth string (tuned to low D in the original) brought back to its customary pitch, while the *Trois rondo brillants*, op. 2, of Dionisio Aguado are cut down to the first and second sections of a single movement and renamed 'Siciliano'.[61] The strength of such serialised collections at their best lay in the more extended pieces, which are not too demanding (but nonetheless have substance), which take the player some way up the fingerboard (but not too often) and which have moments where the lowest strings participate in the melodic writing (Fig. 35).

Fig. 35 Quintet from Rossini's opera *Il Turco in Italia*, arranged for guitar by Mauro Giuliani as his third *Rossiniana*, op. 123; published in Felix Horetzky's *L'Aurore, ou journal de guitare*, no. 1 (1827), 12.

Some amateur players – perhaps most – chose to perform songs among friends, not to hold the attention of a company with an instrumental piece such as Giuliani's arrangement of Rossini. In April 1827 Marianne

Dyson of the Hampshire gentry received a letter from her friend Anne Sturges Bourne describing the performance of a guest, Lady Frances, who sang a series of accompanied songs in several languages:

> Since I wrote last the guitar is come and she [Lady Frances] sings to us every evening, the prettiest collection of things, Italian, German, Spanish, light and grave, and the voice is so sweet and so flexible, and the words so clear and the face so smiling, and the figure so binding, and the whole thing so perfectly lovely that in short there is no going to bed.[62]

These songs in Italian, German and Spanish may well have included items composed or arranged by Carlo Michelangelo Sola, known in England as Charles Sola, another indefatigable arranger and composer of accompanied song for the guitar.[63] Sola was principally known as a flautist and singing teacher of some distinction, serving the landed gentry,[64] but by 1817 the *Hampshire Chronicle* can describe him as a musician whose 'singing and guitar playing are too well known in London to require any comment from us'.[65] On the strength of that reputation, Sola published his *Instructions for the Spanish Guitar* in 1820 and song arrangements that were frequently issued in sets, such as *Six Italian Canzonets with an Accompaniment for the Guitar* (1820?), *Six French Songs Composed with an Accompaniment for the Spanish Guitar* (1823), various series of 'Spanish airs' and some English ballads such as Joseph Wade's 'Meet me by the moonlight' and 'Your heart and lute: A Ballad [with words] Written by a Lady'.[66] Many of Sola's arrangements have accompaniments 'for the piano forte or Spanish guitar'. Sure of his market, he consistently produced accompaniments well accommodated to the needs of the amateur, and as a result rarely drew praise from the critics; by 1842 a journalist in Leeds had 'a faint recollection' that someone called Sola had once been 'an arranger of airs for the guitar'.[67]

The absence of any reference to French songs in Anne Sturges Bourne's letter quoted above is puzzling, for they were much in demand. Where Italian songs inevitably evoked the social milieu of London's Italian Opera, quarried as early as 1807 by Bortolazzi, a taste for imported French song was more vividly cosmopolitan; there was even, perhaps, a tang of sea air and holiday about such *chansons* and *romances*, for they belonged with other interests that one could easily make a cross-Channel jaunt to pursue.

If singers performed them really well, they were likely to have other Francophile interests, which declared to all that they had been to Paris, and suggested they would go again. A scene in Marianne Spencer Hudson's satirical novel *Almack's* of 1826, named after the most exclusive assembly room in London, shows 'a dozen new French romances for the guitar' arriving from London at a country house, together with new designs for embroidery, some political pamphlets, a bonnet *à la jolie femme* and a novel, all in the same packet. The parcel is addressed to a young woman, whose time spent time in the French capital has become a talking point in the county.[68] In reality, such a consignment would have included the *romances* available from the London agents of Parisian sellers, such as A. Petit and A. Meissonnier, who supplied material to English players wishing to look beyond the publications of a major firm such as Chappell. These elegant French productions usually offered a single *romance* with a guitar accompaniment, and the constituency for them was certainly wider than *Almack's* suggests; Sophia Broadwood, born into the famous family of pianoforte-makers in 1805 and therefore into the London artisan class, collected them with interest.[69]

In the English songs, as in the French and Italian, everything is geared towards the amateur who cannot be asked to show more dexterity than is required for rolling quaver or semiquaver arpeggios. Nor are players expected to occupy themselves over much with the differences that distinguish genres according to melodic form or subject, for, although a critic of 1824 uses the terms *bolero*, *barcarole*, *canzonetta* and *romance* in a review of recent material for the guitar, he or she quickly reveals that they all have much the same character: 'the gaiety, softness, tenderness, and chivalry, which we associate with the troubadours, the gay squires, and sprightly dames, of the early ages of poetry and music'.[70] Such songs, whether accompanied by the guitar or the pianoforte, were sometimes reviewed under the heading 'new ballads' in the periodical press; that is probably the best way to conceive them, for the term 'ballad' captures much of what these songs provide. The melodies seem generally designed to give the singer a chance to display feeling but not necessarily virtuosity, while the verse is often decorously sentimental or nostalgic with a narrative opening ('Gaily the Troubadour touch'd his Guitar / When he was hastening home from the war').[71] The point of view expressed is mostly masculine: in these poems women are variously adored, reproached, invited to moonlit assignations or reassured that they will still be loved when time has turned them into a 'dear ruin'.[72] G. T. May's *Instructions for the Spanish Guitar* offers a representative if superior example, arranged by May from an original for voice and pianoforte by the well-known Irish composer Sir John Andrew Stevenson (Ex. 30). In the poem a man lectures his beloved on the importance of tears (hers, not his) as a means to teach a feeling heart. The setting responds to the line 'and if those sighs be love!' with discreet word painting in bar 8, while the D sharp in bar 10 adds a pungency to the seventh chord as the voice is given the affective repetition 'thy heart, thy heart'. Such small moments have significance in this modest but companionable art.

The guitar has never been given its due for the encouragement it gave to amateur composition.[73] Bennett's method gives fingerboard diagrams of the chords I, IV and V in various major and minor keys, so that the player can devise accompaniments for 'simple Italian and French melodies', while Derwort's manual invites the reader to contemplate devising 'an Accompaniment, to any air sung by another person'. He observes that the three basic chords I, IV and V will allow anyone to 'compose a song which may be correct and good'.[74] (Too many composers of the period came to the same conclusion; a great many have done so since.) Poems in newspapers and journals also show that guitarists were creating their own repertoire; in 1831 *La Belle Assemblée* published verses entitled 'Song for the Guitar: imitated from the Spanish', which issues an obvious invitation, while two years later *The Giulianiad* printed a 'Guitar Song' and called upon the reader 'to exercise his or her judgement in giving the effect in music, unassisted'.[75] Each stanza of the 'Guitar Song' appears with a guide to the character of the music required ('A light breathing cadence is played', 'A low air, in imitation of a voice'). Many other poems of the day call upon the player to try composition, including 'Ode to the Guitar' ('Hail, soft guitar, the Spaniard's joy'), 'The Spanish Guitar' ('My gay guitar, my gay guitar / When sleep the furious sounds of war') and 'Stanzas to my Guitar, by a Lady' ('Companion of the exiled brave').[76]

The players who set such material were eventually paid the tribute of being fictionalised in Benjamin Disraeli's novel *Henrietta Temple* of 1833. The heroine takes up her guitar and sings a ballad beginning 'Yes, weeping is madness, / Away with this tear'. A house guest named Ferdinand, an accomplished singer and guitarist himself, is impressed, and Henrietta's father swiftly assures him that the air is Henrietta's own:

Ex. 30 'Oh! if those eyes deceive me not', from G. T. May's *Instructions for the Spanish Guitar*, 2nd edn (n.d. [c.1830]), 14.

'The music', said Ferdinand, full of enthusiasm, 'is—'

'Henrietta's,' replied her father.

'And the words?'

'Were found in my canary's cage,' said Henrietta Temple, rising and putting an end to the conversation.[77]

Henrietta pretends that the poem of her song was found at the bottom of a birdcage, where torn sheets of newspaper might serve as a lining; not wishing to admit she wrote the poem herself, she implies that it was a piece of newspaper verse.

Henrietta Temple contains numerous accounts of social life in the opulent houses of the leisured and political classes, and is therefore a prime example of what is commonly termed 'silver-fork' fiction. Yet there are so many references to guitars in this, as in Disraeli's other novels, that 'Spanish-guitar' fiction would do just as well to describe his contributions to the genre, and might, indeed, be better. For while the indoor sociability of luncheons and dinners, with elegant silver service, is prominent in Disraeli's writing, his books abound in references to sketching parties and excursions to abbeys, castles and country villas, where a guitar could be a beguiling companion. Despite their elite and self-consciously genteel settings, such episodes rest on a general expansion of horizon that also affected the middle ranks of life from which Disraeli himself, once an articled clerk in a solicitor's office, sprang. The age of guitars stowed in the holds of steamships and rowing boats, or laid out on the grass for picnic parties, is now just beginning.

EIGHT

The Guitar Going Places

O long unharmed
May all its agèd boughs o'er-canopy
The small round basin, which this jutting stone
Keeps pure from falling leaves!

Samuel Taylor Coleridge, 'Inscription for a
Fountain on a Heath' (1802), lines 2–5

A detached leaf from a scrapbook, probably from the late 1820s or 1830s, shows a couple at a fountain beneath a canopy of leaves (Fig. 36). A guitar lies between them. The man wears a kilt and a grandly feathered hat, the woman a decidedly indoor dress. The setting is Romantic in the sense that it evokes both the dramatic landscape of Scotland (there is a suggestion of mountainous terrain) and the Mediterranean (if it is, indeed, a *pin parasol* that overshadows the lady). The fountain seems to be in a cultivated but nonetheless remote place; it may even be on an island, given the man's careful tread to find dry land amid the enveloping waters. The man gestures towards his companion, perhaps inviting her to play the guitar, but she smilingly demurs. All around this central scene, the unknown compiler has pasted small printed images; some are crude wood engravings of the kind to be found in the double-column penny magazines, while others, carefully kept apart, use the relatively new technique of steel engraving and are considerably more accomplished.

The details of the central picture with the guitar are so specific that we may suspect some episode from an unidentified novel lies behind them, or

Fig. 36 Page from a scrapbook, probably from the late 1820s or 1830s, by an unknown compiler. Pride of place in the assemblage of rural vistas of castles, ruins and modest cottages is given to a scene of romance played out around a guitar. Private collection.

perhaps the theatre set for a melodrama based on something from Sir Walter Scott. Penny magazines in the 1830s often published wood engravings of such scenes, and the newspapers record many ephemeral productions that might come into question. Yet the meaning of the page as a whole is broader, to the point where the importance of any specific allusion we might suspect takes second place to a pervasive sense of the *scenic*. The surrounding images show the remains of ancient buildings, cottages and riverine scenes, gratifying a taste for the pastoral and picturesque.[1] The printed captions that came with these images have all been carefully kept, with their range of terms indicating a directed gaze: 'a *Scene* near Wisbech', 'a *Prospect* in Sussex', 'a *View* near St. Ives' (my emphasis).

Getting out

The late Georgians developed a keen sense of the pleasure and well-being to be gained from outings to beauty spots, the countryside or the coast. This was not the solitary communion with nature that inspired William Cowper to recognise, in shadows cast by a winter sun, that he himself was 'but a fleeting shade', or that prompted Wordsworth, in the countryside above Tintern Abbey, to ponder 'Thoughts of more deep seclusion'.[2] The Georgian outing was public and convivial. Towards 1800 the word 'excursion' began to be employed in the sense of 'a journey ... undertaken for the sake of pleasure or health', a development hastened by the fashion for taking the waters at spas or coastal villages such as Cheltenham or Brighton.[3] At about the same time, 'picnic', unknown to Samuel Johnson's *Dictionary* of 1755, began to be used of a shared outdoor meal at a scenic spot – it previously meant a repast where each party contributed to the supply of food.[4] Contemporary artists responded eagerly to this opportunity for a new kind of pastoral, where the napkins and sketchbooks of the middle classes replaced the spinning wheels and homespun fabrics of rural cottagers. A coloured engraving of 1823 by Charles Heath shows a view of Richmond, a favourite picnic place alongside the meandering Thames, with elegant men and women strolling or sitting in various couples and groups; a lady sketches the view and another reads to her companions, a guitar lying nearby on the grass.[5]

A musical instrument that did not encumber anyone on the journey, but could offer full resources of harmony when the party paused or reached its destination, was such an obvious need that one of the most resourceful inventors of stringed instruments in Georgian England, Edward Light (d. 1832), set about the task of creating nearly half a dozen new types that would serve. These inventions combined features of existing instruments to create hybrids such as the 'harp-guitar'.[6] As Light emphasised in some of his many advertisements, his new instruments were easy to carry and were good company, even on the long journeys or voyages that might be necessary for commerce. In 1801 he even commended his harp-guitar for being so 'very light and portable' that it could be taken as far as the Indies; Light assured his customers that they need have no anxieties about taking a fragile object made in London to lands between the Tropics, for it was built 'to stand the test of different climates', just as it was designed to 'amuse and delight on the journey or passage'.[7] He also envisaged less ambitious itineraries or excursions, for the smaller examples of his harp-guitar could easily fit 'within a coach seat or portmanteau'. Admirably suited to 'all purposes of amusement' at home and in the garden, his inventions were 'exceedingly convenient for the watering places'.[8]

Edward Light increasingly found himself battling against the rising fashion for the Spanish guitar, already commended in 1801 by Bonaventura Sperati for being 'so convenient to travel with, so pleasing in the solitude of the Country'.[9] Light eventually had to make an explicit counter-claim; with a degree of exaggeration that seems remarkable even by the standards of Georgian advertising, he announced another creation in 1817 which was 'not larger than a Spanish guitar, and in every respect the most desirable little instrument ever invented'.[10] As Light knew very well, the Spanish guitar was the equal of all his inventions in its capacity for harmony and its ability to produce a harp-like sound from strings of gut and overspun silk. The guitar was also eminently portable; as one enthusiastic commentator remarked in 1833, the year after Light's death, it was even possible to play while journeying in a carriage, 'to dissipate the ennui of travel'.[11]

The guitar seemed the ideal instrument for the picnics commonly called 'gypsy parties', where those who took part affected to live, for some little while, a nomadic life, with tents and kettles hanging on chains over wood fires. The term 'gypsy party' is first recorded in 1816 and therefore joins 'excursion', in the sense of a trip for pleasure, and 'pic-nic' as a token of new outdoor pursuits and ventures. An article in *The Giulianiad* captures the character of such occasions, and the guitar's place in them, with that journal's customary note of evangelical enthusiasm:

> In a gipsy party, also – where there must be a sprinkling of romance, and an oblivion of the dull cares of the world . . . what instrument can be listened to with so much reverence and buoyant pleasure? . . . In all such situations of festive mirth and convivial recreation, the guitar is the instrument of joy and gladness.[12]

As the fashion for excursions and picnics caught on, caricaturists and sketch writers began to show men and women from the middle ranks of life suffering all kinds of rural mishap during the jaunts on which they take their guitars. These unfortunate holidaymakers – who are mainly City of London tradesmen, incautiously venturing out of their shops with friends and families – often appear to be courting disaster by aspiring to pleasures somewhat above their station, for the comic figures of the aspiring City tradesman and his sharply status-conscious wife were deeply etched by now in English traditions of satire and comedy. James White's story 'Preparations for Pleasure or a Picnic' (1829) has Mr Claudius Bagshaw, a retired silk merchant from Cheapside in the heart of London, settling on Richmond for a picnic and inviting Miss Euphemia Grouts to join the excursion with her guitar.[13] This lady is socially somewhat above him, for she is the daughter of a corn chandler, who received a knighthood for presenting an address to George III. The music for the outing is carefully planned, with a handwritten programme; Miss Grouts is down to offer a 'Grand aria, with variations', presumably something like Matteo Carcassi's variations upon the well-known air 'Di tanti palpiti' from Rossini's *Tancredi*, the kind of piece liable to outstay its welcome, and perhaps especially impractical for performance on a small boat as it passes under Blackfriars Bridge. In the event, the performance is impossible because three of the strings on the lady's guitar break (a facile joke at the guitar's expense, which Charles Dickens will stoop to repeat). As a substitute offering, Miss Grouts bravely tries to sing the aptly entitled ballad 'O leave me to my sorrow', accompanying herself on the three strings left, but quickly abandons the attempt.

The greatest of all satires in this vein is 'The Steam Excursion', an early story by Charles Dickens, originally published in the *Monthly Magazine* for October 1834 and subsequently collected into *Sketches by Boz*. The young Dickens here captures everything that made the guitar a good (if sometimes unreliable) companion on the day trips that the new steamships made feasible; the resistance of these vessels to the vagaries of wind or tide made a fixed timetable possible, at least for departure, and ensured a passage sufficiently stable (if the weather held) for food to be served – as in Dickens's story – during what was effectively a waterborne picnic with constantly changing scenic views.[14] The characters in 'The Steam Excursion', heading out to the mouth of the Thames estuary and back, are mostly lower-middle-class Londoners connected with the legal profession, so often associated in Dickens's imagination with the dingiest alleys and darkest courts of London, from which the possibility of escape sometimes seems so distant. They engage a band for dancing, 'and then, whoever we know that's musical, you know, why they'll make themselves useful and agreeable'. As the company boards ship, *The Endeavour*, the Briggs sisters arrive with three guitars and 'two immense portfolios of music, which it would take at least a week's incessant playing to get through'. They set off from London Bridge Wharf:

> 'Now,' said Mr. Percy Noakes, who had just ascended from the fore-cabin, where he had been busily engaged in decanting the wine, 'if the Misses Briggs will oblige us with something before dinner, I am sure we shall be very much delighted'. The three Misses Briggs looked modestly at their mamma, and the mamma looked approvingly at her daughters ... The Misses Briggs asked for their guitars, and several gentlemen seriously damaged the cases in their anxiety to present them. Then, there was a very interesting production of three little keys for the aforesaid cases, and a melodramatic expression of horror at finding a string broken; and a vast deal of screwing and tightening, and winding, and tuning, during which Mrs. Briggs expatiated to those near her on the immense difficulty of playing a guitar ... At length, the Misses Briggs began in real earnest. It was a new Spanish composition, for three voices and three guitars. The effect was electrical. All eyes were turned upon the captain, who was reported to have once passed through Spain with his regiment, and who must be well acquainted with the national music.

Dickens here comically overstates the effect that multi-voice boleros, with their ebulliently rhythmical accompaniments, could no doubt sometimes produce, though Cruikshank's illustration to the story suggests that the 'national music' of Spain is here receiving a demurely English and well-drilled, rather than a flamboyant, performance (Fig. 37). As shown in Chapter 5, the vogue for such boleros using several voices and guitar arose in England during the Peninsular War, a conflict that may still be in the minds of Dickens's characters as they listen; during the performance some fix their eyes on a military man among them who is rumoured to have 'passed through Spain with his regiment'.[15]

Fig. 37 Illustration by George Cruikshank from Charles Dickens, 'The Steam Excursion', *Sketches by Boz* (1836), etching. The three Misses Briggs are performing 'a new Spanish composition, for three voices and three guitars. The effect was electrical' (254).

The resorts

In 1800, before the steamships began to run, a resort like Margate on the Kentish coast could not be visited in the kind of day trip described by Dickens in 'The Steam Excursion'. In difficult conditions, the sloops that ran from London to Margate could take more than thirty-six hours on a churning sea to reach their destination, a journey that could be a severe test of the passenger's endurance. Nonetheless, Margate had become a residential watering place by the beginning of the nineteenth century, with a choice of polite pursuits, which included 'strumming on a guitar', according to a description of the town in 1802; the author associates the instrument with the hours after dinner, and regards it as an alternative to playing the pianoforte or visiting the libraries to look over the newspapers, magazines and novels.[16] Guitars might even be played in those same libraries, which were often used as evening venues for music; in 1803 William Robinson's verse satire *A Trip to Margate* mocked the 'vile strumming' to be heard at Betterson's Library in the town.[17] By 1828 the introduction of steam packets finally allowed London excursionists to make a day trip (or better a weekend break) to the resort, and in that year Charles Cochrane, in disguise as the Spanish minstrel Juan de Vega, saw 'about a thousand city folk' arriving at Margate pier for a long weekend; Cochrane found abundant employment in the resort and received various invitations to give lessons on the guitar.[18]

Although Margate was doing well, none of the coastal resorts in the ascendant by 1800 prospered quite like Brighton in Sussex, already an established watering place by the 1750s, with assembly rooms, substantial inns, coffee-houses and a theatre.[19] The town was extended westwards with the Regency building campaigns of the Brunswick estate, and eastwards with the efforts of the property speculator Thomas Kemp.[20] The public coach service from London could reach Brighton in six hours by the 1820s, and the Chain Pier, completed during that decade, allowed steamships to dock for tours around the south coast or trips across the Channel to Dieppe. The social world of the guitar in Brighton was shaped by two seasons that were notionally quite distinct: the summer months were for tradesmen and others from the City of London, while the winter was for the gentry and nobility, who could form, at their most exalted, a transplanted court.[21] Thus anyone who wished to enjoy the 'fashionable entertainments' of the resort arrived in mid-November. The result was a high concentration of elite visitors in a resort that was *out* of season', as the expression is now understood. The shutters were in place on the windows against wind and storm, the steamships were laid up until the spring and all was set fair 'for a snug and comfortable winter season . . . Signor Sagrini does the guitar, and it is all as nice as may be'.[22]

Passing references in novels, satirical verse and newspapers reveal amateur guitar playing in Brighton during both seasons, but principally in the winter, when the town was an elite playground. Charles Cochrane received several requests to give lessons when he toured the town as Juan de Vega and met various guitar players there, both male and female, amateur and professional.[23] Disraeli's novel *The Young Duke* of 1831 features a count 'who daily brought his guitar' to a house in Kemptown – a fictional account that does not exaggerate the elite clientele for which the new quarter of Brighton was built and which it occasionally found.[24] The anonymous verse satire 'A Trifle from Brighton' (1827), whose title alludes to the cheap souvenirs on sale in the town, confirms the place of the guitar among the diversions of the cold season:

> Then albums, souvenirs and the newest quadrilles,
> *La Belle Assemblée*'s latest pattern for frills.
> The harp, the piano, the tinkling guitar
> All help to kill time – for both *Miss* and *Mamar*.[25]

Guitars could be purchased at local auctions of household goods in Brighton, often the contents of houses in prestigious streets such as Grand Parade facing the Royal Pavilion, and 'superior' guitars were for sale or hire at Wright's Music Warehouse on the corner of North Street and New Road (Fig. 38). Together with the assembly room of the Old Ship Inn (which still stands), Wright's emporium was a hub of musical life in Brighton, and with 'the increased extent of the town westward' (meaning the Brunswick estate) its operations were expanded in 1828 with a new Reading Room and a Musical Repository. Offers of guitar lessons appeared frequently in the Brighton papers, sometimes addressed to visitors who settled in the town during the summer, when teachers with mainstream musical positions in London might find themselves free; the principal cellist of Drury Lane advertised lessons on the guitar in July 1826.[26] Some were also language teachers, such as Signora Straccia and G. Vally, both of whom advertised in *The Watering Places of Great Britain and Fashionable Directory* of 1831 as Brighton teachers of Italian and the guitar.[27] Such was the vogue for the guitar in a resort where the instrument was likely to go out of tune even faster than in London, a victim of damp sea air.

Winter aficionados of the guitar could enjoy performances in Brighton by noted professional guitarists including Trinidad Huerta, Ferdinand Pelzer, Giulio Regondi ('a fine child, only eight years of age'), Luigi Sagrini, the Schulz family, Charles Sola and Philippe Verini.[28] This roster of professional visitors, all of them foreigners, had no rival anywhere in England outside

Fig. 38 Wright's Music Warehouse, Colonnade, Brighton, by Wilfred Alfred Delamotte, 1853, watercolour. The premises were a focus of musical activity in the town. Royal Pavilion and Museums, Brighton and Hove.

London and the port of Bristol. Advertisements in the press, though revealing, provide only a reduced account of their activities, for much happened that there was no cause to announce. One of the great players, Ferdinand Pelzer, announces his arrival in Brighton in November 1835 then promptly vanishes from the newspaper record, presumably because he had secured the pupils and engagements he sought by leaving his details (as his advertisement explains) at Wright's in the town. Many of the engagements that gave visiting guitarists their second stream of income were private affairs arranged informally, like the soirée at Kemptown in 1827 where Trinidad Huerta played (see below) or the 'evening parties' that the child prodigy Giulio Regondi was ready to attend with his father in 1831. Charles Cochrane soon learned that the evening was the best time for making money; a professional French guitarist whom he met at Brighton was able to support a wife and family (though times were sometimes hard) without playing during the day.[29]

The less eminent players, primarily using the guitar to accompany their singing and perhaps rarely offering a solo piece, usually performed just one or two items within the standard miscellaneous programmes of the period.[30] Luigi Sagrini, however, was sufficiently well known and admired in Brighton to venture a *Grande concertante* for pianoforte and guitar, among other works.[31] In 1829 he took the unusual step for a guitarist of mounting a concert himself, but it was not given in one of the major concert venues of the town: the location was a private house, 23 Brunswick Terrace, one of a row of Georgian mansions in Hove.[32] Sagrini engaged instrumentalists and various singers, including the Misses Kean, whose own concert at the Old Ship assembly room in 1829 featured 'a simple but pretty duet' by Molina, identifiable as 'The Rural Ballad of Lelillo / Canción del Lellilo' from Molina's guitar method, *The Spanish Lyre* (1825) (Ex. 31).[33]

Ex. 31 Excerpt from 'The Rural Ballad of Lelillo / Canción del Lellilo', from F. V. Molina's *The Spanish Lyre* (1825), 18–19.

Some professionals on the road

Two of the most influential guitarists on the Western European scene, Ferdinando Carulli and Matteo Carcassi, visited London in the 1820s. This was such stuff as dreams are made on for devotees of the guitar who were able to hear them, but the two masters left barely a rack behind. Neither was ready to hazard a tour, perhaps for want of the necessary contacts or any appetite for the planning required to balance the costs of travel and accommodation against revenue from ticket sales, which were always uncertain. Carulli came in 1823 and played his variations (op. 209) on a theme from Pierre-Alexandre Monsigny's opera *Aline, reine de Golconde* at the King's Theatre, but the only musical deposit of his brief visit is *Forty* [actually fourteen] *Easy Pieces and Eight Short Preludes for the Guitar Composed for the Use of Beginners*, which appeared with the subtitle *Op. 1 of Works Composed in London*.[34] The collection offers some fine examples of Carulli's salon manner at its most companionable. In 1827 Carcassi played at a West End mansion 'in a style of excellence we have never seen surpassed if ever equalled', but his printed legacy is also modest, comprising *Twelve Easy Pieces for the Spanish Guitar Composed for the Use of Beginners* of 1828, and *Twelve Popular Airs . . . Arranged for the Spanish Guitar* from the same year, which mostly used melodies of English songs such as 'Love was once a little boy' and 'Your heart and lute'.[35]

If a visiting virtuoso had something particular to offer – best of all if he was a child prodigy – then more ambitious itineraries were possible. The printed programme for a 'Vocal Concert' of 1825, given at the house of John Capel in west London's Russell Square, contains various handwritten additions noting performances by the Schulz family.[36] At this time the Schulz trio, father and sons (who were barely teenagers), had only recently arrived in England; the Russell Square concert is the first trace of them in London before their debut at the Argyll Rooms and their performances before the king at Carlton House. Perhaps they had been invited to play at other venues, after the programmes had been printed, on the strength of the reputation they were beginning to acquire and which continued to mount; by 1826 the young Leonard Schulz was acknowledged to be 'one of the best performers on the guitar we ever heard', and 'quite a miracle of his age'.[37] From London, the trio travelled to Manchester and Liverpool; Schulz senior apparently suspected that audiences would wish to indulge their curiosity about such child prodigies only once, and kept the boys on the move, using a well-trodden route for musicians to the north-west and then across to Dublin.

The English career of Trinidad Huerta (Fig. 39) shows a virtuoso touring in the late 1820s, just before the railway networks transformed the opportunities for moving between distant towns (see Appendix 2). Huerta combined occasional appearances in major London venues with performances at provincial town halls, meeting rooms in the hotels of watering places and a library. He travelled as a professional guitar player but also, in a sense, as a professional Spaniard, exploiting British sympathies for the Spanish political

Senor Heurta of Ouhuela a provine of Valencia 1829 GC

Fig. 39 *Señor Huerta of Orihuela*, by George Cumberland, 1829, pencil sketch. Trinidad Huerta visited Bristol for a week in mid-April 1829 and gave a concert on the 14th; Cumberland sketched the guitarist during that visit. City of Bristol Museum and Art Gallery, K3082/64.

refugees of the later 1820s, some of whom lived in poverty 'amidst the sordid and varied miseries of toil and ignorance'.[38] When Charles Cochrane impersonated a Spanish military refugee and mendicant guitarist in 1828–9, he met a Frenchman who advised him to invent a story about his life, for the English, being 'very romantic', would believe it and the tale would work to his advantage.[39] Huerta did, indeed, allow a colourful tale about his past to circulate, which has him leaving home 'with a guitar under his arm, when a boy', then wandering to the West Indies, 'where he gave a concert *to the blacks*' (original emphasis), to Mexico, the United States (that part is true) and Egypt, before turning to 'different parts of the Mediterranean' and finally England.[40]

Those travels – part real and part imaginary – over, Huerta had arrived in London by 8 February 1827, where he began building the reputation that would provide the basis for his extensive touring in the south. At the Argyll Rooms, he took part in a concert, where his playing was described as 'altogether wonderful'.[41] In the same year, a contributor to the *New Monthly Magazine and Literary Journal*, presumably asked to provide a puff, took him to be the new Sor, for here was another exceptional artist from Iberia, triumphing over the limitations of the guitar:

> Those who merely cultivate the guitar as an accompaniment, without any conception of its capabilities as an instrument, should have heard Sor, who astonished all the musical circles in London some years ago; or since that is no longer possible, they ought to hear the young Spaniard Huerta, who has lately arrived in this country: his superiority in clearness and brilliance of touch, the power, the rapidity, the facility, the grace of his execution, the depth and variety of tone he can call forth, are incredible, inconceivable to those who have not heard him; he gives to the puny instrument in his hand an effect like that of a band of music, heard through some diminishing medium.[42]

Huerta needed an influential friend and found one in Nicolas Mori, a distinguished musician who ran a music-publishing business in London's New Bond Street with his partner, Henry Louis Lavenu. Mori swiftly discerned how the firm and Huerta together could exploit the vogue for the Spanish guitar to the benefit of all concerned. The tickets for Huerta's first London concert were available exclusively from Mori and Lavenu's shop, and although it was an evening of vocal and instrumental music featuring fifteen artists the event was announced as 'Mr. Huerta's Concert'.[43] Huerta played a 'Grand Fantasia', which was perhaps his *Nouvelle grande fantaisie*, op. 64, together with the *Grand March of Don Rafaell dell Riego*, a 'Grand Overture' and a fandango. The march was the piece he used to imitate a full military band, an effect much admired,[44] while the 'Grand Overture' was his fantasia on the overture to Rossini's *Semiramide*; the published score of that work (1829), with its extended runs and rapidly sounded octaves, provides some sense of the virtuosity that won him many admirers (Fig. 40). The fandango, sometimes described in programmes and reviews as a

Fig. 40. Introduction to Huerta's fantasia on the overture to Rossini's *Semiramide* (1829).

work performed 'extempore', was no doubt another show-stopper. Huerta must have been a flamboyant player, for it is a rare thing to find a guitarist praised for the 'power' of his playing; he was also clearly a virtuoso of a recognisable kind, catering for a public in love with the idea of Paganini, a performer with whom Huerta explicitly compared himself on more than one occasion.

Mori and Lavenu briskly issued a method, *A Complete Book of Instructions for the Spanish Guitar* (1829), 'approved by A. T. Huerta' and designed to exploit Huerta's fame without suggesting that he was the author of a serviceable but routine piece of work.[45] The Mori–Huerta association was still going strong in December 1828, when the firm advertised guitars for sale 'on the improved plan of Signor Huerta, Plain and in Rosewood from 4 to 12 guineas'. [46] This is the time when Louis Panormo began to call himself 'the only maker of guitars in the Spanish style' on his labels, probably in consultation with Huerta, who married Panormo's daughter Angelina that same year.[47] Several London makers were keen to capitalise on Huerta's name and on public sympathy for the Spanish 'exiled brave'.[48]

With a metropolitan reputation established, Huerta ventured forth late in 1827, beginning with a tour of the southern resorts (Fig. 41). After a brief stop at Hastings, to play at Diplock's Marine Library, he was in Brighton by the third week of November, and performed twice during the winter at the assembly room of the Old Ship Inn, now called the Paganini Room after a more famous musician who also played there. He was engaged to play one evening at 22 Sussex Square in Kemptown, the home of Thomas Kemp, the property speculator who financed the building of the estate (and ruined himself in the process).[49] The French memoirist Auguste, comte de La Garde,

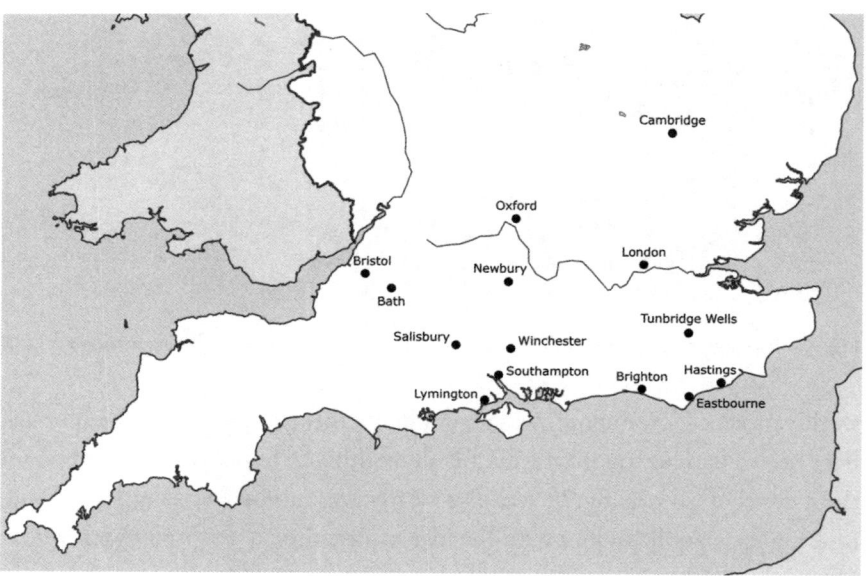

Fig. 41 The concert venues of Trinidad Huerta, as recorded in the London and provincial press, 8 February 1827 to 7 June 1830.

was present on that occasion, and although his report of the evening is clearly designed to persuade French families to take houses in Kemptown (many of which were still unoccupied) he was impressed with Huerta's performance. The guitarist played in the drawing room 'avec une perfection admirable'.[50]

In 1828 Huerta visited Cambridge and Oxford in speculative sorties – the former taking him far from his usual circuit south of the Thames – but it seems that neither experiment was repeated. There is no record of the response at Cambridge, but at Oxford, his 'scientific, and indeed wonderful performance', given twice, failed to attract a good audience, for which the *Oxford and City Herald* blamed the inter-collegiate boat races of that summer week in June.[51] The spas of Bath and Tunbridge Wells proved more dependable, while Winchester and Salisbury, as cathedral towns, offered promising venues for many kinds of music; there were also opportunities in smaller coastal places such as Eastbourne, where Huerta played for the monthly dinner of the Melodists' Club at the Freemasons' Tavern, and Lymington, where a local worthy, Colonel Shedden, acted as the patron.[52] An entry for 27 March 1830 in the diary of Emma Austen-Leigh shows that Huerta also visited the market town of Newbury in Berkshire ('Went to a morning concert at Newbury – Senhor Huerta on the Guitar – his wife played the Piano Forte and sung').[53] This was a small affair, as were many of Huerta's concerts in quieter places, for the only performers were Huerta and his wife, Angelina (née Panormo).

Huerta's provincial performances were generally given in what may be loosely defined as assembly rooms, as at Salisbury, where the premises are now a capacious shop, while in the university towns he played in the neo-classical town halls, which eventually yielded to Victorian developers; some of the other venues were in hotels or inns, such as The Albion in Brighton. While some of these spaces were opulent, like the assembly room in Bristol's Clifton Hotel, others could be very unassuming. At Hastings, Huerta probably played in the billiard room on the first floor of Diplock's Marine Library (a modest stage for an artist billed, for that event, as 'the first guitar player in the world'), while the assembly room at Lymington, where he appeared, was built on a humble scale. Nonetheless, these travels made Huerta the outstanding professional guitarist in the English public's experience before the Victorian period, and the musician who first showed those beyond London and Bath that such a profession could exist.

NINE

Women and Men

We have seen a throwing-off young gentleman . . .
volunteer a Spanish air upon the guitar when he
had previously satisfied himself that there was not
such an instrument within a mile of the house.

Charles Dickens, 'The "Throwing-Off" Young
Gentleman', *Sketches of Young Gentlemen* (1838)

In poetry of the Romantic period, women and the guitar achieve a shared apotheosis in the lines that Percy Bysshe Shelley wrote for his friend Jane Williams in 1821 and presented to her, together with a guitar he bought in Pisa, which still survives.[1] In two poems, but especially in 'With a Guitar, To Jane', Shelley praises the instrument as an embodiment of Nature.[2] Far from being a piece of lifeless timber, it is made of living wood from the Apennine forests; blown in the 'summer winds', it is the ultimate Aeolian harp, and long before its materials ever reached the maker's bench Nature had imbued them with her softest sounds:

> Whispering in enamoured tone
> Sweet oracles of woods and dells,
> And summer winds in sylvan cells;
> For it had learnt all harmonies
> Of the plains and of the skies,
> Of the forests and the mountains,
> And the many-voicèd fountains;
> The clearest echoes of the hills,

The softest notes of falling rills,
The melodies of birds and bees,
The murmuring of summer seas,
The pattering rain, and breathing dew . . .

In presenting the guitar to Jane Williams, Shelley assumes that only the touch and sensibility of a woman – or this particular woman – will truly reveal what Nature has conferred upon its materials. His poem therefore offers a rapturous understanding of the common association in Georgian England between music and the way Nature had constituted 'the fair sex' with especial care for what was calming and nurturing.

A 'particular display of figure'

The most prominent amateur guitarist in the drawing rooms of the 1820s and 1830s was, in fact, a man – the prolific lyricist Thomas Moore (d. 1852), who sang the verses he had composed for pre-existing airs. The results of his work with Irish tunes were published in the rapturously received *Irish Melodies* of 1808–34, with arrangements for the pianoforte by Sir John Andrew Stevenson, though the poems attracted many other composers. Moore sometimes sang his songs to the guitar, and much of his work was published in arrangements for voice and guitar by Charles Sola, among others.[3] Yet there is no doubt that many literary and pictorial sources suggest that some ability with the guitar, as with the harp or pianoforte, was considered a fit accomplishment for women in a very particular and gendered condition: they were of marriageable age and had been schooled since girlhood to please. References to men in the same kinds of source, reinforced by diaries and letters, suggest that musical interests and talents were markedly less prominent in the lives of males.[4] Already by 1801 periodicals such as the *Lady's Magazine* had begun to publish copies of Parisian fashion plates in which women (but not men) occasionally appear playing the Spanish guitar; and miscellaneous engravings, lithographs and mezzotints appeared showing only female guitar players, some derived from portraits now lost, forming a kind of visual companion to the fashion for the instrument. Some resembled the mass-produced 'Spanish señorita' pictures that can still be seen in some British homes; others were cut in steel for the new and popular albums and keepsake books, such as *Fisher's Drawing Room Scrapbook*.[5] In 1827 a reviewer declared that the guitar had 'gradually made its way into the circles of fashion, and is now pretty generally to be found in the saloons of *her* fair votaries' (my emphasis), where even the guitar itself is female.[6]

Given the limited musical horizons of the guitar, relative to the pianoforte and harp, we might be tempted to associate it with a particularly acute instance of the charge, evoked by Mary Wollstonecraft in *A Vindication of the Rights of Woman* (1792), that musical accomplishments confined women in a gilded cage – one where they had 'nothing to do but to plume themselves, and stalk with mock majesty from perch to perch'.[7] Shelley's poem, in which all the available space is filled with his voluble and exhilarated male voice, is not really about Jane's capacity to wield an eloquence denied to the poet as a man. The invocation of the guitar, so closely associated with song, shows that Shelley's true concern lies elsewhere: he summons a euphoric pantheism or religion of Nature to the cause that women should 'always inhabit the place of silence, or at most make it echo with their singing'.[8]

The fact that Shelley bought the guitar he gave to Jane Williams in Pisa may have no bearing on the meaning of the poem, but it offers an important reminder that we should distinguish lands north of the Alps and Pyrenees from Spain and Italy, where guitars were so deeply ingrained in musical life that they were played by both men and women as a matter of course. Viewed in that light, the place of the guitar in Georgian England may seem to offer a particularly entrenched opposition between a sportive masculinity, suspicious of artistic pursuits or foreign ways, and a femininity prettified by accomplishment, by the shallow cosmopolitanism of fashionable pastimes, and by the need to please the male eye. For although the guitar offered some women an art in which they could rival the finest professional and male practitioners – just as they did in some surviving examples of shell-work and embroidery[9] – the aspect of a woman's guitar playing most often emphasised by male writers and artists in Georgian England is the 'particular display of figure' that performance on the guitar could allow, in contrast to the pianoforte, where the player might find herself with her back to the company and her face turned against the wall:

> In choosing a musical instrument for a young girl, we should take into
> consideration her talents for it, her opportunities for their indulgence, and

her appearance – actually, her appearance. The Piano is the most generally suitable, in the latter respect, the attitude of the performer not requiring any particular grace, or making any particular display of figure. But this instrument, the least interesting of all in its tones, is costly and cumbrous, requires immense practice to excel on, and with common playing is not worth listening to . . . For more general use, with the voice, I know nothing comparable to the Spanish Guitar . . . a tolerable ear and a year's practice would form a performer on this instrument, more attractive than after three times the study on any other. Once acquired, its facility is scarcely injured by intervals of disuse; and to that it is little liable, from its extreme portability. Add to all this, its gracefulness, and powers for displaying exquisite taste.[10]

The emphasis in this passage, presumably written for the guidance of parents, is as much upon the player's aspect as the music she may produce. Whereas the pianoforte, somewhat unexpectedly described as 'the least interesting' of the instruments an amateur might cultivate, suits a player who can make no great 'display of figure', the guitar invites 'gracefulness' and 'powers for displaying exquisite taste'. The quality of touch, so vital in an instrument like the guitar, where both hands are in direct contact with the sounding element, is here on the verge of assuming an erotic aspect. In one of the papers published in the *Giulianiad* from 1833, indeed, the eroticism of a woman's touch on the guitar is taken about as far the editors dared:

An instrument seems fully conscious of the difference between being struck by a hammer, or a maiden's fingers . . . on the guitar, the feeling is instantaneous and electrical . . . Who that has once felt the true sentiment of love, but does not know the impression of the mind in the mere touch of the beloved object? . . . The taper [*sic*] fingers of the lady too are admirably adapted for this instrument . . . they find a ready ingress and egress . . .[11]

The strings recognise the touch of a woman (as opposed to the stroke of a pianoforte hammer) and quiver in response.

Contrary to what is often supposed, however, music held no universally agreed place among the arts that young women were encouraged to use in Georgian England, either to fill their time or to form their character.[12] Even some of the most voluble manuals compiled for their edification, such as *The Young Woman's Companion; or, Female Instructor*, published in various editions from 1814 onwards, make scarcely any reference to it. What is more, there was an influential school of thought that they would do better to abandon music studies altogether.[13] Married life for many women was ruled by the daily business of running a household, and at least one satirist associated the disappointments of wedlock with the end of the guitar in no uncertain

Fig. 42 Unknown artist, *Three Weeks after Marriage*, c.1835, coloured aquatint. The swift demise of romance is graphically represented by the fate of the guitar. Private collection.

terms (Fig. 42). It was not always an advantage, during a social gathering, to have a talent that could bring family, class or generational rivalries to light, and as standards of amateur performance rose in the decades around 1800 the hours of practice required to merit a hearing, even in an amateur context, rose to a level that some considered excessive, even immoral.

The question of whether a young woman would be set to study the guitar or any other musical instrument therefore depended as much upon *who* she was as upon *what* she was in the simple sense of her gender. This distinction embraced the development of her character, as assessed by her parents or her guardian, the particular nature of her prospects in life, and her connections, both in the home and in society, many of which might arise in a fortuitous manner. The question of her natural talent was, perhaps, the last matter to be considered. Elizabeth Spence's novel *The Spanish Guitar* of 1814 was written to advise female children on the verge of their teens that the guitar could be such an absorbing pastime it should be encouraged only in tandem with a constant monitoring of their character and sense of Christian duty by a parent. A young woman's station in life was just as important: if it allowed her to envisage some measure of freedom from overseeing the housemaids and the cook, or from exceptional devotion to occupations that she might one day need so as to make her own way in the world, such as fine embroidery, then she could devote time to the guitar as 'an alternative amusement to relieve the graver parts of musical studies' on the pianoforte or harp.[14]

Much also depended upon chance connections and family background, for guitar lessons and instruments sometimes passed between networks of relatives, close friends and associates. In 1831 the actress and memoirist Fanny Kemble bought her sister a guitar, which she thought a beauty, with a 'sweet, low, soft voice'.[15] Many young women received their general education from their mother and some found there a role model that encouraged them to play, as Mary Martha Sherwood had done in the days of the English guitar.[16] Just as many, perhaps, did not. A governess might have the talent, so too a friend or associate, or again they might not. Catherine Hutton learned the English guitar because a neighbour, who also acted as her chaperone to various balls, plays and exhibitions, could play it,[17] while Emily Maynard in *The Spanish Guitar* is fortunate (or in her mother's eyes, until events develop, unfortunate) to be presented with her first guitar as a gift from 'a lady in the neighbourhood'.

The heavy predominance of female players in contemporary images of guitars in use – both English and Spanish – is impressive, but Georgian painters and engravers, even those touched by genius, were in some measure taught to see by their predecessors, and learned to approach what had already been shown

Fig. 43 Some of the most striking images of the Spanish guitar transported back to the 'olden time' show female players. This anonymous mezzotint of c.1830 shows a young woman dozing beside a lattice window in a chair of Stuart-period design; the table is carpeted, the floor is of bare flagstones. Around her are the materials used in her daily lessons: the globe, the pair of compasses on the floor, the books and a guitar. Private collection.

to be approachable (Fig. 43).[18] For all the differences of medium, composition and emphasis that individualise their work, most artists assimilated the female guitar player to essentially the same archetype of the leisured lady, shown finely dressed (see frontispiece and Figs 11–13, 21). The conventionalised character of such imagery, at least in portraits put up for exhibition, had become cause for comment by the 1830s.[19] There are various examples of the motif in the guitar methods printed in England, for, until the mid-1820s, depictions of players that might imply a wider constituency for the guitar, encompassing actresses, street musicians or, indeed, males, are rare in those books as they are in general.

So where are the men?

The belief that the figure-of-eight shaped guitar has 'a certain womanish quality', a 'je ne scai quoi d'efféminé', which is innate and not socially conditioned, reaches back to at least the 1640s in France.[20] Six decades later, a man who can play the Spanish guitar in Thomas Baker's comedy *Tunbridge Walks, or, The Yeoman of Kent; a Comedy* of 1703 is an openly homosexual fop named Maiden, who avoids the taverns where he fears he will be taken for a male prostitute or molly (see above, p. 26). He finds an echo in a newspaper article of 1777 that ridicules a former ensign of the guards, who had become a footman in the service of Georgiana Cavendish, the flamboyant Duchess of Devonshire;[21] the individual concerned had once passed for a man but was now thought to be 'of the *female kind*' since returning from Paris, where she (or he) had learned to play the guitar, hung round the neck with a blue ribbon. This may be one of the macaronis – the males often believed to be of doubtful gender and dubious sexual inclination – whose clothes of bright French textiles were a scandal of the age.[22] Soldiers and footmen also played a prominent part in the homosexual culture of the eighteenth-century capital, which adds another layer to this report of a guardsman who returned from the land of the foppish and effeminate French able to use a muff and play the guitar.

In contrast to the Spanish guitar, the English instrument had seemed essentially domestic and British, its stained wood and metal fittings redolent of mahogany card-tables, brass door-locks and Anglo-Scottish ballads. Although the relation between men and this polite instrument, as between men and politeness more generally, was a conflicted matter in the later eighteenth century, nothing quite so acrid emerged in relation to the English guitar as surrounds the foreign, Spanish guitar in the attempt just recounted to pillory (I choose the word advisedly) a former guardsman. While some French guitars manufactured in the second half of the eighteenth century might be called chaste in appearance, at least in the sense that they were unadorned, they retained the curvaceous form that wantonly seeks attention in a way that the lute's gracious curve does not. The more elaborate instruments might also have leafy sprays or scrolls growing from either end of the combined bridge–saddle, a chequered edging running all round the body, elaborate inlay on the fingerboard and matching designs around the aperture in the belly.[23] The guitar's adornments, combined with its *ease*, made it seem libertine and even perhaps a little meretricious in the strict sense of the word. By saying the guitar had a 'je ne scai quoi d'effeminé', the Bordeaux lawyer Pierre Trichet intended to capture a certain allure without giving a compliment.

Yet to be a man was to have choices, and for those inclined to music the guitar was a choice a man could make without reference to anyone's expectations of the form his life should take. In 1808 the writer and diarist Melesina Trench found a 'tolerable Spanish Guittar' while clearing her London house, and suggested to her husband, who came from a baronial family, that he might wish to learn it.[24] She showed no desire to play it herself. A letter written the following year shows a man seeking to negotiate with his guitar-maker, but principally preoccupied with news from the unmistakably male world of boxing: the author, John Jarvis, writes to tell a male friend among the Derbyshire gentry that the celebrated pugilist Jem Belcher has just been confined to prison for causing an affray;[25] the letter ends with a scribbled postscript, and an abrupt change of subject, announcing that Jarvis has ordered several guitars from a joiner named Jack Twigg in the Derbyshire village of Hopton. He hopes that his correspondent, Philip Gell, will have a word with the maker, for while one guitar is of excellent quality another needs the soundboard thinned to give its best: 'I have sent to Jack Twigg for 2 more guittars. I wish you would tell him to make the belly thinner and not to mortice but only glue it on flat; the other is planed thinner and is really quite a capital instrument.'[26] A connoisseur of prizefighting here seems to know what a responsive guitar requires.

Extending the search to the named individuals responsible for published guitar music soon uncovers Antonio Francalanza, master of an art that allowed a male to show his skill in the use of 'the manly foils'.[27] Francalanza was a fencing master who served the Royal Military College at

High Wycombe and then the Scottish Military and Naval Academy, where he taught recruits to acquire 'a manly, and gentlemanly carriage'.[28] In 1812 he completed a three-part subscription series of guitar-accompanied songs, *A Collection of Italian and French Canzonets with Accompaniments for the Spanish Guitar or Piano Forte*, dedicated to Prince Augustus Frederick, Duke of Sussex (Ex. 32).[29] Francalanza went on to enjoy a distinguished career in Edinburgh, where *Blackwood's Edinburgh Magazine* praised him in 1826 for being 'delightful on his guitar . . . and every inch a man'.[30]

The material becomes more abundant, as we would expect, in the 1820s. A newspaper notice of 1821 announces that a 'Gentleman of Classical Education' offers lessons on the Spanish guitar and will gladly serve as a 'Private Tutor or Companion' to a family venturing abroad, since he has travelled widely himself.[31] This sounds like a graduate, or perhaps a young

Ex. 32 Excerpt from 'Per amare abiamo il core', from Antonio Francalanza, *A Collection of Italian and French Canzonets with Accompaniments for the Spanish Guitar or Piano Forte*, 3 vols (1811–12), vol. ii, 11. The pianoforte accompaniment is the work of William Crotch.

man schooled by a home tutor. The following year, a single gentleman 'of regular and domestic habits' sought board and lodging in London, closing his advertisement with the note that it is addressed to 'amateurs in music, where the Spanish guitar is played'.[32] A young man seeking a position as a private secretary, amanuensis or companion, who had lived long in Portugal (perhaps a Peninsular veteran), advertised his willingness to teach the guitar and flute in 1823, and six years later a guitar professor in London claimed that the instrument he taught was 'fashionable for Gentlemen as well as ladies'.[33] It is also in the 1820s that the illustrated title pages of Georgian guitar methods begin to show male players; the earliest appeared in Molina's bilingual book *The Spanish Lyre* (1825, a man and a woman, both with guitars, wearing Spanish national dress), followed by Duvernay's *A Complete Instruction Book for the Guitar* (1828, a man alone; Fig. 44) and finally Bennett's *Instructions for the Spanish Guitar* (1829, a man and a woman playing a duet for two guitars).

The indulgences a man was prepared to allow himself while he was still an apprentice, at school or travelling abroad would not necessarily survive the change to an autonomous manhood or the return home. Something similar might be said for the years at university – a uniquely male experience at this date. Parents and guardians were much concerned that university life could draw young men away from habits of temperance and prudence; a poem by Hartley Coleridge in his volume of 1833 – a farewell to the Lake District at the end of the long university vacation – is accompanied by an extensive note about the figure an Oxford or Cambridge undergraduate cuts in the country, all with a university friend in mind, who will long be remembered in the village of Grasmere for his 'green-ribboned guitar'. Such a young man would not necessarily have continued to play in later life, and Coleridge seems to regard it as a complement to the youthfulness of student days.[34]

These sources, and indeed everything mentioned in this section reaching back to John Jarvis's letter of 1809, fall within the period of the Peninsular War or in the years of its developing reputation as a great victory. In Iberia, British and Irish soldiers saw guitars played in social contexts where differences of talent and social class between players were more conspicuous than differences of gender. Save for a remark by Lieutenant Charles Crowe, who hailed from rural Suffolk, that a wounded English officer who played the guitar very well was a 'decided coxcomb' (meaning 'A vain, conceited, or pretentious man; a man of ostentatiously affected mannerisms or appearance;

Fig. 44 Frontispiece to Flamini Duvernay's method, *A Complete Instruction Book for the Guitar* (1828), lithograph. The image is an early example of a representation of a male player of the guitar.

a fop'),[35] the issue of gender roles never seems to arise in the veterans' memoirs and letters. The experience of campaigning was well calculated to wear down gendered suppositions about the guitar among men who were far from home and who every day encountered new social customs, landscapes and ecologies.

The association between the guitar and returning soldiers from the Peninsular campaign, mentioned above in relation to the 1820s, remained strong during the 1830s; like the flag of a participating regiment hung in a country church, it offered a simplified memory that was beyond alteration, but not beyond the ravages of time. The professional guitarists behind *The Giulianiad* were well aware of it in 1833, when one of their contributors, carried away by sentiment and patriotism, imagines the soldiers playing their guitars in the camp, thinking of their beloveds at home: 'Perhaps, while yet *bivouaching* in the soft twilight, conjuring in imagination the one dear form of her he left in his native land, touching in sympathy the strings of his guitar, might the mandate be given to arouse and prepare for the expected battle!'[36] Under the influence of Spanish skies and the guitar, the members of Wellington's army seem to be turning into troubadours, who sing of their far-away amours as they wait for the call to combat.

Such reveries outlasted the Georgian period and survived into the reign of Victoria. When Giuseppe Anelli sought to establish himself in Exeter during the year 1839, he reminded readers of the *Exeter and Plymouth Gazette* that the guitar had recently been introduced into England 'by the valiant British Officers from that country, who were delighted with the uncommon touching effects of an Instrument so admirably well calculated to accompany the voice with exquisite effect in every style of Music'.[37] There was a strain in the guitar's appeal by now that went beyond the civilian comforts of sofa and *fauteuil*; it reached, instead, the wide horizon and the moonlit bivouac of the serving soldier.[38] When males who were indisputably true warriors played the guitar, such as Lord Saltoun, who survived the carnage of Waterloo, and when other 'Peninsular heroes' took up the instrument or learned it from a Spanish officer such as Molina or de Bruguera, the way was open to reconcile the guitar with a martial masculinity deployed in a heroic cause.

The Sketch Book of Geoffrey Crayon, a collection of essays and short stories in which a fictional American, confident in his country's future, explores the more traditional aspects of England, captures and gently satirises this vision of soldierly manhood. The author, Washington Irving, describes an educated veteran of the Napoleonic Wars, an officer, given a lightly cosmopolitan and perhaps even a chivalric air by his soldiering and talents, including some mastery of the guitar, which he acquired abroad:

He was tall, slender, and handsome, and, like most young British officers of late years, had picked up various small accomplishments on the Continent: he could talk French and Italian, draw landscapes, sing very tolerably, dance divinely, but, above all, he had been wounded at Waterloo. What girl of seventeen, well read in poetry and romance, could resist such a mirror of chivalry and perfection? The moment the dance was over he caught up a guitar, and, lolling against the old marble fireplace in an attitude which, I am half inclined to suspect, was studied, began the little French air of the Troubadour.[39]

This veteran brings a young woman's reading of verse and novels to life, or so Irving claims, for what girl 'of seventeen, well read in poetry and romance, could resist such a mirror of chivalry and perfection?'[40]

The association between the guitar and a venturesome manliness led some male players to disdain the plodding pedantry (as they saw it) of the published guitar methods and, indeed, the whole business of learning the guitar in a literate, methodical manner. Their approach was distinctively male and class-based, in the sense that it derided methodical guitar lessons conducted with music masters, who were not considered gentlemen. The case of Charles Cochrane shows how readily a gentleman in the later 1820s might consider it part of his gentlemanliness to acquire the art of the guitar, pursued to a reasonably ambitious level, and yet scorn the formal process of taking paid lessons.[41] Cochrane (d. 1855) was born in Madras, the illegitimate son of the Hon. Basil Cochrane; in 1828, when he set out across Great Britain in disguise as the 'Spanish minstrel' Juan de Vega, the music in his repertoire included some waltzes and a Spanish *contredanse*, but among his best pieces was the divertimento dedicated to Huerta by that 'exquisite composer Signor Verini, of Bentick [*sic*] Street'. Cochrane was therefore far from being a novice.[42] (He mentions being present at Verini's 'very delightful musical re-unions' at the latter's London address; he may first have heard the divertimento there.)[43] The songs and instrumental pieces that Cochrane took on tour were therefore those of his own repertoire as a gentleman amateur in the later 1820s and were only on temporary loan, so to speak, to his alter ego, Juan de Vega. Despite his interest in the guitar, Cochrane associated lessons from guitar masters with a female regime of study, and mentions what he dismissively calls 'the preliminaries that masters make such a fuss about ... dilating largely and pedantically on the manner of holding the guitar, the arm, and a great number of *et ceteras*' only in relation to an attractive young woman who asked him to teach her. This he was scarcely able to do, for he was not even musically literate, as he unblushingly admits.[44] He claims to have acquired his 'little facility' with the guitar in Colombia, suggesting an authentic practice learned by ear during an exotic and gentlemanly adventure, not by grinding through scales with a teacher.[45]

Men, the guitar and the 'olden time'

In 1818 a contributor to the *Literary Gazette* pondered the best choice of instrument for males. He believed that the Spanish guitar was the ideal instrument for them, for it is 'easily acquired, easily retained, and easily supplied in case of accidents': it is an excellent capital resource, in other words, that must appeal to rational men of business and affairs.[46] Yet the same commentator takes a very different tack when he celebrates the guitar for being as 'rapturous and romantic as the most resolute enthusiast in sensibility and serenading can desire'. Late Georgian males, according to this journalist, led 'hurried and adventurous' lives – the word 'adventurous' being tinged with the Romantic medievalism of Walter Scott's fiction: the 'high spirit of military fame, personal adventure, and whatever could distinguish them as the Flower of Chivalry' (*Ivanhoe*, introduction). It seems a grand term for the commerce and trade that occupied many men in the middle ranks of life, yet perhaps that is the point; with a touch of seemingly good-natured irony, the writer gives a chivalric colour to the investment and risk-taking that produced both victors and vanquished, as the lists of bankrupts in the newspapers reveal. To judge by his remarks, men wanted the guitar to charge their imagination when they played, and to create flickering images of themselves transformed, just as much as women, who were commonly supposed to possess especially fertile imaginations, which drew them to the guitar.[47]

The soldier of the Napoleonic Wars was apt to be regarded, in the manner of Walter Scott on the Peninsular conflict, as a medieval knight in modern garb. In Britain it was an eighteenth-century discovery that between the ancient world of Greece and Rome on one hand and the age of street lighting, racetracks and newspapers on the other there lay a very long stretch of time: a Middle Age whose remains offered a potent and long-misunderstood alternative to the culture of Antiquity.[48] It was readily apparent that many important chapters of Britain's national story lay in that alternative phase of European history where Chaucer, Spenser and Shakespeare were imagined, for many non-specialist purposes, as writing more or less simultaneously with Cervantes, Ariosto, Tasso and others. This was the 'olden time'.

The olden time had left many literary and archaeological traces in Britain including the ballads published by Thomas Percy and others,[49] the ruins of Gothic abbeys to visit in search of the picturesque, and romances to sift for information about 'manners and customs' that Walter Scott recycled to immense acclaim in his narrative poems and novels. It was Scott's narrative verse that provided much of the inspiration for one of the highest expressions of Regency medievalism, John Keats's *Eve of St. Agnes* from 1819, with its reference to a 'hollow lute':

> A casement high and triple-arch'd there was,
> All garlanded with carven imag'ries
> Of fruits, and flowers, and bunches of knot-grass,
> And diamonded with panes of quaint device,
> Innumerable of stains and splendid dyes,
> As are the tiger-moth's deep-damask'd wings;
> And in the midst, 'mong thousand heraldries,
> And twilight saints, and dim emblazonings,
> A shielded scutcheon blush'd with blood of queens and kings . . .
>
> Awakening up, he took her hollow lute . . .[50]

It is an open question what the poet meant by the 'hollow lute'. Many lesser talents than Keats, however, committed themselves to the guitar by name, the principal fretted and plucked instrument of the day, when setting stories or poems in the olden time. 'The Guelf and the Ghibelline: A Romance of the Middle Ages', published in an issue of *La Belle Assemblée* of 1824, shows how readily the guitar could find a place in a medieval setting, just as it reveals the scope such narratives offered for presenting male guitarists. The hero is a knight, who repeatedly espies a young woman as he returns with other youths from the joust, their glittering helmets 'flaming in the sunshine'; he goes to her garden at night to serenade her, and there 'his fond guitar was as regular as convent vesper hymn beneath her lattice'.[51] This is very much the scene and setting favoured by the first article ever published in the niche magazine for guitar enthusiasts, *The Giulianiad*, where a contributor makes the case for the guitar as 'the instrument of romance and sentiment', one whose name has been 'handed down to us associated with deeds of chivalry and love … awakening in the memory a thousand traditions of its enchanting power'.[52]

Similar 'olden time' associations found musical and visual expression in one of the most popular songs of the 1820s, Joseph Barnet's 'The Light Guitar' for voice and pianoforte:

> I'll tell thee how the maiden wept
> When her true knight was slain,
> And how her broken spirit slept
> And never woke again.
>
> I'll tell thee how the steed drew nigh
> And left his lord afar,
> But if my tale should make thee sigh
> I'll strike the light guitar,
>
> *I'll sing thee songs of happier days*
> *And strike the light guitar.*

Originally composed for the comic drama *The Epaulette*, first performed in 1825, 'The Light Guitar' enjoyed a remarkably long life, as witness the fact that Charles Dickens mentions it in works published at both extremes of his literary career.[53] A few years later, John Barnett produced *The Songs of the Minstrels* for voice and pianoforte, subsequently arranged for voice and guitar by Carl Eulenstein (1828?) and widely advertised in the newspapers with a paragraph about the 'olden time [when the] Troubadour was a welcome guest in the halls of nobles'.[54] To reinforce the impression of re-creating that time, even of reliving it if the singer used a guitar as a latter-day lute, the songs are presented as a sequence of pieces sung by the members of an international gathering of minstrels in a great lord's castle, each performing one of his national airs.

The same associations found visual expression in images showing both man and woman. *The Minstrel*, a lithograph published in 1832 after a painting by C. Tomkins, shows a male guitar player holding the attention, and presumably winning the admiration, of court women in a woodland scene. A castle appears on the top of a hill, looking Romantic more than ominously Gothic, and one young woman wears a pendant crucifix: this is the olden time understood as the Catholic Middle Ages of feudal dependence but also of freedom, represented by the wandering minstrel (Fig. 45). The image recalls a passage in Wordsworth's

Fig. 45 *The Minstrel*, 1832, lithograph by Louis Haghe after a painting by C. Tomkins. The print perfectly portrays the role of the guitar in the Romantic conception of minstrelsy in the 'olden time'. Private collection.

poem *The Excursion* (1814), where the Romantic notion of the poet as minstrel – valued and supported by all who receive him, as free to speak truth to power as to roam the open road – finds perhaps its supreme expression.[55]

The Giulianiad, which began publication in 1833, shows how easily aficionados of the guitar could move between detailed accounts of the current guitar scene and Romantic reveries about the olden time, without any sense of dislocation. Despite the mock-heroic title of *The Giulianiad*, modelled on Homeric epic, its literary ambitions are easily overlooked today, but it published several prose ventures and poems that reveal a more literary enjoyment of the guitar than the contributors' insistent (and self-interested) commendation of its purely practical advantages might suggest. 'The Farewell Gift', a poem published in the second number of 1833, shows a warrior who departs for battle leaving behind the guitar over which his 'skilful hand had roved'; the setting is once more the Catholic Middle Ages (a pilgrim appears, peasants cross themselves and the lovelorn lady, left by her knight, pines in a 'lonely hall' with a 'mouldering tower').[56] 'The Fancy Ball', a prose tale, begins with an epigraph invoking 'knights and dames' from Lord Byron's *Lara* (1814), and proceeds to give a highly coloured account of a masquerade.[57] The abundant music published with the magazine even includes a song with a text that could almost be a description of the minstrel in Figure 45:

> I a poor minstrel gay
> Through the world find my way . . .
> Sweet is my shelter free,
> Under the Greenwood tree.[58]

The guitar players of the olden time evoked in *The Giulianiad* are all male.

The wandering and wooing troubadour of the olden time was a medieval version of the serenader, the most venerable of all identities for the male guitar player, and the one most closely associated with the warm south.[59] Late Georgian observers readily confounded the southern (and especially the Spanish) associations of the guitar with the olden time, so an essayist of 1824 can eagerly praise the Spanish bolero for having 'all the gaiety, softness, tenderness, and chivalry, which we associate with the troubadours, the gay squires, and sprightly dames, of the early ages of poetry and music'.[60] The male guitarist in the late Georgian parlour or drawing room could think himself a minstrel, a troubadour or even a knight, his armour put aside, with as much seriousness, or as much playful irony, as his inclinations and the situation seemed to warrant. The danger that onlookers would suspect his pose was studied (to paraphrase Washington Irving) all too often came to pass, to judge by the readiness with which the satirists exposed such affectations. Late in 1830 various provincial newspapers ran a droll article, largely devoted to the guitar, describing it as an instrument much in fashion 'with gentlemen of lank, attenuated fingers who have pretensions to a romantic bearing'; the piece comes with a comic warning that the guitar is indeed 'the instrument to make a sensation in the drawing room' but cannot be recommended 'to men weighing more than fifteen stone from the difficulty of assuming an appropriate troubadour air'.[61]

The humour of that piece provides a timely reminder that Georgian England was in some respects a strange place for such an instrument as the Spanish guitar to flourish, and the English an unlikely people to be playing it. 'After taking the air in a stiff North-east wind in January', wrote a reviewer in 1824, 'we are feelingly persuaded that ours is not a serenading climate, at least not at all seasons of the year.'[62] This note of national self-mockery was often sounded in relation to the guitar, for there is a sense in which the Georgians were never really at ease with the quality of sheer *fancy* that was often associated with the guitar in France. There, Michel Corrette could begin a guitar method of 1762, *Les dons d'Apollon*, with an exuberant mythological romance without courting ridicule; in Britain, the romance of the guitar could feel perilously close to the absurd if the conditions were right (or, rather, if they were wrong). Thus in 1829 another caricaturist satirised the male guitar players who fancied themselves, in whatever spirit, to be figures of the olden time. William Heath's *Morning, Noon, Night* (Fig. 46) shows a young gentleman taking coffee in the morning and reading a number of the *Literary Gazette*. By noon, he is out and about. At night, with his abundant hair curled to imitate a full wig of the seventeenth century, complemented by a bowed cravat of the same period and black hose, he is a young man of Charles II's court: a 'resolute enthusiast in sensibility', indeed, he is so 'rapturous and romantic' that only the whites of his eyes can be seen as he sings. Such a dandy, who is all indulgence, may seem to be the antithesis of the soldier, who is nominally all obedience, but both were required to take great care over their respective uniforms, to be highly attentive to their grooming, to be slim and to dance well.[63]

MORNING   NOON   NIGHT

Fig. 46 William Heath, *Morning, Noon, Night*, 1829, hand-coloured etching. The young dandy's day culminates with a Romantic evening performance in which he sings to his own accompaniment on the guitar.

As the dandified appearance of the guitarist in Heath's cartoon suggests, the situation never arose in earlier nineteenth-century England in which a man could confidently expect to win only admiration if he played the guitar well. Anne Manning's novel of 1833, *Village Belles*, shows how quickly a male playing the guitar, especially one with a bohemian or otherwise unconventional air, could come into conflict with established notions of the English male as sportive and robustly philistine. Rosina meets a painter named Mr Huntley, a devotee of opera who has studied the guitar with an Italian teacher and is widely read in several languages. To Rosina this is all quite enticing, for it shows her that certain interests she has been taught to regard as the sequestered concerns of women are considerably less gendered, in a confining sense, than she supposed. Others in the novel, however, take a different view. A common ideal of English manhood shunned the foppery of the Frenchman, the idleness of the Spaniard and the excitability of the Italian; the guitar courted associations with all three nations, and Rosina's brother in *Village Belles* treats the news that Mr Huntley plays the guitar with the appropriate scorn: 'How ridiculous, how contemptible', he cries, 'for a man, an Englishman, to play on a guitar! I would as soon play on a penny whistle!' [64]

A few years earlier, however, Henry Heath had published a comic sketch that not only depicts a dandy guitarist but also expresses an expansive sense of the social changes that had made such a figure possible. The drawing appeared as part of a series entitled *Old Way's and New Way's*, contrasting antiquated fashions with their modern counterparts, and generally making fun of both. The old and new ways 'of performing a Concert' are shown in Figure 47,

Fig. 47 'The Old way of performing a Concert', contrasted with 'The New way . . .', from a set of drawings by Henry Heath advertised under the title *Old Way's and New Way's, or, A Comparison of Ancient and Modern Customs and Manners exemplified in Seventy Humorous Groups for Scrap Books*, 1829, hand-coloured etchings. Youth, elegance, conviviality and lightness of touch characterise the 'New Way'. Private collection.

Chapter Nine

neither drawing showing an actual ensemble but both consisting of a collage of the various instruments one might expect to see in what is presumably a private and domestic concert. The musicians of the new way are mostly slimmer and younger than their predecessors in the old; there are more women in their company and the bassoon and cello, staples of the clubbable male amateur in the later eighteenth century, have vanished, to be replaced by the lighter plucked sounds of harp and guitar. The young men wear their own hair in flamboyant styles, suggesting a quality of self-regard and grooming with a more overtly narcissistic edge than in the days of the powdered wig, which their significantly older and more corpulent colleague has retained. Even the music stands have become elegant pieces of Regency furniture rather than simple easels. The guitarist makes a great show of the slender and flexible legs that will draw the admiring gaze of all when he dances a quadrille. A male guitarist here serves as a vivid emblem of the way an age had come to see itself.

TEN

The Guitar and the Working Classes

His wife had laid by fourpence (their whole remaining stock) to pay for the baking of a shoulder of mutton and potatoes, which they had in the house, and on her return home from some errand, she found he had expended it in purchasing a new string for a guitar.

William Hazlitt, *On the Want of Money* (1826)

When William IV was crowned monarch of the United Kingdom in September 1831, the girl destined to succeed him, Princess Victoria, was firmly kept at home. Her mother, the Duchess of Kent, had far-reaching plans for her daughter (as for herself), and they did not include associating Victoria with 'the dissolute regime of the late Hanoverian monarchy'.[1] The principal radical newspaper of the 1830s, the *Poor Man's Guardian*, immediately published an ironic letter to the duchess, praising her for recognising that all coronations are 'ridiculous and barbarous' ceremonies.[2] The letter concludes that Princess Victoria, with such a wise mother to guide her, will henceforth be taught to 'despise all the pomp and vanities of this wicked world' instead of learning how to dance and play the guitar.

The guitar and the *Poor Man's Guardian*

The *Poor Man's Guardian* began life in 1831 with the incendiary claim that it would 'excite hatred and contempt' from the government for exercising tyranny over the working man – a tyranny enforced by means of laws made behind his back and unintelligible to him when he was apprised of them.[3] Although the paper was illegal because the editor refused to pay the stamp duty,[4] it achieved a circulation of between 12,000 and 15,000 copies per week; many were transmitted in secret, packed with shoes or in chests of tea, to be sold by individuals who risked imprisonment. It is hardly surprising that such a paper would present the guitar as a toy of the middle classes and above; in newspapers such as the *Morning Chronicle*, widely available in coffee shops, labourers, small artisans and petty clerks could learn that the cheapest guitars on sale in London cost enough to buy them their breakfast for half a year.

Some working people had no idea what a guitar was, if the reports of the prankster Charles Cochrane can be trusted. In 1829 he played to regulars at the Coopers Arms in Rochester, and found them puzzled by what they thought was a kind of fiddle sounded with the fingers; he also played to a girl selling cakes at Tunbridge Wells, who told him she had never seen such an instrument before.[5] In 1832, however, the *Poor Man's Guardian* carried an advertisement showing that the guitar, flute and violin were being taught as part of a far-reaching project to improve the prospects of boys, the sons of small artisans and tradesmen. A panel on the final page of the issue for 3 October records that an otherwise unknown Mr Wise has just reopened his school in London's Poland Street, offering an education that could be completed (or so the advertisement maintained) by literate youths of reasonable aptitude within three years. For a fee of 13s. per quarter there are classes in astronomy, chemistry, geography, algebra, logarithms, arithmetic and writing. For the musical side of their studies boys may choose between the violin, flute and guitar, but it is mandatory that they learn to copy music and 'to sing correctly the rational and liberal songs now published'.[6] Sessions for adults were to be held in the evenings and on Sundays, when the subjects covered were presumably the same as during the week.

MR. WISE'S SCHOOL was re-opened on Monday, October the 8th. The Children will be taught Popular Astronomy, Chemistry, Geography, Algebra, Logarithms, Arithmetic, Writing, Violin, Flute, or Guitar, to copy Music, and to sing correctly the rational and liberal songs now published; and to read in French, and perfectly understand some of the best works of J. J. Rosseau. Any boy who can read well may acquire easily the whole of the above in three years. A Sunday morning class for Adults, and also every Evening from 6 to 10.

Terms, 13s. per quarter, and taken in Labour Notes. – 50, Poland Street, Oxford Street.

Mr Wise's syllabus assigns the guitar a place in the collective endeavour of artisans and tradesmen to acquire, both for their sons and for themselves, the elements of an education denied them by the circumstances of their birth; for working men, this often involved attendance at a Sunday school such as the one Wise opened as a satellite to his main establishment.[7] Such enterprises developed widely during the 1830s, but Mr Wise's school served a specific radical project. Situated at number 50 Poland Street, it stood just down the road from the First Western Co-operative Union at no. 59, one of many such organisations that emerged around 1830 as a response to high food prices, wage reductions and competition.[8] Further down the same street, at no. 69, the same co-operative union opened an institute, where the members hosted meetings, held social events, and took part in public debates that held the existing social order, including all denominational religions, up to scrutiny. The immediate purpose of such co-operative associations, and their accompanying shops, was to create a mutually supportive network of working people and enable them to enjoy *all* the profit from what they could manufacture in their spare time. A small manufacturer could deposit his surplus production in the co-operative store (perhaps a pair of shoes, a looking-glass or a coffee pot) and take out something estimated to be of equivalent labour value made by another artisan (perhaps a shirt, a kettle or a hat). Alternatively, he might receive one of the 'Labour Notes' mentioned in Wise's advertisement, which represented the labour value of his goods and could be used, within the community, as a form of currency.[9] By these means, as one contributor to the *Poor Man's Guardian* fervently hoped, there would be 'a mighty revolution . . . in the moral and physical condition of the only *useful* classes in Society by the *universal* establishment of Labour Exchanges in which the producers will have money . . . of their own in the shape of Labour Notes'.[10] So it was in the Poland Street school. A shoemaker could pay for his guitar lessons with shoes and a hatmaker with hats.

There was a wealth of music to get by ear, including airs performed on the operatic and comic stage, which found their way swiftly into the repertoire of singers engaged in the public houses and street musicians with fiddles, wind instruments and barrel organs. When, around 1860, there finally appears a guitar method designed for players with 'a good ear, and ordinary aptitude' but only modest funds – *Ciebra's Handbook for the Guitar* – it offers that kind of repertoire. Yet there could be keener and more contentious purposes for the guitar when used to accompany voices, as suggested by Mr Wise's reference to 'the rational and liberal songs now published'. Radical papers such as the *Manchester Observer*, especially issues published after the Peterloo Massacre of August 1819, show how often poetry was called to the aid of political protest, appearing side by side with sharply radical editorials in prose. The 1830s also brought forward one of the best-known radical poets, the 'pragmatic, propagandistic, newspaper-taught anti-religionist' Ebenezer Elliott, whose *Corn Law Rhymes* opposed the legislation that kept grain prices high for the benefit of domestic producers; some of Elliott's poems use well-known tunes such as 'Robin Adair' and 'Rule Britannia', both found in arrangements for the guitar.[11]

At their most radical, the 'rational and liberal songs' taught at Mr Wise's academy anticipated a new social order based on communitarian living in egalitarian settlements, each member a rational being freed from obsequiousness either to his fellow men or to God. Taken more broadly, the 'rational songs' of the period expressed a variety of positions, from the deism espoused by the founder of the *Poor Man's Guardian*, Henry Hetherington, to the rationalism and secularism associated with the originator of the co-operative movement, Robert Owen.[12] *Co-operative Songs*, probably published in 1832, offers the texts of two such lyrics in the cheap form of a single sheet: 'Each for all', to be sung to the tune of 'Rule Britannia', and 'Hail the great, the glorious plan' to the melody of 'Auld lang syne'.[13] Since both texts were printed to celebrate the co-operative ideal and were intended for singing, they have a strong claim to represent the kind of 'rational and liberal songs now published' that Wise mentions. They are celebratory pieces, notably 'Hail the great, the glorious plan', which hymns the aims of Robert Owen with millenarian rapture. A version can be reconstituted, with a closely contemporary accompaniment for the guitar, using the musical setting (to different words) in Matthias von Holst's *Selection of the Most Favorite Scottish Melodies*, published c.1825–7 (Ex. 33).

Ex. 33 'Hail the great, the glorious plan', text from *Co-operative Songs* (1832?) set to a traditional melody ('Auld lang syne'); this version, with guitar accompaniment, comes from Matthias von Holst, *A Selection of the Most Favorite Scottish Melodies* (n.d. [*c.*1825–7]), 24–5.

Mr Wise's academy was probably short-lived, for there seems to be no further trace of it in the *Poor Man's Guardian* or anywhere else. A specific and recoverable context for the use of guitars by working people, in relation to a radical project, therefore vanishes with him, though only at this one address: there were many kinds of co-operative experiment, some of them explicitly Owenite, throughout England.[14]

THE MARCH OF INTELLECT

Fig. 48 *The March of Intellect*, later 1820s?, anonymous lithograph. In this harsh piece of social commentary, the broken-down washerwoman neglects her menial occupation to pursue her unlikely ambition to become a guitarist. Private collection.

The caricatured guitarist

The guitar was never entirely confined to drawing rooms, parlours or palaces, and it had long known the life of the street (see Fig. 22). The notebooks of the organist R. J. S. Stevens (1757–1837) record how a young girl was heard one evening playing upon a guitar 'and singing very pleasantly with it' in London's Upper Harley Street; a notable resident of that elite quarter, Lady Anne Simpson (d. 1821), was eager to hear about the young woman's predicament and invited her into the drawing room. There the girl gave such 'a pitiable account of the distress of her family' that the ladies of the house commissioned Stevens to educate her in preparation for the musical career they believed she could have.[15] Perhaps the most remarkable report of a pauper guitarist, however, concerns an albino girl named Sarah Rixford, who

Pub by A. PARK. 47 Leonard S.º Finsbury

MUSIC HATH CHARMS.

" How much betterer, that air is then vhistlin—Bobby !— and doin it on the Shovel —"
.Bobby. Aint it Bet — and missis is axed me to play it ewerry night under her vinder ven master's a snoring !. "

Fig. 49 *Music hath Charms*, 1840?, hand-coloured lithograph. 'How much betterer, that <u>air</u> is then vhistlin – Bobby! – and doin it on the Shovel –'[.] Bobby. 'Aint it Bet – and missis is axed me to play it ewerry night under her vinder ven master's a snoring! –'. The descent of the once genteel guitar to the lower classes of servant and housemaid is satirised in this print, which puts the instrument in the hands of a figure as far down the social scale as it was possible to go: a child blackened from his work as a chimney sweep. Private collection.

applied to be admitted to the parochial workhouse at Whitechapel in east London in 1835. The parochial committee was so struck by her 'most singular and interesting appearance' that they immediately assigned funds to meet her immediate needs and keep her out of the institution. When asked about her employment hitherto, Rixford replied that 'a gentleman had made her a present of a guitar, and given her lessons on it, so that she was enabled to play it pretty well'. Nothing further is known of this anonymous benefactor, who may have intended to exhibit her as a natural curiosity. Unfortunately, she had been unable to earn enough money with her guitar, and when the family lacked bread altogether she had pawned it for 8s.[16]

The spread of the guitar to those in lowly trades was swiftly noticed, and is exaggerated, by several caricaturists; they associate it with working-class aspiration to pleasures that were formerly beyond the reach of workers but which could not be ridiculed in any simple way because the technological progress that was changing the world so fast relied, in part, upon a general aspiration to leisure and convenience. Figure 48 shows one of the most lurid examples of the caricaturists' approach.[17] The title, *The March of Intellect*, consists of an expression widely used to denote any aspect of progress in technology or education (especially if it seemed to be dissolving social boundaries) that some commentator might wish to evoke with amusement, admiration or alarm.[18] A laundress sits in a rough dwelling with the casement windows typical of old London; laundry boils in a pot on the range, while more hangs beneath the stained and patched ceiling. Undernourished, her clothes washed to rags, she plays a guitar that shows many points of resemblance to the six-string Longman instruments made in London around 1810.[19] The score of her song lies on the floor, showing that she is singing the popular ballad 'My heart with love is beating'.

A later print, also unsigned and entitled *Music hath Charms*, shows a chimney sweep or 'climbing boy' (his dustpan and brush hang beside him) playing to an appreciative scullery maid in the kitchen at night – the candle is lit – when the day's work is over (Fig. 49). The print probably appeared in 1840, the year of the Chimney Sweepers and Chimneys Regulation Act; the dialogue shows the substandard grammatical forms and the substitution of 'v' for 'w' (and vice versa) associated with the London proletariat.

It is easy to mistake the tone of these two caricatures. Both may appear contemptuous, even vicious, for in one a laundrywoman struggles to learn the guitar despite the raw and chapped hands of her trade, while in the other a smiling chimney sweep wears a cancerous coating of coal dust and presumes to serenade a kitchen maid. Yet both prints are touched by the kind of satire that became increasingly common in the first third of the nineteenth century, with the rise of the comical literary or visual sketch bemused and curious about the signs of social change.

Laundresses ranked as a low form of domestic servant, and the real target of the laundress lithograph is probably young women of the servant class. Although such domestics were housebound for much of the working week, they increasingly joined the mass public for kinds of entertainment that were emerging in late Georgian England.[20] One such servant comes to light in an issue of London's leading music magazine, the *Musical World*, for 1836. Like some other periodicals of the day (and many of the penny magazines) the *Musical World* lightened its tone with miscellaneous anecdotes or reflections; this example, introduced as a tale which 'may be relied on as a fact', tells how a young woman applied for a position as housemaid in one of the various schools in the London suburb of Somers Town. During her interview, she asks her potential employer if she may absent herself to take the guitar lessons for which she has paid in advance:

MUSIC IN THE KITCHEN

A lady, who kept a seminary in Somers Town, was in want of a housemaid; she advertised, and many called to offer their services. The lady was pleased with the appearance of one, and entered into an agreement with her, request-ing her to come to her place without delay. The girl seemed as if she had something on her mind; and, after a grand effort, she said that she would require to go out twice a week for the first month. 'Oh! (said the lady) you attend some particular chapel, I conclude?' – 'No, Ma'am, (simpered the girl) but I am learning the guitar, and have paid for a quarter's instruction in advance; so I should not like to lose my lessons.' – 'Where do you intend to practise?' said the lady. – 'In the kitchen, I suppose,' answered Sappho Cobwebbo. – 'Oh! I shall grow distracted; (said the lady); what with the young ladies thumping up stairs, and you thrumming below; – you won't suit me. Good day to you.'[21]

As it appears in the *Musical World*, this story concerns a particular kind of presumption that seeks to overturn established barriers of class and calling. A presentable but nonetheless lowly young woman, who will have little leisure in a well-run home, wishes to learn the guitar in a way that will necessarily entail some reduction in her service to her employer. The story was widely reprinted in the provincial press, so from Dorset to Staffordshire readers were invited to marvel at a 'march of intellect' that could lead a servant to suppose her interests might ever, in any circumstance, take precedence over her employer's requirements.[22] The setting in Somers Town seems particularly apt, given that this London suburb was about to be riven by the creation of three mainline railway stations: an excursion by rail would soon be added to the painted panoramas, exhibitions, comedies, lectures and guitar lessons that competed for the spare money of the servant class.[23]

In 1834 the guitar made an appearance in the *Casket of Literature, Science and Entertainment*, one of many miscellanies sold for a penny, and printed in double columns 'like a tract or even a broadside[,] in ways that deliberately evoked the cultural history' of both.[24] Such publications helped to diffuse and democratise polite tastes and pursuits, notably in their crude, wood-engraved copies of famous paintings and their abridgements of novels such as Victor Hugo's *Hunchback of Notre-Dame*. An article entitled 'The Conveniences of the Guitar', which appeared in the magazine's regular closing section 'Varieties', commends the 'many desirable qualifications' of the guitar as 'an accompaniment to the voice'. It is easy to tune when affected by variations in temperature, and its pitch can be adjusted to suit any singer or instrumentalist with whom the guitarist wishes to play. It is also excellent for accompanying weak voices that the pianoforte will drown, especially in the works of 'noisy composers' such as Rossini. The whole passage was taken verbatim (with due acknowledgement) from *The Giulianiad*, where it formed part of an essay on the comparative merits of the guitar and pianoforte, published the previous year.[25]

In the same year the *Penny Magazine of the Society for the Diffusion of Useful Knowledge* also commended the guitar. This was not a publication that the *Poor Man's Guardian* held in high regard, for the Society for the Diffusion of Useful Knowledge was overseen by a board of 'esquires' and Church of England clergy, betraying its true character as a paternalistic, middle-class enterprise. Yet with its miscellaneous articles on science, art, literature and history, the *Penny Magazine* achieved a circulation of 200,000 in its first year, placing it 'at the centre of the explosion of the reading public in the 1830s'.[26] On 17 May 1834 the magazine ran an article pondering the ways in which working people might acquire some knowledge of the physics of musical sound and notation, given that instruments were expensive and 'the greater part of musical books of instruction are very obscure'. The author's first thought is that some kind of monochord might teach the foundations of music to his readers, but he also invites those with mechanical skill to invent a device that might achieve the same objective; it should cost no more than 5s., should have a compass of at least two octaves with all the intermediate semitones, should allow the player to reproduce 'simple airs' and must not be 'very loud or full'. Turning to existing instruments as a third option, the writer suggests that they 'be made sufficiently cheap, if possible, for the working classes of this country' to afford them, and decides to recommend the guitar, this time on the grounds that it can provide the player with harmony. He also notes that much may be done with 'a proper book of instructions', a passing remark that associates some of the demand for such methods with the drive for self-improvement in an unusually explicit manner. For although

> the guitar admits of very little, either of tone or execution, yet that little is what is technically called harmony; that is, proper combinations of notes can be struck at once, and in this it would be superior to the flute or clarionet, which only produces melody; that is, the simple consecutive notes which make up the air. Next, the little that an ordinary player can ever hope to do on the guitar can be soon done; a very few lessons, with a proper book of instructions, would suffice to enable the beginner to please himself and others.[27]

The guitar's fitness for accompanying the voice will allow 'a very ordinary singer' within half a year to reach a standard where he may entertain himself and others pleasantly. The goal is not some fine instrument with 'endless screws for adjustment, and its mother-of-pearl bordering', but something with 'a more humble degree of finish, which might, nevertheless, discourse very tolerable music in proper hands'.[28]

Buying, learning and singing

In 1838 the Society for the Diffusion of Useful Knowledge had further dealings with the guitar in the eleventh volume of its *Penny Cyclopædia*, a work published in twenty-seven volumes and three supplements between 1828 and 1843. The (unsigned) entry for the guitar gives succinct but accurate details of stringing and compass, together with a comprehensive set of measurements, in a manner perhaps designed to appeal to the artisan. The entry ends with advice that the 'best and cheapest guitars are made in Germany' and can be purchased in London 'at a moderate price'.[29] This is clearly a recommendation.

Instruments could also be obtained from pawnbrokers' shops, as the story of Sarah Rixford has already revealed. She never went to redeem her pledge, so it could legally have been sold, after a year and a day, at the pawnbroker's counter or at auction.[30] There were many other ways in which guitars, including those belonging to persons far above Sarah Rixford in the social scale, might find their way to the pawnbroker; all that was needed was for some rash gamble or over-ambitious business venture to fail. According to Charles Dickens, those on the gradual slide towards the debtors' prison would pawn watches, rings and 'the more expensive articles of dress' first, then turn to items such as musical instruments, dressing cases and writing desks next.[31] The handling of stolen goods added yet more instruments to the stock, for there was an unfortunate side to the ease with which the guitar could be carried. In 1831 an unnamed individual hired a guitar from Wright's Musical Repository in Brighton and promptly pawned it 'for a trifling sum', while in May 1832 a man posing as a French aristocrat stole a guitar from Benedetto Ventura and took it directly to a pawnbroker.[32]

Unredeemed pledges generally fetched a poor price – often little more than the initial loan – as the pawnbrokers were fond of complaining, so instruments could be had cheaply. A revealing tale, taken from the *Working Man's Companion* and published in an issue of the *Manchester Times and Gazette* in 1831, shows a hatter abandoning his noxious trade and buying a guitar for 3 guineas in the hope of becoming a singer, perhaps at first a street musician, then moving on to public-house concerts and higher ambitions still. Unfortunately, he was compelled to pawn the instrument for 7s. to support his drinking, and could never afford to reclaim the pledge.[33] Thus a 3 guinea guitar would come on sale for a small fraction of the original purchase price.

Working-class autobiographies suggest that fiddles and flutes, some of them no doubt homemade, were the principal instruments of the disadvantaged in the 1820s and 1830s and we must wait until about 1860 for a guitar method to appear that was specially devised for the shallow pockets of those engaged in 'this work a-day world'.[34] Yet for the housemaid who paid for lessons in advance, for the friend of William Hazlitt who went without his dinner to buy a guitar string, and for the hatter who hoped for a musical career, the guitar fulfilled its true and highest destiny: to provide the working classes with access to 'what is technically called harmony', often for the first time in their lives.

Conclusion

At a time when musicians like William Crotch (d. 1847) were seeking to guide public taste towards a silent and in a sense solitary encounter with Austro-German instrumental masterworks,[1] the guitar stood for the pleasures of song, entertainment and conviviality. No doubt it would be an exaggeration to suggest that guitar aficionados consciously resisted the critics who sought to educate them, or that the best amateur singers with a guitar played to a musical faction that knew what it liked, yet when Crotch praises the Philharmonic Concerts for giving professional musicians an opportunity to choose 'the music *they* admire' (original emphasis) there is clearly some sense of opposing parties.[2] The contrast is sharpened further by a journalist's remark in an issue of the *Literary Gazette* for 1818 that the power of vocal music is so great that some trifling air with guitar accompaniment will almost always entice a company away from one of 'Beethoven's crudities' on the pianoforte.[3] The tone of that attack, which would have seemed less extraordinary in 1818 than it does now,[4] is hard to judge, though it does identify a self-consciously partisan and unrepentant preference for the pleasures of guitar-accompanied song over the most innovative of the Austro-German masterworks, just as it may suggest a certain impatience with their advocates.

The principal weakness of the guitar in the matter of sound, judged in relation to all mainstream instruments, was the source of a power that it exercised over the fancy as much as the ear. To the aficionado, the delicacy of the guitar's voice was an invitation to bring 'the most searching scrutiny and minutest examination' to its music,[5] especially to the qualities of light and shade, in timbre and dynamics, that were as highly valued by connoisseurs of the guitar as by admirers of the pianoforte. The most discerning enthusiasts valued the guitar's subtle gradations within a spectrum of low-intensity sound, which had been admired for hundreds of years, but which parted company with mainstream compositional practice during the eighteenth century – as witness the gradual disappearance of lutes from most larger ensembles as the century proceeded.

An evocative reminiscence of that older and quieter sound world partly explains the association, increasingly marked during the 1830s, between the guitar and an 'olden time' encompassing the Middle Ages but often extending to the period of Shakespeare and Cervantes. This generously broad understanding of the 'olden time' was therefore innocent of the now familiar, if somewhat antiquated, distinction between 'the Middle Ages' (a long-established term) and 'the Renaissance' (not traced by the *OED* before 1836). The breadth of the Georgian conception reflects a sense, well established by 1800, that there was a European canon of literature, an imaginary museum of literary works, which the explosion of translations and cheap editions had done much to foster in Britain during the eighteenth century. The close association between the literary canon and the guitar, perhaps unique among the musical instruments of the Georgian period, owed much to the emphatic presence of the lute, both as instrument and emblem, in many major works of that canon, including a great wealth of Elizabethan poetry and the plays of Shakespeare.[6] There was material here for another kind of partisan opposition – between an emerging corpus of 'classical' instrumental music and the guitar. The critic and music historian George Hogarth, for example, can have had only the most diaphanous idea in 1835 of what 'the graceful canzonets and roundelays sung by the accomplished cavaliers and fair ladies of the olden time' had actually sounded like as *songs*, but he believed they evoked feelings that 'the most elaborate compositions of Mozart or Beethoven will never awake, in the youthful heart'. What is more, those canzonets and roundelays had been accompanied on the lute, 'a word in which there is a thousand times more poetry than in the names of all the instruments in the Philharmonic Orchestra'. Hogarth regarded the guitar as the most 'romantic' of all modern instruments because, as many believed, it was the 'direct offspring of the lute'.[7]

A vein of imagery in Georgian poetry confounded strings, gently or meditatively stirred, with the soft respiration of the wind and fading sounds. The association with the breeze explains the contemporary interest in Aeolian harps, played by the hand of Nature herself, Romanticism's chief deity.[8] Such imagery was readily transferred to the Spanish guitar:

> The room was low and lone, but linger'd there,
> In careless loveliness, the marks of mind . . .
> And there lay a guitar, whose silvery string
> Breathed to the wind . . . [9]

Conclusion

A frequently mined vein of imagery associated the plucked strings, including those of the guitar, with the oncoming night and a mood of darkling reverie:

> The garden in which they had joined him was the favourite scene of all at the close of day ... here they delighted, amidst the fragrance of exhaling plants and flowers, to watch the sun gradually fading from the summits of the mountains, the evening yielding the world to night; and to listen to the soft and expiring sounds, so well according with the fading scenery ... Hither Elizabeth frequently brought her guitar and harp.[10]

In this passage from R. M. Roche's novel *The Discarded Son* (1807), the sound of plucked strings blends with the fleeting (both light and sound are dying) and the nocturnal, recurrent preoccupations of Romantic art.[11] These may seem rich meanings to discern in an instrument often condemned by its critics for being impoverished, but they begin to explain why Hector Berlioz, with an exquisite sensitivity to instrumental colour, judged the sound of the guitar to be inherently melancholic and dreamy: *mélancolique et rêveur*.[12]

The guitar was called a 'romantic' instrument in England well before the 1840s when Giulio Regondi and Johann Kaspar Mertz first began to compose works that might be judged to show elements of a Romantic musical idiom, such as a more experimental palette of harmony or long-breathed melody. In 1818 one commentator described the guitar as 'rapturous and romantic', while in 1824 a reviewer noted that players often associated their guitars with 'romantic ideas'.[13] To some extent these may, indeed, be musical judgements alluding to the boleros adapted to English taste and published for the Spanish guitar in London during the Peninsular War; with their Spanish words, their ebullient figurations and even the explicit requirement on some scores that the player should strum the strings 'in the Spanish style', these pieces go well beyond the usual idiom of material published for the guitar in Britain (see Exx. 21 and 23). For those on the home front, whether they supported the war or not, such pieces offered a sonorous distillation of Spain, with

> the haughty orientalism of the Mussulmans, and the rude struggles of ardent and courageous adventurers for freedom, – the knight-errantry of

the chivalric ages, – the music of the *trobadores*, – all in action among high mountains, mighty streams, the surrounding sea, the unclouded heaven, and conveyed through a language singularly poetical and sonorous.[14]

The guitar's associations with Spain, fortified by the Peninsular War of 1807 to 1814, made it the instrument of a country where the satanic mills of industrialism that blighted the landscape of contemporary England were as yet unknown.[15] No one called upon Spain, as John Hanmer summoned England in a sonnet of 1840, to 'Arise up . . . from the smoky cloud / That covers thee',[16] and there were no brick kilns around Madrid or Valencia like those that were rapidly defacing John Keats's rural walk from Hampstead to Walthamstow. In Spain, Romanticism's greatest antagonist, industrial modernity, was a rough beast whose hour had yet to strike.

Spain was also a country where the theatre of political life seemed, when viewed from Britain, to be staging the drama of revolutionary and counter-revolutionary conflict with the guitar as a prop. It was a guitar that a guerilla fighter played at the gates of Salamanca to taunt the French, according to a widely circulated report in the English metropolitan and provincial press, and a guitar that Byron's Maid of Saragossa hangs on a willow in the first canto of *Childe Harold's Pilgrimage* so that her hands may be free to work the guns against the invader. Pablo Rosquellas, a Spanish expatriate who played an important role in London celebrations to mark the Liberal Constitution of 1812, issued by the Cortes of Cádiz, published a guitar method probably in 1813, and a former officer 'in the independent cause', de Bruguera, taught the guitar in Liverpool. A serving 'Officer in the Spanish Army', Molina, published a guitar method in London in 1825, and at the end of the same decade Charles Cochrane, in disguise as an expatriate Spanish officer with only a guitar to win his livelihood, could still hope to exploit a lively sympathy for the political and military toils of the Spanish and Hispano-American people. A guitar, even when laid on a sofa in a parlour or drawing room, never quite lost the air of something that a professional soldier in liberty's cause or an impassioned patriot had just put down in a hurry, and the memoirs of Peninsular veterans reinforced the sense that the guitar was the authentic, chosen instrument of the Spanish people in their free and natural condition. Their musical life was reported to be spontaneous and unreflecting: about as far from the ethos of an ideal symphonic concert as could be imagined.[17]

To call the guitar 'romantic' in 1818 or 1824 was to enlist the core sense of the word: something that might figure in extravagant forms of narrative fiction, including novels (often called 'romances' at this date) and the florid tales of love and heroism serialised in magazines such as *La Belle Assemblée*. The setting chosen was often an exotic Mediterranean environment, enlisting images of the warm south for an Atlantic readership, for some of these stories exploit the guitar's long-standing literary associations, from Restoration drama onwards, with Mediterranean street life and the serenade. These were contexts in which a violin might seem too mundane (being so securely professional) and where a pianoforte would be no more appropriate than a hat-stand. In 1811 *La Belle Assemblée* published a serialised tale, *The Chateau of Rousillon*, with a scene of moonlight, nightingales and a company, 'embowered amid citrons, oranges and myrtles', hearing the sound of a guitar on the evening air.[18] The appeal of the guitar is here intertwined, as it so often was, with the romance of the Mediterranean, variously imagined as paradisiacal but dangerous, inspiring but corrupting.[19]

In 1830, the year when George IV died, the first railway built to carry passengers opened for business, running between Liverpool and Manchester. The coming of the railways is one of the various developments in the 'March of Intellect' – not synchronised but cumulative – that identify the 1830s (where this book closes), as the key decade 'marking the transition from one cultural configuration to another', which may be called 'Victorian'.[20] The guitar did not become obsolete in England during the 1830s – there is a Victorian history still to be written – but the intensity of the vogue for the instrument did begin to decline later in that decade. Despite the potency of its associations, the guitar was a novelty and therefore, by definition, ephemeral. Or rather, as the long-term history of the guitar shows, its appeal was cyclical: a phase of intense interest would lead to a protracted lull (but never extinction) until a new cycle, often coinciding with some arresting modification of the guitar's resources, began. There was one such phase in England, a vogue for the four-course guitar, between about 1545 and 1580, and later a period of strong enthusiasm for the five-course instrument between about 1660 and 1700.[21] The great vogue for the new guitar of six single strings, between about 1800 and 1835, conforms to this pattern of forty years or so of higher favour followed by recession.

The fashion for recitals, in which an audience might expect to hear works of high difficulty played with great panache, posed problems for those guitarists, certainly in the majority, who had neither the technical ability for such fireworks nor any repertoire that imposed demands of the necessary severity. To be sure, there were some notable successes by recitalists; the Spanish player–composer Julián Arcas (1832–1882) gave a well-received concert lasting two hours in Brighton Pavilion in 1862, having recently performed at Apsley House by permission of the 2nd Duke of Wellington.[22] Yet the earliest instance of the expression 'guitar recital' in the London press appears in the *Morning Post* for 23 June 1847 and shows Don R. de Ciebra advertising his act like a circus showman: he will play the grand overture to *William Tell*, a 'great work, exceeding in difficulty and effect all others ever attempted on the guitar'. In 1842 Signor Malgarini attempted to hold an audience for two hours, one December night, at the northern coastal resort of Scarborough; it was a quixotic venture, perhaps one of most misconceived musical occasions on record, and it was duly damned in the local press.[23]

Despite the continuing activity of a few artists, such as Arcas, into the 1840s and beyond, by 1845 the 'elegant and fashionable instrument' of newspaper advertisements placed by teachers, players and instrument-makers in search of custom was more likely to be a concertina than a guitar.[24] This was the instrument on which two of the most durable survivors of the great guitar vogue in England, Giulio Regondi (d. 1872) and Madame Pratten (née Pelzer; d. 1895) both relied for part of their livelihood. Old stagers hoping to trade on their former reputations could face disappointment in changing times. When Huerta returned to England in the mid-1860s, he failed on one occasion to raise an audience in Brighton, a town where he was much admired decades earlier.[25] Some prominent players of the vogue days, like Luigi Sagrini, settled down, in their declining years under Victoria, to quiet lives mostly devoted to teaching, while stalwarts like Charles Sola and George Derwort, prolific arrangers of songs for voice and guitar in the 1820s, were soon forgotten; Derwort abandoned England for America some time after the spring of 1836, and now lies in a cemetery in Charleston, South Carolina.

Much later, in 1877, when the guitar, the banjo and the mandolin were increasingly finding a place in a great institution of high-Victorian musical life – namely, the local amateur concert in aid of some good cause – a journalist remarked that a slow revival of interest in the guitar was under way, which seemed likely to bring back the days of Lord Byron (d. 1824) and Thomas Moore's romance of *Lalla Rookh* (1817).[26] The comment is facetious, but not without a certain nostalgia, perhaps, for a time when an instrument often to be heard, in his day, in national schoolrooms and in church halls, with teas and speeches from the rector, had seemed 'rapturous and romantic'. The new ladies' guitar and mandolin bands, whose ethos was often decidedly genteel, even aristocratic, restored a measure of novelty, perhaps of excitement, towards the end of the century; yet these orchestras, which might unite as many as fifty plucked instruments, retained little of what the guitar's devotees had admired when the great vogue had been a decidedly Romantic affair.

Sources for the Term 'English guit(t)ar'

The term 'English guitar' probably arose as a translation of French *guitarre angloise*, which is found in continental documents by 1770 (see below). The English counterpart appears in the advertisements of immigrant teachers and players such as Merch. (1774), L.-F.-M. Grumaille (1779, 1789), Joseph Boruwlaski (1782), Monsieur Prador (1790) and Monsieur Brillaud de Lonjac (1793), all of whom are listed below. The expression probably spread to the general public in the normal course of trading, but this seems to have happened only to a very limited extent. Between 1755 and 1800 English and Spanish guitars were simply 'guit(t)ars' to the vast majority of English-language speakers in Britain; 'English guitar' was the specialised usage of those with a commercial interest in the instrument and its music.

Some contemporaries were displeased that these instruments had taken the name of 'guitar' (see Chapter 2). In 1769 Elizabeth Harris of Salisbury was careful to specify 'the true Spanish guitar' in one of her letters (her emphasis; see D. Burrows and R. Dunhill, eds, *Music and Theatre in Handel's World: The Family Papers of James Harris, 1732–1780* (Oxford: Oxford University Press, 2002), 552), while Sir John Hawkins thought it showed mere ignorance to use the term 'guitar' in this way (*A General History of the Science and Practice of Music*, 5 vols (1776), vol. iv, 112 n., 113, 173; vol. v, Index, s.v. 'cittern').

Newspapers

Any attempt to base a quantitative survey on electronic databases must be fallible, given the limitations of the software and the often very damaged state of the original type from which the electronic text has been scanned, but the results from a search for the terms 'English guitar' and 'English guittar' are nonetheless strikingly thin. (For the sources consulted, see 'Electronic Resources' in the Bibliography, pp. 289–90.) A reference to 'the English and Spanish guitar' in an advertisement placed by a teacher in the *London Chronicle* for 24 July 1760 offers the earliest known instance. The term later appears in the *Morning Herald and Daily Advertiser* for 5 March 1781, the *Bath Chronicle and Weekly Gazette* for 8 April 1790, and *World* for 9 October 1790. The Burney database of seventeenth- and eighteenth-century newspapers yields five examples, but the first three are replicas of a single advertisement for an event in 1788 (*The World*, 24 May 1788), and the remaining two comprise the same advertisement placed by a teacher of the instrument (*Oracle and Public Advertiser*, 28 January 1796). The term 'common guitar', found in some sources, is extremely rare in the newspapers (see, for example, *Morning Chronicle*, 24 August 1793).

Published literary works

This category excludes newspapers but is otherwise broadly defined, taking in fiction, non-fiction, poetry, drama, instrumental methods, etc.

Eighteenth Century Collections Online contains more than 180,000 titles (200,000 volumes) and more than 33 million pages; when a date filter of 1750–1800 is applied, the database returns 2,243 texts where the term 'guitar' appears at least once (taking together results with both the single and double consonant, 'guitar' and 'guittar'). A search for the term 'English guitar' (with both spellings of the second word) returns just a single hit of 1800 (a music publisher's catalogue). However, this turns out to be a phantom: the term does not actually appear in the document.

The financial accounts of Christian Clauss

Christian Clauss was an instrument-maker in the Soho area of London. Covering the period from June 1783 to April 1786, his accounts are of value since Clauss was a specialist in making English guitars. The term 'common guitar' appears twenty-four times in the documents, and appears to be used in opposition to 'Spanish guitar' (appearing four times) and perhaps to 'pianoforte guitar'. There is no instance of the term 'English guitar' in the accounts (J. Nex, 'The Business of Musical-Instrument Making in Early Industrial London', doctoral diss., Goldsmiths, University of London, 2013, Appendix 3).

A chronological list of references to 'English guit(t)ar', 1760–1814

1760
London Chronicle, 24 July. Signor Giuseppe Passerini proposes 'to Lecture and Instruct young Ladies and Gentlemen' on several musical instruments including 'the English and Spanish Guittar'.

1770
Anon., *Bibliographie parisienne, ou Catalogue d'ouvrages de sciences, de littérature et de tout ce qui concerne les beaux-arts, année 1770* (Paris, 1772), p. i, Table alphabétique; p. xi 'Méthode très facile pour la Guitarre Angloise ou Allem.'

1774
Public Advertiser, 8 January. Signor Merchi, 'being just come from the West Indies', advertises lessons in singing and accompaniment with both the Spanish and English guitar, but recommends the Spanish, 'for though it be a more difficult Instrument than the English Guitar, yet it is more harmonious and pleasing'.

1779
Almanach Musical, 5 (1779), 202, an annual publication for Paris. Names Grumaille in a list of teachers of 'Cistre: ou guitarre allemande ou Angloise'.

1781
Morning Herald and Daily Advertiser, 5 March.

1782
Morning Herald and Daily Advertiser, 25 May. Announces that Boruwlaski will give a recital on the English guitar.

1787
Mlle Woos advertises at Liège, offering to teach harp, 'guitare espagnole, guitare anglaise et du cistre à boyaux dans le goût de Paris' (J. Quitin, *La musique à Liège entre deux révolutions: 1789–1830* (Sprimont: Mardaga, 1997), 36).

1788
The World, 24 May.

1789

Anon., *Catalogue de livres anglois et français* (Ghent, 1789), unpaginated. Announces the sale of 'Une Guitarre angloise, meilleure fabrique'.

World, 3 June. Carries an advertisement for the sale of various instruments including 'An exceeding good Spanish Guittar', to be seen at the premises of Mr Grumaille, 'Professor of the Cistre, Spanish guitar and English guittar'.

The instrument-maker Juan Puyol, active in Madrid, advertises instruments equipped with a keyboard mechanism (the so-called 'pianoforte guitars') and calls them 'guitarras a la inglesa que se tocan con teclas' (K. Kenyon de Pascual, 'Ventas de instrumentos musicales en Madrid durante la segunda mitad del siglo XVIII, II', *Revista de Musicología*, 6 (1983), 299–308, at 304).

1790

Bath Chronicle and Weekly Gazette, 8 April.

World, 9 October. Carries the advertisement of Monsieur Prader ('a Native of France, and where he has always resided') offering lessons on the Spanish guitar, 'which is totally different from the English, and which is at present very much in vogue in France'.

M. Hayebin advertises at Liège, as 'musicien professeur de cistre ou guitare anglaise' (Quitin, *La musique à Liège*, 36).

1793

Courier de Londres, 17 May. M. Brillaud de Lonjac of Marylebone, who has been in London for two years, offers lessons in singing, the 'guitarre anglaise' and the art of accompaniment. He addresses himself 'à toutes les familles respectables réfugiées dans cette ville'.

1796

Oracle and Public Advertiser, 28 January. Advertisement of [J. A.] Stevenson, 'Professor of the French and English Guitar'.

1804

Morning Post, 18 April. Advertisement for lessons on 'The Pedal Harp, Lute, Lyre and English Guitar, Taught by a LADY'.

1805–10

Anon., *Instructions for the Harp, Lute, Lyre, Spanish and English Guittar* (E. Stenstadvold, *An Annotated Bibliography of Guitar Methods, 1760–1860* (Hillsdale, NY: Pendragon Press, 2010), 25).

1814

Morning Post, 25 March. Advertisement for lessons on the harp, pianoforte, Spanish and English guitar, offered by 'a Lady'.

APPENDIX 2

Trinidad Huerta's Concerts and Other Activities in England, 1827–30

The travels of Trinidad Huerta reveal the movements of a solo guitarist who often looked beyond London (where he was well known) for his engagements. The relatively narrow scope of his activity suggests the constraints that pressed upon such itinerant soloists before the coming of the railways. In the following list, all performances were given by Huerta alone, unless otherwise indicated. (See also Fig. 41.)

1827

LONDON

8 February, concert at the Argyll Rooms (*The Times*, 6 February)

26 March, Mori and Lavenu advertise a guitar method 'approved by A. T. Huerta' (*Morning Post*, 26 March)

16 May, concert at the house of Sir Frances Burdett (*Morning Chronicle*, 15 May)

18 May, concert at Almack's Rooms (*The Harmonicon*, 5 (1827), 149)

25 May, concert at the Argyll Rooms, in which Franz Liszt also takes part (*The Age*, 6 May)

4 June, concert for the Royal Society of Musicians, in which Huerta takes part (*Morning Post*, 30 May)

6 June, concert at the Argyll Rooms (*The Times*, 7 June)

19 June, concert at the Green Man, Blackheath (*Bell's Life in London and Sporting Chronicle*, 17 June)

19 June, concert at the Argyll Rooms (*Morning Post*, 14 June)

22 June, concert at the Argyll Rooms (*Morning Post*, 19 June)

16 July, concert at Willis's Rooms (*Morning Post*, 16 July)

HASTINGS

21 October, concert at Diplock's Marine Library (*Sussex Advertiser*, 22 October)

BRIGHTON

19 November, concert announced by Huerta (*Brighton Gazette*, 15 November)

Winter soirée (date unspecified) at 22 Sussex Square, Kemptown (A. L. C. de La Garde, *Brighton: scènes détachées d'un voyage en Angleterre* (Paris and London, 1834), 220)

18 December, concert at the Old Ship assembly room (*Brighton Herald*, 22 December)

1828

BRIGHTON

21 January, concert at the Old Ship assembly room (*Brighton Gazette*, 17 January)

LONDON

15 February, Huerta announces that he is to open an academy for teaching the guitar, with the guitarist F. Gómez (*Morning Post*, 15 February)

9 March, announcement of Huerta's return from Brighton (*Bell's Life in London and Sporting Chronicle*, 9 March)

BRISTOL

20 March, concert (venue unspecified), in which Huerta takes part (*Bristol Mercury*, 24 March)

BATH

'Two concerts were given last week at Bath and Bristol', in which Huerta takes part (*The Standard* (London), 28 March)

LONDON

31 March, concert at Freemasons' Hall in aid of the New Musical Fund, in which Huerta takes part (*Morning Post*, 28 March)

6 May, concert at Willis's Rooms, in which Huerta takes part (*Morning Post*, 30 April)

CAMBRIDGE

13 May, concert in the town hall (poster in the Royal Academy of Music, York Gate Collection)

EASTBOURNE

29 May, Huerta plays for the monthly dinner of the Melodists' Club at the Freemasons' Tavern (*The Standard*, 30 May)

OXFORD

2 June and 4 June, concerts in the Town Hall (*Oxford University and City Herald*, 31 May, 7 June)

LONDON

6 June, concert at the Argyll Rooms (*Morning Post*, 19 May; *The Harmonicon*, 6 (1828), 168)

13 June, concert at the Theatre Royal, Covent Garden, in which Huerta takes part (*Morning Post*, 9 June)

16 June, concert at the Argyll Rooms, in which Huerta takes part (*Morning Post*, 6 June)

23 June, concert at Blackheath assembly room (*Morning Post*, 20 June)

11 July, concert at Willis's Rooms (*Morning Post*, 1 July)

TUNBRIDGE WELLS

28 August, concert at Mr Nash's Assembly Room (*Brighton Gazette*, 4 September 1828)

4 September, concert at Mr Nash's Assembly Room (*South Eastern Gazette*, 4 September)

BRISTOL

27 November, concert at the Theatre Royal (*Bristol Mirror*, 22 November)

LONDON

7 December, Mori and Lavenu offer for sale guitars 'on the improved plan of Signor Huerta, Plain and in Rosewood from 4 to 12 guineas' (*The Age*, 7 December)

1829

BATH

10 February, Huerta is too ill to play at a concert for Spanish and Italian refugees (*Bristol Mercury*, 10 February)

April, concert (date and venue unspecified) (J. Suárez-Pajares and R. Coldwell, eds, *A. T. Huerta (1800–1874), Life and Works* (San Antonio, TX: DGA Editions, 2006), 15)

BRISTOL
9 April, concert at Clifton assembly rooms (*Bristol Mercury*, 14 April)

WINCHESTER
5 November, concert at St John's House (*Hampshire Chronicle*, 2 November)

SOUTHAMPTON
26 November and 28 November, concerts for the Southampton Choral Society at their rooms (*Hampshire Telegraph and Sussex Chronicle*, 2 November, and other newspapers)

BRIGHTON
19 December, concert at the Old Ship assembly room (*Brighton Gazette*, 17 December)
22 December, select dinner party at The Albion hotel, at which Huerta is a guest (*Brighton Gazette*, 24 December)

1830

SOUTHAMPTON
19 January, concert at the Long Rooms (*Hampshire Advertiser*, 16 January)

BRIGHTON
Madame Sala's concert (date and venue unspecified) (*Brighton Gazette*, 21 January)

LYMINGTON
9 February, concert at the assembly room (*Hampshire Advertiser*, 13 February)

SOUTHAMPTON
9 March, concert at the Freemasons' Hall (*Hampshire Advertiser*, 27 February)

SALISBURY
10 March, concert at the assembly room (*Salisbury and Winchester Journal*, 8 March)
15 March, morning concert at the assembly room (*Salisbury and Winchester Journal*, 15 March)

BRISTOL
20 March, concert at the Clifton Hotel (*Bristol Mercury*, 9 March)

NEWBURY
27 March, morning concert (venue unspecified) (diary of Emma Austen-Leigh, Hampshire Record Office, Winchester, 23M93/87/1/15)

LONDON
22 May, benefit concert for Huerta at the Great Room of the King's Theatre (*The Times*, 24 May). The orchestra advertised was unable to appear (Huerta, letter to *The Times*, 26 May)
24 May, concert at the mansion of John Penn Esq. 'au benefice d'un homme de lettres', in which Huerta takes part (*Morning Post*, 21 May)
3 June, concert (venue unspecified), in which Huerta takes part (*Morning Post*, 4 June)
7 June, concert at the King's Theatre, in which Huerta takes part (*Morning Post*, 28 May)

Notes

For a list of abbreviations used in the notes, see pp. 10–11. The place of publication for books is London, unless otherwise indicated.

Introduction

1. *Dorset County Chronicle*, 26 January 1832.

2. For contemporary polemics against the guitar see A. Britton, 'The Guitar in the Romantic Period: Its Musical and Social Development with Special Reference to Bristol and Bath', doctoral diss., Royal Holloway, University of London, 2010, 88–98, which is particularly good on the generally unqualified attacks in new musical journals; and, more comprehensively, E. Stenstadvold, '"We hate the guitar": Prejudice and Polemic in the Music Press in Early 19th-Century Europe', *EM*, 41 (2013), 595–604.

3. Among the writings that have accompanied and enhanced this revival of interest, T. F. Heck, *Mauro Giuliani: Virtuoso Guitarist and Composer* (Columbus, Ohio: Editions Orphée, 1995), and J. Tyler and P. Sparks, *The Guitar and its Music from the Renaissance to the Classical Era* (Oxford: Oxford University Press, 2002), set new standards for the study of guitar history in general and for the nineteenth-century craze in particular. E. Stenstadvold, *An Annotated Bibliography of Guitar Methods, 1760–1860* (Hillsdale, NY: Pendragon Press, 2010), does the same for its materials, while J. Westbrook, 'Guitar Making in Nineteenth-Century London: Louis Panormo and his Contemporaries', doctoral diss., University of Cambridge, 2013, takes the organology of nineteenth-century guitars to a new level. G. Wade, *The Traditions of the Classical Guitar* (Calder, 1980), is a thoroughly dependable account; and H. Turnbull, *The Guitar from the Renaissance to the Present Day* (Batsford, 1974), remains one of the best of general histories. Recent works with a continental focus include R. Aleixo, *La guitarra en Madrid (1750–1808) con un catálogo de la música de ese periodo conservada en bibliotecas madrileñas* (Madrid: Spanish Society of Musicology, 2016); J. van Amersfoort, '"Extra fine guitars after the newest fashion": Guitar- and Cittern-Making in the Northern Netherlands, 1750–1800', *EM*, 46 (2018), 35–53; and J. van Amersfoort, '"The notes were not sweet till you sung them": French Vocal Music with Guitar Accompaniment, c.1800–1840', *EM*, 41 (2013) 605–19; L. Briso de Montiano, 'Una parte de la biblioteca personal de Dionisio Aguado en el legado de Rosaio Huidobro', *Roseta*, 12 (2018),

115–64; P. Poulopoulos, 'The Impact of François Chanot's Experimenta Violins on the Development of the Earliest Guitar with an Arched Soundboard by Francesco Molino in the 1820s', *EM*, 45 (2018), 67–86; K. Sparr, 'Barthélemy Trille Labarre: professeur de guitare et compositeur, élève d'Haydn', *Soundboard Scholar*, 4, (2018), 22–4 K. Sparr, '*Journal des troubadours avec accompagnement de guitare ou lyre*, with its Unusual Dating Code and Ferdinando Carulli as Composer and Arranger', at www.tablatura.com/Journal%20des%20Troubadours2.pdf; E. Stenstadvold, 'A Bibliographical Study of Antoine Meissonnier's Periodicals for Voice and Guitar, 1811–27', *Notes*, 2nd ser., 58 (2001), 11–33; and Stenstadvold, '"We hate the guitar"'. See also K. Hartdegen, 'Fernando Sor's Theory of Harmony Applied to the Guitar: History, Bibliography and Context', 3 vols, doctoral diss., University of Auckland, 2011; T. Hindricks, *Zwischen 'leerer Klimperey' und 'wirklicher Kunst': Gitarrenmusik in Deutschland um 1800* (Münster: Waxmann, 2012); B. Jeffery, *Fernando Sor: Composer and Guitarist*, 2nd edn (Tecla Editions, 1994); P. Pérez Díaz, 'Los tratados de Dionisio Aguado y Fernando Sor como fuentes para la interpretación del repertorio de la guitarra clásico-romantica', in B. Lolo, ed., *Campos Interdisciplinares de la Musicología: Actas del V Congreso de la Sociedad Española de Musicología (Barcelona, 25–28 de octubre de 2000)*, 2 vols (Madrid: Sociedad Española de Musicología, 2001), 683–98; D. Ribouillault-Bibron, 'La technique de la guitare en France dans la première moitié du XIXe siècle', doctoral diss., Université de Paris, Sorbonne, 1980; R. Savino, 'Essential Issues in Performance Practices of the Classical Guitar, 1770–1850', in V. A. Coelho, ed., *Performance on Lute, Guitar and Vihuela: Historical Practice and Modern Interpretation* (Cambridge: Cambridge University Press, 1997), 195–219; P. Valois, 'Les guitaristes français entre 1770 et 1830', thesis, Laval University, Quebec, 2009; L. Verrett, *The Early Romantic Guitar*, at www.earlyromanticguitar.com. The Oxford University Press journal *Early Music* has devoted two issues to the early nineteenth-century guitar and its congeners: 41/4 (2013) and 46/1 (2018). For publications of the Consortium for Guitar Research at Sidney Sussex College, Cambridge, see https://guitarconsortium.wordpress.com.

4. S. W. Button, 'The Guitar in England, 1800–1924', doctoral diss., University of Surrey, 1984, was a pioneering study, but is now in need of revision. See also Britton, 'The Guitar in the Romantic Period', and A. Britton, 'The Guitar and the Bristol School of Artists', *EM*, 41 (2013), 585–604; the former is a remarkable study, which offers, in its first part, a survey of guitar history in Western Europe that manages to be both compendious and succinct. See also S. Clarke, 'An Early Victorian Amateur Guitarist', *EM*, 47 (2019), 99–111; N. Confalone, 'Scene di vita vittoriana dalle memorie di Madame Sidney Pratten e di sua sorella Giulia Pelzer', *Il Fronimo*, 181 (January 2018), 21–30; D. Martín Gil, 'The Guitarist behind *La Guitaromanie*: Charles de Marescot', *Soundboard Scholar*, 4 (2018), 4–16; C. Page, 'Being a Guitarist in late Georgian England', *EM* 46 (2018), 3–16; C. Page, 'New Light on the London Years of Fernando Sor', *EM*, 41 (2013), 557–60; C. Page, 'The Spanish Guitar in the Newspapers, Novels, Drama and Verse of Eighteenth-Century England', *RMARC*, 44 (2013), 1–18; E. Stenstadvold, 'Fernando Sor on the Move in the Early 1820s', *Soundboard Scholar*, 1 (2015), 16–25; E. Stenstadvold, 'Mariano Castro de Gistau (*d.* 1856) and the Vogue for the Spanish Guitar in Nineteenth-Century Britain', *Nineteenth-Century Music Review* (2017), 1–21 (a major survey of social, cultural and professional issues); E. Stenstadvold, '"The worst drunkard in London": The Life and Career of the Guitar Virtuoso Leonard Schulz', *Soundboard*, 38/4 (2012), 9–16, 52; T. Takeuchi, 'Rediscovering the Regency Lute: A Checklist of Musical Sources and Extant Instruments', *EM*, 46 (2018), 17–34; J. Westbrook, 'General Thompson's Enharmonic Guitar', *Soundboard*, 38/4 (2012), 45–52; Westbrook, 'Guitar Making'; J. Westbrook, 'Louis Panormo: "The only maker of guitars in the Spanish style"', *EM*, 41 (2013), 571–84.

5. *Morning Post*, 16 February 1802: 'the guitar is admired "in most of the circles of fashion". Guitar teachers naturally used the same language – thus F. Duvernay, *A Complete Instruction Book for the Guitar* (1828), 4: 'that pleasing instrument (the Guitar) has of late years become so extremely fashionable'.

6. For the guitar in Hispanic territories during the eighteenth century see Tyler and Sparks, *The Guitar and its Music*, 193–8, 212–17; see also Aleixo, *La guitarra en Madrid*. There are many relevant articles, too numerous to list, in the Spanish journal *Hispánica Lyra*.

7. See Appendix 1. The term 'English guitar', though now widely accepted, is in some respects unfortunate since it occludes the contribution of makers, arrangers and publishers in Edinburgh, Aberdeen and Dublin to the instrument's good fortune for some three generations after about 1750; for a report of the plausible (but as yet not fully substantiated) suggestion that the 'English' guitar was introduced into England from Scotland, see Tyler and Sparks, *The Guitar and its Music*, 206 n. The term 'English guitar' is appropriate

in the sense that makers such as Johan Friedrich Hintz, Michael Rauche and John Frederick Zumpe, though all immigrants, made London a major centre for the manufacture of such guitars, and even the French were prepared to acknowledge the existence of the 'Guitthare Angloise': see J. Carpentier, *1er Recueil de menuets, allemandes etc. entremêlés d'airs agréables à chanter avec leurs accompagnemens* (Paris, 1770), 6; see also A. Devriès-Lesure, *Dictionnaire des éditeurs de musique français*, vol. i (Geneva: Minkoff, 1979), cat. no. 32 (Cousineau, 1781): 'Sonates pour le Sixtre ou Guitarre Angloise'. In 1789 the Madrid instrument-maker Juan Puyol advertised examples equipped with a keyboard mechanism (the so-called 'pianoforte guitars') and called them 'guitarras a la inglesa que se tocan con teclas': K. Kenyon de Pascual, 'Ventas de instrumentos musicales en Madrid durante la segunda mitad del siglo XVIII, II', *Revista de Musicología*, 6 (1983), 299–308, at 304.

8. Such tunings were occasionally also employed on the Spanish guitar during the period of the great vogue, but they never became standard. For more on the English guitar, with bibliography, see Chapter 2.

9. E. Johnson, 'The Death and Second Life of the Harpsichord', *Journal of Musicology*, 30 (2013), 180–214, at 180.

10. When the term 'amateur', which will often be used in this book, appears in Georgian sources it is sometimes printed there in italics, marking it as a loan word borrowed from French with a precious, perhaps somewhat affected, air. In the later eighteenth century the word was often associated with a liberal gentleman's interest in architecture, painting and sculpture, fostered during the Grand Tour. As late as 1803 this was still a widespread sense; Rees's *Cyclopædia* defines an 'amateur' as someone with the discriminating taste for the fine arts that the word 'connoisseur', another French loan, also conveyed (*OED*, s.v. 'amateur', *n.*, 2.a., gives the quotation from Rees; see also ibid., s.v. 'connoisseur', *n.*, quotations from 1719). Yet the discernment implied by 'amateur' was generally held to be of a less precious kind than anything conveyed by 'connoisseur', and the word was easily and rapidly extended beyond a discerning love of the fine arts to an informed enthusiasm, even perhaps a passion, for anything pursued or approached in a disinterested manner (i.e. without financial interest).

11. *Musical World*, 2 (1836), 41–2, reviewing a performance by Philippe Verini at Willis's Rooms of a guitar fantasia on favourite airs from Vincenzo Bellini's *I Puritani*. The concert room was about 100 feet in length by 40 feet in width (approximately 30.5 × 12 metres).

12. For a survey of this repertoire see P. Pieters, *De literatuur voor gitaar met piano gedurende de eerste helft van de negentiende eeuw* (Ghent: Universiteit Gent

Faculteit Letteren en Wijsbegeerte, Vakgroep Kunst-, Muziek- en Theaterwetenschappen, 1994).

13. For the morphological characteristics of guitars from the late eighteenth century into the nineteenth, including X-rays showing internal bracings and harmonic bars, see J. Westbrook, *The Century that Shaped the Guitar: From the Birth of the Six-String Guitar to the Death of Tárrega* (Hove: James Westbrook, 2005); and for guitars made in London during the great vogue see Westbrook, 'Guitar Making in Nineteenth- Century London'.

14. Experiment also shows that modern and marketed equivalents, such as overspun synthetics, are not a satisfactory substitute for the originals; the higher partials of the modern strings are more prominent, and the sound louder.

15. *The Harmonicon*, 7 (1829), 300.

16. *The Examiner*, 13 May 1827.

17. An anonymous commentator who surveyed the concert life of London in 1823 found that there were 'many amateurs among the families both at the West End of the Town, and in the City' who could stand comparison with the leading professional players: Anon., 'Sketch of the State of Music in London, 1823', *Quarterly Musical Magazine and Review*, 5 (1823), 241–75. For further commentary see especially D. Golby, *Instrumental Teaching in Nineteenth-Century Britain* (Aldershot: Ashgate, 2004); and for the broader picture see S. McVeigh, *Concert Life in London from Mozart to Haydn* (Cambridge: Cambridge University Press, 1993).

18. Surveys of these development include Sparks, in pt iii of Tyler and Sparks, *The Guitar and its Music*, pursued in a trans-European context, and foundational. For Spain see Aleixo, *La guitarra en Madrid*; for France there is Valois, 'Les guitaristes français entre 1770 et 1830'. For the chronology of developments in England see Britton, 'The Guitar in the Romantic Period'; Westbrook, 'Guitar Making in Nineteenth-Century London'; and Westbrook, *The Century that Shaped the Guitar*.

19. I am indebted to Yang Yuanzheng, of the Department of Music, University of Hong Kong, for information about Chinese string practices. Strings of silk, presumably without the overwinding, were known in the West by the fourteenth century: C. Page, *Voices and Instruments of the Middle Ages* (Dent, 1987), 216, 238, 240–41.

20. For Spanish instruments see Chapter 3.

21. Aleixo, *La guitarra en Madrid*, 183ff.; Sparks, in pt iii of Tyler and Sparks, *The Guitar and its Music*. Stenstadvold, *An Annotated Bibliography*, 3–4, lists the number of strings assumed by the French methods (many of which are precisely or approximately dated) during the formative period; see also Westbrook, 'Guitar Making in Nineteenth-Century London', 46ff.

22. The discussion in M. Butler, *Romantics, Rebels and Reactionaries: English Literature and its Background, 1760–1830* (Oxford: Oxford University Press, 1981), 57–68, remains unrivalled.

23. I borrow the term from S. G. Marks, *The Information Nexus: Global Capitalism from the Renaissance to the Present* (Cambridge: Cambridge University Press, 2016). There are many useful studies of the eighteenth-century press, including H. Barker, 'Catering for Provincial Tastes? Newspapers, Readership and Profit in Late-Eighteenth-Century England', *Historical Research*, 69 (1996), 42–61; H. Barker, *Newspapers, Politics, and Public Opinion in Late-Eighteenth-Century England* (Oxford: Oxford University Press, 1998); and C. Dean, 'Court Culture and Political News in London's Eighteenth-Century Newspapers', *ELH*, 73 (2006), 631–49.

24. A search for the spelling 'guittar' adds just over a hundred more.

25. *New Monthly Magazine and Literary Journal* (1827), no. 1, 95–6.

Chapter One

1. As recorded by Samuel Pepys: R. Latham and W. Matthews, eds, *The Diary of Samuel Pepys: A New and Complete Transcription*, 11 vols (1971–83), entry for 8 June 1660.

2. A. Hamilton, *Mémoires de la vie du comte de Grammont* (Rotterdam, 1716); relevant extracts and discussion in *GISE*, 8c–84.

3. For discussion see J. Lombard, *Courtilz de Sandras et la crise du roman à le fin du grand siècle* (Paris: Presses Universitaires de France, 1980).

4. E. S. de Beer, ed., *The Diary of John Evelyn*, 6 vols (Oxford, 2000), vol. iv, 360. For the Restoration vogue and beyond see *GISE*, ch. 3.

5. *GISE*, 164, quoting Mark Goldie.

6. Ibid., 122.

7. Nederlands Muziek Instituut, The Hague, MS Kluis D I. *GISE*, ch. 7, with bibliography; M. Hall, 'Princess An's Lute Book and Related English Sources of Music for the 5-Course Guitar', *The Consort*, 66 (2010), 18–34.

8. *The Levellers* is a genuine work of 1703, when it was advertised for sale in the press (e.g. in *The Observator* for 28 August – 1 September 1703). The earliest copy of the text, however, appears to be the reprint in *The Harleian Miscellany*, 5 (1745), 417–33.

9. P. Borsay, *The English Urban Renaissance: Culture and Society in the Provincial Town, 1660–1770* (Oxford: Clarendon Press, 1989), 205; P. Langford, *A Polite and Commercial People: England, 1727–1783* (Oxford: Clarendon Press, 1989), 72–3.

10. Act II, scene i; *LS*, vol. ii, 105.

11. A system of public credit overseen by the Bank of England, founded in 1694, allowed some money scriveners to become aldermen, Justices of the Peace or even Lord Mayor of London: J. G. A. Pocock, *Virtue, Commerce, and History: Essays on Political Thought and History, Chiefly in the Eighteenth Century* (Cambridge: Cambridge University Press, 1985), 68ff., 108ff. Other sources of the early 1700s include a poem of 1710 by one of the most exuberant satirists, Edward Ward, evoking a young wife who spends the money of her miserly husband on imported silks and cosmetics, passing her time by thrumming a guitar and singing:

> I find but what I fear'd, this 'tis to wed
> A proud *Virago* so profusely bred,
> Humour'd at Home, and taught at Dancing-School
> To scorn, for foreign Silks, your native Wooll;
> To turn your Toes, to bridle up your Head,
> And move, like formal Clock-work, as you tread;
> To tune your Voice, to thrum on your Gittar,
> And wash and paint, to make your looks more fair.

(E. Ward, 'Dialogue between a Wealthy Niggard, and his Generous Termagant', *Nuptial Dialogues and Debates*, 2 vols (1710), vol. i, 51). In Daniel Defoe's novel *The History and Remarkable Life of the Truly Honourable Colonel Jaque* (1722), 238, the hero, pardoned by George I (r. 1714–27) for various crimes, receives the attentions of a woman whom he can see across the narrow London court where they both live, singing and playing the guitar.

12. W. Darrel, *A Supplement to the First Part of The Gentleman Instructed* (1708), 61.

13. J. Trenchard, *Cato's Letters*, 4 vols (1723), vol. iii, 260.

14. Anon., *The Ladies Cabinet Broke Open* (1710), 5. The word 'thrum(b)', meaning a strumming action, had a well-established erotic sense; G. Williams, *A Dictionary of Sexual Language and Imagery* (Athlone Press, 1994), s.v. 'thrum', in the sense 'to couple with'.

15. For the female wits see L. A. Finke, 'The Satire of Women Writers in "The Female Wits"', *Restoration: Studies in English Literary Culture, 1660–1700*, 8 (1984), 64–71; for Philips and Lawes see *GISE*, 110–12.

16. Act I, scene i; *LS*, vol. ii, 31; S. Staves, 'A Few Kind Words for the Fop', *Studies in English Literature*, 22 (1982), 413–28, at 415.

17. The evidence is all continental: P. Barbieri, 'Roman and Neapolitan Gut Strings, 1550–1950', *GSJ*, 59 (2006), 147–81; M. Peruffo, 'Italian Violin Strings in the Eighteenth and Nineteenth Centuries: Typologies, Manufacturing Techniques and Principles of Stringing', *Recercare*, 9 (1997), 155–203.

18. *Daily Post*, 28 March 1724, and subsequently; see also P. Barbieri, 'An Assessment of Musicians and Instrument-Makers in Rome during Handel's Stay: The 1708 Grand Taxation', *EM*, 37 (2009), 597–619.

19. *Stamford Mercury*, 21 March 1723; *Newcastle Courant*, 20 October 1764.

20. *London Gazette*, 29 April – 2 May 1700.

21. *Post Man and the Historical Account*, 13–16 September 1701.

22. R. Rasch, *The Music Publishing House of Estienne Roger and Michel-Charles Le Cène, 1696–1743*, at http://docplayer.net/6666597-The-music-publishing-house-michel-charles-le-cene-1696-1743-of-estienne-roger-and-my-work-on-the-internet-volume-four-rudolf-rasch.html, iv/2, 14.

23. For a facsimile of Derosiers's *Les principes de la guitarre* (1689) see J. Saint-Arroman and C. Delume, eds, *Méthodes et traités*, 18: *Guitare*, ser. I: *France, 1600–1800*, 2 vols (Courlay, 2003), vol. i, 39–45; another was published in Bologna in 1975. Around 1724 Derosiers's music and his tutor appeared again in a London catalogue, this time in a list issued by John Brotherton of Threadneedle Street, who was launching a music-publishing arm of an established business with imported material from Étienne Roger's stock; L. Brotherton, *An Account of Printed Musick, for Violins, Hautboys, Flutes, and other Instruments, by Several Masters* (n.d. [c.1724]), final page: 'Lessons for the Guittar. / Mr. *Derosiers* / Instructions by *Ditto*'. On this document see P. Holman, *Life After Death: The Viola da Gamba in Britain from Purcell to Dolmetsch* (Woodbridge: Boydell, 2010), 91–3; J. B. Young, 'An Account of Printed Musick', *Fontes Artis Musicae*, 29 (1982), 93–113.

24. *GISE*, fig. 23, with discussion at 200. The scene is a polite bacchanalia of gentlemen, mostly Whig politicians of the day.

25. Visitors to the Smithfield fair could be sure of seeing dancers or comedians playing Scaramouche amid the general noise and turmoil. At various times in the last years of William III (d. 1702) or soon after, the King's Head and Mitre Music Booth at the fair featured 'two Scaramouths' (*sic*) and 'a *Scaramouch* done by a boy of seven years old to admiration', while other booths offered 'two figures that dance Sarramouch [*sic*] after a new *Grotesque* fashion' and 'A new *Scaramouch*, more civil than the former . . . '. Quoted from the music-booth bills, Harvard University, Houghton Library, TS 932.3. See also S. Rosenfeld, *The Theatre of the London Fairs in the 18th Century* (Cambridge: Cambridge University Press, 1960). The surviving bills for the music booths of the great London fairs, especially Bartholomew Fair at Smithfield and Southwark Fair, reveal an extraordinarily varied range of musical and visual entertainment on offer around 1700, including tumbling, rope-dancing and puppetry, as well as music. The bills virtually never indicate what instruments

took part, but it would be a significant departure from seventeenth-century precedent if the 'Spaniard' who danced 'a Sarabrand with castinets incomparably well' at the King's Head and Mitre Music Booth (Smithfield) did not have a guitar, and likewise 'a Woman that dances a *Sarraband* with Castinets beyond expectation' at Root's Booth. All these are to be found in the volume of documents in the Houghton Library. For non-English representations of Scaramouche with a guitar, see M. Chilton, *Harlequin Unmasked: The Commedia dell'arte and Porcelain Sculpture* (New Haven and London: Yale University Press, 2001), pls 144, 145, 280, 287, 305, 399, 400.

26. For Sorine, whose name is spelled in various ways in contemporary documents, see *BD*, vol. xiv, s.v. 'Sorin, Joseph', also 'Sorine, Mr'. The Drury Lane accounts mentioning Sorine are transcribed in L. R. N. Ashley, 'The Theatre-Royal in Drury Lane, 1711–1716, under Colley Cibber, Barton Booth and Robert Wilks', doctoral diss., Princeton University, 1955. Sorine is occasionally mentioned in works on pantomime and theatre music: see M. Goff, '"Actions, Manners, and Passions": Entr'acte Dancing on the London Stage, 1700–1737', *EM*, 26 (1998), 213–28; M. Goff, 'John Rich, French Dancing, and English Pantomimes', in B. Joncus and J. Barlow, eds, *The Stage's Glory: John Rich, 1692–1761* (Newark: University of Delaware Press, 2011), 85–98, at 89; Rosenfeld, *The Theatre of the London Fairs*, 76, 111; R. Semmens, *Studies in the English Pantomime, 1712–1733* (Hillsdale, NY: Boydell & Brewer, 2017), 4, 132–3; J. Thorp, 'From Scaramouche to Harlequin: Dances "in Grotesque Characters" on the London Stage', in K. Lowerre, ed., *The Lively Arts of the London Stage, 1675–1725* (Farnham: Ashgate, 2014), 13–128, at 116–17. See also J. O'Brien, *Harlequin Britain: Pantomime and Entertainment, 1690–1760* (Baltimore: Johns Hopkins University Press, 2004); P. Sawyer, 'The Popularity of Pantomime on the London Stage, 1720–1760', *Restoration and Eighteenth-Century Theatre Research*, 5 (1990), 1–16.

27. Anon., *A Comparison between the Two Stages* (1702), 47.

28. Rosenfeld, *The Theatre of the London Fairs*, ch. 4.

29. Alexander Pope, *The Dunciad in Four Books*, ed. V. Rumbold, rev. edn (Harlow: Pearson Longman, 2009), Book III, lines 235–6.

30. When Jean de Castillion of Ghent compiled a handsome manuscript collection of music for the guitar in 1730 he conceded, in an extensive preface, that the instrument once fashionable at the court of Louis XIV of France had now entered upon a period of decline (Jean de Castillion, *Recueil des pieces de guitarre*, Preface: 'Mais comme dans ce Monde tout est sujet à la vicissitude, il paroit que Louïs XIV. ce grand Roi soit le dernier qui s'y est exercé, et que ce soit presentement le tour de la Guitarre de languir'); see

the facsimile (Brussels, 1979) and Saint-Arroman and Delume, *Méthodes et traités*, vol. i, 51–61. Fifteen years later Charles Philippe d'Albert de Luynes described the guitar as 'no longer in use'; see C.-P. d'Albert, *Mémoires du duc de Luynes sur la cour de Louis XV*, 17 vols (Paris, 1860–65), vol. vi, 386.

31. A. Boyer, *The History of the Life and Reign of Queen Anne* (1722), 715–16; J C. Pepusch, *A Short Explication of such Foreign Words, as are made Use of in Musick Books* (1724), s.v. 'Guitarra'.

32. J. Hawkins, *A General History of the Science and Practice of Music*, 5 vols (1776), vol. iv, 74. According to Hawkins, the notice carried a crude drawing of a guitar and the poorly spelled commendation: 'De delectabl music calit Chittara fit for te gantleman e ladis camera.'

33. E. Chamberlayne, *The Present State of England* (1683), 89.

34. *OED*, s.v. 'thrum', *v.3*: 'To play on a stringed instrument . . . in an idle, mechanical, or unskilful way; to strum'.

35. *GISE*, 81.

36. D. Defoe, *A Journal of the Plague Year* (1722), 19; B. A. Atkinson, *Good Princes Nursing Fathers and Nursing Mothers to the Church. A Sermon Preach'd in London, May 2, 1736. On the Marriage of His Royal Highness* (1736), 16.

37. The author was Jean-Benjamin de La Borde. We owe the identification to Charles Burney (A. Rees, *The Cyclopædia: or, Universal Dictionary of Arts, Sciences, and Literature*, 41 vols (1810–24), vol. xvii, s.v. 'Guitarra'), who notes the suitability of the guitar for 'vandevilles [*sic*], pastorials and brunettes' and attributes that assessment to 'M. Laborde'. The observation is found, made in precisely these terms, in the *Encyclopédie* entry; facsimile in Saint-Arroman and Delume, *Méthodes et traités*, vol. i, 63–5.

38. Act III, scene i; *LS*, vol. iii, 66.

39. *BD*, vol. x, s.v. 'Palmer, Mrs.'.

40. M. J. M. Ezell, ed., *Poems and Prose of Mary, Lady Chudleigh* (Oxford, 1993).

41. M. Spring, *The Lute in Britain: A History of the Instrument and its Music* (Oxford: Oxford University Press, 2001), 308–13. 'Huntly's Chimes' and 'Price's Gavott' are both a mystery; the latter's connection to any dancing masters or musicians named Price, past or present (if there is one to be found), remains unknown.

42. Text in A. Baines, 'Fifteenth-Century Instruments in Tinctoris's De inventione et usu musicae', *GSJ*, 3 (1950), 19–26, 23. This is still the most serviceable text of the passage.

43. *GITE*, 37.

44. J. Loftis, *The Spanish Plays of Neoclassical England* (New Haven: Yale University Press, 1973). A direction in Dryden's play *An Evening's Love* of 1668 set in Madrid, calls for 'Musick and Guitars tuning on the other side of the Stage' in Act II, and again for the scene in Act III where Spanish ladies give 'an Essay of their Guittars'. The play is indebted to Calderón de la Barca's comedy *El astrólogo fingido* (1632), among other sources.

45. Anon., *Choice Novels and Amorous Tales* (1652), 79, where 'Spanish Gittar' renders 'chitarra Spagnuola' in the story's Italian source (G. Brusoni, *Delle novelle amorose libri quattro* (Venice, 1655), 25). For the Spanish associations of the guitar in the Jacobean period, see *GISE*, ch. 1.

46. Appendix, 7.

47. C. T., *A Short Account and Character of Spain in a Letter from an English Gentleman now Residing at Madrid to his Friend in London* (1701), 15. See further P. Shaw, 'Sensual, Solemn, Sober, Slow and Secret: The English View of the Spaniard: 1590–1700', in C. C. Barfoot, ed., *Beyond Pug's Tour: National and Ethnic Stereotyping in Theory and Literary Practice* (Amsterdam, and Atlanta, Ga: Rodopi, 1997), 99–114

48. T. Salmon, *Modern History: or, The Present State of all Nations*, vol. xiii (1731), 22.

49. Anon, *A Trip to Spain: or, A True Description of the Comical Humours, Ridiculous Customs, and Foolish Laws, of that Lazy Improvident People the Spaniards* (1705), 8.

50. G. Carleton, *The Military Memoirs of Captain George Carleton* (1743), 279; *ODNB*, s.v. 'Carleton, George'. These memoirs have been attributed in the past to Daniel Defoe and Jonathan Swift, among others, but they are now widely accepted to be a genuine record of Carleton's life, albeit one perhaps ghosted for him by an unknown hand. See R. M. Baine, 'Daniel Defoe and Robert Drury's Journal', *Texas Studies in Literature and Language*, 16 (1974), 479–91. A century later, some observers believed that the guitar owed much of its popularity in the 1830s to British servicemen who fought in another Spanish campaign, the Peninsular War of 1807–14, and who returned with instruments in their kit bags (see Chapter 5).

51. *Brice's Weekly Journal*, 24 December 1725.

52. *Daily Journal*, 26 August 1728.

53. *Penny London Post or The Morning Advertiser*, 4 February 1747. This satire of 1719, whose original printing has not been found, was sharply relevant in 1747, and merited a reprinting, for the hopes of the Young Pretender, Charles Edward Stuart, Bonnie Prince Charlie, of gaining the throne of Great Britain, had recently been shattered at the Battle of Culloden (1746). For the date of Alberoni's support for the Old Pretender see M. M. McKerracher, *The Jacobite Dictionary* (Glasgow: Neil Wilson, 2007), s.v. 'Alberoni, Giulio'.

Chapter Two

1. Act II; *LS*, vol. iv, 360. For context see I. Kelly, *Mr Foote's Other Leg: Comedy, Tragedy and Murder in Georgian London* (Picador, 2012), 175–6.

2. *Manuscripts of Sir William Fitzherbert, Bart., and Others*, HMC, 13th Report, Appendix vi (1893), 201. For Miss Macklin see *BD*, x, 31–7. For Foote and Delaval see Kelly, *Mr Foote's Other Leg*, 173ff.

3. *BD*, x, 33.

4. Anon., *Memoirs of the Bedford Coffee-House* (1763), 71.

5. P. Sparks, 'The Mandolin in Britain, 1750–1800', *EM*, 46 (2018), 55–66.

6. The major study of these instruments is P. Poulopoulos, 'The Guittar in the British Isles, 1750–1810', doctoral diss., University of Edinburgh, 2011, which lists all significant works up to the date of its completion in 2011. (Poulopoulos follows the convention, not observed here, of using the spelling 'guittar' to indicate the English guitar, and the spelling 'guitar' for the gut-strung or Spanish instrument.) The indispensable online checklists of printed repertoire for the instrument are: G. Boye, *Chronological List of Tablatures from the 1700's*, at https://applications.library.appstate.edu/music/lute/C18/1700.html; and J. Kloss, *The 'Guittar' in Britain, 1753–1800*, at www.justanothertune.com/html/guittarinbritain.html. See also J. van Amersfoort, 'Miss Sara Burgerhart's English *Guittar*: The 'guitarre Angloise' in Enlightenment Holland', *Tijdschrift van de Koninklijke Vereniging voor Nederlandse Musiekgeschiedenis*, 64 (2014), 76–102; P. Coggin, '"This easy and agreeable instrument": A History of the English Guittar', *EM*, 15 (1987), 205–20; R. MacKillop, 'The Guitar, Cittern and Guittar in Scotland: An Historical Introduction up to 1800', in M. Lustig, ed., *Michaelsteiner Konferenzberichte*, vol. lxvi: *Gitarre und Zister-Bauweise, Spieltechnik und Geschichte bis 1800* (Blankenburg: Stiftung Kloster Michaelstein, 2004), 121–48; P. Poulopoulos, 'A Comparison of Two Surviving Guittars by Zumpe and New Details Concerning the Involvement of Square Piano Makers in the Guittar Trade', *GSJ*, 64 (2011), 49–59; P. Poulopoulos, '"A Complete Accompanyment to the Female Voice": The Guittar and its Role in the Culture of Georgian England', *Phoibos*, 1 (2012), 97–120; P. Poulopoulos, 'The Influence of Germans in the Development of "This Favourite Instrument the Guittar" in England', *Soundboard*, 38/4 (2012), 62–75; P. Poulopoulos, '"Wha sweetly Tune the Scottish Lyre": A Guitar by Rauche and Hoffmann and its Connection to Robert Burns', *GSJ*, 47 (2014), 40–44, 143–70; M. Spring, 'Benjamin Milgrove, the Musical "Toy Man", and the "Guittar" in Bath, 1757–1790', *EM*, 41 (2013), 317–29. F. Geminiani, *The Art of Playing the Guitar or Cittra* (1760), ed. P. Holman, is an edition of Geminiani's English guitar tutor with a thorough study.

For various aspects of the fashion for these instruments see also J. Nex, 'The Business of Musical-Instrument Making in Early Industrial London', doctoral diss., Goldsmiths, University of London, 2013, esp. 116ff.

7. *Public Advertiser*, 2 March 1754.

8. *Public Advertiser*, 24 September 1755. Johan Friedrich Hintz, an influential maker of both furniture and English guitars, advertised himself in 1755 as 'the Original Maker of that Instrument call'd The Guittar or Zittern', while in later advertisements from 1766 he claimed to be the 'first Inventor' of the guitar: Poulopoulos, 'The Guittar in the British Isles', 62, 81–2, 397–8, 586.

9. For discussion and photographs see Poulopoulos, 'The Guittar in the British Isles', 51ff.

10. J. Hawkins, *A General History of the Science and Practice of Music*, 5 vols (1776), vol. iv, 112 n., 113, 173; vol. v, Index, s.v. 'cittern'. Makers sometimes referred to English guitars as 'common' guitars, a name that is revealing in itself; for examples see Nex, 'The Business of Musical-Instrument Making', 349–50, 381, 390.

11. A notable source is the illustration and description in the *Neu-eröffneter theoretisch- und pracktischer Music-Saal*, compiled by Joseph Maier, organist at the church of St Catharine in the free imperial city of Schwäbisch Hall, now in the German state of Baden-Württemberg. In 1732, when the first edition of the work appeared, Maier felt free to ignore such instruments, but by 1741 they had won 'so many devotees' that he decided to include an example in his second edition. He explains that it has six courses, for the most part; the lowest two are overspun with a silver alloy, the next three are double courses of brass, tuned to a unison, while the top course, which is single, may either be of steel or be a lute chanterelle of gut. The tuning is variable, but Maier observes that it is closely related to the open major chord of the viola d'amore. Maier provides an illustration, reproduced in Poulopoulos, 'The Guittar in the British Isles', 66.

12. Poulopoulos, 'The Guittar in the British Isles'; see also P. Holman, *Life after Death: The Viola da Gamba in Britain from Purcell to Dolmetsch* (Woodbridge: Boydell, 2010), ch. 4. On Moravian music see S. Eyerly, 'Mozart and the Moravians', *EM*, 47 (2019), 161–82; P. Vogt, 'Listening to "Festive Stillness": The Sound of Moravian Music according to non-Moravian Visitors', *Moravian Music Journal*, 44 (1999), 15–23. For broader historical surveys see C. Podmore, *The Moravian Church in England, 1728–1760* (Oxford: Clarendon Press, 1998); G. Stead and M. Stead, *The Exotic Plant: The History of the Moravian Church in Britain* (Peterborough: Epworth Press, 2003). Hintz, the noted maker of English guitars, was at one time an evangelist for the Moravians: L. Boynton, 'The Moravian Brotherhood and the Migration of Furniture Makers in the Eighteenth Century', *Furniture History*, 29 (1993), 45–58;

L. Graf, 'John Frederick Hintz, Eighteenth-Century Moravian Instrument Maker, and the Use of the Citter in Moravian Worship', *Journal of Moravian History*, 5 (2008), 7–39; L. Graf, 'Moravians in London: A Case Study in Furniture-Making', *Furniture History*, 40 (2004), 1–52. It is doubtful whether the cause of the English guitar was furthered by Moravian *worship*, for it has not been established that Moravians in England used the instruments with any consistency in that context.

13. Call made substantial bequests to the Moravian ministers at Pudsey, in Yorkshire, and Bedford (TNA, PROB 11/898/208 (1)).

14. For performances of *The Englishman in Paris* in April 1755 see *LS*, vol. iv, 477, with cast list at 442; for Call's advertisement see *Public Advertiser*, 24 September 1755.

15. See the following, all in the *Public Advertiser*. For 1754: 2 March, 1 May (in neither does Call name either himself or Foote's play). For 1755: 24 September (Call identifies himself, names Foote's play and Miss Macklin, and he also alludes to the music scene; for the play's 'so portable, and so soft and so silly', Call has 'so portable, its Sound so acute, and yet withal so soft and sweet'), 1 October, 11 November. For 1756: 13 and 15 January, 26 August, 5 and 12 November. Call's advertisements were long and leisurely, sometimes vaunting himself over 'any other teacher that has yet appeared in public' and offering instruments 'at a very small expense'.

16. For Cloes's claim to be the princess's teacher on the pandola see J. C. Greene, *Theatre in Dublin, 1745–1820: A Calendar of Performances*, 2 vols (Bethlehem, PA: Lehigh University Press, 2011), vol. i, 401. On 19 March 1753 Cloes placed an advertisement for a forthcoming benefit concert (his own) in the *Public Advertiser*, using a separate line to announce that the 'chief airs' would be accompanied on the pandola. The panel appeared with a manicule pointing to that part of the text as if Cloes anticipated that it would be of particular interest.

17. For other English guitar repertoire presented in this form see, for example, T. Call, *The Tunes and Hymns as they are used at the Magdalen Chapel, Properly Set for the Organ, Harpsichord and Guittar* (n.d. [c.1760]).

18. See J. Munns, 'Celebrity Status: The Eighteenth-Century Actress as Fashion Icon', in T. Potter, ed., *Women, Popular Culture, and the Eighteenth Century* (Toronto: University of Toronto Press, 2012), 70–91. Two portraits provide further evidence for the use of hand-held, plucked and fretted instruments at the early Georgian court. In the three versions of Philippe Mercier's painting of Frederick, Prince of Wales, as a musician, dating from 1733 (Royal Collection, National Portrait Gallery, National Trust), the prince plays the cello, while his sister Anne sits at the harpsichord and Princess Amelia plays a small mandolin; Amelia

took lessons on the instrument from Francisco Weber, who also featured the mandolin in several London concerts after 1724 and composed twelve sonatas for *mandolino* and continuo. As the painting attests, it was considered attractive to associate instruments of the two cohorts, the plucked instrument required being almost invariably a small one, assigned a treble line that was also playable on the violin or the flute (for which it was principally intended), and at times requiring some virtuosity. In 1751, the year in which the Prince of Wales died, George Knapton painted a portrait of Augusta, Princess of Wales, and her offspring (Royal Collection), where Princess Elizabeth Caroline plays what seems to be essentially a small lute with eight pegs, perhaps implying four double courses, frets extending onto the belly and a rose placed surprisingly far towards the fingerboard.

19. *Manchester Mercury*, 9 January 1770; the advertisement is dated 26 December 1769.

20. C. S. Roberts, 'Music and Society in Eighteenth-Century Yorkshire', doctoral diss., University of Leeds, 2014, 168.

21. *Manchester Mercury*, 26 February 1760.

22. For surveys of the repertoire arranged by date of publication see Boye, *Chronological List of Tablatures*; Kloss, *The 'Guittar' in Britain*, section III.

23. *Public Advertiser*, 11 May 1754: 'This instrument differs nothing from the Mandalien, unless in Tuning; easier to play, and yet more copious, having two strings more than the Mandalien.' On the affinity with the mandolin, see Sparks, 'The Mandolin in Britain', 56.

24. For full details see Poulopoulos, 'The Guittar in the British Isles', 133–4.

25. S. Birkett and P. Poletti, 'Reproduction of Authentic Historical Soft Iron Wire for Musical Instruments', in T. Steiner, ed., *Instruments à claviers: expressivité et flexibilité sonore. Actes des Rencontres Internationales Harmoniques, Lausanne 2002* (Bern: Lang, 2004), 259–72; J. Carpentier, *Methode distribuée par leçons pour apprendre en peu de temps à joüer de l'instrument appellé cytre où guitthare allemande* (Paris, 1771), 5; facsimile in J. Saint-Arroman and C. Delume, eds, *Méthodes et traités*, 18: *Guitare*, ser. I: *France, 1600–1800*, 2 vols (Courlay, 2003), vol. i, 177.

26. A. Ford, *Lessons and Instructions for Playing on the Guitar* (1761), 7. For Gainsborough's portrait of Ann Ford with an English guitar see H. Belsey, *Thomas Gainsborough: The Portraits, Fancy Pictures and Copies after Old Masters*, 2 vols (New Haven: Yale University Press, 2019), vol. ii, 807–9.

27. B. Robins, ed., *The John Marsh Journals: The Life and Times of a Gentleman Composer (1752–1828)*, 2 vols (1998, 2013), vol. i, 154. The family of Miss [Ann] Littlejohn (née Chafy) included a canon of Salisbury

Cathedral, portrayed by Gainsborough playing the cello (Ann acquired the portrait as a legacy), while in the next generation the same clan produced a master of Sidney Sussex College, Cambridge.

28. Geminiani, *The Art of Playing the Guitar*, ed. Holman.

29. C. Avison, *An Essay on Musical Expression* (1752), 73.

30. F. Geminiani, *The Art of Playing the Guitar or Cittra* (1760), p. [1].

31. P. Langford, 'The Uses of Eighteenth-Century Politeness', *Transactions of the Royal Historical Society*, 6th ser., 12 (2002), 311–31, at 313, with bibliography. On the economic and social bases of politeness see P. Langford, *A Polite and Commercial People: England, 1727–1783* (Oxford: Clarendon Press, 1989), 61–121; see also L. E. Klein, 'Politeness and the Interpretation of the British Eighteenth Century', *Historical Journal*, 45 (2002), 869–98.

32. D. Herd, *The Ancient and Modern Scots Songs, Heroic Ballads, etc. Now First Collected into one Body* (Edinburgh, 1769), p. iii.

33. Ibid., p. ii.

34. J. S. Ackerman, *The Villa: Form and Ideology of Country Houses* (Thames and Hudson, 1990), 216. See also M. McMordie, 'Picturesque Pattern Books and Pre-Victorian Designers', *Architectural History*, 18 (1975), 43–59; N. Reynolds, 'Cottage Industry: The Ladies of Llangollen and the Symbolic Capital of the *Cottage Ornée*', *Eighteenth Century*, 51 (2010), 211–27.

35. E. Clark, *Ermina Montrose; or, The Cottage of the Vale*, 3 vols (1800), vol. i, 104.

36. For the success of this poem in a great many editions, often illustrated, see S. Jung, 'Print Culture, High-Cultural Consumption, and Thomson's "The Seasons", 1780–1797', *Eighteenth-Century Studies*, 44 (2011), 495–514.

37. J. Thomson, 'Autumn', *The Seasons*, ed. J. Sambrook (Oxford: Clarendon Press, 1981), line 340.

38. *OED*, s.v. 'silly', *adj.*, *n.*, and *adv.*, III.5.c.

39. F. Parfaict *et al.*, *Dictionnaire des théâtres de Paris*, vol. vi (1756), 83. For some reason Francis Delaval, who was present at the first night of *The Englishman in Paris*, reports that Miss Macklin sang 'an Italian song' (*Manuscripts of Sir William Fitzherbert, Bart.*, 201).

40. On the pastoral and imitation of the bagpipe drone see I. Ken'ichiro, 'Siciliano in der Instrumentalmusik Joseph Haydns und seiner Zeitgenossen: Untersuchungen zur kompositorischen Auseinandersetzung mit dem Topos im klassischen Stil', doctoral diss., Julius-Maximilians-Universität, Würzburg, 2014, 70ff.

41. C. Page, 'An Essay of 1824 on the Guitar', *Soundboard*, 38/4 (2012), 53–60, 75, at 57; see also J. Girdham, *English Opera in Late Eighteenth-Century London: Stephen Storace at Drury Lane* (Oxford: Clarendon Press, 1997), 103ff.

42. Note the eagerness of William Wilson (*A New Selection of the Most Admired Songs for the Guittar* (Aberdeen and Edinburgh, n.d. [*c*.1780])) to advertise, on his title page, the fact that he has provided true accompaniments rather than the method that 'HAS been used of playing the same notes that the Voice Sung'.

43. C. Cudworth, 'The Vauxhall "Lists"', *GSJ*, 20 (1967), 24–42; see also S. C. Foster, '"To Entertain the Fancy": The Orchestral Concert Song in England, 1740–1800', doctoral diss., Goldsmiths, University of London, 2013. D. Coke and A. Borg, *Vauxhall Gardens: A History* (New Haven and London: Yale University Press, 2011), offers a lavish account.

44. Anon., *Eliza: or, The History of Miss Granville*, 2 vols (1766), vol. i, 169–70; J. Raithby, *Delineations of the Heart; or, The History of Henry Bennet*, 3 vols (1792), vol. ii, 14. For a persuasive interpretation of the reputation and social importance of Blair's sermons, see W. St Clair, *The Reading Nation in the Romantic Period* (Cambridge: Cambridge University Press, 2004), 270–74.

45. *St. James's Chronicle or the British Evening Post*, 11–13 August 1761.

46. J. F. Hintz, *A Choice Collection of Psalm and Hymn Tunes set for the Cetra or Guittar* (n.d. [1760?]); T. Call, *The Tunes and Hymns as they are used at the Magdalen Chapel, Properly Set for the Organ, Harpsichord and Guittar* (n.d. [*c*.1760]).

47. A. Britton, 'The Guitar in the Romantic Period: Its Musical and Social Development with Special Reference to Bristol and Bath', doctoral diss., Royal Holloway, University of London, 2010, 79–80; Poulopoulos, 'The Guittar in the British Isles', 106ff.

48. For other eighteenth-century images of male guitar players, see Poulopoulos, 'The Guittar in the British Isles', 102–5.

49. For the issue of the English guitar and gender see Britton, 'The Guitar in the Romantic Period', 79–82, where the account is in places too reliant upon R. Leppert, *Music and Image: Domesticity, Ideology and Socio-Cultural Formation in Eighteenth-Century England*, new edn (Cambridge: Cambridge University Press, 1993).

50. See, for example, M. Cohen, '"Manners Make the Man": Politeness, Chivalry, and the Construction of Masculinity, 1750–1830', *Journal of British Studies*, 44 (2005), 312–29.

51. Anon., *The Feelings of the Heart; or, The History of a Country Girl*, 2 vols (1772), vol. ii, 71; C. Anstey, *The Mercenary Marriage*, 2 vols (1776), vol. i, 54.

52. Robins, ed., *The John Marsh Journals*, vol. i, 108–9: Marsh meets Miss Brown, his future wife; he spends an evening in a party that includes her, and tunes her guitar for her, she having 'just been taught a little on it' by Mr Blake, 'a gentleman at the excise Office, London'. The reverse situation, in which a man receives instruction from a woman, is rarely described. In *Eliza: or, The History of Miss Granville*, Miss Lennox plays at a gentleman's request and enslaves him with the combined beauty of her person and her playing; Eliza (whose beauty has taught her to be as contemptuous of male admiration as she is keen to excite it) reports that the gentleman was besotted with Miss Lennox and became her 'creature' as he sat down for some impromptu guitar lessons. His eyes were so engaged in gazing on her face 'that he profited little by her instructions' (vol. i, 121–2).

53. Anon., *Hartlebeurn Castle: A Descriptive English Tale*, 2 vols (1793), vol. i, 210.

54. O. Goldsmith, *The Vicar of Wakefield: A Tale*, 2 vols (1766), vol. i, 44.

55. A. M. Lysaght, *Joseph Banks in Newfoundland and Labrador, 1766: His Diary, Manuscripts and Collections* (Berkeley: University of California Press, 1971), 236. The repertoire Banks names in his letter was standard fare. 'Lady Coventry's Minuet' appears in *A Pocket Book for the Guitar* (*c*.1771), while 'In Infancy' is an air from Arne's opera *Artaxerxes*. For Banks as a macaroni see P. McNeil, *Pretty Gentlemen: Macaroni Men and the Eighteenth-Century Fashion World* (New Haven and London: Yale University Press, 2018).

56. Private collection. For related hairdresser images in other media, including porcelain, see McNeil, *Pretty Gentlemen*, 138–9.

57. C. H. Beale, ed., *Reminiscences of a Gentlewoman of the Last Century: Letters of Catherine Hutton* (Birmingham, 1891), 7–8.

58. Examples by all these artists, and more, are reproduced in Poulopoulos, 'The Guittar in the British Isles'.

59. E. Bonhôte, *Olivia; or, Deserted Bride*, 3 vols (1787), vol. iii, p. 140; Anon., *Belleville Lodge*, 2 vols (1793), vol. i, 80.

60. H. Man, *The Trifler* (1775) (Dublin, 1779), 189; Anon., *Montrose, or The Gothic Ruin*, 3 vols (1799), vol. i, 256.

61. Anon., *Eliza: or, The History of Miss Granville*, vol. i, 218.

62. S. Kelly, ed., *The Life of Mrs. Sherwood* (1854), 21–2.

63. Ibid., 136.

64. The song was published by Maurice Hime (Dublin, n.d. [*c*.1790]).

65. The seminal work was Thomas Percy's three-volume collection *Reliques of Ancient English Poetry: Consisting of Old Heroic Ballads, Songs and other Pieces of our Earlier Poets* (1765). Many of the ballads in this collection are bleak. A princess, disguised in homely array, makes her way to a secret assignation in a wood, not knowing that her lover has been murdered by robbers ('The King of France's Daughter'). A lover is poisoned by his rival ('Fair Rosamond'). A hunt on the Scottish borderlands leads to a murderous war ('Chevy Chase'). Such poems inspired many imitations, including the ballad often called 'The Hermit', written by Percy's friend Oliver Goldsmith and probably first published privately in 1765. In a novel of 1789, *The Vicar of Lansdowne* by Regina Maria Roche, material from Goldsmith's imitation of Percy's balladry is sung to a guitar (vol. i, 84). For a modern edition of Goldsmith's poem see R. Lonsdale, *The Poems of Thomas Gray, William Collins, Oliver Goldsmith*, new edn (1976), 596–605, with illuminating commentary at 596–7.

66. *Mary's Dream, or, Sandy's Ghost . . . set to Music by J. Relfe* (London, 1794).

67. G. Sheldrick, ed., *The Accounts of Thomas Green: Music Teacher and Tuner of Musical Instruments, 1742–1790* (Ware: Hertfordshire Record Society, 1992), 17–18. At this early date Green calls the English guitar the 'citron'. In addition to the accounts published by Sheldrick, there are Green's fair copies of his poems and other materials of interest in Hertfordshire Archives and Local Studies, D/EHX F56.

68. For a rich array of such portraits see C. S. Smith, *Eighteenth-Century Decoration: Design and the Domestic Interior in England* (New York: H. N. Abrams, 1993).

69. J. R. Harris, 'French Industrial Espionage in Britain in the Late Eighteenth Century', *RSA Journal*, 137 (1989), 629–34. All these metallic elements are discussed in detail, with photographs, in Poulopoulos, 'The Guittar in The British Isles'.

70. Derbyshire Record Office, D239 M/F 367.

71. Nottinghamshire Archives, DD/SY/169/xii. The writer comments that the piece 'may be had at Chelmsford'.

Chapter Three

1. A. Rees, *The Cyclopædia: or, Universal Dictionary of Arts, Sciences, and Literature*, 41 vols (1810–24), vol. xvii, s.v. 'Guitarra'. This is one of numerous articles on the historical and technical aspects of music that Burney wrote between 1801 and 1805, when he was an elderly man. He had notes going back many years to the period when he compiled his most celebrated work, *A General History of Music*, 4 vols (1776–89), supplemented by the memories of performers and personalities he had accumulated during his long and eventful life. At many points, as here, Burney's work for *The Cyclopædia* is all the more informative for his willingness to reminisce. For an illuminating discussion of Burney's work on the entries see R. Lonsdale, ed., *Dr. Charles Burney: A Literary Biography* (Oxford: Clarendon Press, 1965), 407–31. The article on the guitar was finally published posthumously in 1819 (Burney died in 1814). Some passages of Burney's multi-layered account of the guitar, though not the material relating to de Meneses, are a close paraphrase of the entry for the guitar in vol. vii of the *Encyclopédie* of Denis Diderot and Jean Le Rond d'Alembert, issued in 1757.

2. Rees, *The Cyclopædia*, vol. xvii, s.v. 'Guitarra': 'About 45 years ago, soon after the conspiracy at Lisbon, of Malagrida and others [December 1758], a Portuguese gentleman, or musician, with the appearance of a gentleman, of the name of Menesis [*sic*], probably involved in the plot, resided some time in London, seemingly as a man of fashion, who performed in a very superior manner on the large Spanish guitar strung with cat-gut or bowel-strings.' The executions of the alleged conspirators were widely reported in the London newspapers (as, for example, *Universal Chronicle, or Weekly Gazette*, 27 January – 3 February 1759). Burney may have been right about the political involvement of de Meneses, given intermarriage between his family and that of de Tavora, the latter the kindred accused and convicted of involvement in the failed assassination attempt. Further on de Meneses see J. Tyler and P. Sparks, *The Guitar and its Music from the Renaissance to the Classical Era* (Oxford: Oxford University Press, 2002), 204.

3. For such instruments see the account by Sparks in Tyler and Sparks, *The Guitar and its Music*, 195, 212–16, 229–32; see also R. Aleixo, *La guitarra en Madrid (1750–1808) con un catálogo de la música de ese periodo conservada en bibliotecas madrileñas* (Madrid: Spanish Society of Musicology, 2016), 194.

4. For the corpus of such sources, on which this chapter is primarily based, see C. Page, 'The Spanish Guitar in the Newspapers, Novels, Drama and Verse of Eighteenth-Century England', *RMARC*, 44 (2013), 1–18. For the Spanish guitar in eighteenth-century Britain, a subject very little explored, see Tyler and Sparks, *The Guitar and its Music*, 206–8.

5. There is a rich literature on the guitar in eighteenth-century France: see, for example, Tyler and Sparks, *The Guitar and its Music*, 198–206; P. Valois, 'Les guitaristes français entre 1770 et 1830', thesis, Laval University, Quebec, 2009. The two volumes of Saint-Arroman and Delume, *Méthodes et traités*, dedicated to the guitar offer facsimiles of some important methods and other materials (J. Saint-Arroman and C. Delume, eds, *Méthodes et traités*, ser. I: *Guitare, 1600–1800*, 2 vols (Courlay, 2003)). The French methods of the eighteenth century are catalogued in E. Stenstadvold, *An Annotated Bibliography of Guitar Methods, 1760–1860* (Hillsdale, NY: Pendragon Press, 2010).

6. For the decline by 1730, as noted by Jean de Castillion, see Saint-Arroman and Delume, eds, *Méthodes et traités*, vol. i, 51. For the guitar in de Garsault's *Notionnaire ou mémorial raisonné* (Paris, 1761) see ibid., 101, which offers a facsimile of the passage ('On s'est dégouté de cet instrument, qui ne peut enter dans aucun concert').

7. In his article on the guitar for vol. vii (1757) of Diderot and d'Alembert's *Encyclopédie*; facsimile of the entry in Saint-Arroman and Delume, eds, *Méthodes et traités*, vol. i, 63.

8. A facsimile of Campion's additions to the copy of his collection is in the edition by F. Lesure, *Nouvelles découvertes sur la guitarre, contenantes plusieurs suittes de pièces sur huit manières différentes d'accorder. Exemplaire augmenté de nombreuses pièces manuscrites de la main de l'auteur (Ms. Bibliothèque Nationale, Paris, Vm7 6221)* (Geneva, 1977)

9. For the testimony of Jean de Castillion see Saint-Arroman and Delume, eds, *Méthodes et traités*, vol. i, 54, mentioning strings partially wound (i.e. in a spiral pattern) with 'un fin filet de laiton ou d'argent, ce dernier en vaut mieux'. Castillion says that he makes his own strings because the ones on sale in the shops are fully wound, which makes the sound 'sec et dure'; he reports that he has been using such strings for a while, but that he does not know any other players who employ them.

10. Saint-Arroman and Delume, eds, *Méthodes et traités*, vol. i, 71 ('Cordes filées sur de la Soye'). I take the date of this treatise from Stenstadvold, *An Annotated Bibliography*, 28. For discussion of this treatise see Aleixo, *La guitarra en Madrid*, 169, 176, 18, etc. For a succinct but useful survey of string-making see Tyler and Sparks, *The Guitar and its Music*, 209–11; see also items by P. Barbieri and M. Peruffo in the bibliography.

11. Saint-Arroman and Delume, eds, *Méthodes et traités*, vol. i, 158.

12. P.-J. Baillon, *Nouvelle méthode de guitarre* (Paris, 1780), 3, with an extensive note explaining other dispositions for courses four and five: a *single* entirely overspun string or a *double* entirely overspun string. Baillon regards the first option as unsatisfactory because the sound is *maigre*, while the second makes it impossible (he claims) to pluck both strings at once. He adds that those who complain of a *féraillement* or 'clang' produced by the disposition he favours should examine the quality of their strings, the gradation of their frets and their plucking action.

13. Rees, *The Cyclopædia*, vol. xvii, s.v. 'Guitarra'. There are few traces of string manufacture using silk in eighteenth-century Britain. In 1774 a silk throwster named Peter Nouaille of Kent patented 'a method of making silk strings for all sorts of musical instruments', but there is no indication that they were overspun, and nothing came of this momentary intersection between the great tradition of Huguenot silk weaving in England and the needs of musicians ('A Method of Making Silk Strings for all Sorts of Musical Instruments', GB patent 1062, first awarded 22 January 1774; I am grateful to James Westbrook and Charles Pardoe for guiding me towards the full text of this patent). Nouaille advertised the strings in the *Gazetteer and New Daily Advertiser* for 19 May 1778. The stock of a London instrument-maker, Joseph Silcock, included two 'Engines for making Silver Strings' in 1742; these were presumably winding machines for producing what the Italian sources call *corde d'argento*: strings with a gut or silk core overspun with silver-plated copper wire (*Daily Advertiser*, 9 December 1742).

14. For further discussion of the arpeggio see A. Britton, 'The Guitar in the Romantic Period: Its Musical and Social Development with Special Reference to Bristol and Bath', doctoral diss., Royal Holloway, University of London, 2010, 38–40.

15. [J.] Deleplanque, *Recueil d'airs . . . pour la harpe* (Paris, n.d.); F. Petrini, *Recueil de pieces et d'airs choisis, avec accompagnement de harpe* (Paris, n.d.).

16. P. Denis, *Troisième et dernière partie de la méthode pour apprendre à jouer de la mandoline sans maître* (Paris, 1773), 3, in which Denis shows how to accompany the voice.

17. Baillon, *Nouvelle méthode*, 5, argues for a notational separation, using staff notation modelled on usage for the harp and the pianoforte, between the bass notes and the accompanying harmony in a guitar arpeggio.

18. F. Campion, *Addition au traité d'accompagnement* (Paris, 1730; repr. Geneva, 1976), 40.

19. [G. or B.] Merchi, *Traité des agrémens de la musique* (Paris, 1777; repr. Geneva, 1981), 10.

20. D. Foskett, *Miniatures: Dictionary and Guide* (Woodbridge: Antique Collectors Club, 1987), 675.

21. *Morning Herald and Daily Advertiser*, 26 February 1782.

22. Ibid., 23 June 1783.

23. *Bath Chronicle*, 12 June 1788.

24. Ibid., 1 February 1787.

25. K. Carpenter, *Refugees of the French Revolution: Émigrés in London, 1789–1802* (Basingstoke: Macmillan Press, 1999).

26. *The World*, 3 June 1789. See J. Carpentier, *Methode distribuée par leçons pour apprendre en peu de temps à jouer de l'instrument appellé cytre où [sic] guitthare allemande* (Paris, 1771) in Saint-Arroman and Delume, eds, *Méthodes et traités*, vol. i, 171.

27. *The World*, 9 October 1790.

28. *RISM* id. 551005037 (accessed 27 November 2018). I am grateful to Damián Martín, who is currently conducting research on Vidal.

29. A. Devriès-Lesure, *L'édition musicale dans la presse parisienne au XVIIIe siècle: catalogue des annonces* (Paris: CNRS Éditions, 2005), 520; for the many publications by Vidal noted or reviewed in contemporary sources, such as the *Journal Général de France*, see ibid., 520–22. For Vidal's methods see Stenstadvold, *An Annotated Bibliography*, 194–5.

30. There are several (unplayable) six-note chords, which must be an error.

31. *Oracle: Bell's New World*, 26 August 1789.

32. Marie-Françoise Henriette Laché sometimes went back and forth as an intermediary for Sainte-Foy between London and Paris; see A. Doyon, 'Maximilien Radix de Sainte-Foy, 1736–1810', *Revue d'Histoire Diplomatique*, 80 (1966), 231–74, 314–54. There is a good summary of her life in J. Major and S. Munden, *An Infamous Mistress: The Life, Loves and Family of the Celebrated Grace Dalrymple Elliott* (Barnsley: Pen & Sword, 2016), 125–7, 139, 190. The title 'St Aubin' remains unexplained, but it is curious that the lady's will, made in England and in English, gives her address in 1804 as St Albans Street in St James's (TNA, PROB 11/1411/242).

33. As revealed by Marie-Françoise Henriette Laché's will (see previous note), where she states that the couple's daughter, Harriet, was born on 13 November 1789. For Harriet see www.thepeerage.com/p2620.htm#i26194 (accessed 24 November, 2018).

34. P. McNeil, *Pretty Gentlemen: Macaroni Men and the Eighteenth-Century Fashion World* (New Haven and London: Yale University Press, 2018), 127.

35. H. L. Piozzi, *Observations and Reflections made in the Course of a Journey*, 2 vols (1789), vol. ii, 235.

36. For images and descriptions of Italian guitars of the late eighteenth century into the nineteenth see L. Frignani, A. Radice and T. Rizzi, *La chitarra in Italia tra la fine del Settecento e l'inizio dell'Ottocento* (Modena: LF Edizioni, 2015).

37. *London Chronicle*, 24–6 July 1760. For Passerini see *BD*, vol. xi, s.v. 'Passerini, Giuseppe'; S. McVeigh, *Concert Life in London from Mozart to Haydn* (Cambridge: Cambridge University Press, 1993), 94, 113, 119, etc.; S. McVeigh, *The Violinist in London's Concert Life, 1750–1784: Felice Giardini and his Contemporaries* (New York: Garland, 1989), 17–18.

38. *Public Advertiser*, 27 February 1753.

39. For Merchi in the Netherlands see Rasch, *Geschiedenis van de Muziek in de Republiek der Zeven Verenigde Nederlanden, 1572–1795*. ch. 13: 'Het concertwezen', at www.let.uu.nl/~Rudolf.Rasch/ personal/Republiek/Republiek13Concerten.pdf (accessed 2 November 2018). I am grateful to Jelma van Amersfoot for this reference. See also *Dizionario biografico degli Italiani*, vol. lxxiii (2009), s.v. 'Merchi'. On 7 April 1766 a panel in the *Public Advertiser* gives his name as G. Merchi; it appears in another advertisement as 'J. Merchi' (*Public Advertiser*, 10 February 1769) and once in full as 'Giacomo Merchi' (ibid., 28 May 1768).

40. *Public Advertiser*, 7 April 1766.

41. Ibid., 10 February 1769.

42. Ibid., 15 January 1774.

43. Ibid., 7 April 1766; see Stenstadvold, *An Annotated Bibliography*, 140.

44. Merchi, *Traité des agrémens*, 2.

45. For an example by Vuillaume and Giron, Troyes, *c.*1790, see J. Westbrook and T. Fuller, *The Complete Illustrated Book of the Acoustic Guitar* (Wigston, Leics.: Lorenz Books, 2012), 186 (right). I am grateful to James Westbrook for the chance to examine this instrument.

46. Merchi, *Traité des agrémens*, 5 ('secs et disgratieux').

47. H. Belsey, *Thomas Gainsborough: The Portraits, Fancy Pictures and Copies after Old Masters*, 2 vols (New Haven: Yale University Press, 2019), vol. ii, 807–9, fig. 872.1.

48. M. New and P. de Voogd, eds, *The Florida Edition of the Works of Laurence Sterne*, vol. viii (Gainesville, Fla: University Press of Florida, 2009), 539: 'my daughter begs a present of me – tis a Guittar – it must be strung with cat gut & of 5 Cords – si chiama in Italiano, "La Chitera di cinque corde" – She cannot get such a Thing at Merseilles – at Paris one may have every thing – would you be so good to my Girl as to make her happy in this affaire, by getting some musical Body to buy one, & send it to her to Avignon directed to Monsr. Teste.'

49. *Bath Chronicle and Weekly Gazette*, 28 December 1768. Merchi had performed in Bath the previous month (ibid., 24 November 1768).

50. Dulwich Picture Gallery, DPG320; Belsey, *Thomas Gainsborough: The Portraits*, vol. ii, 555–7. It should be noted that Gainsborough painted the portrait in 1771–2 but retouched it substantially in 1785 at the request of Mary Linley (seated to the viewer's right), partly to bring the sisters' clothing and hairstyles into accord with current fashions (J. Ingamells, *Dulwich Picture Gallery Collections: British* (Unicorn Press, 2008), 134). Traces of the earlier version may still be seen and they suggest that the guitar on which Elizabeth leans was moved to the right at this stage; it remains unknown what other changes were made, but close inspection of the original shows that the instrument has five strings, which it may have possessed from the beginning or acquired in the retouching.

51. *Gazetteer and New Daily Advertiser*, 31 January 1780, and repeatedly thereafter.

52. B. Robins, ed., *The John Marsh Journals: The Life and Times of a Gentleman Composer (1752–1828)*, 2 vols (1998, 2013), vol. i, 252–3.

53. *Morning Chronicle and London Advertiser*, 13 April 1785.

54. For Noferi see R. Southey, 'Commercial Music-Making in Eighteenth Century North-East England: A Pale Reflection of London?', doctoral diss., 2 vols, University of Newcastle upon Tyne, 2001, vol. i, 125, etc.; S. D. I. Fleming, 'A Century of Music Production in Durham City, 1711–1811: A Documentary Study', doctoral diss., University of Durham, 2009, 99–100, 336. See also *BD*, vol. xi, s.v. 'Noferi, Giovanni Battista'; C. Price, J. Milhous and R. D. Hume, *Italian Opera in Late Eighteenth-Century London*, vol. i: *The King's Theatre, Haymarket, 1778–1791* (Oxford: Clarendon Press, 1995), 438, 447, 450–52, 457.

55. *Public Advertiser*, 25 February 1782.

56. J. T. Dillon, *Letters from an English Traveller in Spain, in 1778* (1781), 4; A. Jardine, *Letters from Barbary, France, Spain, Portugal, etc. by an English Officer*, 2 vols (1788), vol. ii, 182.

57. H. Swinburne, *Travels through Spain, in the Years 1775 and 1776* (Dublin, 1779), 83, 92. Some travellers, however, did express admiration for the music and guitars that Swinburne and others denounced. Francis Carter's travelogue *A Journey from Gibraltar to Malaga*, 3 vols (1777) admires the 'tuneful Seguidillas' that he heard and the 'sprightly fandango' (vol. iii, 428), while *A journey from London to Genoa, through England, Portugal, Spain, and France*, 4 vols (1770), by Giuseppe Baretti, a writer well known to Boswell and Johnson, finds the fandango greatly exhilarating and notes its seductive character (vol. ii, 48–9).

58. *BD*, vol. xiii, s.v. 'Ross, Mme'. The act was widely publicised and admired.

59. *London Chronicle*, 11–13 June 1778; *Morning Chronicle and London Advertiser*, 6 October 1785.

60. *True Briton*, 4 May 1796.

61. Price, Milhous and Hume, *Italian Opera*, vol. i, 286, 321.

62. *Gazetteer and New Daily Advertiser*, 14 February 1784.

63. *Morning Post*, 26 June 1784.

64. Robins, ed., *The John Marsh Journals*, vol. i, 309–10.

65. The cost of printing was borne by Culliford, Rolfe and Barrow, a partnership that had just opened a warehouse in Cheapside offering 'Grand and small Piano Fortes, Harpsichords, and Guitars, of every

description'; they may have commissioned *Compleat Instructions* as their 'house' method for the guitar to accompany a new stock of instruments (*Morning Chronicle*, 30 May 1795). The firm also advertised their warehouse in the French émigré newspaper *Courier de Londres* for 16 June 1795, announcing the sale of pianofortes of various sizes and 'diverses autres instrumens de leur manufacture'.

66. *BD*, vol. iii, s.v. 'Chabran, Francesco [Felice?]'. See also J. Milhous, G. Dideriksen and R. D. Hume, *Italian Opera in Late Eighteenth-Century London*, vol. ii: *The Pantheon Opera and its Aftermath, 1789–1795* (Oxford: Clarendon Press, 2001), 46, 100, 400ff. For this and other methods by Chabran see Stenstadvold, *An Annotated Bibliography*, 75–7.

67. B. Trowell, 'Mozart's Fandango', *Music and Letters*, 50 (1969), 427–8.

68. R. Twiss, *Travels through Portugal and Spain, in 1772 and 1773* (1775), between pp. 156 and 157.

69. For Stangate Street as a musicians' quarter see J. Doane, *A Musical Directory for the Year 1794* (1794; repr. 1993), 11, 15, 34, 41–2 (two examples), 62; see also D. A. Rohr, *The Careers of British Musicians, 1750–1850: A Profession of Artisans* (Cambridge: Cambridge University Press, 2001), 57. Chabran took out an insurance policy in August 1794 to cover his house, clothing and musical instruments: London Metropolitan Archives, MS 11936/401/620765, 18 August 1794.

70. Lambeth Archives, LBL/DCEPS/SL/1/351.

71. *GISE*, 201–2.

72. *Blouzelind*, stipple engraving and etching after Henry William Bunbury (1792), London, British Museum, 1878,0511.831.

73. This air was also associated with the text 'Sawney will never be my love again'; see *GISE*, 90, 226; C. M. Simpson, ed., *The British Broadside Ballad and its Music* (New Brunswick, NJ: Rutgers University Press, 1966), 632–5.

74. 'Pleyel' (F. Chabran, *Compleat Instructions for the Spanish Guitar* (1795), 14) is from *Symphonie concertante* in E flat, for violin, viola, violoncello and oboe concertant, second movement, 'Andante grazioso', first section; R. Benton, *Ignace Pleyel: A Thematic Catalogue of his Compositions* (New York: Pendragon Press, 1977), 11–17, lists numerous adaptations and arrangements, but not this one. 'Air, Pleyel' (ibid., 18) is from the second section, 'Thema con Varia', of the first quartet in a set of six; Benton, *Ignace Pleyel*, 114–19. 'Air. Pleyel' (ibid., 21) is from a string quartet, second section, 'Andante ma non troppo, Variationi'; Benton, *Ignace Pleyel*, 99–105. The third of these airs was published in a vocal version entitled 'The Miniature' (n.d. [1794?]) with a texted and purely monophonic version for English guitar.

Chapter Four

1. For the material and technical aspects of the guitar in England at this time see J. Westbrook, 'Guitar Making in Nineteenth-Century London: Louis Panormo and his Contemporaries', doctoral diss., University of Cambridge, 2013, 27ff.

2. M. Latcham, 'Harpsichord-piano', in *Oxford Music Online*, www.oxfordmusiconline.com (accessed 4 April 2019); M. Latcham, 'Pianos and Harpsichords', ibid.

3. *Public Advertiser*, 15 January 1774.

4. *Morning Post*, 23 August 1800. The term used is 'Spanish mandolin', perhaps a *mandolino* or a *bandurria*, a plucked and fretted instrument of Portugal, which was then strung with gut and commonly played with a plectrum; but the instrument may have been an Italian mandolin, for such instruments (also gut-strung) were widely available in later eighteenth-century Spain. See K. Kenyon de Pascual, 'Ventas de instrumentos musicales en Madrid durante la segunda mitad del siglo XVIII, II', *Revista de Musicología*, 6 (1983), 299–308, at 302, noting a number of Italian mandolins being offered for sale in the Spanish capital.

5. A. Rees, *The Cyclopædia: or, Universal Dictionary of Arts, Sciences, and Literature*, 41 vols (1810–24), vol. xvii, s.v. 'Guitarra'; 'Sir B. Sketchwell', *London Characters: or, Fashions and Customs of the Present Century*, 2nd edn, 2 vols (1809), vol. i, 293–4.

6. [E. W. Buckham], *A Personal Narrative of Adventures in the Peninsula during the War in 1812–1813, by an Officer* (1827), 228; the letter is dated 26 July 1811, but was probably rewritten for publication.

7. *A Fireside Book*, 59. The story is set in the first years of the eighteenth century, but the musical fashions assumed are those of late Georgian England.

8. *Morning Herald*, 28 June 1799.

9. For the first six-string guitars in London see J. Westbrook, *The Century that Shaped the Guitar: From the Birth of the Six-String Guitar to the Death of Tárrega* (Hove: James Westbrook, 2005), 45–8.

10. National Portrait Gallery, London, NPG 1770. For Burney's remarks see Rees, *The Cyclopædia*, vol. xvii, s.v. 'Guitarra'.

11. J. Beresford, *The Miseries of Human Life*, 2 vols (1807), vol. ii, 90. He is presumably referring to old and worn strings of overspun silk.

12. For the exhibition see *Morning Post*, 3 May 1802; for Mrs Mountain see *ODNB*, s.v. 'Mountain [née Wilkinson], Rosemund'. *The Gipsey Prince*, a collaboration between Thomas Moore and Michael Kelly, was performed at the Theatre Royal in the Haymarket; at one point there is the stage direction 'Enter Antonia singing to the accompaniment of her Guittar', while another specifies that she 'Strikes the Chords of her Guittar'. For a facsimile of the text of *The Gipsey Prince* see https://romantic-circles.org/editions/gipsy_prince. The cast list is printed in the *Union Magazine and Imperial Register*, 2 (June–December 1801), 57.

13. [G.] Merchi, *Le guide des écoliers de guitarre* (Paris, 1761; repr. Geneva, 1981), p. iv. The *Methode pour aprendre a joüer de la guitarre* by Don *** (Paris and Madrid, 1758) uses both notation and tablature, but makes no comment on that practice (facsimile in J. Saint-Arroman and C. Delume, eds, *Méthodes et traités*, 18: *Guitare*, ser. I: *France, 1600–1800*, 2 vols (Courlay, 2003), vol. i, 69–100). For the situation in eighteenth-century Spain, almost certainly the compiler's homeland, see R. Aleixo, *La guitarra en Madrid (1750–1808) con un catálogo de la música de ese periodo conservada en bibliotecas madrileñas* (Madrid: Spanish Society of Musicology, 2016), 270–89. Burney's entry on the guitar in Rees, *The Cyclopædia*, vol. xvii, s.v. 'Guitarra', drafted between 1801 and 1805, discusses tablature extensively, suggesting that Burney was using very old notes (or recollections) and was working under pressure. For a wider discussion see E. Stenstadvold, 'The Evolution of Guitar Notation, 1750–1830', *Soundboard*, 31/2–3 (2005), 11–29; J. Tyler and P. Sparks, *The Guitar and its Music from the Renaissance to the Classical Era* (Oxford: Oxford University Press, 2002), 198–202.

14. In Spain guitars with six double courses had appeared by the 1760s, and although at least one such instrument rapidly made its way to Britain (see Fig. 13) they were not widely received beyond Iberia. The lyres that were fashionable in the decades either side of 1800, especially in France, were often equipped with six strings, sometimes more; these instruments were shaped like antique lyres and supplied with fingerboards, but it is unclear whether it makes sense to speak of their influence upon the guitar, since they were themselves effectively guitars, redesigned to gratify neoclassical taste. The earliest surviving example is French and dates from 1785 (Yale University, Belle Skinner Collection, 4581). For an account of the lyre and a diagram showing six strings see C. Doisy, *Principes généraux de la guitare*, 2 pts (1801; pt i repr. Geneva, 1979), 70–74; for extant instruments see S. Bonner, *The Classic Image: European History and Manufacture of the Lyre Guitar, 850–1840* (Harlow: Bois de Boulogne, 1972); U. Wedemeier, *Gitarre, Zister, Laute* (Hanover: Verlag Ulrich Wedemeier, 2012), 24, 26. There are numerous representations in French art, notably J.-A.-D. Ingres, *Portrait of the Family of Lucien Bonaparte*, 1815 (Harvard Art Museums / Fogg Museum, Bequest of Grenville L. Winthrop).

15. The *Morning Chronicle*, 23 January 1801, advertised a separate publication, *Four Canzonets, with a Spanish Guitar Accompaniment, by Mrs Dussek*, published by

Monzani and Cimador at the Opera Music Warehouse, but it is not known to survive.

16. Lolli was buried in the cemetery of St Mary, Paddington Green, 30 August 1805; London Metropolitan Archives, P87/MRY/060.

17. For periodical publication in the Georgian period see Y. L. An, 'The Periodical Music Collections of John Bland', in M. Kassler, ed., *The Music Trade in Georgian England* (Farnham: Ashgate, 2011), 195–229.

18. In contrast to many guitarists before him, Sperati was a trained musician, a cellist who played at various times in the orchestras of the King's Theatre, the Pantheon, and the Antient Music in Tottenham Street. For Sperati as a cellist see Anon., *Concerts of Antient Music, under the Patronage of Their Majesties as Performed at the New Rooms, Tottenham-Street* (1792), p. xv; for Sperati as an arranger for the keyboard see D. Corri, *Select Collection of the most Admired Songs, Duetts, etc. from Operas in the Highest Esteem, and from other Works*, 4 vols (1795), vol. iv, 90, 92. Sperati's will, proved 19 June 1846, is TNA, PROB/11/2038/384.

19. Sperati's *Periodical Collection* is presumably to be identified with the 'Eleven Numbers of the Spanish Guitar' advertised by the collection's publishers, Monzani and Cimador, in the *Morning Post* on 15 May 1801 and described there (for what it may be worth) as 'just published'. The 'Eleven Numbers' would be nos 2–12, no. 1 being Sperati's method (see note 21). The two songs to French texts, nos 8 and 9, 'O douce paix' and 'Sous le nom d'amitié', may both refer to the peace negotiations with Napoleon, which were under way by mid-1801 and which led to the short-lived Treaty of Amiens in 1802.

20. B. Sperati, *A Periodical Collection*, no. 12 (1802), 2.

21. E. Stenstadvold, *An Annotated Bibliography of Guitar Methods, 1760–1860* (Hillsdale, NY: Pendragon Press, 2010), 184–5, with much useful information. For some reason the appearance of the method was delayed, for it was not advertised until 1802 (*Morning Post*, 9 April), while the musical numbers (nos 2–12) had started to appear in 1801.

22. Surrey History Centre, Woking, 2185/JB/42/4, 28 September 1807. Miss Thomas of 35 Parliament Street was either Jane or Mary Thomas, who were sisters then living at this address; their father was a clerk in the Poll Office in His Majesty's Exchequer, so this was a family of the middling sort. The father's will, mentioning both daughters and describing the testator as formerly of Parliament Street, is TNA, PROB/11/1506/454.

23. R. J. S. Stevens, forty-second lecture on musical history, delivered at Gresham College, in 1829, Corporation of London, Guildhall Library, London, G. Mus. 472, box 4, p. 71. For the dating of Viganoni's performances, remembered by Stevens, see T. Fenner,

Opera in London: Views of the Press, 1785–1830 (Carbondale: Southern Illinois University Press, 1994), 167–8; *BD*, vol. xv, s.v. 'Viganoni, Giuseppe'. There may be a trace of Viganoni's repertoire in S. Mayr, *Three Cavatine for Voice and an Accompaniment, either for Piano Forte, Harp, or Spanish Guitar, the Last with a Flute, or Violin Obligato, Composed . . . for . . . Mr Viganoni by S. Mayr* (n.d. [1805?]), Killerton House, Devon (National Trust).

24. *Morning Post*, 21 December 1802. For Rovedino, see below, p. 260 (Chapter 7, n. 63).

25. *Morning Post*, 4 April 1810. The term 'French guitar', not often found in English sources, is commonly taken to mean a guitar with single strings (see T. F. Heck, 'The Vogue of the *chitarra francese* in Italy: How French? How Italian? How Neapolitan?', *Soundboard*, 38/4 (2012), 18–24, 44). There are at least three published songs composed by Luigi Gianella for Tramezzani, with guitar arrangements: 'Un Cestellin di fiori: Canzonetta, with an Accompaniment for the Piano Forte or Spanish Guitar' and 'Vien qua Dorina bella: Canzonetta, with an Accompaniment for the Piano Forte or Spanish Guitar Composed Expressly for Signor Tramezzani' are both in the British Library and are duly listed in I. Gammie, *Nineteenth-Century Guitar Songs: An Idiosyncratic Survey* (St Albans: Corda Music Publications, 2017), 75; these two songs, with a third ('Ve chi sprezza'), are also in the Arts and Social Sciences Library, Bristol, Special Collections, STORE 607780, Songs III.

26. Earl of Mount Edgcumbe, *Musical Reminiscences*, 3rd edn (1828), 96.

27. Byron, *Don Juan*, Canto XIII, stanza 83. See S. McVeigh, *Concert Life in London from Mozart to Haydn* (Cambridge: Cambridge University Press, 1993), 54–5; W. Weber, 'La culture musicale d'une capitale: l'époque du beau monde à Londres, 1700–1870', *Revue d'Histoire Moderne et Contemporaine*, 49 (2002–3), 119–39'.

28. H. More, *Strictures on the Modern System of Female Education*, 3rd edn, 2 vols (1799), vol. ii, 138. For a contemporary view of the routs, by one who was caught up (unwillingly) in the new fashion for them, see A. Bell, *The Cabinet: A Series of Essays Moral and Literary*, 2 vols (1835), vol. i, 30–38. Compare I. Taylor, *Music in London and the Myth of Decline: From Haydn to the Philharmonic* (Cambridge: Cambridge University Press, 2010), 116–24.

29. For the notion of the beau monde see H. Greig, *The Beau Monde: Fashionable Society in Georgian London* (Oxford: Oxford University Press, 2013); for more specifically musical reflections see Weber, 'La culture musicale d'une capitale'; W. Weber, *The Great Transformation of Musical Taste: Concert Programming from Haydn to Brahms* (Cambridge: Cambridge University Press, 2008), 21–3.

30. *Morning Chronicle*, 4 March 1799.

31. Emma Hamilton was a noted and influential exponent of the art. For her portraiture in this context see Q. Colville and K. Williams, eds, *Emma Hamilton: Seduction and Celebrity* (Thames and Hudson, 2016), 140–41, 160ff. On 19 March 1798 an article in the *Evening Mail* noted that the 'management of the *Tambourine* is becoming an accomplishment in the female world of fashion. Nothing is better calculated to *set* off an elegant figure by displaying the person in the most beautiful attitudes.' For Adam Buck's portrait *Tambarina* see P. Darvall, *A Regency Buck: Adam Buck (1759–1833)* (Oxford: Ashmolean Museum, 2015), 44.

32. *Morning Herald*, 14 May 1792.

33. British Museum, London, 1867,0713.413

34. *Morning Post*, 29 May 1801. Emma Hamilton had encountered the guitar during her time in Naples, where she had resided with her husband, the ambassador Sir William Hamilton. During her time there, Giuseppe Aprile dedicated his *Sei canzoncine*, with accompaniment for violin and a 'Chitarra francese' to 'Miledi Hamilton', perhaps as a wedding gift. The title page is reproduced in Heck, 'The Vogue of the *chitarra francese* in Italy', 21. For Emma's performances in Naples, and her deep immersion in the musical culture of the city, see J. M. Kelly, 'A Classical Education: Naples at the Heart of European Culture', in Colville and Williams, eds, *Emma Hamilton: Seduction and Celebrity*, 108–37, at 128–32, 274 n. 7.

35. Zaniboni may only recently have begun to teach and play the six-string guitar when this collection was published; a surviving guitar of *c*.1800, now in the collection of Edinburgh University, bears the label 'A Zaniboni', almost certainly the same individual; there are eight peg-holes in the head but the ebony nut is set for six strings; see A. Myers, ed., *Historic Musical Instruments in the Edinburgh University Collection: Catalogue of the Edinburgh University Collection of Historic Musical Instruments*, 9 pts (Edinburgh: Edinburgh University Collection of Historic Musical Instruments, 1997–2007), 2/B, pt ii, 36–7, inv. no. 2330; for the possibility that such guitars were tuned to a major chord, like the English guitar, see Westbrook, 'Guitar Making in Nineteenth-Century London', 33 (who discusses the Zaniboni instrument).

36. *Morning Post*, 16 June 1801.

37. Fenner, *Opera in London*, 286, 333.

38. *Morning Post*, 12 February 1802.

39. *Morning Post*, 16 February 1802.

40. H. Sugimoto, 'The Harp-Lute in Britain, 1800–1830: A Study of the Inventor Edward Light and his Instruments', doctoral diss., 2 vols, University of Edinburgh, 2015, 144; T. Takeuchi, 'Rediscovering the Regency Lute: A Checklist of Musical Sources and Extant Instruments', *EM*, 46 (2018), 17–34.

41. *Wiener Zeitung*, 17 October 1804. I am grateful to Gerhard Penn for this reference.

42. The date of the inception of the English series is confirmed by a spin-off publication entitled *Three Ariettes ... Extracted from the Periodical Amusements*, comprising items from three different numbers of the series (6, 7, 9) with a watermark of 1807 (private collection). Complete sets of the *Periodical Amusements* are rare. A set in its original binding (with 'Bortolazzi's Spanish Music' stamped on the cover) is currently in private hands. The set in the Bayerische Staatsbibliothek in Munich, which has the subscribers' list attached to the twelfth number, may be viewed on the library's site at https://opacplus.bsb-muenchen.de/metaopac/search?&query=periodical%20amusements (accessed 7 July 2018). Another set is in the Spencer Collection, Royal Academy of Music, London; this was the property of a Miss Ashburner, who bound the individual parts with her name embossed in gold on a leather label. Her family seems to have had some personal connection to Bortolazzi. She is very likely to be one of the daughters of William Ashburner, who died in Bombay in 1790; two of the Ashburner sisters married into a family called Forbes, and Bortolazzi published *Waltz with Six Easy Variations for a Spanish Guitar and Flute Accompt. ad libitum Composed and Dedicated to Miss Elisabeth Forbes* (*c*.1807), presumably of the same family.

43. The list of subscribers appeared at the end of the twelfth number, but was discarded before some of the surviving sets were bound (see previous note).

44. As revealed by Louis Spohr in his autobiography, recounting an evening he spent at the duke's home. Most English readers knew the relevant passage from the anonymous translation, *Louis Spohr's Autobiography: Translated from the German* (1865), 90–91: 'During a conversation we had upon the subject of English national songs, the Duke even sent for his guitar and sang to me some English and Irish national songs, which afterwards suggested to me the idea of working up some of the most popular of these as a pot-pourri for my instrument, and of introducing the same at my concert.' The duke later received the dedication of guitar-accompanied songs by Antonio Francalanza and of a guitar method by Charles Sola, but he is best remembered for the favour he showed a far greater guitarist, namely Fernando Sor. For his connections with Francalanza, see p. 197 below; for Sor's own account of his connections to the duke see B. Jeffery, *Fernando Sor: Composer and Guitarist*, 2nd edn (Tecla Editions, 1994), 129.

45. Fenner, *Opera in London*, 210, 288–9.

46. Reproduced in C. Page, 'New Light on the London Years of Fernando Sor, 1815–1822', *EM*, 41 (2013), 557–60, at 559.

47. A. Pitman, *The Miseries of Music Masters* (1815).

Chapter Five

1. This was partly in the hope of preventing the Spanish American colonies, an object of considerable economic and quasi-imperial interest to the British, from falling into French hands: R. C. Heinowitz, *Spanish America and British Romanticism, 1777–1826: Rewriting Conquest* (Edinburgh: Edinburgh University Press, 2010), 132. For British conceptions of Iberia during the romantic period see J. M. Almeida, ed., *Romanticism and the Anglo-Hispanic Imaginary* (Amsterdam and New York: Rodopi, 2010); D. Saglia, *Poetic Castles in Spain: British Romanticism and Figurations of Iberia* (Amsterdam: Rodopi, 2000); D. Saglia, 'War Romances, Historical Analogies and Coleridge's Letters on the Spaniards', in P. Shaw, ed., *Romantic Wars: Studies in Culture and Conflict, 1793–1822* (Aldershot: Ashgate, 2000), 138–60.

2. *Morning Post*, 28 July 1808.

3. C. Kennedy, *Narratives of the Revolutionary and Napoleonic Wars: Military and Civilian Experience in Britain and Ireland* (Basingstoke: Palgrave Macmillan, 2013), 171–8. For the vastness of the war effort see R. Knight, *Britain Against Napoleon: The Organization of Victory, 1793–1815* (Allen Lane, 2013).

4. Quoted in S. Valladares, *Staging the Peninsular War: English Theatres, 1807–1815* (Abingdon: Routledge, 2015), 1.

5. Ibid., 132–3, 427 (calendar of performances of *The Castle of Andalusia*).

6. D. B. Oleksijczuk, *The First Panoramas: Visions of British Imperialism* (Minneapolis: University of Minnesota Press, 2011), 6. For the songs and dance tunes see E. Buurman and O. C. Jensen, '"Dancing the Waterloo Waltz": Commemorations of the Hundred Days – Parallels in British Social Dance and Song', in K. Astbury and M. Philp, eds, *Napoleon's Hundred Days and the Politics of Legitimacy* (Basingstoke: Palgrave Macmillan, 2018), 209–32.

7. *Morning Chronicle*, 4 August 1809. In eighteenth-century sources the term seems only to appear in the (variously spelled) name of the tune *Lillibolero*.

8. *Morning Post*, 17 May 1810.

9. *Bath Chronicle and Weekly Gazette*, 19 March 1812. The advertisement adds that this is 'the first time an opportunity has been offered of hearing this peculiar style of Music in England' (where 'peculiar' carries its established but now specialised sense of 'special' or 'distinctive': *OED*, s.v. 'peculiar', *adj.* and *n.*, A.1.a.).

10. J. A. Junco, 'The Formation of Spanish Identity and its Adaptation to the Age of Nations', *History and Memory*, 14 (2002), 13–36.

11. *Manchester Mercury*, 16 October 1810; *Kentish Gazette and Canterbury Journal*, 5 October 1810.

12. The passage was much admired and was quoted in various periodicals and newspapers: see *La Belle Assemblée*, 1 March 1812; *Morning Chronicle*, 14 March 1812.

13. *Kentish Gazette and Canterbury Journal*, 30 July 1813.

14. E. Stenstadvold, *An Annotated Bibliography of Guitar Methods, 1760–1860* (Hillsdale, NY: Pendragon Press, 2010), 171–2.

15. Kennedy, *Narratives of the Revolutionary and Napoleonic Wars*, 28.

16. *The Times*, 11 June 1812.

17. Ibid., 31 August 1812.

18. A. B. Granville, *Autobiography of A. B. Granville*, 2nd edn, 2 vols (1874), vol. i, 57.

19. See, for example, *Carlisle Patriot*, 22 November 1817; *Chester Chronicle*, 21 November 1817; *Hereford Journal*, 19 November 1817; *Lancaster Gazette*, 29 November 1817. This obituary is quoted in the earliest of the independent memoirs (E. Hamilton, *A Record of the Life and Death of Her Royal Highness Princess Charlotte* (1817), 4).

20. A. Aspinall, ed., *Letters of the Princess Charlotte, 1811–1817* (1949), 72 (19 November 1817). On 4 November 2008 a guitar of *c.*1800, 'reputedly thought to have belonged to H.R.H. Princess Charlotte', was sold at Bonhams (www.bonhams.com/auctions/16013/lot/13).

21. J. W. Kaye, ed., *Autobiography of Miss Cornelia Knight, Lady Companion to the Princess Charlotte of Wales*, 3rd edn, 2 vols (1861), vol. i, 232; R. Fulford, ed., *The Autobiography of Miss Knight, Lady Companion to Princess Charlotte* (1960), 31. Charlotte also used the Vaccaris to practise her Italian (Aspinall, ed., *Letters of the Princess Charlotte*, 74).

22. A second number appears to be known only from a single copy, which has no title page and yet appears to be complete. I am grateful to James Westbrook for the loan of this publication. Charlotte received the dedication of music by another Spanish exile in London, the pianist Mariano Rodríguez de Ledesma: *Three Italian Ariettes, with an Accompaniment for Spanish Guitar and Piano Forte* (1814).

23. Aspinall, ed., *Letters of the Princess Charlotte*, 79.

24. For studies of the Peninsular War memoirs see G. Daly, *The British Soldier in the Peninsular War: Encounters with Spain and Portugal, 1808–1814* (Basingstoke and New York: Palgrave Macmillan, 2013); J. G. C. Fernández, 'La mirada del Inglés: historia y vivencias sociales del los combatientes británicos en España y Portugal', *Historia Social*, 72 (2012), 23–47; Kennedy, *Narratives of the Revolutionary and Napoleonic*

Wars; C. Santacara, *La Guerra de la Independencia vista por los británicos, 1808–1814* (Madrid: Antonio Machado Libros, 2005); J. R. Watson, *Romanticism and War: A Study of British Romantic Period Writers and the Napoleonic Wars* (Basingstoke and New York: Palgrave Macmillan, 2003), 197. Valladares, *Staging the Peninsular War*, 9 n., lists other recent studies in Spanish. See also B. Jeffery, *España de la guerra: The Spanish Political and Military Songs of the War in Spain, 1808 to 1814* (Tecla Editions, 2017). For the considerable impact of the Peninsular War on the home-front interest in Spain, including its literary inflections, see especially S. Bainbridge, ed., *British Poetry and the Revolutionary and Napoleonic Wars: Visions of Conflict* (Oxford: Oxford University Press, 2003), 148–89.

25. Cited in Daly, *The British Soldier in the Peninsular War*, 22. Further on the war, servicemen's reading and *Gil Blas* see Kennedy, *Narratives of the Revolutionary and Napoleonic Wars*, 20, 22, 96–7.

26. G. Bell, *Rough Notes by an Old Soldier, during Fifty Years' Service*, 2 vols (1867), vol. i, 18–19.

27. M. Sherer, *Recollections of the Peninsula* (1823), 121–2. Compare Kennedy, *Narratives of the Revolutionary and Napoleonic Wars*, 88–9. Lieutenant John Cooke was struck by a scene in the Alentejo region of Portugal during 1811, as if in a theatre set: 'a solitary Portuguese', entirely alone in the landscape like a single figure on stage before scenery, was 'striking an old battered guitar with all his fingers (as on a tambourine) and hallooing forth some ditty loud enough to be heard in the distant valleys' (J. Cooke, *Memoirs of the Late War*, 2 vols (1831), vol. i, 73).

28. Sherer, *Recollections of the Peninsula*, 26.

29. J. Patterson, *The Adventures of Captain John Patterson* (1837), 184–5.

30. W. Stothert, *A Narrative of the Principal Events of the Campaigns of 1809, 1810 and 1811 in Spain and Portugal* (1812), 122–3.

31. R. K. Porter, *Letters from Portugal and Spain written during the March of the British Troops under Sir John Moore, with a Map of the Route, and Appropriate Engravings* (1809), 53. When the Revd James-Wilmot Ormsby heard songs for a fandango and bolero, sung by two ladies accompanied on a guitar, at the house of their father, presumably at a *tertulia*, he was sorry to learn that the words were of a 'seductive tendency' (*An Account of the Operations of the British Army, and of the State and Sentiments of the People of Portugal and Spain, during the Campaigns of the Years 1808 and 1809 in a Series of Letters*, 2 vols (1809), vol. ii, 48–9). Some found the fandango and bolero simply absurd. After a bullfight at Truxillo, John Patterson saw peasants pairing off 'in the fandango or bolero, with some fair sweetheart, putting themselves through the most ridiculous antics, while accompanied by the music

of an old cracked guitar, or broken winded clarionet, performed on by some wretched artist' (Patterson, *The Adventures of Captain John Patterson*, 212–13).

32. Cooke, *Memoirs of the Late War*, vol. i, 219.

33. R. N. Buckley, ed., *The Napoleonic War Journal of Captain Thomas Henry Browne, 1807–1816* (1987), 224; *ODNB*, s.v. 'Browne, Sir Thomas Henry'. For songs in praise of Wellington see Jeffery, *España de la guerra*, 180, 244, 247–8, 251, etc.

34. Buckley, ed., *The Napoleonic War Journal*, 220.

35. [E. W. Buckham], *A Personal Narrative of Adventures in the Peninsula during the War in 1812–1813, by an Officer* (1827), 228.

36. W. Grattan, *Adventures with the Connaught Rangers from 1808 to 1814* (1902), 272; Sherer, *Recollections of the Peninsula*, 86. Lieutenant John Cooke was impressed to find that, as a matter of course, 'towards evening the streets are thronged by merry dancers and songstresses; the tinkling of the guitar is heard from the casements, balconies and verandas' (Cooke, *Memoirs of the Late War*, vol. i, 194).

37. P. Hawker, *Journal of a Regimental Officer during the Recent Campaign in Portugal and Spain under Lord Viscount Wellington* (1810), 79.

38. F. S. Larpent, *The Private Journal of Judge-Advocate Larpent* (1854), 47; *ODNB*, s.v. 'Larpent, Francis Seymour'.

39. *ODNB*, s.v. 'Wellesley, Arthur, first duke of Wellington'.

40. Buckley, ed., *The Napoleonic War Journal*, 180, 202.

41. The distinguished chronicler of the Peninsular War W. F. P. Napier records that Wellington had a number of informers 'amongst the Spaniards who were living within the French lines'; one of them was 'a guitar player of celebrity, named Fuentes', who repeatedly brought information from Madrid (*History of the War in the Peninsula and the South of France from the Year 1807 to the Year 1814*, 6 vols (1828–40), vol. iii, 119).

42. G. Landman, *Recollections of my Military Life*, 2 vols (1854), vol. i, 229.

43. W. Henry, *Trifles from my Port-folio, or, Recollections of Adventures during Twenty-Nine Years' Military Service in the Peninsular War and Invasion of France, the East Indies, Campaign in Nepaul, St. Helena during the Detention and until the Death of Napoleon, and Upper and Lower Canada*, 2 vols (Quebec, 1839; repr. 2011), vol. i, 88.

44. E. Costello, *The Adventures of a Soldier . . . Comprising Narratives of the Campaigns in the Peninsular [sic] under the Duke of Wellington, and the Recent Civil Wars in Spain*, 2nd edn (1852), 139.

Notes to Chapter Five

45. G. Glover, ed., *An Eloquent Soldier: The Peninsular War Journals of Lieutenant Charles Crowe of the Inniskillings, 1812–14* (Barnsley, 2011), 166.

46. R. Southey, *History of the Peninsular War*, 3 vols (1823–32), vol. ii, 328.

47. Anon., 'The Westminster Review and the Guitar', *The Giulianiad*, 1/2 (February 1833), 18–20, at 18, referring to those who lodge 'to this day, with the families of those countries', meaning Spain and Portugal.

48. An instrument of 1809 by Josef Pagés (possibly identifiable with this one) is listed among goods for auction in the London *Morning Post*, 2 June 1898.

49. The information given in this list is provisional, since it has not been possible to examine all the instruments and their labels in person.

50. *Sligo Champion*, 3 December 1859.

51. *Wiltshire Independent*, 17 August 1837; *Birmingham Mail*, 23 January 1882, 15 August 1891.

52. See, for example, *Hampshire Telegraph and Sussex Chronicle*, 26 August 1811; *Cheltenham Chronicle*, 3 July 1817; *Manchester Courier and Lancashire General Advertiser*, 20 May 1826.

53. Spencer Collection, Royal Academy of Music, London, MS 605, with inventory. For discussion of the manuscript, often with special reference to the songs by Fernando Sor therein, see Jeffery, *España de la guerra*, 398–9; B. Jeffery, ed., *Fernando Sor: Seguidillas*, 2 vols (1976, 1999), vol. [i], 13–14.

54. O. G. C. Bridgeman, ed., *Letters from Portugal, Spain, Sicily, and Malta: in 1812, 1813, and 1814* (1875), 64–5.

55. J. de Kloe, ed., *Fernando Sor: Music for Voice and Guitar* (Heidelberg, 2005), nos 27–9 (no. 28 is a second version of no. 27). For the context of these songs and bibliographical details see Jeffery, *España de la guerra*.

56. *New-York Mirror*, 8 July 1830, 19.

57. C. Bashford, 'Historiography and Invisible Musics: Domestic Chamber Music in Nineteenth-Century Britain', *JAMS*, 63 (2010), 291–360, at 292.

58. W. Gardiner, *Music and Friends: or, Pleasant Recollections of a Dilettante*, 2 vols (1838), vol. ii, 692.

59. A. Fraser, *The Frasers of Philorth*, 3 vols (1879), vol. i, 285. Georgiana McCrae, who knew Saltoun well, records in her journal that in addition to being a good guitarist he was also the patron of an unnamed Spanish officer who was particularly admired for his playing and singing. An entry in her diary for 2 January 1828 records how that soldier arrived at Gordon Castle one evening by coach. There came 'from Elgin & Inverness a *protégé* of Lord Saltoun's – a Spanish officer who is

forte on the Guitar – He gave us some beautiful songs & stirring pieces, which the Gordons pronounced "splendidly played!" – Till now I had never any idea of the capabilities of the guitar having supposed it to be merely adapted for accompanying the voice, while it can give Martial music most effectively – Lord Saltoun is a capital performer on the Guitar – having learnt to play while in Spain with his regiment' (B. Niall, ed., *Georgiana: A Biography of Georgiana McCrae, Painter, Diarist, Pioneer* (1994), 55).

60. Lord Saltoun's collection of guitar music, 1810–50, Library of Congress, Washington, DC.

61. Ibid., Box Folder 1/7.

62. Gardiner, *Music and Friends*, vol. ii, 692. One can scarcely forbear to mention here the dedication of Charles Doisy's *Principes généraux de la guitare* (1801) to Madame Buonaparte, and Napoleon's gift of a guitar to one of his generals (J. Westbrook, 'Guitar Making in Nineteenth-Century London: Louis Panormo and his Contemporaries', doctoral diss., University of Cambridge, 2013, 252).

63. Wellington's niece Georgiana Frederica Fitzroy (d. 1821), became the Marchioness of Worcester by marriage, and is the 'Poor Lady Worcester' whom the Earl of Essex believed to be the only titled lady he could think of in 1821 who had cultivated the guitar within recent years (P. Delaforce, *Wellington the Beau: The Life and Loves of the Duke of Wellington* (Moreton-in-Marsh: Windrush Press, 1990), 187–99; C. Page, 'New Light on the London Years of Fernando Sor, 1815–1822', *EM*, 41 (2013), 557–60, 565–6).

Chapter Six

1. E. Spence, *The Spanish Guitar: A Tale for the Use of Young Persons* (1814), esp. 76ff; *ODNB*, s.v. 'Spence, Elizabeth Isabella'.

2. *Carlisle Journal*, 20 May 1815.

3. For the inns, T. Burke, *English Inns* (W. Collins, 1943) still has much to offer. For more recent work see M. C. Borer, *The British Hotel through the Ages* (Guildford: Lutterworth Press, 1972). For the local theatres see P. Borsay, *The English Urban Renaissance: Culture and Society in the Provincial Town, 1660–1770* (Oxford: Clarendon Press, 1989), 119–21 and Appendix 3; G. Garlick, 'Theatre Outside London, 1660–1775', in J. Donohue, ed., *The Cambridge History of British Theatre*, vol. ii (Cambridge, 2004), 165–82. For often candid comments on the failings and vicissitudes of management see the entries for a series of provincial theatres, with illustrations, in J. Winston, *The Theatric Tourist* (1805).

4. *Hereford Journal*, 11 March 1812.

5. *Manchester Mercury*, 29 April 1800. This individual may be the G. Asker who composed and paid for the

printing of *The Youth that I Love: A Ballad sung with Great Applause by Miss Larkman, at the Theatre Royal Liverpool* (1807).

6. L. T. Rede, *The Road to the Stage* (1827), 15–16, 58–63.

7. *Courier and Evening Gazette*, 8 August 1800.

8. For Rosemund Mountain see p. 92 and Fig. 19. Another local figure, Miss Johnston, sang to the Spanish guitar during a new *Pas-Seul* at the Theatre Royal Manchester in 1811, selling tickets from her lodgings in the town (*Manchester Mercury*, 16 April 1811).

9. *Hull Advertiser and Exchange Gazette*, 9 July 1803.

10. *Northampton Mercury*, 8 September 1804.

11. *Norfolk Chronicle*, 9 March 1811.

12. *Kentish Weekly Post or Canterbury Journal*, 25 March 1814.

13. *Carlisle Journal*, 20 May 1815.

14. *Royal Cornwall Gazette, Falmouth Packet & Plymouth Journal*, 28 January 1815.

15. A. B. Granville, *Autobiography of A. B. Granville*, 2nd edn, 2 vols (1874), vol. i, 213.

16. Ibid., 214.

17. Anon., 'To the Editor of *The Giulianiad*', *The Giulianiad*, 1/5 (July 1833), 27–8.

18. For Fernando Sor in England see L. Briso de Montiano, *Información sobre el guitarrista Fernando Sor (1778–1839)*, at http://fernandosor.es/author/luis-briso-de-montiano/ ; B. Jeffery, *Fernando Sor: Composer and Guitarist*, 2nd edn (Tecla Editions, 1994), 39–73; J. M. Mangado, 'Fernando Sor (1778–1839), documenti inediti: riflessioni e ipotesi', *Il Fronimo*, 174 (April 2016), 33–43; C. Page, 'New Light on the London Years of Fernando Sor, 1815–1822', *EM*, 41 (2013), 557–60'; E. Stenstadvold, 'Fernando Sor on the Move in the Early 1820s', *Soundboard Scholar*, 1 (2015), 16–25, esp. 16–18. For Sor's broader ambitions see W. Moser, 'Fernando Sor: The Life and Works of a Reluctant Guitarist', *Classical Guitar*, 26/3 (2007), 20–24; 26/4 (2007), 20–25.

19. The works published in London are listed in Jeffery, *Fernando Sor*, 57–9.

20. *Morning Post*, 5 May 1817.

21. The account of Sor's career in the *Encyclopédie pittoresque de la musique* (Paris, 1835), edited by A. Ledhuy and H. Bertini, is dominated by the report of the Montserrat years, told in the first person and clearly based on a personal memoir; for a facsimile of the entry see Jeffery, *Fernando Sor*, 118–31.

22. For the text of Sor's reminiscence of the experience see Jeffery, *Fernando Sor*, 119; for the composition see

D. Pujol, ed., *Mestres de l'Escolania de Montserrat . . . Joan Cererols*, 3 vols (Monestir de Montserrat, 1930), vol. i, 133–41. Sor misremembers the name as 'Céréols'.

23. For the delicate matter of Sor's political convictions see E. Olcina, 'Fernando Sor como demócrata revolucionario: trasfondo político de sus canciones patrióticas', in L. Gásser, ed., *Estudios sobre Fernando Sor*, 2nd edn (Madrid: Ediciones del ICCMU, 2010), 73–80, which refers (at 75) to Sor's 'political schizophrenia'; see also Jeffery, *Fernando Sor*, 12–13. If Sor had a consistent position, he was a liberal in the sense of the word that then prevailed in Spain, not necessarily implying either republican politics or freedom of thought in matters of the Catholic faith: see J. F. Sebastián, 'Toleration and Freedom of Expression in the Hispanic World: Between Enlightenment and Liberalism', *Past and Present*, 211 (2011), 159–97.

24. *Morning Chronicle*, 27 September 1814.

25. Granville, *Autobiography*, vol. ii, 9. For an edition of the composition see B. Jeffery, ed., *Fernando Sor: Seguidillas*, 2 vols (1976, 1999), vol. [i], 30–31. Lady Westmorland played the guitar herself, according to the diary of Lady Charlotte Bury (*Diary Illustrative of the Times of George the Fourth*, 2 vols (Paris, 1838–9), vol. i, 64). Her daughter, Lady Georgiana Fane, is the dedicatee of Verini's bolero 'Ten piedad vida mia' for two voices and guitar (see Ex. 23).

26. J. Mackintosh, *Memoirs of the Life of the Rt. Hon. Sir James Mackintosh*, 2 vols (1835), vol. ii, 315.

27. W. H. Pyne, *The History of the Royal Residences of Windsor Castle, St. James's Palace, Carlton House, Kensington Palace, Hampton Court, Buckingham House, and Frogmore*, 3 vols (1819), vol. iii, 1–92.

28. For a detailed description room by room see P. Egan, *Life in London* (1823), 259–71.

29. *Morning Post*, 8 May 1815.

30. Ibid.

31. C. Brown, *Classical and Romantic Performing Practice, 1750–1900* (Oxford: Oxford University Press, 1999), 365.

32. It is the kind of progression that he explicitly repudiates; see F. Sor, *Méthode pour la guitare* (1830), 15: 'je ne ferai jamais marcher la basse et le dessus par des octaves directes'.

33. Ashe Collection, Bodleian Libraries, Oxford, 17405 d.11 (17). This is the only programme in this very extensive archive that names Sor.

34. Lady Langham's events are sometimes mentioned in contemporary diaries – for example, the unpublished journals of Emma Smith, who married into the family of Jane Austen somewhat after that author's death. Between 1818 and 1820 Emma mentions a quadrille

party (with music from the well-known tenor Pierre Begrez), a concert and ball, and an Italian ball and concert, all held at Lady Langham's in the month of May. Hampshire Record Office, 23M93/87/1/4–6, comprising 1818 diary (entry for 4 May), 1819 diary (entry for 17 May) and 1820 diary (entry for 29 May).

35. *Morning Post*, 5 May 1817.

36. In 1815 the Davenports resided at Hertford Street, in 1818 at Lower Brook Street, and in January 1819 at Lower Grosvenor Street. Miss Davenport appeared at the Duchess of Wellington's assembly in 1820, at Princess Esterhazy's party in 1821, and at the French ambassador's ball in 1823, to mention only those events among the beau monde where she is named in the press (*Morning Post*, 18 May 1820, 5 March 1821, 8 March 1823).

37. Ibid., 16 May 1823.

38. Earl of Essex to Miss Tiler, 6 August 1821, Surrey History Centre, Woking, 3677/3/77a–b. I am grateful to Julian Pooley for his assistance with this letter. For Carlos Sor in London in 1820–21 see J. M. Mangado, *La guitarra en Cataluña, 1769–1939* (Tecla Editions, 1998), 16–17.

39. T. Longstaffe-Gowan, *The London Square: Gardens in the Midst of Town* (New Haven: Yale University Press, 2012), 105.

40. Names of occupants of houses in the two squares are recorded in Anon., *The Royal Blue Book and Fashionable Directory and Canvassing Guide for 1822* (1822), 41, 44.

41. A. Langton, *The History of the Life of the Squire Marcos de Obregon . . . by Vincent Espinel . . . translated into English from the Madrid Edition of 1618*, 2 vols (1816), vol. i, pp. xxxvi–xxxvii.

42. B. Jeffery, 'Sor, Teaching, and the Enlightenment', at https://tecla.com/fernando-sor/sor-and-the-enlightenment (accessed 26 March 2020).

43. Sor, *Méthode pour la guitare*, 22.

44. A little-known anecdote about Sor's years in England shows that he preferred to use French in England when there was no chance of Spanish or Catalan being understood. Mrs Matthews, *A Continuation of the Memoirs of Charles Matthews*, 2 vols (Philadelphia, 1839), vol. i, 149–50, shows Sor meeting that noted actor, whom he admired, and trying to express himself; the anecdote mimics Sor's poor English.

45. For new light on Sor's departure see Stenstadvold, 'Fernando Sor on the Move'.

46. *The Examiner*, 6 April 1823.

47. *La Belle Assemblée*, 1 October 1820.

Chapter Seven

1. Old Bailey, *The Proceedings of the Old Bailey: London's Central Criminal Court, 1674 to 1913*, at www.oldbaileyonline.org, t18230910-107 (10 September 1823: theft by Alexander Ward and John Brown Bowden on 21 August of a guitar worth 20s.). On the use of this source for the contents of interiors see J. Styles, 'Lodging at the Old Bailey: Lodgings and their Furnishing in Eighteenth-Century London', in A. Vickery and J. Styles, eds, *Gender, Taste and Material Culture in Britain and North America, 1700–1830* (New Haven and London: Yale University Press, 2006), 61–80.

2. *The Proceedings of the Old Bailey*, t18270712-80 (12 July 1827: theft by John Battes on 17 June of a guitar worth £5); t18291029-24 (29 October 1829: theft by John Phillips, posing as an organist at Greenwich, on 20 October of a guitar worth £4; also reported in *Bell's Life in London and Sporting Chronicle*, 1 November 1829, where Phillips is referred to as 'an imbecile and an eccentric character'; and in *John Bull*, 2 November 1829); t18310630-304 (30 June 1831: theft by William Ellis on 18 May of a guitar worth £2); t18320517-162 (17 May 1832: theft by Julius Picard on 3 April of a guitar worth £4).

3. For a list of the English methods see E. Stenstadvold, *An Annotated Bibliography of Guitar Methods, 1760–1860* (Hillsdale, NY: Pendragon Press, 2010), 1–2.

4. *New Monthly Magazine and Literary Journal* (1827), no. 1, 95.

5. *Morning Post*, 16 September 1823. There is no complete catalogue of published music for the guitar, though the extent of the song material can now be conveniently gauged from I. Gammie, *Nineteenth-Century Guitar Songs: An Idiosyncratic Survey* (St Albans: Corda Music Publications, 2017). Filtered searches of *Library Hub Discover* (https://discover.libraryhub.jisc.ac.uk) provide a dependable guide to relevant material in United Kingdom and Irish libraries.

6. [T. P. Thompson], 'Gardiner's Music of Nature', *Westminster Review*, 17 (July–October 1832), 345–68, at 356. The editor(s) of *The Giulianiad* eagerly reprinted material from this article (Anon., 'The Westminster Review and the Guitar', *The Giulianiad*, 1/2 (February 1833), 18–20). For Thompson see *ODNB*, s.v. 'Thompson, Thomas Perronet'; for Thompson's politics see M. J. Turner, 'Radical Opinion in an Age of Reform: Thomas Perronet Thompson and the "Westminster Review"', *History*, 86 (2001), 18–40. For Thompson and the guitar see J. Westbrook, 'General Thompson's Enharmonic Guitar', *Soundboard*, 38/4 (2012), 45–52; J. Westbrook, 'Guitar Making in Nineteenth-Century London: Louis Panormo and his Contemporaries', doctoral diss., University of Cambridge, 2013, 183–200. A guitar method by Thompson is catalogued in Stenstadvold, *An Annotated Bibliography*, 189.

7. *John Bull*, 29 April 1822. For the speech as reported in Hansard and for discussion see D. Wahrman,

Imagining the Middle Class: The Political Representation of Class in Britain, c.1780–1840 (Cambridge: Cambridge University Press, 1995), 253–4. See also D. Cannadine, *Class in Britain* (New Haven and London: Yale University Press, 1988), 76–9; and for the emergence of a middle-class identity see L. Davidoff and C. Hall, *Family Fortunes: Men and Women of the English Middle Class, 1780–1850* (London and New York: Routledge, 2002).

8. *Mayo Constitution*, 1 February 1830.

9. *London Magazine*, 4 (1821), 650.

10. [E. Caswall], 'The Young Lady who Sings', *Sketches of Young Ladies* (1837).

11. For the guitar laid on the sofa see Anon., *Waldegrave: A Novel*, 2 vols (New York, 1829), vol. i, 192: 'The moon, which beamed through this little retreat, was reflected bright on the waters, lighting up the soft bay and islands, and sparkling from the white villages and gliding skiffs. On a sofa lay a guitar, which Lady Hermione playfully took up, and passed her fingers over the strings: "Here is my lyre," said she, placing herself on the sofa.'

12. S. Stickney, *Pictures of Private Life* (1833), 15.

13. *New Monthly Magazine and Literary Journal* (1827), no. 2, 95.

14. P.-F. Le Courayer, 'Second Love: A Tale', *Lady's Monthly Museum*, 2 (January 1813), 31–4, at 31.

15. *Quarterly Musical Magazine and Review*, 9 (1827), 538.

16. The work of the continental guitar-makers was too accomplished, and too accessible through the port of London, for English craftsmen to compete: *GITE*, 60–78; *GISE*, 47–9.

17. *The Age*, 9 April 1826. There was a guitar at Dover Custom House in 1821, one of numerous expensive foreign items, largely French, on which the importer(s) had not paid the duty: *Kentish Weekly Post or Canterbury Journal*, 10 September 1821.

18. Westbrook, 'Guitar Making in Nineteenth-Century London', ch. 2.

19. *Literary Gazette*, 3 January 1818, 394.

20. Anon., 'Guitar Professors, and Guitar Makers and Sellers', *The Giulianiad*, 1/5 (July, 1833), 44–5. Giuseppe Anelli was still making similar complaints, albeit with a vested commercial interest, in 1833: G. Anelli, *Singing Academy Prospectus with the Origin of the Spanish Guitar* (Clifton, 1834), 22ff.

21. G. H. Derwort, *A New Method of Learning the Spanish Guitar* (1825), 8.

22. Westbrook, 'Guitar Making in Nineteenth-Century London', 67–200; J. Westbrook, 'Louis Panormo: "The

only maker of guitars in the Spanish style"', *EM*, 41 (2013), 571–84.

23. Fernando Sor, *Méthode pour la guitare* (1830), 7.

24. Westbrook, 'Louis Panormo', 578.

25. *The Proceedings of the Old Bailey*, t18310630-304 (30 June 1831: theft by William Ellis on 18 May of a guitar worth £2).

26. *Bristol Mercury*, 1 May 1820; *The Proceedings of the Old Bailey*, t18230910-107 (10 September 1823).

27. Westbrook, 'Guitar Making in Nineteenth-Century London', 104.

28. *Morning Chronicle*, 24 April 1816; *Morning Post*, 24 October 1818.

29. *Quarterly Musical Magazine and Review*, 9 (1827), 538.

30. For Bath see A. Britton, 'The Guitar in the Romantic Period: Its Musical and Social Development with Special Reference to Bristol and Bath', doctoral diss., Royal Holloway, University of London, 2010. *Aris's Birmingham Gazette*, 2 March 1829; *Cheltenham Chronicle*, 7 August 1828; *Chester Courant*, 10 January 1826; *Coventry Herald*, 24 July 1829; *Exeter Flying Post*, 22 September 1825; *Hereford Journal*, 11 February 1818; *Kentish Weekly Post or Canterbury Journal*, 12 December 1826; *Leamington Spa Courier*, 16 May 1829; *Leeds Mercury*, 25 April 1812; *Leicester Chronicle*, 1 July 1826; *Liverpool Mercury*, 3 July 1818; *Manchester Courier and Lancashire General Advertiser*, 10 July 1830; *Norfolk Chronicle and Norwich Gazette*, 8 April 1826; *Royal Cornwall Gazette*, 4 February 1815; *Sheffield Independent*, 21 January 1826; *Worcester Journal*, 29 January 1829; *Yorkshire Gazette*, 9 October 1830.

31. *Aris's Birmingham Gazette*, 2 March 1829. Lambley's method has not been found.

32. *Liverpool Mercury*, 14 May 1824. On 7 May the same paper introduced de Bruguera as 'a colonel in the independent army of South America', currently unable to claim his patrimony in Spain, where his family resided, owing to the unsettled state of that country. By the mid-1820s there was at least one guitar-maker in Liverpool. On 15 December 1826 the *Liverpool Mercury* announced that James Cowlan had recruited 'a young man of considerable experience' in building guitars, among other instruments, for his Musical Instrument Repository; this individual is probably the same as the 'Cowland' found in 1837 by Westbrook ('Guitar Making in Nineteenth-Century London', 469).

33. S. Y. Griffith, *Griffith's New Historical Description of Cheltenham and its Vicinity*, 2nd edn, 2 vols (1826).

34. *Cheltenham Chronicle*, 1 September 1814.

35. Ibid., 29 August 1816, 12 September 1816, 26 June 1817; see also the issue for 28 June 1818, where a teacher,

Mr Slatter, capitalises on the late Princess Charlotte's cultivation of the guitar.

36. J. Hughes, *An Itinerary of Provence and the Rhone made during the Year 1819* (1822), 193.

37. *Coventry Herald*, 24 July 1829. The more trustworthy teachers undertook to achieve results in twenty-five lessons; others promised significant progress in twelve. For further references to several of the masters mentioned here, see E. Stenstadvold, 'Mariano Castro de Gistau (d. 1856) and the Vogue for the Spanish Guitar in Nineteenth-Century Britain', *Nineteenth-Century Music Review*, 16 (2017), 1–21, at 12 and see n. 52.

38. Stenstadvold, *An Annotated Bibliography*, 184. An otherwise unknown teacher of Spanish named J. Toby published a guitar method around 1835 (ibid., 190). The whereabouts of the copy sold by Bloomsbury Auctions in 2010 as lot 542 are currently unknown; I know of no other copy.

39. Hampshire Record Office, 9M55/F4/14.

40. Ibid., 9M55/F4/16.

41. *ODNB*, s.v. 'Emidy, Joseph Antonio'.

42. Ibid., s.v. 'Lacy, Michael Rophino'.

43. *Liverpool Mercury*, 3 July 1818.

44. *Brighton Gazette*, 20 July 1826.

45. For a detailed study of a hitherto unknown itinerant guitarist see Stenstadvold, 'Mariano Castro de Gistau'.

46. *Bristol Mercury*, 16 December 1828. For Anelli's West Country career see Britton, 'The Guitar in the Romantic Period', and for guitar-making in Bristol see Westbrook, 'Guitar Making in Nineteenth-Century London', 495–7.

47. M. J. Peterson, 'The Victorian Governess: Status Incongruence in Family and Society', *Victorian Studies*, 14 (1970), 7–26. There are several general surveys of the governess, including R. Brandon: *Governess: The Lives and Times of the Real Jane Eyres* (New York: Walker & Co., 2008); A. Renton, *Tyrant or Victim: A History of the British Governess* (Weidenfeld & Nicolson, 1991).

48. *Morning Post*, 10 November 1834, 16 April 1804.

49. *Morning Post*, 18 August 1832, 31 July 1835.

50. N. Jauralde, *A Complete Preceptor for the Spanish Guitar* (1828), 5.

51. F. Duvernay, *A Complete Instruction Book for the Guitar* (1828), 7.

52. For the textual history of this book see Stenstadvold, *An Annotated Bibliography*, 142.

53. *Morning Post*, 18 June 1825.

54. *The Times*, 14 July 1834.

55. Anon, 'Idea of a New Court for Domestic Grievances', *New Monthly Magazine and Literary Journal* (1833), no. 2, 476–9, at 477. For suburban developments, on which there is a rich literature, see also S. Bilston, '"They congregate . . . in towns and suburbs": The Shape of Middle-Class Life in John Claudius Loudon's *The Suburban Gardener*', *Victorian Review*, 37 (2011), 144–59; E. McKellar, ed., *Landscapes of London: The City, the Country and the Suburbs, 1660–1840* (New Haven: Yale University Press, 2013).

56. B. Maidment, 'Dinners or Desserts? Miscellaneity, Illustration and the Periodical Press, 1820–1840', *Victorian Periodicals Review*, 153 (2010), 353–87, at 357; on the fashion for albums see also W. St Clair, *The Reading Nation in the Romantic Period* (Cambridge: Cambridge University Press, 2004), 229–32.

57. Despite producing a method and a steady stream of arrangements for voice and guitar, Derwort was unable to keep himself from debt; he was discharged from Fleet Prison by order of the Court for Relief of Insolvent Debtors on 4 February 1829. He eventually emigrated to the United States, teaching the guitar and giving concerts with his children, and eventually died there.

58. A case could be made that the pieces are graduated, for the first is undoubtedly the simplest and the last offers two versions of a passage, one of them marked 'Easy'. There were other low- to mid-price collections presenting the works of the acknowledged masters and various minor figures, such as F. Alberti's *The Apollon, Containing National Gems for the Spanish Guitar from the Works of Giuliani, Carulli, Eulenstein, . . .* (n.d. [1820?]).

59. Westbrook, 'Guitar Making in Nineteenth-Century London', 393.

60. John William Millais also left *Eight Airs and Waltzes and a March for the Spanish Guitar* (1827).

61. F. Horetzky, *L'Aurore, ou journal de guitare: choix des plus beaux morceaux composés pour cet instrument* (1827), pt 2, 23; pt 1, 14.

62. Hampshire Record Office, 9M55/F5/13.

63. There is currently no catalogue of Sola's many publications, and the many dedicatees of his works, such as 'Miss Birkett of Railhead House, Isleworth', are as yet no more than names, leaving his extensive network of pupils and patrons in shadow. Gammie, *Nineteenth-Century Guitar Songs*, 167–71, gives a census of the Sola songs in the British Library. The situation is complicated by the fact that some songs are known in very few copies, or perhaps only one, which may be in private hands (the unpaginated notes that introduce B. Jeffery, ed., *English Romantic Songs and Ballads of the Early Nineteenth Century with Guitar Accompaniments of the Period* (Tecla Editions, 2004) are illuminating

in this regard), while the Sola prints and collections in at least one major repository remain uncatalogued at present. A manuscript collection of guitar-accompanied songs in manuscript, now in the Dolmetsch Library, Haslemere (MS 11 C 27), contains copies of Sola's French and Italian sets just mentioned, probably copied by the 'G. Rovedino' whose name often appears. This is probably the 'Rovedino junior' who sang and accompanied himself on the Spanish guitar at Bath in 1802 (see above, p. 97) and almost certainly the G. Rovedino who taught the guitar in Bath during the later 1820s, and then in Cheltenham.

64. Sola appears in the diary of Emma Austen-Leigh, for example, giving singing lessons to a young woman from the Hampshire gentry: Hampshire Record Office, 23M93/87/1/7, entry for 23 February 1821 (arranges for singing lessons with Sola); 23M93/87/1/11, entry for 27 January 1826 (receives a lesson from Sola).

65. *Hampshire Chronicle*, 6 October 1817. I am grateful to Erik Stenstadvold for a reference to Sola in *Allgemeine Musikalische Zeitung*, 15 December 1819, col. 861; the author of the piece thought Sola conspicuous for his talent on the Spanish guitar in a country where, as the writer believed, that instrument was not much favoured.

66. *Meet me by the moonlight, a Ballad Written & Composed by J. A. Wade: Arr[anged] with an Accomp[animent] for the Spanish Guitar ... by C. M. Sola* (n.d. [*c*.1827]); *Your heart and lute: A Ballad Written by a Lady, Composed by F. W. Crouch Arranged with an Accomp[animent] for the Spanish Guitar by C. M. Sola* (1828).

67. *Leeds Times*, 12 November 1842.

68. M. S. Hudson, *Almack's: A Novel in Three Volumes* (1826), vol. i, 50–51.

69. Sophia Broadwood's substantial collection of guitar-accompanied French songs was bequeathed to an aunt, whence it passed into the Broadwood archive, where it remains as part of the Surrey History Centre, Woking.

70. C. Page, 'An Essay of 1824 on the Guitar', *Soundboard*, 38/4 (2012), 53–60, 75, at 58.

71. In Jeffery, ed., *English Romantic Songs and Ballads*, 27–9, 36–8.

72. Very little of this material has been published, hence Jeffery, ed., *English Romantic Songs and Ballads*, is particularly valuable.

73. Pablo Rosquellas's method (1813?) gives a brief melody in the key of C, followed by twelve ways to accompany it with different arpeggio patterns, using the chords I, IV and V$_7$ in various inversions (P. Rosquellas, *A Complete Tutor for the Spanish Guitar* (n.d. [1813?]), 14–15). Sola in 1820 gives 'Six different methods of ARPEGGIO on the same Melody' (C. M. Sola,

Instructions for the Spanish Guitar (1820), 16–17). May provides essentially the same information with his 'Examples of different Styles of Accompanying', comprising thirty-two ways to fill a measure with a single chord of C major (G. T. May, *Instructions for the Spanish Guitar* (*c*.1824?), 2nd edn (n.d. [*c*.1830])). J. M. Ciebra, whose manual survives in a late edition of about 1860, assures his readers that the three basic chords of I, IV and V$_7$ are 'the groundwork to many Operatic, and to nearly all popular Airs', so they will enable players 'with a good ear, and ordinary aptitude, to execute an impromptu Accompaniment to almost any melody' (J. M. Ciebra, *Ciebra's Handbook for the Guitar* (n.d. [*c*.1860]), 9).

74. Derwort, *A New Method of Learning the Spanish Guitar*, 6–7.

75. *La Belle Assemblée*, 1 May 1831; *The Giulianiad*, 1/2 (February 1833), 17.

76. *The Olio, or Museum of Entertainment*, 3 (January–July 1829), 234; *The Atheneum: or Spirit of the English Magazines*, 1 (October–March 1828–9), 125–6; *The Giulianiad*, 1/1 (January 1833), 6.

77. B. Disraeli, *Henrietta Temple* (1837), Book II, ch. 6.

Chapter Eight

1. See J. D. Hunt, 'Picturesque Mirrors and the Ruins of the Past', *Art History*, 4 (1981), 254–70; M. Andrews, *The Search for the Picturesque*. A character in Benjamin Disraeli's novel *Vivian Grey* (1826) describes a spot as one that 'Nature herself' has intended for picnics: a landscape with a ruined abbey, 'discovered by a knight, in the middle ages, following the track of a stag' (vol. v, 8).

2. W. Cowper, 'The Winter Morning Walk', *The Task*, in *The Poems of William Cowper*, ed. J. D. Baird and C. Ryskamp, vol. ii (Oxford: Oxford University Press, 1995), 212, line 13; W. Wordsworth, 'Lines Composed a Few Miles above Tintern Abbey', in *The Poetical Works of William Wordsworth*, ed. E. de Selincourt, 2nd edn, vol. ii (Oxford: Oxford University Press, 1952), 260, line 7.

3. *OED*, s.v. 'excursion', *n.*, 5 (quotation, 1779); see also ibid., s.v. 'ramble', *n.*, 1.a.: 'a walk or wander (formerly) any excursion or journey without definite route or other aim than recreation or pleasure; (now) *esp.* one taken in the country'. The term was taken up by satirists who were quick to see the humour of excursions viewed in terms of cockney expeditions into rural landscapes, where things could easily go amiss for the ramblers – as, for example, in Joseph William Coyte, *A Cockney's Adventures during a Ramble into the Country* (1811). The same theme proved a fertile one for printmakers.

4. *OED*, s.v. 'picnic', *n.*, *adj.*, and *adv.*, A.1.a; see Anna Letitia Barbauld, *A Legacy for Young Ladies Consisting*

of *Miscellaneous Pieces in Prose and Verse by the late Mrs. Barbauld* (1826), 192: "'Pray, mamma, what is the meaning of *pic-nic*? I have heard lately once or twice of a *pic-nic* supper, and I cannot think what it means; I looked for the word in Johnson's Dictionary and could not find it.' 'I should wonder if you had, the word was not coined in Johnson's time.'" For the rise of the picnic see A. Hubbell, 'How Wordsworth Invented Picnicking and Saved British Culture', *Romanticism*, 12 (2006), 44–51. Note that 'scenic', as a quality of landscape 'providing attractive or picturesque scenery' (as opposed to 'having the quality of a staged drama'), is first recorded by the *OED* in 1784 (s.v. 'scenic', *adj.*, 3.a.).

5. Reproduced in C. Page, 'Being a Guitarist in Late Georgian England', *EM* 46 (2018), 3–16, at 4.

6. For Light and his instruments, with special reference to his harp-lute, see H. Sugimoto, 'The Harp-Lute in Britain, 1800–1830: A Study of the Inventor Edward Light and his Instruments', doctoral diss., 2 vols, University of Edinburgh, 2015.

7. *Morning Post*, 28 February 1801.

8. Ibid., 2 May 1801.

9. B. Sperati, *New and Complete Instructions for the Spanish Guitar with Six Strings* (1802), 1.

10. *Morning Post*, 12 June 1817. This was probably Light's 'Patent British Lute-Harp'; Sugimoto, 'The Harp-Lute in Britain', 39.

11. Anon., 'On the Capabilities of the Guitar', *The Giulianiad*, 1/1 (January 1833), 3–5, at 4.

12. Anon., 'Public Concerts', *The Giulianiad*, 1/5 (July 1833), 46–8, at 48.

13. *New Monthly Magazine and Literary Journal* (1829), no. 2, 372–90.

14. J. Armstrong and D. M. Williams, 'The Steamship as an Agent of Modernisation, 1812–1840', *International Journal of Maritime History*, 19 (2007), 145–60.

15. For later examples see, for instance, F. Gómez, *Boleras de sociedad for Three Voices with an Accompaniment for the Piano Forte or Spanish Guitar* (n.d. [c.1826]).

16. *Morning Post*, 18 September 1802.

17. W. A. Robinson, *A Trip to Margate* (1803), 23.

18. [C. Cochrane], *Journal of a Tour made by Señor Juan de Vega, the Spanish Minstrel of 1828–9, through Great Britain and Ireland, a Character assumed by an English Gentleman*, 2 vols (1830), vol. i, 95–108. For the day trip to Margate on the steam packet see J. Armstrong and D. M. Williams, 'The Steamboat and Popular Tourism', *Journal of Transport History*, 26 (2005), 61–77, at 67; see also Armstrong and Williams, 'The Steamship as an Agent of Modernisation'.

19. S. Berry, *Georgian Brighton* (Chichester: Phillimore, 2005).

20. A. Dale, *Fashionable Brighton, 1820–1860* (London: Country Life, 1947).

21. Anon., 'A Trifle from Brighton', a satirical poem of 1827, facetiously separates Brighton's visitors into 'the high *Occidentals*' of London's West End, and those who lived in the City to the east of them, 'the low *Orientals*' (*Lancaster Gazette and General Advertiser*, 21 April 1827).

22. *John Bull*, 23 November 1829.

23. [Cochrane], *Journal of a Tour made by Señor Juan de Vega*, vol. i, 242–310.

24. B. Disraeli, *The Young Duke*, 3 vols (1831), vol. ii, 99–100.

25. *Lancaster Gazette and General Advertiser*, 21 April 1827.

26. *Brighton Gazette*, 20 July 1826. See above, p. 159.

27. Anon., *The Watering Places of Great Britain and Fashionable Directory* (1831), 11.

28. The *Morning Post*, 25 January 1820, announces that Bertioli, 'professor of the Spanish guitar' and pupil of Caroulli (*sic*), who also teaches singing, has just returned from giving concerts for the nobility in Brighton. Alexander Bertioli produced a simplified version of Carulli's method (E. Stenstadvold, *An Annotated Bibliography of Guitar Methods, 1760–1860* (Hillsdale, NY: Pendragon Press, 2010), 69–70). In the *Brighton Gazette*, 24 September 1829, Ferdinand Pebzer (*sic*, for Pelzer) offers guitar lessons. The *Brighton Gazette*, 29 September 1831, announces the arrival of 'the little Giulio Regondi', who will play at evening parties; his father, who is with him, will give lessons. The *Brighton Gazette*, 26 November 1829, refers to Madame Ferrari's annual concert, with Sagrini playing the guitar (see also 19 November 1829 for a concert by Sagrini at 29 Brunswick Terrace, residence of Mrs West). The *Brighton Guardian*, 23 January 1833, records Madame Sala's concert, at which the Schulz family trio was admired. And the *Brighton Gazette*, 16 October 1828, notes that Verini is giving lessons in the town. For Huerta, see below.

29. [Cochrane], *Journal of a Tour made by Señor Juan de Vega*, vol. i, 126, 284.

30. For example, Signor Pagliardini, who in 1825 sang 'Donne belle' to his own accompaniment on the Spanish guitar at the Old Ship assembly room (*Brighton Gazette*, 29 September 1825).

31. *Brighton Gazette*, 28 October 1830 (the *Grande concertante* is presumably identifiable with *Variazione concertante sopra un tema originale di Rossini, per chitarra e piano forte*); *Brighton Gazette*, 20 January 1831 (a fantasia for guitar and piano is presumably identifiable with *Fantaisie pour la guitare avec accompagnement*

de piano sur l'air: O cara memoria de Carafa, dédiée à Madame la Marquise de Bristol et composé par Luigi Sagrini). For these pieces see R. Coldwell, *Luigi Sagrini Works*, at www.digitalguitararchive.com/2013/02/sagrini-works.

32. *Brighton Gazette*, 19 November 1829.

33. Ibid., 22 January 1829.

34. *Morning Chronicle*, 20 May 1823, carries an advertisement for a concert at the King's Theatre, where Carulli will play, 'by particular desire ... "Des Variations sur le theme d'Aline," his own composition'; M. Torta, *Catalogo tematico delle opere di Ferdinando Carulli*, 2 vols (Lucca: Libreria Musicale Italiana, 1993), op. 1[b]. Perhaps this master consented to give lessons while in England, for in 1827 a lady seeking a position as a governess claimed to be one of his pupils (*Morning Post*, 27 June 1827).

35. *Morning Post*, 2 June 1827. The performance took place in the house of Dr Granville in Grafton Street, physician-in-ordinary to the Duke of Clarence. Granville's circle of distinguished acquaintances was undoubtedly extensive. The Duke of Sussex, whose name runs like a silk thread through the history of the guitar in early nineteenth-century England, was present.

36. J. Capel, *Books of the Words of Ten Private Concerts held at the House of J. Capel*, 10 pts (1817–28). There are other manuscript references to the Schulz family in this printed source, and in W. Hawes, *Programmes, Books of Words, etc., of the Annual Concerts given by W. Hawes in 1814, 1819, 1824–39, and by W. and M. B. Hawes in 1840–41: With MS. Notes by Sir G. T. Smart* (1818–41). For the Schulz trio in Bristol see A. Britton, 'The Guitar and the Bristol School of Artists', *EM*, 41 (2013), 585–604, at 587–8; see also, more broadly, E. Stenstadvold, '"The worst drunkard in London": The Life and Career of the Guitar Virtuoso Leonard Schulz', *Soundboard*, 38/4 (2012), 9–16, 52.

37. *Morning Post*, 21 June 1825; *Bristol Mercury*, 13 March 1826.

38. *Leicester Chronicle*, 6 October 1827.

39. [Cochrane], *Journal of a Tour made by Señor Juan de Vega*, vol. i, 311; see also vol. i, 76, where Cochrane claims to be 'un official en el exercito constitucional'.

40. *Liverpool Mercury*, 28 November 1828, quoting the London Press; see also *The Standard*, 15 July 1828; *Brighton Gazette*, 24 July 1828; *Oxford University and City Herald*, 26 July 1828.

41. *Bell's Life in London and Sporting Chronicle*, 11 February 1827; see also *Morning Post*, 9 February 1827. The principal source for Huerta's career is J. Suárez-Pejares and R. Coldwell, *A. T. Huerta (1800–1874), Life and Works* (San Antonio, TX: DGA Editions, 2006),

which includes a list of works and an appendix of scores; its engagement list for Huerta's English years is here expanded; see also Britton, 'The Guitar and the Bristol School of Artists', 588–90.

42. *New Monthly Magazine and Literary Journal* (1827), no. 1, 95–6, a survey of new fashions. See also *Quarterly Musical Magazine and Review*, 9 (1827), 254–5: 'Thanks to the efforts of Messrs. Sor, Sola, Huerta, and other professors, the guitar instead of remaining an almost unknown instrument, or at least considered only as proper to the romantic cavaliers of Spain, and Spanish serenades, has gradually made its way into the circles of fashion, and is now pretty generally to be found in the saloons of her fair votaries.'

43. *The Times*, 6 February 1827.

44. See, for example, the review in *Brighton Gazette*, 4 September 1828, where the imitation is judged 'truly splendid'.

45. Stenstadvold, *An Annotated Bibliography*, 23.

46. *The Age*, 7 December 1828.

47. For Louis Panormo and Huerta, see J. Westbrook, 'Louis Panormo: "The only maker of guitars in the Spanish style"', *EM*, 41 (2013), 571–84, at 578–9.

48. In an attempt to exploit his renown for his own ends, Huerta announced a plan in February 1829 to open an academy for teaching the guitar with Francisco Gómez, a player who, in retrospect, seems a much less distinguished figure than Huerta, though his *Boleras de sociedad for Three Voices with an Accompaniment for the Piano Forte or Spanish Guitar* (n.d. [c.1826]) rode the contemporary wave of interest in Spanish song as successfully as any (*Morning Post*, 15 February 1828).

49. *Sussex Advertiser*, 21 October 1827; *Brighton Gazette*, 15 November 1827.

50. A. L. C. de La Garde, *Brighton: scènes détachées d'un voyage en Angleterre* (Paris and London, 1834), 221.

51. *Oxford and City Herald*, 7 June 1828.

52. Hastings: *Sussex Advertiser*, 22 October 1827. Bristol: *Bristol Mercury*, 24 March 1828 (among other sources). Bath: *The Standard*, 28 March 1828. Cambridge: poster, bearing the date Tuesday 13 May [1828], in the York Gate Collection, Royal Academy of Music, London. Eastbourne: *The Standard*, 30 May 1828. Oxford: *Oxford University and City Herald*, 31 May 1828. Tunbridge Wells: *Brighton Gazette*, 4 September 1828; *South Eastern Gazette*, 4 September 1828. Winchester: *Hampshire Chronicle*, 2 November 1829. Lymington: *Hampshire Advertiser and Salisbury Guardian*, 13 February 1830. Salisbury: *Salisbury and Winchester Journal*, 15 March 1830.

53. Hampshire Record Office, 23M93/87/1/15; Page, 'Being a Guitarist in Late Georgian England', 10, illus. 5.

Chapter Nine

1. The guitar is in the Bodleian Library, Oxford.

2. The two relevant poems, which can be read in numerous editions, are 'With a Guitar, To Jane' and 'To Jane: The keen stars were twinkling'. For images of the guitar and of Jane Williams, see S. Hebron and E. C. Denlinger, ed., *Shelley's Ghost: Reshaping the Image of a Literary Family* (Oxford: Bodleian Library, 2010), 96–7; for a technical survey of the strings found in the case see E. Segerman, 'Shelley's Guitar and 19th Century Stringing Practices', *FoMRHI Quarterly*, no. 67 (April 1992), suppl., communication 1096, p. 41. Shelley had originally hoped to buy Jane a harp in Paris: F. L. Jones, ed., *The Letters of Percy Bysshe Shelley*, 2 vols (Oxford, 1964), letters 678, 692, 699.

3. For Moore as a guitar player see A. Britton, 'The Guitar in the Romantic Period: Its Musical and Social Development with Special Reference to Bristol and Bath', doctoral diss., Royal Holloway, University of London, 2010, 128, 156, 159; at 227–8 Britton discusses some of the references to guitar playing in Moore's journal. See also the essays in S. McCleave and B. Caraher, eds, *Thomas Moore and Romantic Inspiration: Poetry, Music and Politics* (New York: Routledge, 2017). Two of Moore's songs, with arrangements for guitar, are in B. Jeffery, ed., *English Romantic Songs and Ballads of the Early Nineteenth Century with Guitar Accompaniments of the Period* (Tecla Editions, 2004), 12–14, 39–41.

4. S. McVeigh, *Concert Life in London from Mozart to Haydn* (Cambridge: Cambridge University Press, 1993), 55–6; see also H. French and M. Rothery, *Man's Estate: Landed Gentry Masculinities, 1660–1900* (Oxford: Oxford University Press, 2012), which, despite being based on a survey of 'between 10,000 and 15,000 family and personal letters' of the period, needs no index entry for 'music'.

5. *Fisher's Drawing Room Scrapbook* (1841), frontispiece, pl. facing 57.

6. *Quarterly Musical Magazine and Review*, 9 (1827), 254–5. The term 'votaries' has been imported from the expression 'votaries of fashion', a cliché of late Georgian journalism.

7. M. Wollstonecraft, *A Vindication of the Rights of Woman* (1792), 118.

8. Hélène Cixous, quoted in L. A. Finke, 'The Satire of Women Writers in "The Female Wits"', *Restoration: Studies in English Literary Culture, 1660–1700*, 8 (1984), 64–71, at 66.

9. C. Edwards, 'Home is where the Art is: Women, Handicrafts and Home Improvements, 1750–1900', *Journal of Design History*, 19 (2006), 11–21; N. Riley, *The Accomplished Lady: A History of Genteel Pursuits, c.1660–1860* (n.p. [West Yorkshire]: Oblong, 2017).

10. Anon., 'Choice of Musical Instruments for Females', *The Portfolio*, 10 (1820), 91–3.

11. Anon., 'On Public Performances on the Guitar', *The Giulianiad*, 1/4 (April 1833), 38–40, at 39–40.

12. For women's engagement with musical art in the eighteenth and nineteenth centuries see, *inter alia*, J. Brooks, 'Musical Moments for the Country House: Music, Collection, and Display at Tatton Park', *Music and Letters*, 91 (2010), 519–20; K. Ellis, 'Female Pianists and their Male Critics in Nineteenth-Century Paris', *JAMS*, l (1997), 353–85; M. Head, '"If the pretty little hand won't stretch": Music for the Fair Sex in Eighteenth-Century Germany', *JAMS*, 52 (1999), 203–54; R. H. Trillini, *The Gaze of the Listener: English Representations of Domestic Music-Making* (Amsterdam: Rodopi, 2008). For the guitar see S. Clarke, 'An Early Victorian Amateur Guitarist', *EM*, 47 (2019), 99–111.

13. For the question of time spent in musical pursuits see Hannah More, *Coelebs in Search of a Wife* (1808), where the issue is repeatedly discussed; and the unsigned, querulous essay in the *Quarterly Musical Magazine and Review*, 1 (1818), 421–8.

14. See C. Page, 'An Essay of 1824 on the Guitar', *Soundboard*, 38/4 (2012), 53–60, 75, at 57.

15. F. A. Kemble, *Records of a Girlhood* (1878), 361–2.

16. See above, pp. 58–9, and R. M. Roche, *The Discarded Son, or, The Haunt of the Banditti*, 5 vols (1807), vol. i, 96: 'Hither Elizabeth frequently brought her guitar and harp, from both of which she had been taught by her mother to draw the most exquisite tones, such as sensibility could not hear without emotion.'

17. C. H. Beale, ed., *Reminiscences of a Gentlewoman of the Last Century: Letters of Catherine Hutton* (Birmingham, 1891), 7–8.

18. At the English court of the later seventeenth century, the art of the guitar was visually coded as a female pastime, for all the guitar players shown in elite portraiture are women. Yet elite males also played the guitar during the Restoration years, including Charles II and his brother James, together with members of the high nobility (notably males of the Ormond clan), royal servants, such as the physician Sir William Waldegrave (see Fig. 3, which was not, however, painted in England), and gentleman administrators in government departments, such as Samuel Pepys. The issue was one of passing as opposed to permanent regard. A male in the 1680s could be seen with a guitar in his hands, at least by those with whom he was intimate, but the fixed and perpetual gaze of formal portraiture was generally thought to be another matter, at least in England. A man might be shown at his ease, but not distracted by a mere pastime. The Restoration images are reproduced in *GISE*.

19. See *Aris's Birmingham Gazette*, 8 November 1830, a review of Frederick Cruickshank's watercolour *Portrait of a Lady Seated in an Armchair* (1830): 'Another inveterate *fac simile* of the fair occupant of a handsome parlour, with all her household gods about her. Her piano, her guitar, her bust of Watt, her china jar . . .'. Guitar methods in which illustrations show a woman only include: F. Chabran, *Compleat Instructions for the Spanish Guitar* (1795); B. Sperati, *New and Complete Instructions for the Spanish Guitar with Six Strings* (1802); C. M. Sola, *Instructions for the Spanish Guitar* (1820); R. Douro, *A Complete Preceptor for the Spanish Guitar* (n.d. [c.1823]); A. Sosson, *A Complete Instruction Book for the Spanish Guitar* (1826); G. T. May, *Instructions for the Spanish Guitar* (c.1824?), 2nd edn (n.d. [c.1830]); P. Verini, *First Rudiments for the Spanish Guitar*, 2 vols (n.d. [c.1825]); G. H. Derwort, *A New Method of Learning the Spanish Guitar* (1825).

20. *GISE*, 109.

21. *Morning Post*, 25 December 1777.

22. P. McNeil, *Pretty Gentleman: Macaroni Men and the Eighteenth-Century Fashion World* (New Haven: Yale University Press, 2018), offers an illustrated account of the macaroni, with special emphasis on the macaroni and Frenchness in ch. 4. More broadly for the sexual underworld see J. White, *London in the Eighteenth Century: A Great and Monstrous Thing* (Bodley Head, 2012), 372–5.

23. For fine illustrations see, for example, A. Michel and P. Neumann, *Gitarren: 17. bis 19. Jahrhundert. Museum für Musikinstrumente der Universität Leipzig: Katalog* (Leipzig: Museum für Musikinstrumente, Leipzig University, 2016). Such finery, so tricked out and mostly foreign to the traditions of the lute and violin, had long been in use; it underlies the joke in John Crowne's comedy *Sir Courtly Nice* of 1686 that the fop of the title is 'the General Guitarre o' the town, inlay'd with every thing Women fancy' (*GISE*, 111).

24. Hampshire Record Office, 23M93/28/51b.

25. For Belcher and his reputation see J. R. Watson, *Romanticism and War: A Study of British Romantic Period Writers and the Napoleonic Wars* (Basingstoke and New York: Palgrave Macmillan, 2003), 14.

26. Derbyshire Record Office, D258/50/30.

27. G. Rolando, *The Modern Art of Fencing*, rev. J. S. Forsyth (1822), p. vii ('manly foils'), p. xv (arms and wrists).

28. *Morning Post*, 10 March 1814. Anon., *Report of the Directors of the Scottish Military and Naval Academy* (1826), 7.

29. I have used the copy in the Spencer Collection, Royal Academy of Music, London, 150433-1001. For the numbers in the British Library see I. Gammie,

Nineteenth-Century Guitar Songs: An Idiosyncratic Survey (St Albans: Corda Music Publications, 2017), s.v. 'Antonio Francalanza'. There is a set in the Special Collections of the University of Glasgow Library, and another in the Library of Killerton House, Devon (National Trust), without shelfmark.

30. *Blackwood's Edinburgh Magazine*, 20 (1826), 329.

31. *The Times*, 3 October 1821.

32. Ibid., 19 October 1822.

33. *Morning Post*, 13 December 1823; *The Times*, 5 March 1829. Between 1811 and 1832, lists of property put up for auction in various parts of the country reveal Spanish guitars among the possessions of a naval officer, a clergyman and a marine officer in Portsmouth dockyard, among others; see *Hampshire Telegraph and Sussex Chronicle*, 26 August 1811; *Derby Mercury*, 2 April 1828; *Berrow's Worcester Journal*, 29 March 1832; *Hampshire Advertiser and Salisbury Guardian*, 26 May 1832; *Leeds Mercury*, 4 May 1833.

34. H. Coleridge, *Poems by Hartley Coleridge* (1833), 167.

35. *OED*, s.v. 'coxcomb', *n.*, 4.b.

36. Anon., 'The Westminster Review and the Guitar', *The Giulianiad*, 1/2 (February 1833), 18–20. The passage is worth quoting further: 'Mixing, as did our warriors, with the people of Spain and Portugal; and domesticated as many of them were, and are to this day, with the families of those countries, it was only natural that they should have discovered the immense influence which the guitar there possessed, and have felt themselves, the witching powers of its fascination. It is not to be denied, that the introduction of this instrument in Britain, has taken place chiefly through the agency of British officers; and we are not risking too much in asserting, that by them and their families, and through their influence, the guitar in England is at the present moment chiefly supported.' This passage was perhaps drafted by Ferdinand Pelzer in German, to judge by the characteristic locution of that language 'It is not to be denied' ('Es ist nicht zu leugnen') at the beginning of a sentence. I am grateful to Gerhard Penn for this observation.

37. *Exeter and Plymouth Gazette*, 26 October 1839.

38. For this imagery see below, p. 201.

39. W. Irving, 'Christmas Eve', *The Sketch Book of Geoffrey Crayon*, no. 5 (New York and elsewhere, 1820); repr. in 2 vols, 2nd edn (London, 1821), vol. ii, 194–5.

40. In 1829 a soldier guitarist appears again. An issue of the *United Service Journal* for that year includes a story ostensibly based on fact, entitled 'Recollections in Quarters' and evoking an accomplished soldier of the Dragoon Guards: 'The Misses De Gray were perfectly fascinated, as of course most young ladies would have been, with an elegant youth, a Captain of Dragoons,

and one, who could fence, and dance quadrilles, ride, and play at chess and billiards, draw, and sing, and "strike the light guitar" and speak French, Italian, and Spanish, as well as his mother-tongue, in which, by the bye, he was especially fluent; besides, he was well read in the modern British Poets' (*United Service Journal* (1829), no. 1, 335). A caricature entitled *The Tender Passion*, seemingly of the later 1820s, shows an officer (as indicated by the epaulettes) proposing to a lady; a guitar lies on the ground and is perhaps to be understood as his rather than her instrument – an element in his suit to her, now abandoned in favour of a more direct appeal (British Museum, London, inv. no. 1935,0522.4.106).

41. Cochrane publicly unmasked himself as the author of *Journal of a Tour made by Señor Juan de Vega, the Spanish Minstrel of 1828–9, through Great Britain and Ireland, a Character assumed by an English Gentleman*, 2 vols (1830), and therefore as the one who had impersonated that 'Spanish minstrel', in an election speech of 1847 reported in *The Times*, 2 July 1847. For an account of Cochrane's later career as a reformer see J. Winter, *London's Teeming Streets, 1830–1914* (Routledge, 1993), 120–34.

42. [Cochrane], *Journal of a Tour made by Señor Juan de Vega*, vol. i, 88; vol. ii, 98, 227, 322.

43. Ibid., vol. i, 270. For an edition of the piece see J. Suarez-Pajares and R. Coldwell, *A. T. Huerta (1800–1874), Life and Works* (San Antonio, TX: DGA Editions, 2006), 180–81.

44. [Cochrane], *Journal of a Tour made by Señor Juan de Vega*, vol. i, 141. Cochrane claims he knew that a piece he played was in E major only because someone told him so (ibid., vol. ii, 32).

45. Ibid., vol. i, 3. The claim to have learned the guitar in Colombia was perhaps an attempt to confuse the reader into supposing that the author was Charles Cochrane's namesake and relative, Charles Stuart Cochrane, who had spent several years in Colombia and wrote of it in *Journal of a Residence and Travels in Colombia during the Years 1823 and 1824*, 2 vols (1825).

46. *Literary Gazette*, 85 (September 1818), 600.

47. Anon., 'On Public Performances on the Guitar', *The Giulianiad*, 1/4 (April 1833), 38–40, at 39; the contributor writes that the guitar 'has been regarded with so much affection by ladies in all countries' because women's imaginations 'are more strongly developed than those of men'.

48. A. Johnston, *The Enchanted Ground: The Study of Medieval Romance in the Eighteenth Century* (Athlone Press, 1964); A. Sanders, *In the Olden Time: The Victorians and the British Past* (New Haven and London: Yale University Press, 2013).

49. For eighteenth-century recoveries of balladry and romance, see Johnston, *The Enchanted Ground*, but

especially M. M. McLane, *Balladeering, Minstrelsy and the Making of British Romantic Poetry* (Cambridge: Cambridge University Press, 2008).

50. J. Keats, *The Eve of St. Agnes* (1819), stanzas 24, 33.

51. Anon., 'The Guelf and the Ghibelline: A Romance of the Middle Ages', *La Belle Assemblée*, 1 February 1824, 62–9, at 62.

52. *The Giulianiad*, 1/1 (January 1833), 1.

53. The song is mentioned in *The Boarding House* (1834) and *Our Mutual Friend* (1865).

54. *The Age*, 15 June 1828; *Newcastle Courant*, 19 July 1828; *The Standard*, 26 August 1828; *Royal Cornwall Gazette, Falmouth Packet & Plymouth Journal*, 13 September 1828.

55. W. Wordsworth, *The Excursion* (1814), Book II, 'The Solitary', lines 1ff.

56. *The Giulianiad*, 1/2 (February 1833), 21.

57. Ibid., 1/3 (March 1833), 30–31.

58. Ibid., 1/4 (April 1833), 41.

59. For imagery of the medieval troubadour, as received in the nineteenth century, see J. Haines, *Eight Centuries of Troubadours and Trouvères: The Changing Identity of Medieval Music* (Cambridge: Cambridge University Press, 2004).

60. Page, 'An Essay of 1824', 58.

61. *The Atlas*, 28 November 1830; *Perthshire Courier*, 2 December 1830; *The Pilot*, 6 December 1830; *Bath Chronicle and Weekly Gazette*, 9 December 1830; *Sherborne Mercury*, 13 December 1830; *Devizes and Wiltshire Gazette*, 16 December 1830. For parlour troubadourism in France see J. van Amersfoort, '"The notes were not sweet till you sung them": French Vocal Music with Guitar Accompaniment, c.1800–1840', *EM*, 41 (2013) 605–19; see also K. Sparr, '*Journal des troubadours avec accompagnement de guitare ou lyre*, with its Unusual Dating Code and Ferdinando Carulli as Composer and Arranger', at www.tabulatura.com/Journal%20des%20Troubadours2.pdf'.

62. Page, 'An Essay of 1824'.

63. For dandyism and the soldiery in caricature see M. D. George, *Hogarth to Cruikshank: Social Change in Graphic Satire* (Penguin Press, 1967), 196ff.

64. A. Manning, *Village Belles*, 3 vols (1833), vol. i, 162. In 'Fanny Fairfield', a tale serialised in three parts by *Blackwood's Edinburgh Magazine* in 1836, Mr Delisle is a guitarist and painter; he is also 'strikingly Byronian', marking him as an attractive and intelligent man of notable artistic talent but questionable sexual morality and politics. He writes poetry (as a Byronic male should), composes airs for his own verses on the Spanish guitar and lives by his principles, 'the very worst that can

be conceived to govern the heart and mind, from which the fear of God and the moral sense of vice and virtue had been long ago cast out as burthensome and inconvenient' (Anon., 'Fanny Fairfield', *Blackwood's Edinburgh Magazine*, 39 (January–June 1836), 198–208, 391–403, 497–513, at 402–3).

Chapter Ten

1. *ODNB*, s.v. 'Victoria (1819–1901), queen of the United Kingdom of Great Britain and Ireland, and empress of India'.

2. *Poor Man's Guardian*, 24 September 1831. For this paper see L. James, *Fiction for the Working Man, 1830–1850: A Study of the Literature Produced for the Working Classes in Early Victorian Urban England* (Oxford: Oxford University Press, 1963); I. J. Prothero, *Artisans and Politics in Early Nineteenth-Century London: John Gast and his Times* (Folkestone: Dawson, 1981), 268.

3. *Poor Man's Guardian*, 9 July 1831.

4. The Stamp Act of 1815 increased the tax payable on British newspapers to 4*d*. per copy. Some publishers refused to add this considerable sum to the cost of their newspaper and therefore evaded paying the stamp duty.

5. [C. Cochrane], *Journal of a Tour made by Señor Juan de Vega, the Spanish Minstrel of 1828–9, through Great Britain and Ireland, a Character assumed by an English Gentleman*, 2 vols (1830), vol. i, 28, 229.

6. *Poor Man's Guardian*, 13 October 1832.

7. See esp. E. Griffin, *Liberty's Dawn: A People's History of the Industrial Revolution* (New Haven: Yale University Press, 2014), ch. 7; B. Maidment, 'Dinners or Desserts? Miscellaneity, Illustration and the Periodical Press, 1820–1840', *Victorian Periodicals Review*, 43 (2010), 353–87; L. Mackay, *Respectability and the London Poor, 1780–1870* (Pickering & Chatto, 2013); J. A. Rose, *The Intellectual Life of the British Working Classes* (New Haven: Yale University Press, 2001), ch. 2.

8. Prothero, *Artisans and Politics*, 239–64.

9. J. C. Langdon, 'Pocket Editions of the New Jerusalem: Owenite Communitarianism in Britain, 1825–1855', doctoral diss., University of York, 2000, 13, 67, 242.

10. *Poor Man's Guardian*, 10 March 1832.

11. E. Elliott, *The Splendid Village: Corn Law Rhymes and Other Poems* (1833), 69–70, 119–20. 'Rule Britannia' appears in Felice Chabran's method of 1795, 'Robin Adair' in his method of 1813 (E. Stenstavold, *An Annotated Bibliography of Guitar Methods, 1760–1860* (Hillsdale, NY: Pendragon Press, 2010), 75–6). Francesco Vaccari has a different arrangement in the second part of his *Miscellaneous Selection for the Spanish Guitar* (n.d.). For context see J. Hildebrand, 'The Ranter and the Lyric: Reform and Genre Heterogeneity in Ebenezer Elliott's "Corn Law Rhymes"', *Victorian*

Review, 39 (2013), 101–24; *ODNB*, s.v. 'Elliott, Ebenezer [called the Corn Law Rhymer]'. Some of the most radical songs in circulation were reprints of firebrand material animated by the example of the French Revolution, including Richard Carlile's *The Wreath of Freedom: Songs in Favour of Public Liberty* (1820; repr. 1832); with abundant allusions to Thomas Paine and *The Rights of Man*, the songs in *The Wreath of Freedom* join vigorously seditious verse to melodies such as 'God save the king', 'Rule Britannia' and traditional tunes such as 'The Vicar of Bray', 'Maggy Lauder' and 'Duncan Grey'. See also A. Morgan, ed., *Ballads and Songs of Peterloo* (Manchester: Manchester University Press, 2018). For later material see K. Bowan and P. A. Pickering '"Songs for the Millions": Chartist Music and Popular Aural Tradition', *Australia Labour History Review*, 74 (2009), 44–63; M. Sanders, '"A jackass load of poetry": The *Northern Star*'s Poetry Column, 1838–1852', *Victorian Periodicals Review*, 39 (2006), 46–66; M. Sanders, '"God is our guide! Our cause is just!" The National Chartist Hymn Book and Victorian Hymnody', *Victorian Studies*, 54 (2012), 679–705.

12. S. J. Cross, 'Geographies of Owenite Socialism in Britain, 1830–1840: Public Lecturing, the Social Institution and the Production of Associational Knowledges', doctoral diss., University of Cambridge, 2003; Langdon, 'Pocket Editions of the New Jerusalem; *ODNB*, s.v. 'Owen, Robert (1771–1858)'; Prothero, *Artisans and Politics*.

13. Senate House Library, University of London, Special collections [G.L] A. 831.

14. Cross, 'Geographies of Owenite Socialism in Britain'.

15. R. J. S. Stevens, 'Anecdotes, Occurrences [*sic*], Extracts, Opinions and Observations', Cambridge University Library, MS 9111/2, 44. In the event, another music master undertook the task, much to Stevens's relief.

16. *Morning Post*, 14 February 1835; *Kentish Gazette*, 3 March 1835, adds various details; see also R. D. Altick, *The Shows of London: A Panoramic History of Exhibitions, 1600–1862* (Cambridge, MA: Harvard University Press, 1978), ch. 19. According to a late but uniquely informative witness, Henry Mayhew, 'a respectable man' whom he interviewed in the later 1840s had begun playing the guitar in the streets at the age of 4 (*Morning Chronicle*, 6 June 1850).

17. This image of a laundress guitarist began life as a cartoon in *Bell's Life in London and Sporting Chronicle*, 14 September 1828. As presented there, it showed an elderly laundress receiving guitar and singing lessons in her hovel from a reluctant music master, unable to pay his laundry bill in any other way.

18. M. D. George, *Hogarth to Cruikshank: Social Change in Graphic Satire* (Penguin Press, 1967), 177–84;

B. Maidment, *Comedy, Caricature and the Social Order, 1820–50* (Manchester: Manchester University Press, 2013); A. Rauch, *Useful Knowledge: The Victorians, Morality, and the March of Intellect* (Durham, NC: Duke University Press, 2001).

19. C. Page, 'Being a Guitarist in Late Georgian England', *EM* 46 (2018), 3–16, at 8–9.

20. L. Jackson, *Palaces of Pleasure. From Music Halls to the Seaside to Football: How the Victorians Invented Mass Entertainment* (London: Yale University Press, 2019).

21. *Musical World* (1836), 12–13.

22. *Berkshire Chronicle*, 1 October 1836; *Worcester Journal*, 6 October 1836; *Sherborne Mercury*, 17 October 1836; *Kentish Gazette*, 25 October 1836; *Staffordshire Advertiser*, 5 November 1836.

23. See, for example, Altick, *The Shows of London*; B. Comment, *The Panorama*, trans. A.-M. Glasheen (1999); and for the cheap magazines B. Maidment, *Into the 1830s: Some Origins of Victorian Illustrated Journalism: Cheap Octavo Magazines of the 1820s and their Influence* (Manchester: Manchester Polytechnic Library, 1992). Rose, *The Intellectual Life of the British Working Classes* provides essential context.

24. Maidment, 'Dinners or Desserts?', 354.

25. *The Casket*, 8 March 1834, 80; the source is the anonymous essay 'On the Comparative Merits of the Piano Forte and Guitar, as an Accompaniment to the Voice', *The Giulianiad*, 1/1 (January, 1833), 9–11.

26. L. Brake and M. Demoor, *Dictionary of Nineteenth-Century Journalism in Britain and Ireland* (Academia Press and the British Library, 2009), 486; S. Bennett, 'The Editorial Character and Readership of "The Penny Magazine": An Analysis', *Victorian Periodicals Review*, 17 (1984), 127–41.

27. *Penny Magazine of the Society for the Diffusion of Useful Knowledge*, 3 (1834), 189.

28. Ibid., 190.

29. The importance granted to German makers is surprising and suggests a memory of circumstances relating to the English guitar in the eighteenth century: P. Poulopoulos, 'The Influence of Germans in the Development of "This favourite instrument the guittar" in England', *Soundboard*, 38/4 (2012), 62–75.

30. Even the genteel recognised that there were bargain instruments to be had in the pawnshops, including some in a poor state that might be perfectly good when reconditioned. See H. Mayhew, *London Labour and the London Poor*, 4 vols (1861–2; repr. 1968), vol. i, 18–19, on pawnbrokers deceived with inferior instruments that they may be unwilling to accept as pledges.

31. C. Dickens, 'Brokers' and Marine-Store Shops', in *Sketches by Boz* (1836).

32. *Satirist; or, the Censor of the Times*, 27 November 1831; *Bell's Life in London and Sporting Chronicle*, 27 May 1832.

33. *Manchester Times and Gazette*, 20 August 1831.

34. J. M. Ciebra, *Ciebra's Handbook for the Guitar* (n.d. [*c.*1860]). The work is certainly Victorian and is commonly assigned to about 1860, which cannot be far wrong since it uses a melody from Verdi's *Rigoletto*, premiered in London in 1853. Priced at 1s., the book was one of the cheapest guitar tutors ever produced up to that time, and was clearly intended for players of very modest means. A flyleaf in the book carries advertisements for even cheaper material: a series of sixpenny tutors for the concertina, violin, cornet, banjo and other instruments. The most explicit passage is contained in the remarkable introduction: '. . . (in this work a-day world) expense *is* a consideration, and it may be not unwelcome intelligence to many that a most respectable guitar can be procured for even less than a Guinea. This, kept nicely clean, and slung round the neck by a ribbon (plain for a Gentleman, and fanciful as fairy work for a Lady), will suffice for beginners whatever may be their position.'

Conclusion

1. H. Irving, *Ancients and Moderns: William Crotch and the Development of Classical Music* (Aldershot: Ashgate, 1999), prints Crotch's lectures of 1818.

2. Ibid., 215.

3. *Literary Gazette*, 20 June 1818, 393.

4. For another reference to Beethoven's 'crudities' in his piano music, referring to his use of dissonance, see *The Harmonicon*, 1 (1823), 112. As Katherine Ellis has remarked in her review of R. Wallace, *Beethoven's Critics* (1986), *Music and Letters* 68 (1987), 293–4, the study by Wallace shows virtually no interest in the British response to Beethoven, for which abundant materials exist (294); see also T. Skowroneck, *Beethoven the Pianist* (Cambridge: Cambridge University Press, 2010), 142–55.

5. Anon., 'On Public Performances on the Guitar', *The Giulianiad*, 1/4 (April 1833), 38–40, at 38.

6. See C. Goodwin, *The Lute in English Renaissance Verse, 1500–1700: An Anthology* (Albury, Guildford: Lute Society, 2007).

7. *Musical World*, 2 (1836), 69–72, at 69; see also *ODNB*, s.v. 'Hogarth, George'. For the Romantic interest in old instruments during the later nineteenth century see S. Kirby, 'Prisms of the Musical Past: British International Exhibitions and "Ancient Instruments", 1885–1890', *EM*, 47 (2019), 393–407.

8. See John Keats, *Ode to Apollo* ('In thy western halls of gold'), lines 34–5. For the theme in lesser hands see H. F. Cary, *Sonnets and Odes* (1788), 23 ('The Dedication

of an Æolian Harp'); G. Goodwin, *Rising Castle, with Other Poems* (1798), 101–2 ('To the Æolian Harp'). On the metaphorical uses of the Aeolian harp in Romantic writing see the enlightening discussion in W. St Clair, *The Reading Nation in the Romantic Period* (Cambridge: Cambridge University Press, 2004), 402–3. The interest in such instruments can be traced well back into the eighteenth century: H. Thorowgood, *A Description of the Æolian-harp, or Harp of Æolus from the Earliest Account to the Present Time* (n.d. [*c*.1754]). For Aeolian harps in lists of property put up for auction see *Gazetteer and New Daily Advertiser*, 17 August 1772 (the stock of the famous furniture- and instrument-maker Johan Friedrich Hintz); *Bath Chronicle*, 16 October 1788; *Morning Chronicle*, 23 March 1807; *Morning Chronicle*, 29 December 1818. For the pragmatic business of buying an Aeolian harp see J. Wescomb Emmerton, letter to his brother, 8 December 1795, Nottinghamshire Record Office, DD/SY/169/xii: 'The Aeolian Harps are a Guinea apiece. They seem to be all of the same size, and will do for any modern window, but mine are not wide enough to receive them. They have twelve strings, all in Unison accept the two outward strings, which are Octaves to the others. Mrs W's pitch-form for the Guitar will give the proper key, and I think she will meet with no difficulty in tuning it. I enquired at Dale's shop opposite the Royal Exchange, where I bought Miss B's Harp, who thought him a reasonable man. If Mrs W. chuses to have one I would advise her to let Mr Townley or some Musical Person buy it, that it may be well toned.'

9. G. Croly, *The Angel of the World . . . with other Poems* (1820), 84–5.

10. R. M. Roche, *The Discarded Son, or, The Haunt of the Banditti*, 5 vols (1807), vol. i, 96.

11. T. Blanning, *The Romantic Revolution* (New York: Modern Library, 2011), 61–107.

12. H. Berlioz, *Grand traité d'instrumentation et d'orchestration modernes*, 2nd edn (Paris, 1855), 86.

13. *Literary Gazette*, 87 (1818), 600. C. Page, 'An Essay of 1824 on the Guitar', *Soundboard*, 38/4 (2012), 53–60, 75, at 50. For a pioneering discussion of the guitar and

Romantic thought see A. Britton, 'The Guitar in the Romantic Period: Its Musical and Social Development with Special Reference to Bristol and Bath', doctoral diss., Royal Holloway, University of London, 2010, 129ff.

14. J. Bowring, ed., *Ancient Poetry and Romances of Spain* (1824), pp. vi–vii.

15. J. A. Junco, 'The Formation of Spanish Identity and its Adaptation to the Age of Nations', *History and Memory*, 14 (2002), 13–36.

16. J. Hanmer, *Sonnets of Sir John Hanmer* (1840), p. i.

17. See, for example, T. Martin, *The Circle of the Mechanical Arts* (1813), 450: 'The Spaniards . . . are so partial to music, and to that of the guitar in particular, that there are few, even of the labouring class, who do not solace themselves with the practice of it. They use the guitar to serenade their mistresses, and there is scarcely an artificer in any of the cities, or principal towns, who, when his work is over, does not entertain himself with his guitar.'

18. *La Belle Assemblée*, 1 June, 1811, 293.

19. R. Holland, *The Warm South: How the Mediterranean Shaped the British Imagination* (London and New Haven: Yale University Press, 2019); see also M. Butler, *Romantics, Rebels and Revolutionaries: English Literature and its Background, 1760–1830* (Oxford: Oxford University Press, 1981), 113–37.

20. M. Hewitt, 'Why the Notion of Victorian Britain Does Make Sense', *Victorian Studies*, 48 (2006), 395–438, at 396.

21. For these phases see *GITE* and *GISE*.

22. *Brighton Gazette*, 29 October, 30 October, 20 November 1862.

23. *Yorkshire Gazette*, 24 December, 1842.

24. See, for example, *Sherborne Mercury*, 5 April 1845.

25. *Brighton Gazette*, 7 December 1865.

26. *Birmingham Mail*, 14 January 1877.

Bibliography

The place of publication for books is London, unless otherwise indicated.

PRIMARY SOURCES

Manuscripts

Cambridge
Cambridge University
Library
MS 9111/2
MS Add. 9098

Cambridge, Mass.
Harvard University,
Houghton Library
TS 932.3

The Hague
Nederlands Muziek
    Instituut
MS Kluis DI

Haslemere
Library of the Dolmetsch
Foundation
MS II C 27

Hertford
Hertfordshire Record Office
D/EHX F56

Kew
The National Archives
PROB 11/898/208 (1)
PROB 11/1411/242
PROB 11/1506/435
PROB 11/2038/384

London
London Metropolitan
Archives
MS 11936/401/630765
Corporation of London
G. Mus. 472
287/MRY/060

London
Royal Academy of Music,
Spencer Collection

Los Angeles
University of California,
William Andrews Clark
Memorial Library
MS f.c.697.M. 4

Maidstone
Kent Archives Office
U269/A518/5

Matlock
Derbyshire Record Office
D239 M/F 367
D258/50/30

Nottingham
Nottinghamshire Record
Office
DD/SY/169/xii.

Oxford
Bodleian Libraries, Ashe
Collection

Preston
Lancashire Record Office
DDB/81/35

Washington, DC
Library of Congress, Lord
Saltoun's collection of guitar
music, 1810–50

Winchester
Hampshire Record Office
9M55/F5/13
9M55/F4/14

9M55/F4/16
23M93/87/1/4–7
23M93/87/1/11
23M93/87/1/15

Woking
Surrey History Centre
2185/JB/42/4
3677/3/77a–b

Worcester
Worcestershire Record
Office
26/M69/1

Printed

*Sources known only from
secondary references, which
are lost or were never printed,
are enclosed in square
brackets.*

Newspapers and Periodicals
Ackermann's Repository
Age, The
Almanach Musical
Aris's Birmingham Gazette
*Atheneum: or Spirit of the
    English Magazines*
Atlas, The
*Bath Chronicle and Weekly
    Gazette*
Belle Assemblée, La
*Bell's Life in London and
    Sporting Chronicle*
Berkshire Chronicle
Birmingham Mail
*Blackwood's Edinburgh
    Magazine*
Brice's Weekly Journal

Brighton Gazette
Brighton Guardian
Bristol Mercury
Bristol Mirror
Caledonian Mercury
Carlisle Journal
Carlisle Patriot
Casket of Literature, Science
    and Entertainment
Cheltenham Chronicle
Chester Chronicle
Chester Courant
Courier and Evening Gazette
Courier de Londres
Coventry Herald
Daily Advertiser
Daily Courant
Daily Journal
Daily Post
Derby Mercury
Devizes and Wiltshire
    Gazette
Diary; or, Woodfall's Register
Dorset County Chronicle
Examiner, The
Exeter and Plymouth Gazette
Exeter Flying Post
Fisher's Drawing Room
    Scrapbook
Freeman's Journal
Gazetteer and New Daily
    Advertiser
General Advertiser
Giulianiad, The
Glasgow Herald
Hampshire Advertiser and
    Salisbury Guardian
Hampshire Chronicle
Hampshire Telegraph and
    Sussex Chronicle
Harmonicon, The
Hereford Journal
Hull Advertiser and Exchange
    Gazette
John Bull
Kentish Gazette and
    Canterbury Journal
Kentish Weekly Post or
    Canterbury Journal
Lady's Monthly Museum
Leamington Spa Courier
Leeds Intelligencer
Leeds Mercury

Leeds Times
Leicester Chronicle
Literary Gazette
Liverpool Mercury
London Chronicle
London Courier and Evening
    Gazette
London Evening Post
London Gazette
London Magazine
Manchester Courier and
    Lancashire General
    Advertiser
Manchester Mercury
Manchester Times and
    Gazette
Mayo Constitution
Mirror of Literature,
    Amusement, and
    Instruction
Morning Chronicle
Morning Chronicle and
    London Advertiser
Morning Herald and Daily
    Advertiser
Morning Post
Musical World
Newcastle Courant
New Monthly Magazine and
    Literary Journal
New-York Mirror
Norfolk Chronicle and
    Norwich Gazette
Northampton Mercury
Observator, The
Olio, or Museum of
    Entertainment
Oracle and Daily Advertiser
Oracle and Public Advertiser
Oracle: Bell's New World
Oxford Journal
Oxford University and City
    Herald
Penny London Post or The
    Morning Advertiser
Penny Magazine of the
    Society for the Diffusion of
    Useful Knowledge
Perthshire Courier
Poor Man's Guardian
Post Man and the Historical
    Account
Public Advertiser

Quarterly Musical Magazine
    and Review
Royal Cornwall Gazette,
    Falmouth Packet &
    Plymouth Journal
St. James's Chronicle or the
    British Evening Post
Salisbury and Winchester
    Journal
Satirist; or, the Censor of the
    Times
Sheffield Independent
Sherborne Mercury
Sligo Champion
South Eastern Gazette
Staffordshire Advertiser
Stamford Mercury
Standard, The
Sussex Advertiser
Times, The
Trewman's Exeter Flying Post
True Briton
United Service Journal
Universal Chronicle, or
    Weekly Gazette
Westminster Review
Wiltshire Independent
Worcester Journal
World
Yorkshire Gazette

Sources Relating to the Spanish Guitar

List of principal works
mentioned; individual songs
are not included.

Aguado, D., Trois rondo [sic]
    brillants, op. 2 (Madrid,
    1825)
Alberti, F., The Apollon,
    Containing National
    Gems for the Spanish
    Guitar from the Works
    of Giuliani, Carulli,
    Eulenstein … (n.d. [1820?])
Anelli, G., Singing Academy
    Prospectus with the Origin
    of the Spanish Guitar
    (Clifton, 1834)
Anonymous, 'Guitar
    Professors, and Guitar
    Makers and Sellers', The

Giulianiad, 1/5 (July, 1833), 44–5

———, 'On Public Performances on the Guitar', *The Giulianiad*, 1/4 (April 1833), 38–40

———, 'On the Capabilities of the Guitar', *The Giulianiad*, 1/1 (January 1833), 3–5

———, 'On the Comparative Merits of the Piano Forte and Guitar, as an Accompaniment to the Voice', *The Giulianiad*, 1/1 (January, 1833), 9–11

———, 'Public Concerts', *The Giulianiad*, 1/5 (July 1833), 46–8

———, 'The Westminster Review and the Guitar', *The Giulianiad*, 1/2 (February 1833), 18–20

———, 'To the Editor of *The Giulianiad*', *The Giulianiad*, 1/5 (July 1833), 27–8

Baillon, P.-J., *Nouvelle méthode de guitarre* (Paris, 1780)

Barnett, J., *The Songs of the Minstrels . . . Arranged with an Accompaniment for the Spanish Guitar . . . by C. Eulenstein*, 2 vols (n.d. [1828?])

B. D. C., *Méthode de guittarre par musique et tablature* (Paris, 1773)

Bennett, A., *Instructions for the Spanish Guitar* (1829)

Bolton, T., *A Collection of Airs, Marches, Dances (with Figures), Waltzes, Pollacas, and Quick Steps . . . The Whole Adapted for the Piano Forte, with Accompaniments and Directions ad libitum for the following Fashionable Instruments: Lyre or Lute, Spanish Guitar, Harp,*

Tambourine, Castanets, Flute or Violin (1808)

Bortolazzi, B., *Periodical Amusements for the Spanish Guitar* (1807–)

———, *Three Ariettes . . . Extracted from the Periodical Amusements* (1807)

Burnett, W., [*Eight Familiar Airs for the Spanish Guitar . . . an Explanation of the Finger Board; the Natural and Cromatic Scales; with the Chords in the Different Keys, and the Manner of Fingering them, by William Burnett, Musician, Belonging to the Coldstream Regiment of Foot Guards* (1784)]

———, [*Six Familiar Airs for the Spanish Guittar, with a Compleat Scale for that Instrument* (1784)] [probably the same as the above]

Campion, F., *Addition au traité d'accompagnement* (Paris, 1730; repr. Geneva, 1976)

———, *Nouvelles découvertes sur la guitarre* (1705), ed. F. Lesure as *Nouvelles découvertes sur la guitarre, contenantes plusieurs suittes de pièces sur huit manières différentes d'accorder. Exemplaire augmenté de nombreuses pièces manuscrites de la main de l'auteur (Ms. Bibliothèque Nationale, Paris, Vm7 6221)* (Geneva, 1977) [with composer's manuscript additions]

Carcassi, M., *Twelve Easy Pieces for the Spanish Guitar Composed for the Use of Beginners* (1828)

———, *Twelve Popular Airs . . . Arranged for the Spanish Guitar* (1828)

Carulli, F., *Forty [recte fourteen] Easy Pieces and Eight Short Preludes for the Guitar Composed for the Use of Beginners: Op. 1 of Works Composed in London* (n.d. [1823?])

Castillion, Jean de, Preface to François Le Cocq, 'Recueil des pieces de guitarre', Brussels, Bibliothèque du Conservatoire Royal de Musique, MS Littera s, no. 5615, 1730, pubd (Brussels, 1979) [facsimile of preface in Saint-Arroman and Delume, eds, *Méthodes et traités . . . Guitare*, vol. i, 47–61]

Chabran, F., *Compleat Instructions for the Spanish Guitar* (1795)

Ciebra, J. M., *Ciebra's Handbook for the Guitar* (n.d. [c.1860])

Corrette, M., *Les dons d'Apollon* (Paris, 1762)

Derosiers, N., *Les principes de la guitarre* (1689) [facsimile in Saint-Arroman and Delume, eds, *Méthodes et traités . . . Guitare*, vol. i, 39–45]

Derwort, G. H., *A New Method of Learning the Spanish Guitar* (1825)

———, *Dolce ed utile: A Melange of Original Compositions, Operatic Airs, Rondos, Waltzes, etc. for the Spanish Guitar . . . Selected for the Use of Amateurs, Corrected and Fingered by Derwort* (n.d. [1828?])

Doisy, C., *Principes généraux de la guitare*, 2 pts (1801; pt i repr. Geneva, 1979)

Dor. ***, *Methode pour aprendre a joüer de la guitare* (Paris and Madrid, 1758)

Douro, R., *A Complete Preceptor for the Spanish Guitar* (n.d. [*c*.1823])

Downes, R. L., *Eight Esteemed Italian, Portuguese and Spanish Songs with an Accompaniment for the Spanish Guitar* (n.d. [*c*.1820])

Dussek, S., [*Four Canzonets, with a Spanish Guitar Accompaniment, by Mrs Dussek* (1801?)]

Dussek, S., with S. Mandini, *Three Favorite Canzonetts, Arranged with Accompaniment for the Piano Forte or Guitar* (1799)

Duvernay, F., *A Complete Instruction Book for the Guitar* (1828)

Francalanza, A., *A Collection of Italian and French Canzonets with Accompaniments for the Spanish Guitar or Piano Forte*, 3 vols (1811–12)

Garsault, F.-A.-P. de, *Notionnaire ou mémorial raisonné* (Paris, 1761)

Gianella, L., *Un cestellin di fiori: Canzonetta, with an Accompaniment for the Piano Forte or Spanish Guitar, and Vien qua Dorina bella: Canzonetta, with an Accompaniment for the Piano Forte or Spanish Guitar Composed Expressly for Signor Tramezzani* (n.d. [*c*.1810])

Giuliani, M., *Le Rossiniane*, opp. 119–24 (Vienna, n.d. [*c*.1822])

Gómez, F., *Boleras de sociedad for Three Voices with an Accompaniment for the Piano Forte or Spanish Guitar* (n.d. [*c*.1826])

Holst, M. von, *A Selection of the Most Favorite Scottish Melodies Arranged for the Voice with Symphonies and Accompaniments for the Spanish Guitar* (n.d. [*c*.1825–7])

Horetzky, F., *L'Aurore, ou journal de guitare: choix des plus beaux morceaux composés pour cet instrument* (1827)

Huerta, A. T., *Grand March of Don Rafaell dell Riego* (1824)

——, *The Celebrated Fantasia founded on Rossini's Overture to Semiramide* (1829)

'Huerta, A. T.', *A Complete Book of Instructions for the Spanish Guitar* (1829)

Jauralde, N., *A Complete Preceptor for the Spanish Guitar* (1828)

Jeffery, B., ed., *Fernando Sor: New Complete Works for Guitar*, 2nd edn, 11 vols (2004)

——, *Fernando Sor: Seguidillas*, 2 vols (1976, 1999)

Kloe, J. de, ed., *Fernando Sor: Music for Voice and Guitar* (Heidelberg, 2005)

[Lambley, J.], *Guide to the Art of Accompanying on the Spanish Guitar* (Birmingham, 1829)]

Ledesma, M. R. de, *Three Italian Ariettes, with an Accompaniment for Spanish Guitar and Piano Forte* (1814)

Lolli, L. B., *Six Italian Canzonetts, with Accompaniments for the Spanish Guitar, or Piano Forte, Two Noturn's [sic] for Two Voices, and Six Easy Divertiments for the Piano Forte or Harp ...* (n.d. [1800?])

Matteis, N., *The False Consonances of Musick or Instructions for the Playing a True Base upon the Guitarre, with Choice Examples and Cleare Directions to enable any Man in a Short Time to Play all Musicall Ayres* (1682)

May, G. T., *Instructions for the Spanish Guitar* (*c*.1824?), 2nd edn (n.d. [*c*.1830])

Mayr, S., *Three Cavatine for Voice and an Accompaniment, either for Piano Forte, Harp, or Spanish Guitar, the Last with a Flute, or Violin Obligato, Composed ... for ... Mr Viganoni* (n.d. [1805?])

Merchi, [G.], *Le guide des écoliers de guitarre*, op. 7 (Paris, 1761; repr. Geneva, 1981)

——, *Raccolta d'ariette francesi ed italiane per la chitarra*, op. 4 (1760)

——, *Scelta d'ariette francesi italiane ed inglesi con accompagnamento di chitarra*, op. 15 (1766)

—— [or Merchi, B.], *Traité des agrémens de la musique* (Paris, 1777; repr. Geneva, 1981)

Millais, I. W. [J. W.], *Eight Airs and Waltzes and a March for the Spanish Guitar* (1827)

Molina, F. V., *Spanish Serenades ... which have been Admired in the First Circles of London ... for the Piano Forte and Guitar* (n.d. [*c*.1825])

——, *The Spanish Lyre* (1825)

Prucilli, P. [pseud. of Robert William Keith], *Rudiments for the Spanish Guitar* (n.d. [*c*.1830])

Rosquellas, P., *A Complete Tutor for the Spanish Guitar* (n.d. [1813?])

Sagrini, L., *Divertissement*, op. 20 [see 'Electronic Resources', Coldwell]

Saint-Arroman, J., and C. Delume, eds, *Méthodes et traités, 18: Guitare*, ser. I: *France, 1600–1800*, 2 vols (Courlay, 2003)

Sola, C. M., *Instructions for the Spanish Guitar* (1820)

——, *Six French Songs Composed with an Accompaniment for the Spanish Guitar* (1823)

——, *Six Italian Canzonets with an Accompaniment for the Guitar* (n.d. [1820?])

Sor, F., [*Fantasia Concertante, Composed of French, Spanish and Tyrolese Airs for the Spanish Guittar, Violin, Viola, Violoncello and Double Bass* (n.d. [c.1816])]

——, *Méthode pour la guitare* (1830) [pubd 1 January 1831]; Eng. trans. A. Merrick as *Method for the Spanish Guitar* (1832)

——, *Second Fantasia for the Spanish Guitar*, [op. 4] (1816)

——, *Six Divertimentos for the Spanish Guitar*, [op. 1] (1816)

——, *Six Divertimentos for the Spanish Guitar*, [op. 2] (1816)

Sosson, A., *A Complete Instruction Book for the Spanish Guitar* (1826)

Sperati, B., *A Periodical Collection of Italian, French and English Songs . . . for the Spanish Guitar of Six Strings*, 12 pts (1801–2)

——, *New and Complete Instructions for the Spanish Guitar with Six Strings* (1802) [no. 1 of the above]

Vaccari, F., *Three Favorite Spanish Boleros as Sung by Madame Vaccari, Arranged with an Accompaniment for Spanish Guitar or Piano Forte* (n.d. [c.1810])

——, *Vaccari's Miscellaneous Selection for the Spanish Guitar Humbly Dedicated to H.R.H. the Princess Charlotte* (n.d. [c.1813])

——, [*Vaccari's Miscellaneous Selection for the Spanish Guitar, II* (n.d.)] [pubd without title page], private collection (unique copy)

Verini, P., *Bolero Arranged as a Duet for Two Voices with an Accompaniment for the Spanish Guitar* (n.d. [c.1820])

——, *Divertimento* (for A. T. Huerta) (n.d. [1820s–1830s])

——, *First Rudiments for the Spanish Guitar*, 2 vols (n.d. [c.1825])

Vidal, M., *Collection of Easy Pieces for the Guitar dedicated to Mrs de St Albain* (n.d. [1791?])

Zaniboni, A., *Six Italian Canzonetts and Eight Divertimentos principally for Spanish Guitar and Bass Accompaniments or any other Instruments, Composed and Dedicated with Permission to the Right Noble Lady Emily Stratford by Antonio Zaniboni* (n.d. [1802?])

Sources Relating to the English Guitar

List of principal works mentioned; individual songs are not included.

Anonymous, *A Pocket Book for the Guitar* (n.d. [c.1770])

——, *The Airs with all the Symphonies in the Opera of Artaxerxes: Corrected, Transpos'd for the German Flute, Violin and Guitar* (1763)

Bremner, R., *Instructions for the Guitar with a Collection of Airs, Songs, and Duets, Fitted for that Instrument* (Edinburgh, 1758)

Call, T., *The Tunes and Hymns as they are used at the Magdalen Chapel, Properly Set for the Organ, Harpsichord and Guittar* (n.d. [c.1760])

Carpentier, J., *1er Recueil de menuets, allemandes etc. entremêlés d'airs agréables à chanter avec leurs accompagnements dont les sujets sont tirés des meilleurs autheurs et arrangés exprès pour le cytre ou guitthare allemande* (Paris, 1770)

——, *Methode distribuée par leçons pour apprendre en peu de temps à joüer de l'instrument appellé cytre où* [sic] *guitthare allemande* (Paris, 1771)

——, *Methode pour apprendre en peu de temps à joüer de l'instrument appellé cytre où guitthare allemande, IIeme partie* (Paris, 1773)

Cloes, N., *One Hundred French Songs Set for a Voice, German Flute, Violin, Harpsicord and Pandola* (n.d. [1749?])

Ford, A., *Lessons and Instructions for Playing on the Guitar* (1761)

Geminiani, F., *The Art of Playing the Guitar*

or Cittra Containing
Several Compositions
with a Bass for
the Violoncello or
Harpsichord (1760; repr.
New York, 1999); ed. P.
Holman (Bologna, 2019)

Giardini, F., *Six Trios for the
Guittar, Violin and Piano
Forte, or Harp, Violin and
Violoncello*, op. 18 (1775)

Hintz, J. F., *A Choice
Collection of Psalm and
Hymn Tunes set for the
Cetra or Guittar . . .* (n.d.
[1760?])

Marella, G. B., *Sixty-Six
Lessons for the Cetra or
Guittar, in Every Key,
both Flat and Sharp*, op.
3 (1758)

Straube, R., *Three Sonatas
for the Guittar, with
Accompanyments for
the Harpsichord or
Violoncello . . . with
an Addition of Two
Sonatas for the Guittar
Accompanyd with the
Violin. Likewise a Choice
Collection of the most
Favourite English, Scotch
and Italian Songs for
One and Two Guittars,
of Different Authors,
properly Adapted for that
Instrument, also Thirty
Two Solo Lessons by
Several Masters* (1768;
repr. Monte Carlo, 1979)

Wilson, W., *A New Selection
of the Most Admired Songs
for the Guittar* (Aberdeen
and Edinburgh, n.d.
[c.1780])

**Other Printed Primary
Material**
Aird, J., *Selection of Scotch,
English, Irish and Foreign
Airs Adapted for the Fife,
Violin or German Flute*
(n.d. [1795?])

Anonymous, *A Comparison
between the Two Stages*
(1702)
——, 'A Trifle from
Brighton', *Lancaster
Gazette and General
Advertiser*, 21 April 1827
——, *A Trip to Spain: or,
A True Description of
the Comical Humours,
Ridiculous Customs, and
Foolish Laws, of that Lazy
Improvident People the
Spaniards. In a Letter to
a Person of Quality by an
Officer in the Royal Navy*
(1705)
——, *Belleville Lodge*, 2 vols
(1793)
——, *Bibliographie
parisienne, ou Catalogue
d'ouvrages de sciences, de
littérature et de tout ce qui
concerne les beaux-arts,
Année 1770* (Paris, 1772).
——, *Catalogue de livres
anglois et français* (Ghent,
1789)
——, *Choice Novels and
Amorous Tales* (1652)
——, 'Choice of Musical
Instruments for Females',
The Portfolio, 10 (1820),
91–3
——, 'Collection of
Admired Italian, French,
German, Spanish,
and English Songs,
with a Progressive
Accompaniment for
the Spanish Guitar; by
George Hervey Derwort',
*Quarterly Musical
Magazine and Review*, 6
(1824), 543–8 [review]
——, *Concerts of Antient
Music, under the
Patronage of Their
Majesties as Performed
at the New Rooms,
Tottenham-Street* (1792)
——, *Co-operative Songs*
(n.d. [1832?])

——, *Eliza: or, The History
of Miss Granville*, 2 vols
(1766)
——, 'Fanny Fairfield',
*Blackwood's Edinburgh
Magazine*, 39 (January–
June 1836), 198–208,
391–403, 497–513
——, *Hartlebourn Castle: A
Descriptive English Tale*,
2 vols (1793)
——, 'Idea of a New
Court for Domestic
Grievances', *New
Monthly Magazine and
Literary Journal* (1833),
no. 2, 476–9
——, *Memoirs of the Bedford
Coffee-House* (1763)
——, *Montrose, or The
Gothic Ruin*, 3 vols (1799)
——, *Musical Directory for
the Year 1794* (1794)
——, *Report of the Directors
of the Scottish Military
and Naval Academy* (1826)
——, 'Sketch of the State
of Music in London,
1823', *Quarterly Musical
Magazine and Review*, 5
(1823), 241–75
——, *The Feelings of the
Heart; or, The History of a
Country Girl*, 2 vols (1772)
——, 'The Guelf and the
Ghibelline: A Romance
of the Middle Ages',
La Belle Assemblée, 1
February 1824, 62–9
——, *The Ladies Cabinet
Broke Open* (1710)
——, *The Levellers: A
Dialogue between Two
Young Ladies, concerning
Matrimony* (1703); repr.
in *Harleian Miscellany*,
5 (1745), 417–33 [known
only from the reprinted
version]
——, *The Royal Blue Book
and Fashionable Directory
and Canvassing Guide for
1822* (1822)

——, *The Watering Places of Great Britain and Fashionable Directory* (1831)

——, *Waldegrave: A Novel*, 2 vols (New York, 1829)

Anstey, C., *The Mercenary Marriage*, 2 vols (1773)

Arnold, S., and J. O'Keeffe, *The Castle of Andalusia* (1782)

Aspinall, A., ed., *Letters of the Princess Charlotte, 1811–1817* (1949)

Astor, G., *Astor's Twenty Four Country Dances for the Year 1803: with Proper Tunes and Directions to each Dance as they are Performed at Court, Bath, and all Public Assemblies* (1803)

Atkinson, B. A., *Good Princes Nursing Fathers and Nursing Mothers to the Church. A Sermon Preach'd in London, May 2, 1736. On the Marriage of His Royal Highness* (1736)

Avison, C., *An Essay on Musical Expression* (1752)

Baines, A., 'Fifteenth-Century Instruments in Tinctoris's De inventione et usu musicae', *GSJ*, 3 (1950), 19–26 [parallel text and trans.]

Baker, T., *Tunbridge Walks, or, The Yeoman of Kent; a Comedy* (1703)

Barbauld, A. L., *A Legacy for Young Ladies Consisting of Miscellaneous Pieces in Prose and Verse by the late Mrs. Barbauld* (1826)

Baretti, G., *A Journey from London to Genoa, through England, Portugal, Spain, and France*, 4 vols (1770)

Beale, C. H., ed., *Reminiscences of a Gentlewoman of the Last Century: Letters of Catherine Hutton* (Birmingham, 1891)

Bell, A., *The Cabinet: A Series of Essays Moral and Literary*, 2 vols (1835)

Bell, G., *Rough Notes by an Old Soldier, during Fifty Years' Service*, 2 vols (1867)

Beresford, J., *The Miseries of Human Life*, 2 vols (1807)

Berlioz, H., *Grand traité d'instrumentation et d'orchestration modernes*, 2nd edn (Paris, 1855)

Bonhôte, E., *Olivia; or, Deserted Bride*, 3 vols (1787)

Bowring, J., ed., *Ancient Poetry and Romances of Spain* (1824)

Boyer, A., *The History of the Life and Reign of Queen Anne* (1722)

—— (trans.), *Memoirs of the Life of Count de Grammont* (1714)

Bridgeman, O. G. C., ed., *Letters from Portugal, Spain, Sicily, and Malta: in 1812, 1813, and 1814* (1875)

Brotherton L., *An Account of Printed Musick, for Violins, Hautboys, Flutes, and other Instruments, by Several Masters* (n.d. [c.1724])

Brown, J., *An Estimate of the Manners and Principles of the Times*, 2nd edn (1757)

Brusoni, G., *Delle novelle amorose libri quattro* (Venice, 1655)

[Buckham, E. W.], *A Personal Narrative of Adventures in the Peninsula during the War in 1812–1813, by an Officer* (1827)

Buckley, R. N., ed., *The Napoleonic War Journal of Captain Thomas Henry Browne, 1807–1816* (1987)

Burnett, W., *Summer Amusement … Twelve Country Dances and Three Cotillons, entirely New, for a Violin and Bass, Harpsichord or Harp* (1782)

——, [*Twenty-Four Military Divertimentos* (1783?)]

Burney, C., *A General History of Music*, 4 vols (1776–89)

Byron, G., *Childe Harold's Pilgrimage* (1812–18)

Capel, J., *Books of the Words of Ten Private Concerts held at the House of J. Capel*, 10 pts (1817–28) [privately printed]

Carleton, G., *The Military Memoirs of Captain George Carleton* (1743)

Carlile, R., *The Wreath of Freedom: Songs in Favour of Public Liberty* (1820; repr. 1832)

Carter, F., *A Journey from Gibraltar to Malaga*, 3 vols (1777)

[Caswall, E.], *Sketches of Young Ladies* (1837)

Chamberlayne, E., *The Present State of England* (1683)

Clark, E., *Ermina Montrose; or, The Cottage of the Vale*, 3 vols (1800)

[Cochrane, C.], *Journal of a Tour made by Señor Juan de Vega, the Spanish Minstrel of 1828–9, through Great Britain and Ireland, a Character assumed by an English Gentleman*, 2 vols (1830)

Coleridge, H., *Poems by Hartley Coleridge* (1833)

Cooke, J., *Memoirs of the Late War*, 2 vols (1831)

Corri, D., *Select Collection of the most Admired Songs,*

Duetts, etc. from Operas in the Highest Esteem, and from other Works, 4 vols (1795)

Costello, E., *The Adventures of a Soldier ... Comprising Narratives of the Campaigns in the Peninsular [sic] under the Duke of Wellington, and the Recent Civil Wars in Spain*, 2nd edn (1852)

Croly, G., *The Angel of the World ... with other Poems* (1820)

C. T., *A Short Account and Character of Spain in a Letter from an English Gentleman now Residing at Madrid to his Friend in London* (1701)

d'Albert, C.-P., *Mémoires du duc de Luynes sur la cour de Louis XV*, 17 vols (Paris, 1860–65)

Darrel, W., *A Supplement to the First Part of The Gentleman Instructed* (1708)

de Beer, E. S., ed., *The Diary of John Evelyn*, 6 vols (Oxford, 2000)

Defoe, D., *A Journal of the Plague Year* (1722)

——, *The History and Remarkable Life of the Truly Honourable Colonel Jaque, Vulgarly Call'd, Colonel Jack, who was Born a Gentleman* (1722)

Deleplanque, [J.], *Recueil d'airs ... pour la harpe* (Paris, n.d.)

Denis, P., *Troisième et dernière partie de la méthode pour apprendre à jouer de la mandoline sans maître* (Paris, 1773)

Dickens, C., *Sketches by Boz* (1836)

Diderot, D., and J. Le Rond d'Alembert, *Encyclopédie, ou dictionnaire raisonné des sciences, des arts et des métiers*, 28 vols (Paris and Neuchâtel, 1751–72) with later supplements and rev. edns

Dillon, J. T., *Letters from an English Traveller in Spain, in 1778* (1781)

Disraeli, B., *Henrietta Temple: A Love Story*, 3 vols (1837)

——, *The Young Duke*, 3 vols (1831)

——, *Vivian Grey*, 5 vols (1826)

Doane, J., *A Musical Directory for the Year 1794* (1794; repr. 1993)

Donaldson, J., *Recollections of the Eventful Life of a Soldier* (Philadelphia, 1845)

Dryden, J., *An Evening's Love* (1668)

Egan, P., *Life in London* (1823)

Elliott, E., *The Splendid Village: Corn Law Rhymes and Other Poems* (1833)

Espinel, V., *Relaciones de la vida del escudero Marcos de Obregón* (Madrid, 1618)

Ezell, M. J. M., ed., *Poems and Prose of Mary, Lady Chudleigh* (Oxford, 1993)

Fletcher, J., *The Chances: A Comedy* (1755)

Foote, S., *The Englishman in Paris* (1753)

Fraser, A., *The Frasers of Philorth*, 3 vols (1879)

Fulford, R., ed., *The Autobiography of Miss Knight, Lady Companion to Princess Charlotte* (1960)

Gardiner, W., *Music and Friends: or, Pleasant Recollections of a Dilettante*, 2 vols (1838)

Glover, G., ed., *An Eloquent Soldier: The Peninsular War Journals of Lieutenant Charles Crowe of the Inniskillings, 1812–14* (Barnsley, 2011)

Goldsmith, O., *The Vicar of Wakefield: A Tale*, 2 vols (1766)

Granville, A. B., *Autobiography of A. B. Granville*, 2nd edn, 2 vols (1874)

Grattan, W., *Adventures with the Connaught Rangers from 1808 to 1814* (1902)

Griffith, S. Y., *Griffith's New Historical Description of Cheltenham and its Vicinity*, 2nd edn, 2 vols (1826)

Hamilton, A., *Mémoires de la vie du comte de Grammont; contenant particulièrement l'histoire amoureuse de la cour d'Angleterre, sous le regne de Charles II* ('Cologne', 1713)

Hamilton, E., *A Record of the Life and Death of Her Royal Highness Princess Charlotte* (1817)

Hanmer, J., *Sonnets of Sir John Hanmer* (1840)

Hawes, W., *Programmes, Books of Words, etc., of the Annual Concerts given by W. Hawes in 1814, 1819, 1824–39, and by W. and M. B. Hawes in 1840–41. With MS. notes by Sir G. T. Smart* (1818–41) [privately printed]

Hawker, P., *Journal of a Regimental Officer during the Recent Campaign in Portugal and Spain under Lord Viscount Wellington* (1810)

Hawkins, J., *A General History of the Science and Practice of Music*, 5 vols (1776)

Hazlitt, W., *On the Want of Money* (1826)

Henry, W., *Trifles from my Port-folio, or, Recollections of Adventures during Twenty-Nine Years' Military Service in the Peninsular War and Invasion of France, the East Indies, Campaign in Nepaul, St. Helena during the Detention and until the Death of Napoleon, and Upper and Lower Canada*, 2 vols (Quebec, 1839; repr. 2011)

Herd, D., *The Ancient and Modern Scots Songs, Heroic Ballads, etc. Now First Collected into one Body* (Edinburgh, 1769)

Hudson, M. S., *Almack's: A Novel in Three Volumes* (1826)

Hughes, J., *An Itinerary of Provence and the Rhone made during the Year 1819* (1822)

Irving, W., *The Sketch Book of Geoffrey Crayon* (1819)

Jardine, A., *Letters from Barbary, France, Spain, Portugal, etc. by an English Officer*, 2 vols (1788)

Jones, F. L., ed., *The Letters of Percy Bysshe Shelley*, 2 vols (Oxford, 1964)

Kaye, J. W., ed., *Autobiography of Miss Cornelia Knight, Lady Companion to the Princess Charlotte of Wales*, 3rd edn, 2 vols (1861)

Kelly, S., ed., *The Life of Mrs. Sherwood* (1854)

Kemble, F. A., *Records of a Girlhood* (1878)

La Garde, A. L. C. de, Comte, *Brighton: scènes détachées d'un voyage en Angleterre* (Paris and London, 1834)

Landman, G. T., *Recollections of my Military Life*, 2 vols (1854)

Langton, A., *The History of the Life of the Squire Marcos de Obregon ... by Vincent Espinel ... translated into English from the Madrid Edition of 1618*, 2 vols (1816)

Larpent, F. S., *The Private Journal of Judge-Advocate Larpent* (1854)

Latham, R., and W. Matthews, eds, *The Diary of Samuel Pepys: A New and Complete Transcription*, 11 vols (1971–83)

Le Courayer, P.-F., 'Second Love: A Tale', *Lady's Monthly Museum*, 1 (December 1812), 306–9; 2 (January 1813), 31–4; 3 (March 1813), 123–6; 4 (May 1813), 251–5; 5 (June 1813), 323–6; 5 (August 1813), 74–8

Lonsdale, R., ed., *The Poems of Thomas Gray, William Collins, Oliver Goldsmith*, new edn (1976)

Mackintosh, J., *Memoirs of the Life of the Rt. Hon. Sir James Mackintosh*, 2 vols (1835)

Man, H., *The Trifler: or, A Ramble among the Wilds of Fancy, the Works of Nature, and the Manners of Men*, 4 vols (1775) (Dublin 1779)

Manning, A., *Village Belles*, 3 vols (1833)

Manuscripts of Sir William Fitzherbert, Bart., and Others, HMC, 13th Report, Appendix vi (1893)

Martin, T., *The Circle of the Mechanical Arts* (1813)

Matthews, Mrs, *A Continuation of the Memoirs of Charles Matthews*, 2 vols (Philadelphia, 1839)

Mayhew, H., *London Labour and the London Poor*, 4 vols (1861–2; repr. 1968)

Miles, Mrs L., 'The Fancy Ball', *The Giulianiad*, 1/3 (March 1833), 30–31

More, H., *Coelebs in Search of a Wife* (1808)

——, *Strictures on the Modern System of Female Education*, 3rd edn, 2 vols (1799)

Motteux, A., *The Novelty: Every Act a Play* (1697)

Mottley, J., *The Widow Bewitch'd: A Comedy* (1730)

Napier, W. F. P., *History of the War in the Peninsula and the South of France from the Year 1807 to the Year 1814*, 6 vols (1828–40)

New, M., and P. de Voogd, eds, *The Florida Edition of the Works of Laurence Sterne*, vol. viii (Gainesville, Fla: University Press of Florida, 2009)

Nial, B., ed., *Georgiana: A Biography of Georgiana McCrae, Painter, Diarist, Pioneer* (1994)

Ormsby, J.-W., *An Account of the Operations of the British Army, and of the State and Sentiments of the People of Portugal and Spain, during the Campaigns of the Years 1808 and 1809 in a Series of Letters*, 2 vols (1809)

Parfaict, F., Q. Godin d'Abguerbe and C. Parfaict, *Dictionnaire des théâtres de Paris*, 7 vols (Paris, 1756)

Patterson, J., *The Adventures of Captain John Patterson* (1837)

Penny Cyclopædia of the Society for the Diffusion of Useful Knowledge, 27 vols, 3 suppls (1828–43)

Pepusch, J. C., *A Short Explication of such Foreign Words, as are made Use of in Musick Books* (1724)

Percy, T., *Reliques of Ancient English Poetry: Consisting of Old Heroic Ballads, Songs and other Pieces of our Earlier Poets*, 3 vols (1765)

Petrini, F., *Recueil de pieces et d'airs choisis, avec accompagnement de harpe* (Paris, n.d.)

Piozzi, H. L., *Observations and Reflections made in the Course of a Journey*, 2 vols (1789)

Pitman, A., *The Miseries of Music Masters* (1815)

Playford, H., *Wit and Mirth; or Pills to Purge Melancholy*, ed. J. Tonson, 6 vols (1719–20) [vols i–ii contain 350 songs by Thomas d'Urfey]

Pope, A., *The Dunciad in Four Books*, ed. V. Rumbold, rev. edn (Harlow: Pearson Longman, 2009)

Porter, R. K., *Letters from Portugal and Spain written during the March of the British Troops under Sir John Moore, with a Map of the Route, and Appropriate Engravings* (1809)

Pujol, D., ed., *Mestres de l'Escolania de Montserrat: obres musicals dels monjos del Monestir de Montserrat, 1500–1800. Joan Cererols: transcripció, revisió i anotació de David Pujol*, 3 vols (Monestir de Montserrat, 1930)

Pyne, W. H., *The History of the Royal Residences of Windsor Castle, St. James's Palace, Carlton House, Kensington Palace, Hampton Court, Buckingham House, and Frogmore*, 3 vols (1819)

Raithby, J., *Delineations of the Heart; or, The History of Henry Bennet*, 3 vols (1792)

Rede, L. T., *The Road to the Stage* (1827)

Rees, A., *The Cyclopædia: or, Universal Dictionary of Arts, Sciences, and Literature*, 41 vols (1810–24)

Robins, B., ed., *The John Marsh Journals: The Life and Times of a Gentleman Composer (1752–1828)*, 2 vols (1998, 2013)

Robinson, W. A., *A Trip to Margate* (1803)

Roche, R. M., *The Discarded Son, or, The Haunt of the Banditti*, 5 vols (1807)

——, *The Vicar of Lansdowne*, 2 vols (1789)

Rolando, G., *The Modern Art of Fencing*, rev. J. S. Forsyth (1822)

Sadler, T., ed., *Henry Crabb Robinson: Diary, Reminiscences, and Correspondence* , 3 vols (1869)

Salmon, T., *Modern History: or, The Present State of all Nations*, 31 vols (1724–38)

Scott, W., *The Vision of Don Roderick* (1811)

Seymour, R., *The Schoolmaster Abroad* (1834)

Sheldrick, G., ed., *The Accounts of Thomas Green: Music Teacher and Tuner of Musical Instruments, 1742–1790* (Ware: Hertfordshire Record Society, 1992)

Sherer, M., *Recollections of the Peninsula* (1823)

'Sketchwell, Sir B.', *London Characters: or, Fashions and Customs of the Present Century* 2nd edn, 2 vols (1809)

Southey, R., *History of the Peninsular War*, 3 vols (1823–32)

Spence, E., *The Spanish Guitar: A Tale for the Use of Young Persons* (1814)

Spohr, L., *Louis Spohr's Autobiography: Translated from the German* (1865)

[Stewart, J. A.], *The Young Woman's Companion; or, Female Instructor*, various edns (1814–)

Stickney, S., *Pictures of Private Life* (1833)

Stothert, W., *A Narrative of the Principal Events of the Campaigns of 1809, 1810 and 1811 in Spain and Portugal* (1812)

Swinburne, H., *Travels through Spain, in the Years 1775 and 1776* (Dublin, 1779)

[Tayler, C. B.], *A Fireside Book: or, The Account of a Christmas spent at Old Court* (1828)

Thomson, J., *The Seasons* (1730), ed. J. Sambrook (Oxford: Clarendon Press, 1981)

Thorowgood, H., *A Description of the Æolian-harp, or Harp of Æolus from the Earliest Account to the Present Time* (n.d. [*c*.1754])

Trenchard, J., *Cato's Letters*, 4 vols (1723)

Twiss, R., *Travels through Portugal and Spain, in 1772 and 1773* (1775)

Vanbrugh, J., *The Confederacy* (1705)

Walker, J. C., *Historical*

Memoirs of the Irish Bards (Dublin, 1786)

Ward, E., *Nuptial Dialogues and Debates*, 2 vols (1710)

Watts, J., *The Musical Miscellany, being a Collection of Choice Songs*, 6 vols (1729–31)

White, J., 'Preparations for Pleasure or a Picnic', *New Monthly Magazine and Literary Journal* (1829), no. 2, 372–90

Winston, J., *The Theatric Tourist* (1805)

Wollstonecraft, M., *A Vindication of the Rights of Woman* (1792)

SECONDARY SOURCES

Printed Materials

Ackerman, J. S., *The Villa: Form and Ideology of Country Houses* (Thames and Hudson, 1990)

Aleixo, R., *La guitarra en Madrid (1750–1808) con un catálogo de la música de ese periodo conservada en bibliotecas madrileñas* (Madrid: Spanish Society of Musicology, 2016)

Almeida, J. M., ed., *Romanticism and the Anglo-Hispanic Imaginary* (Amsterdam and New York: Rodopi, 2010)

Altick, R. D., *The Shows of London: A Panoramic History of Exhibitions, 1600–1862* (Cambridge, MA: Harvard University Press, 1978)

Amersfoort, J. van, '"Extra fine guitars after the newest fashion": Guitar- and Cittern-Making in the Northern Netherlands, 1750–1800', *EM*, 46 (2018), 35–53

——, 'Miss Sara Burgerhart's English *Guittar*: The 'guitarre Angloise' in Enlightenment Holland', *Tijdschrift van de Koninklijke Vereniging voor Nederlandse Musiekgeschiedenis*, 64 (2014), 76–102

——, '"The notes were not sweet till you sung them": French Vocal Music with Guitar Accompaniment, c.1800–1840', *EM*, 41 (2013), 605–19

An, Y. L., 'The Periodical Music Collections of John Bland', in M. Kassler, ed., *The Music Trade in Georgian England* (Farnham: Ashgate, 2011), 195–229

Andrews, M., *The Search for the Picturesque: Landscape Aesthetics and Tourism in Britain, 1760–1800* (Aldershot: Scolar Press, 1989)

Armstrong, J., and D. M. Williams, 'The Steamboat and Popular Tourism', *Journal of Transport History*, 26 (2005), 61–77

——, 'The Steamship as an Agent of Modernisation, 1812–1840', *International Journal of Maritime History*, 19 (2007), 145–60

Ashley, L. R. N., 'The Theatre-Royal in Drury Lane, 1711–1716, under Colley Cibber, Barton Booth and Robert Wilks', doctoral diss., Princeton University, 1955

Bainbridge, S., ed., *British Poetry and the Revolutionary and Napoleonic Wars: Visions of Conflict* (Oxford: Oxford University Press, 2003)

Baine, R. M., 'Daniel Defoe and Robert Drury's Journal', *Texas Studies in Literature and Language*, 16 (1974), 479–91

Barbieri, P., 'An Assessment of Musicians and Instrument-Makers in Rome during Handel's Stay: The 1708 Grand Taxation', *EM*, 37 (2009), 597–619

——, 'Roman and Neapolitan Gut Strings, 1550–1950', *GSJ*, 59 (2006), 147–81

Barker, H., 'Catering for Provincial Tastes? Newspapers, Readership and Profit in Late Eighteenth-Century England', *Historical Research*, 69 (1996), 42–61

——, *Newspapers, Politics, and Public Opinion in Late Eighteenth-Century England* (Oxford: Oxford University Press, 1998)

Bashford, C., 'Historiography and Invisible Musics: Domestic Chamber Music in Nineteenth-Century Britain', *JAMS*, 63 (2010), 291–360

Bessey, H., *Thomas Gainsborough: The Portraits, Fancy Pictures and Copies after Old Masters*, 2 vols (New Haven: Yale University Press, 2019)

Bennett, S., 'The Editorial Character and Readership of "The Penny Magazine": An Analysis', *Victorian Periodicals Review*, 17 (1984), 127–41

Benton, R., *Ignace Pleyel: A Thematic Catalogue of his Compositions* (New York: Pendragon Press, 1977)

Berry, S., *Georgian Brighton* (Chichester: Phillimore, 2005)

Bilston, S., '"They congregate . . . in towns and suburbs": The Shape of Middle-Class Life in John Claudius Loudon's *The Suburban Gardener*', *Victorian Review*, 37 (2011), 144–59

Birkett, S., and P. Poletti, 'Reproduction of Authentic Historical Soft Iron Wire for Musical Instruments', in T. Steiner, ed., *Instruments à claviers: expressivité et flexibilité sonore. Actes des Rencontres Internationales Harmoniques, Lausanne 2002* (Bern: Lang, 2004), 259–72

Blanning, T., *The Romantic Revolution* (New York: Modern Library, 2011)

Bonner, S., *The Classic Image: European History and Manufacture of the Lyre Guitar, 850–1840* (Harlow: Bois de Boulogne, 1972)

Borer, M. C., *The British Hotel through the Ages* (Guildford: Lutterworth Press, 1972)

Borsay, P., *The English Urban Renaissance: Culture and Society in the Provincial Town, 1660–1770* (Oxford: Clarendon Press, 1989)

Bowan, K., and P. A. Pickering, '"Songs for the Millions": Chartist Music and Popular Aural Tradition', *Australia Labour History Review*, 74 (2009), 44–63

Boynton, L., 'The Moravian Brotherhood and the Migration of Furniture Makers in the Eighteenth Century', *Furniture History*, 29 (1993), 45–58

Brake, L., and M. Demoor, *Dictionary of Nineteenth-Century Journalism in Britain and Ireland* (Academia Press and the British Library, 2009)

Brandon, R., *Governess: The Lives and Times of the Real Jane Eyres* (New York: Walker & Co., 2008)

Briso de Montiano, L., 'Una parte de la biblioteca personal de Dionisio Aguado en el legado de Rosaio Huidobro', *Roseta*, 12 (2018), 115–64

Britton, A., 'The Guitar and the Bristol School of Artists', *EM*, 41 (2013), 585–604

——, 'The Guitar in the Romantic Period: Its Musical and Social Development with Special Reference to Bristol and Bath', doctoral diss., Royal Holloway, University of London, 2010

Brooks, J., 'Musical Moments for the Country House: Music, Collection, and Display at Tatton Park', *Music and Letters*, 91 (2010), 519–20

Brown, C., *Classical and Romantic Performing Practice, 1750–1900* (Oxford: Oxford University Press, 1999)

Burke, T., *English Inns* (W. Collins, 1943)

Burrows, D., and R. Dunhill, eds, *Music and Theatre in Handel's World: The Family Papers of James Harris, 1732–1780* (Oxford: Oxford University Press, 2002)

Bury, Charlotte, *Diary Illustrative of the Times of George the Fourth*, 2 vols (Paris, 1838–9)

Butler, M., *Romantics, Rebels and Reactionaries: English Literature and its Background, 1760–1830* (Oxford: Oxford University Press, 1981)

Button, S. W., 'The Guitar in England, 1800–1924', doctoral diss., University of Surrey, 1984

Buurman, E., and O. C. Jensen, '"Dancing the Waterloo Waltz": Commemorations of the Hundred Days – Parallels in British Social Dance and Song', in K. Astbury and M. Philp, eds, *Napoleon's Hundred Days and the Politics of Legitimacy* (Basingstoke: Palgrave Macmillan, 2018), 209–32

Cannadine, D., *Class in Britain* (New Haven and London: Yale University Press, 1988)

Carpenter, K., *Refugees of the French Revolution: Émigrés in London, 1789–1802* (Basingstoke: Macmillan Press, 1999)

Chilton, M., *Harlequin Unmasked: The Commedia dell'arte and Porcelain Sculpture* (New Haven and London: Yale University Press, 2001)

Clarke, S., 'An Early Victorian Amateur Guitarist', *EM*, 47 (2019), 99–111

Coelho, V. A., ed., *Performance on Lute, Guitar and Vihuela:*

Historical Practice and Modern Interpretation (Cambridge: Cambridge University Press, 1997)

Coggin, P., '"This easy and agreeable instrument": A History of the English Guittar', *EM*, 15 (1987), 205–20

Cohen, M., '"Manners make the man": Politeness, Chivalry, and the Construction of Masculinity, 1750–1830', *Journal of British Studies*, 44 (2005), 312–29

Coke, D., and A. Borg, *Vauxhall Gardens: A History* (New Haven and London: Yale University Press, 2011)

Colville, Q., and K. Williams, eds, *Emma Hamilton: Seduction and Celebrity* (Thames and Hudson, 2016)

Comment, B., *The Panorama*, trans. A.-M. Glasheen (Reaktion, 1999)

Confalone, N., 'Scene di vita vittoriana dalle memorie di Madame Sidney Pratten e di sua sorella Giulia Pelzer', *Il Fronimo*, 181 (January 2018), 21–30

Cross, S. J., 'Geographies of Owenite Socialism in Britain, 1830–1840: Public Lecturing, the Social Institution and the Production of Associational Knowledges', unpublished doctoral diss., University of Cambridge, 2003

Cudworth, C., 'The Vauxhall "Lists"', *GSJ*, 20 (1967), 24–42

Dale, C., *Fashionable Brighton, 1820–1860* (Country Life, 1947)

Daly, G., *The British Soldier in the Peninsular War: Encounters with Spain and Portugal, 1808–1814* (Basingstoke: Palgrave Macmillan, 2013)

Darvall, P., *A Regency Buck: Adam Buck (1759–1833)* (Oxford: Ashmolean Museum, 2015)

Davidoff, L., and C. Hall, *Family Fortunes: Men and Women of the English Middle Class, 1780–1850* (London and New York: Routledge, 2002)

Dean, C., 'Court Culture and Political News in London's Eighteenth-Century Newspapers', *ELH*, 73 (2006), 631–49

Delaforce, P., *Wellington the Beau: The Life and Loves of the Duke of Wellington* (Moreton-in-Marsh: Windrush Press, 1990)

Devriès-Lesure, A., *Dictionnaire des éditeurs de musique français*, 3 vols (Geneva: Minkoff, 1979–88)

——, *L'édition musicale dans la presse parisienne au XVIIIe siècle: catalogue des annonces* (Paris: CNRS Éditions, 2005)

Doyon, A., 'Maximilien Radix de Sainte-Foy, 1736–1810', *Revue d'Histoire Diplomatique*, 80 (1966), 231–74, 314–54

Dubois, P., *Music in the Georgian Novel* (Cambridge: Cambridge University Press, 2015)

Edwards, C. 'Home is where the Art is: Women, Handicrafts and Home Improvements, 1750–1900', *Journal of Design History*, 19 (2006), 11–21

Eisenhardt, L., *Italian Guitar Music of the Seventeenth Century: Battuto and Pizzicato* (Woodbridge: Boydell & Brewer, 2015)

Ellis, K., 'Female Pianists and their Male Critics in Nineteenth-Century Paris', *JAMS*, 50 (1997), 353–85

——, Review of R. Wallace, *Beethoven's Critics* (1986), *Music and Letters*, 68 (1987), 293–4

Everly, S., 'Mozart and the Moravians', *EM*, 47 (2019), 161–82

Fenner, T., *Opera in London: Views of the Press, 1785–1830* (Carbondale: Southern Illinois University Press, 1994)

Fernández, J. G. C., 'La mirada del Inglés: historia y vivencias sociales de los combatientes británicos en España y Portugal', *Historia Social*, 72 (2012), 23–47

Firke, L. A., 'The Satire of Women Writers in "The Female Wits"', *Restoration: Studies in English Literary Culture, 1660–1700*, 8 (1984), 64–71

Fleming, S. D. I., 'A Century of Music Production in Durham City, 1711–1811: A Documentary Study', doctoral diss., University of Durham, 2009

Foskett, D., *Miniatures: Dictionary and Guide* (Woodbridge: Antique Collectors Club, 1987)

Foster, S. C., '"To Entertain the Fancy": The Orchestral Concert Song in England, 1740–1800', doctoral diss., Goldsmiths, University of London, 2013

French, H., and M. Rothery, *Man's Estate: Landed Gentry Masculinities, 1660–1900* (Oxford: Oxford University Press, 2012)

Frignani, L., A. Radice and T. Rizzi, *La chitarra in Italia tra la fine del Settecento e l'inizio dell'Ottocento* (Modena: LF Edizioni, 2015)

Fulford, T., *Romanticism and Masculinity: Gender, Politics and Poetics in the Writings of Burke, Coleridge, Cobbett, Wordsworth, De Quincey and Hazlitt* (Basingstoke: Macmillan Press, 1999)

Gammie, I., *Nineteenth-Century Guitar Songs: An Idiosyncratic Survey* (St Albans: Corda Music Publications, 2017)

Garlick, G., 'Theatre Outside London, 1660–1775', in J. Donohue, ed., *The Cambridge History of British Theatre*, vol. ii (Cambridge, 2004), 165–82

Gásser, L., ed., *Estudios sobre Fernando Sor*, 2nd edn (Madrid: Ediciones del ICCMU, 2010)

George, M. D., *Hogarth to Cruikshank: Social Change in Graphic Satire* (Penguin Press, 1967)

Girdham, J., *English Opera in Late Eighteenth-Century London: Stephen Storace at Drury Lane* (Oxford: Clarendon Press, 1997)

Goff, M., '"Actions, manners, and passions": Entr'acte Dancing on the London Stage, 1700–1737', *EM*, 26 (1998), 213–28

——, 'John Rich, French Dancing, and English Pantomimes', in Joncus and Barlow, eds, *'The Stage's Glory'*, 85–98

Golby, D., *Instrumental Teaching in Nineteenth-Century Britain* (Aldershot: Ashgate, 2004)

Goodwin, C., *The Lute in English Renaissance Verse, 1500–1700: An Anthology* (Albury, Guildford: Lute Society, 2007)

Graf, L., 'John Frederick Hintz, Eighteenth-Century Moravian Instrument Maker, and the Use of the Citter in Moravian Worship', *Journal of Moravian History*, 5 (2008), 7–39

——, 'Moravians in London: A Case Study in Furniture-Making', *Furniture History*, 40 (2004), 1–52

Greene, J. C., *Theatre in Dublin, 1745–1820: A Calendar of Performances*, 2 vols (Bethlehem, PA: Lehigh University Press, 2011)

Greig, H., *The Beau Monde: Fashionable Society in Georgian London* (Oxford: Oxford University Press, 2013)

Griffin, E., *Liberty's Dawn: A People's History of the Industrial Revolution* (New Haven: Yale University Press, 2014)

Grunfeld, F. V., *The Art and Times of the Guitar: An Illustrated History of Guitars and Guitarists* (New York and London: Macmillan, 1969)

Haines, J., *Eight Centuries of Troubadours and Trouvères: The Changing Identity of Medieval Music* (Cambridge:

Cambridge University Press, 2004)

Hall, M., *'Princess An's Lute Book* and Related English Sources of Music for the 5-course Guitar', *The Consort*, 66 (2010), 18–34

Harris, J. R., 'French Industrial Espionage in Britain in the Late Eighteenth Century', *RSA Journal*, 137 (1989), 629–34

Hartdegen, K., 'Fernando Sor's Theory of Harmony Applied to the Guitar: History, Bibliography and Context', 3 vols, doctoral diss., University of Auckland, 2011

Head, M., '"If the pretty little hand won't stretch": Music for the Fair Sex in Eighteenth-Century Germany', *JAMS*, 52 (1999), 203–54

Hebron, S., and E. C. Denlinger, eds, *Shelley's Ghost: Reshaping the Image of a Literary Family* (Oxford: Bodleian Library, 2010)

Heck, T. F., *Mauro Giuliani: Virtuoso Guitarist and Composer* (Columbus, OH: Editions Orphée, 1995)

——, 'The Vogue of the *chitarra francese* in Italy: How French? How Italian? How Neapolitan?', *Soundboard*, 38/4 (2012), 18–24, 44

Heinowitz, R. C., *Spanish America and British Romanticism, 1777–1826: Rewriting Conquest* (Edinburgh: Edinburgh University Press, 2010)

Hewitt, M., 'Why the Notion of Victorian Britain Does Make

Sense', *Victorian Studies*, 48 (2006), 395–438

Hildebrand, J., 'The Ranter and the Lyric: Reform and Genre Heterogeneity in Ebenezer Elliott's "Corn Law Rhymes"', *Victorian Review*, 39 (2013), 101–24

Hindricks, T., *Zwischen 'leerer Klimperey' und 'wirklicher Kunst': Gitarrenmusik in Deutschland um 1800* (Münster: Waxmann, 2012)

Holland, R., *The Warm South: How the Mediterranean Shaped the British Imagination* (New Haven and London: Yale University Press, 2019)

Holman, P., *Life after Death: The Viola da Gamba in Britain from Purcell to Dolmetsch* (Woodbridge: Boydell Press, 2010)

——, 'The Lute Family in Britain in the Eighteenth and Nineteenth Centuries', *Lute News*, 84 (December, 2007), 7–21

——, and R. Cowgill, eds, *Music in the English Provinces, 1690–1914* (Aldershot: Ashgate, 2007)

Hubbell, A., 'How Wordsworth Invented Picnicking and Saved British Culture', *Romanticism*, 12 (2006), 44–51

Hunt, J. D., 'Picturesque Mirrors and the Ruins of the Past', *Art History*, 4 (1981), 254–70

Ingamells, J., *Dulwich Picture Gallery Collections: British* (Unicorn Press, 2008)

Irving, H., *Ancients and Moderns: William Crotch and the Development of Classical Music* (Aldershot: Ashgate, 1999)

Jackson, L., *Palaces of Pleasure. From Music Halls to the Seaside to Football: How the Victorians Invented Mass Entertainment* (New Haven and London: Yale University Press, 2019)

James, L., *Fiction for the Working Man, 1830–1850: A Study of the Literature Produced for the Working Classes in Early Victorian Urban England* (Oxford: Oxford University Press, 1963)

Jeffery, B., *English Romantic Songs and Ballads of the Early Nineteenth Century with Guitar Accompaniments of the Period* (Tecla Editions, 2004)

——, *España de la guerra: The Spanish Political and Military Songs of the War in Spain, 1808 to 1814* (Tecla Editions, 2017)

——, *Fernando Sor: Composer and Guitarist*, 2nd edn (Tecla Editions, 1994)

Johnson, E, 'The Death and Second Life of the Harpsichord', *Journal of Musicology*, 30 (2013), 180–214

Johnston, A., *The Enchanted Ground: The Study of Medieval Romance in the Eighteenth Century* (Athlone Press, 1964)

Joncus, B., and J. Barlow, eds, *'The Stage's Glory': John Rich, 1692–1761* (Newark: University of Delaware Press, 2011)

Junco, J. A., 'The Formation of Spanish Identity and its Adaptation to the Age of Nations', *History and Memory*, 14 (2002), 13–36

Jung, S., 'Print Culture, High-Cultural Consumption, and Thomson's "The Seasons", 1780–1797', *Eighteenth-Century Studies*, 44 (2011), 495–514

Kelly, I., *Mr Foote's Other Leg: Comedy, Tragedy and Murder in Georgian London* (Picador, 2012)

Kelly, J. M., 'A Classical Education: Naples at the Heart of European Culture', in Colville and Williams, eds, *Emma Hamilton: Seduction and Celebrity*, 108–37

Ken'ichiro, I., 'Siciliano in der Instrumentalmusik Joseph Haydns und seiner Zeitgenossen: Untersuchungen zur kompositorischen Auseinandersetzung mit dem Topos im klassischen Stil', doctoral diss., Julius-Maximilians-Universität, Würzburg, 2014

Kennedy, C., *Narratives of the Revolutionary and Napoleonic Wars: Military and Civilian Experience in Britain and Ireland* (Basingstoke: Palgrave Macmillan, 2013)

Kenyon de Pascual, K., 'Ventas de instrumentos musicales en Madrid durante la segunda mitad del siglo XVIII, II', *Revista de Musicología*, 6 (1933), 299–308

Kirby, S., 'Prisms of the Musical Past: British International Exhibitions and "Ancient

Instruments", 1885–1890', *EM*, 47 (2019), 393–407

Klein, L. E., 'Politeness and the Interpretation of the British Eighteenth Century', *Historical Journal*, 45 (2002), 869–98

Knight, R., *Britain Against Napoleon: The Organization of Victory, 1793–1815* (Allen Lane, 2013)

LaMay, T., ed. *Musical Voices of Early Modern Women: Many-Headed Melodies* (Aldershot: Ashgate, 2005)

Langdon, J. C., 'Pocket Editions of the New Jerusalem: Owenite Communitarianism in Britain, 1825–1855', doctoral diss., University of York, 2000

Langford, P., *A Polite and Commercial People: England, 1727–1783* (Oxford: Clarendon Press, 1989)

——, 'The Uses of Eighteenth-Century Politeness', *Transactions of the Royal Historical Society*, 6th ser., 12 (2002), 311–31

Latcham, M., 'Pianos and Harpsichords for Their Majesties', *EM*, 36 (2008), 359–96

Leppert, R., *Music and Image: Domesticity, Ideology and Socio-Cultural Formation in Eighteenth-Century England*, new edn (Cambridge: Cambridge University Press, 1993)

Loftis, J., *The Spanish Plays of Neoclassical England* (New Haven and London: Yale University Press, 1973)

Lombard, J., *Courtilz de Sandras et la crise du roman à la fin du grand siècle* (Paris: Presses Universitaires de France, 1980)

Longstaffe-Gowan, T., *The London Square: Gardens in the Midst of Town* (New Haven: Yale University Press, 2012)

Lonsdale, R., *Dr. Charles Burney: A Literary Biography* (Oxford: Clarendon Press, 1965)

Lovejoy, A. O., 'The Meaning of Romanticism for the Historian of Ideas', *Journal of the History of Ideas*, 2 (1941), 257–78

Lysaght, A. M., *Joseph Banks in Newfoundland and Labrador, 1766: His Diary, Manuscripts and Collections* (Berkeley: University of California Press, 1971)

McCleave, S., and B. Caraher, eds, *Thomas Moore and Romantic Inspiration: Poetry, Music and Politics* (New York: Routledge, 2017)

Mackay, L., *Respectability and the London Poor, 1780–1870* (Pickering & Chatto, 2013)

McKellar, E., ed., *Landscapes of London: The City, the Country and the Suburbs, 1660–1840* (New Haven: Yale University Press, 2013)

McKerracher, M. M., *The Jacobite Dictionary* (Glasgow: Neil Wilson, 2007)

MacKillop, R., 'The Guitar, Cittern and Guittar in Scotland: An Historical Introduction up to 1800', in M. Lustig,

ed., *Michaelsteiner Konferenzberichte*, vol. lxvi: *Gitarre und Zister-Bauweise, Spieltechnik und Geschichte bis 1800* (Blankenburg: Stiftung Kloster Michaelstein, 2004), 121–48

McLane, M. M., *Balladeering, Minstrelsy and the Making of British Romantic Poetry* (Cambridge: Cambridge University Press, 2008)

McMordie, M., 'Picturesque Pattern Books and Pre-Victorian Designers', *Architectural History*, 18 (1975), 43–59

McNeil, P., *Pretty Gentlemen: Macaroni Men and the Eighteenth-Century Fashion World* (New Haven and London: Yale University Press, 2018)

McVeigh, S., *Concert Life in London from Mozart to Haydn* (Cambridge: Cambridge University Press, 1993)

——, *The Violinist in London's Concert Life, 1750–1784: Felice Giardini and his Contemporaries* (New York: Garland, 1989)

Maidment, B., *Comedy, Caricature and the Social Order, 1820–50* (Manchester: Manchester University Press, 2013)

——, 'Dinners or Desserts? Miscellaneity, Illustration and the Periodical Press, 1820–1840', *Victorian Periodicals Review*, 43 (2010), 353–87

——, *Into the 1830s: Some Origins of Victorian Illustrated Journalism: Cheap Octavo Magazines of the 1820s and their Influence* (Manchester:

Manchester Polytechnic Library, 1992)

Major, J., and S. Munden, *An Infamous Mistress: The Life, Loves and Family of the Celebrated Grace Dalrymple Elliott* (Barnsley: Pen & Sword, 2016)

Mangado, J. M., 'Fernando Sor (1778–1839), documenti inediti: riflessioni e ipotesi', *Il Fronimo*, 172 (October 2015), 45–54; 173 (January 2016), 18–31; 174 (April 2016), 33–43; 175 (July 2016), 9–24; 176 (October 2016), 34–45

——, *La guitarra en Cataluña, 1769–1939* (Tecla Editions, 1998)

Marks, S. G., *The Information Nexus: Global Capitalism from the Renaissance to the Present* (Cambridge: Cambridge University Press, 2016)

Martin, D., ' The Early Wire-Strung Guitar', *GSJ*, 59 (2006), 123–37, 252–6

Martín Gil, D., 'The Guitarist behind *La guitaromanie*: Charles de Marescot', *Soundboard Scholar*, 4 (2018), 4–16

Medina, Á, 'La guitarra fronteriza de Vargas y Guzmán y su particular notación para el rasgueado', *Hispánica Lyra*, 20 (June 2015), 7–15

Michel, A., and P. Neumann, *Gitarren: 17. bis 19. Jahrhundert. Museum für Musikinstrumente der Universität Leipzig: Katalog* (Leipzig: Museum für Musikinstrumente, Leipzig University, 2016)

Milhous, J., G. Dideriksen and R. D. Hume, *Italian Opera in Late Eighteenth-Century London*, vol. ii: *The Pantheon Opera and its Aftermath, 1789–1795* (Oxford: Clarendon Press, 2001)

Morgan, A., ed., *Ballads and Songs of Peterloo* (Manchester: Manchester University Press, 2018)

Moser, W., 'Fernando Sor: The Life and Works of a Reluctant Guitarist', *Classical Guitar*, 26/3 (2007), 20–24; 26/4 (2007), 20–25

Munns, J., 'Celebrity Status: The Eighteenth-Century Actress as Fashion Icon', in T. Potter, ed., *Women, Popular Culture, and the Eighteenth Century* (Toronto: University of Toronto Press, 2012), 70–91

Myers, A., ed., *Historic Musical Instruments in the Edinburgh University Collection: Catalogue of the Edinburgh University Collection of Historic Musical Instruments*, 9 vols (Edinburgh: Edinburgh University Collection of Historic Musical Instruments, 1997–2007)

Nex, J., 'The Business of Musical-Instrument Making in Early Industrial London', doctoral diss., Goldsmiths, University of London, 2013

O'Brien, J., *Harlequin Britain: Pantomime and Entertainment, 1690–1760* (Baltimore: Johns Hopkins University Press, 2004)

Olcina, E., 'Fernando Sor como demócrata revolucionario: trasfondo político de sus canciones patrióticas', in Gásser, ed., *Estudios sobre Fernando Sor*, 73–80

Oleksijczuk, D. B., *The First Panoramas: Visions of British Imperialism* (Minneapolis: University of Minnesota Press, 2011)

Page, C., 'An Essay of 1824 on the Guitar', *Soundboard*, 38/4 (2012), 53–60, 75

——, 'Being a Guitarist in Late Georgian England', *EM*, 46 (2018), 3–16

——, 'New Light on the London Years of Fernando Sor, 1815–1822', *EM*, 41 (2013), 557–60

——, *The Guitar in Stuart England: A Social and Musical History* (Cambridge: Cambridge University Press, 2017)

——, *The Guitar in Tudor England: A Social and Musical History* (Cambridge: Cambridge University Press, 2015)

——, 'The Spanish Guitar in the Newspapers, Novels, Drama and Verse of Eighteenth-Century England', *RMARC*, 44 (2013), 1–18

——, *Voices and Instruments of the Middle Ages* (Dent, 1987)

Parker, R., '"As a stranger give it welcome": Musical Meanings in 1830s London', in J. S. Walden, ed., *Representation in Western Music* (Cambridge: Cambridge University Press, 2013), 33–46

Penn, G., 'Matteo Bevilacqua (1768–1821):

compositore, chitarrista e poeta', *Il Fronimo*, 180 (October 2017)

Pérez Díaz, P., 'Los tratados de Dionisio Aguado y Fernando Sor como fuentes para la interpretación del repertorio de la guitarra clásico-romantica', in B. Lolo, ed., *Campos Interdisciplinares de la Musicología: Actas del V Congreso de la Sociedad Española de Musicología (Barcelona, 25–28 de octubre de 2000)*, 2 vols (Madrid: Sociedad Española de Musicología, 2001), 683–98

Peruffo, M., 'Italian Violin Strings in the Eighteenth and Nineteenth Centuries: Typologies, Manufacturing Techniques and Principles of Stringing', *Recercare*, 9 (1997), 155–203

——, 'The Mystery of Gut Bass Strings in the Sixteenth and Seventeenth Centuries: The Role of Loaded-Weighted Gut', *Recercare*, 5 (1993), 115–151

Peterson, M. J., 'The Victorian Governess: Status Incongruence in Family and Society', *Victorian Studies*, 14 (1970), 7–26

Pieters, P., *De literatuur voor gitaar met piano gedurende de eerste helft van de negentiende eeuw* (Ghent: Universiteit Gent Faculteit Letteren en Wijsbegeerte, Vakgroep Kunst-, Muziek- en Theaterwetenschappen, 1994)

Pocock, J. G. A., *Virtue, Commerce, and History: Essays on Political Thought and History, Chiefly in the Eighteenth Century* (Cambridge: Cambridge University Press, 1985)

Podmore, C., *The Moravian Church in England, 1728–1760* (Oxford: Clarendon Press, 1998)

Poulopoulos, P., 'A Comparison of Two Surviving Guittars by Zumpe and New Details Concerning the Involvement of Square Piano Makers in the Guittar Trade', *GSJ*, 64 (2011), 49–59

——, '"A complete accompanyment to the female voice": The Guittar and its Role in the Culture of Georgian England', *Phoibos*, 1 (2012), 97–120

——, 'The Guittar in the British Isles, 1750–1810', doctoral diss., University of Edinburgh, 2011

——, 'The Impact of François Chanot's Experimental Violins on the Development of the Earliest Guitar with an Arched Soundboard by Francesco Molino in the 1820s', *EM*, 45 (2018), 67–86

——, 'The Influence of Germans in the Development of "This favourite instrument the guittar" in England', *Soundboard*, 38/4 (2012), 62–75

——, '"Wha sweetly tune the Scottish lyre": A Guitar by Rauche and Hoffmann and its Connection to Robert Burns', *GSJ*, 47 (2014), 40–44, 143–70

Price, C., J. Milhous and R. D. Hume, *Italian Opera in Late Eighteenth-Century London*, vol. i: *The King's Theatre, Haymarket, 1778–1791* (Oxford: Clarendon Press, 1995)

Prothero, I. J., *Artisans and Politics in Early Nineteenth-Century London: John Gast and his Times* (Folkestone: Dawson, 1981)

Quitin, J., *La musique à Liège entre deux révolutions: 1789–1830* (Sprimont: Mardaga, 1997)

Rauch, A., *Useful Knowledge: The Victorians, Morality, and the March of Intellect* (Durham, NC: Duke University Press, 2001)

Renton, A., *Tyrant or Victim: A History of the British Governess* (Weidenfeld & Nicolson, 1991)

Reynolds, N., 'Cottage Industry: The Ladies of Llangollen and the Symbolic Capital of the *Cottage Ornée*', *Eighteenth Century*, 51 (2010), 211–27

Ribouillault-Bibron, D., 'La technique de la guitare en France dans la première moitié du XIXe siècle', doctoral diss., Université de Paris, Sorbonne, 1980

Riley, N., *The Accomplished Lady: A History of Genteel Pursuits, c.1660–1860* (n.p. [West Yorkshire]: Oblong, 2017)

Roberts, C. S., 'Music and Society in Eighteenth-Century Yorkshire', doctoral diss., University of Leeds, 2014

Rohr, D. A., *The Careers of British Musicians, 1750–1850: A Profession of Artisans* (Cambridge: Cambridge University Press, 2001)

Rose, J. A., *The Intellectual Life of the British Working Classes* (New Haven and London: Yale University Press, 2001)

Rosenfeld, S., *The Theatre of the London Fairs in the 18th Century* (Cambridge: Cambridge University Press, 1960)

Saglia, D., *Poetic Castles in Spain: British Romanticism and Figurations of Iberia* (Amsterdam: Rodopi, 2000)

——, 'War Romances, Historical Analogies and Coleridge's Letters on the Spaniards', in P. Shaw, ed., *Romantic Wars: Studies in Culture and Conflict, 1793–1822* (Aldershot: Ashgate, 2000), 138–60

St Clair, W., *The Reading Nation in the Romantic Period* (Cambridge: Cambridge University Press, 2004)

Sanders, A., *In the Olden Time: The Victorians and the British Past* (New Haven and London: Yale University Press, 2013)

Sanders, M., '"A jackass load of poetry": The *Northern Star*'s Poetry Column, 1838–1852', *Victorian Periodicals Review*, 39 (2006), 46–66

——, '"God is our guide! Our cause is just!" The National Chartist Hymn Book and Victorian Hymnody', *Victorian Studies*, 54 (2012), 679–705

Santacara, C., *La Guerra de la Independencia vista por los británicos, 1808–1814* (Madrid: Antonio Machado Libros, 2005)

Savino, R., 'Essential Issues in Performance Practices of the Classical Guitar, 1770–1850', in Coelho, ed., *Performance on Lute, Guitar and Vihuela*, 195–219

Sawyer, P., 'The Popularity of Pantomime on the London Stage, 1720–1760', *Restoration and Eighteenth-Century Theatre Research*, 5 (1990), 1–16

Sebastián, J. F., 'Toleration and Freedom of Expression in the Hispanic World: Between Enlightenment and Liberalism', *Past and Present*, 211 (2011), 159–97

Segerman, E., 'Shelley's Guitar and 19th Century Stringing Practices', *FoMRHI Quarterly*, no. 67 (April 1992), suppl., communication 1096, p. 41

Semmens, R., *Studies in the English Pantomime, 1712–1733* (Hillsdale, NY: Boydell & Brewer, 2017)

Shaw, P., 'Sensual, Solemn, Sober, Slow and Secret: The English View of the Spaniard, 1590–1700', in C. C. Barfoot, ed., *Beyond Pug's Tour: National and Ethnic Stereotyping in Theory and Literary Practice* (Amsterdam, and Atlanta, Ga: Rodopi, 1997), 99–114

Simpson, C. M., ed., *The British Broadside Ballad and its Music* (New Brunswick, NJ: Rutgers University Press, 1966)

Skowroneck, T., *Beethoven the Pianist* (Cambridge: Cambridge University Press, 2010)

Smith, C. S., *Eighteenth-Century Decoration: Design and the Domestic Interior in England* (New York: H. N. Abrams, 1993)

Southey, R., 'Commercial Music-Making in Eighteenth Century North-East England: A Pale Reflection of London?', 2 vols, doctoral diss., University of Newcastle upon Tyne, 2001

Sparks, P., 'The Mandolin in Britain, 1750–1800', *EM*, 46 (2018), 55–66

Sparr, K., 'Barthélemy Trille Labarre: professeur de guitare et compositeur, élève d'Haydn', *Soundboard Scholar*, 4, (2018), 22–4

Spitzer, J., and N. Zaslaw, *The Birth of the Orchestra: History of an Institution* (Oxford: Oxford University Press, 2005)

Spring, M., 'Benjamin Milgrove, the Musical "Toy Man", and the "Guittar" in Bath, 1757–1790', *EM*, 41 (2013), 317–29

——, *The Lute in Britain: A History of the Instrument and its Music* (Oxford: Oxford University Press, 2001)

Staves, S., 'A Few Kind Words for the Fop', *Studies in English Literature*, 22 (1982), 413–28

Stead, G., and M. Stead, *The Exotic Plant: The History of the Moravian Church in Britain* (Peterborough: Epworth Press, 2003)

Stenstadvold, E., 'A Bibliographical Study of Antoine Meissonnier's Periodicals for Voice and Guitar, 1811–27', *Notes*, 2nd ser., 58 (2001), 11–33

——, *An Annotated Bibliography of Guitar Methods, 1760–1860* (Hillsdale, NY: Pendragon Press, 2010)

——, 'Fernando Sor on the Move in the Early 1820s', *Soundboard Scholar*, 1 (2015), 16–25

——, 'Mariano Castro de Gistau (d 1856) and the Vogue for the Spanish Guitar in Nineteenth-Century Britain', *Nineteenth-Century Music Review*, 16 (2017), 1–21

——, 'The Evolution of Guitar Notation, 1750–1830', *Soundboard*, 31/2–3 (2005), 11–29

——, '"The worst drunkard in London": The Life and Career of the Guitar Virtuoso Leonard Schulz', *Soundboard*, 38/4 (2012), 9–16, 52

——, '"We hate the guitar": Prejudice and Polemic in the Music Press in Early 19th-Century Europe', *EM*, 41 (2013), 595–604

Styles, J., *The Dress of the People: Everyday Fashion in Eighteenth-Century England* (New Haven and London: Yale University Press, 2007)

——, 'Lodging at the Old Bailey: Lodgings and their Furnishing in Eighteenth-Century London', in Vickery and Styles, eds, *Gender, Taste and Material Culture*, 61–80

Suárez-Pajares, J., and R. Coldwell, eds, *A. T. Huerta (1800–1874), Life and Works* (San Antonio, TX: DGA Editions, 2006)

Sugimoto, H., 'The Harp-Lute in Britain, 1800–1830: A Study of the Inventor Edward Light and his Instruments', 2 vols, doctoral diss., University of Edinburgh, 2015

Takeuchi, T., 'Rediscovering the Regency Lute: A Checklist of Musical Sources and Extant Instruments', *EM*, 46 (2018), 17–34

Taylor, I., *Music in London and the Myth of Decline: From Haydn to the Philharmonic* (Cambridge: Cambridge University Press, 2010)

Tebbutt, M., *Making Ends Meet: Pawnbroking and Working-Class Credit* (Leicester: Leicester University Press, 1983)

[Thompson, T. P.], 'Gardiner's Music of Nature', *Westminster Review*, 17 (July–October 1832), 345–68

Thorp, J., 'From Scaramouche to Harlequin: Dances "in Grotesque Characters" on the London Stage', in K. Lowerre, ed., *The Lively Arts of the London Stage, 1675–1725* (Farnham: Ashgate, 2014), 13–128

Torta, M., *Catalogo tematico delle opere di Ferdinando Carulli*, 2 vols (Lucca: Libreria Musicale Italiana, 1993)

Trillini, R. H., *The Gaze of the Listener: English Representations of Domestic Music-Making* (Amsterdam: Rodopi, 2008)

Trowell, B., 'Mozart's Fandango', *Music and Letters*, 50 (1969), 427–8

Turnbull, H., *The Guitar from the Renaissance to the Present Day* (Batsford, 1974)

Turner, M. J., 'Radical Opinion in an Age of Reform: Thomas Perronet Thompson and the "Westminster Review"', *History*, 86 (2001), 18–40

Tyler, J., and P. Sparks, *The Guitar and its Music from the Renaissance to the Classical Era* (Oxford: Oxford University Press, 2002)

Valladares, S., *Staging the Peninsular War: English Theatres, 1807–1815* (Abingdon: Routledge, 2015)

Valois, P., 'Les guitaristes français entre 1770 et 1830', doctoral diss., Laval University, Quebec, 2009

Vickery, A., and J. Styles, eds, *Gender, Taste and Material Culture in Britain and North America, 1700–1830* (New Haven and London: Yale University Press, 2006)

Vogt, P., 'Listening to "Festive Stillness": The Sound of Moravian Music according to non-Moravian Visitors', *Moravian Music Journal*, 44 (1999), 15–23

Vries, J. de, *The Industrious Revolution: Consumer Behaviour and the Household Economy, 1650 to the Present* (New York: Cambridge University Press, 2008)

Wade, G., *The Traditions of the Classical Guitar* (Calder, 1980)

Wahrman, D., *Imagining the Middle Class: The Political Representation of Class in Britain, c.1780–1840* (Cambridge: Cambridge University Press, 1995)

Wallace, R., *Beethoven's Critics: Aesthetic Dilemmas and Resolutions during the Composer's Lifetime* (Cambridge: Cambridge University Press, 1986)

Watson, J. R., *Romanticism and War: A Study of British Romantic Period Writers and the Napoleonic Wars* (Basingstoke and New York: Palgrave Macmillan, 2003)

Weber, W., 'La culture musicale d'une capitale: l'époque du beau monde à Londres, 1700–1870', *Revue d'Histoire Moderne et Contemporaine*, 49 (2002–3), 119–39

——, *The Great Transformation of Musical Taste: Concert Programming from Haydn to Brahms* (Cambridge: Cambridge University Press, 2008)

Wedemeier, U., *Gitarre, Zister, Laute* (Hanover: Verlag Ulrich Wedemeier, 2012)

Westbrook, J., 'General Thompson's Enharmonic Guitar', *Soundboard*, 38/4 (2012), 45–52

——, 'Guitar Making in Nineteenth-Century London: Louis Panormo and his Contemporaries', doctoral diss., University of Cambridge, 2013

——, 'Louis Panormo: "The only maker of guitars in the Spanish style"', *EM*, 41 (2013), 571–84

——, *The Century that Shaped the Guitar: From the Birth of the Six-String Guitar to the Death of Tárrega* (Hove: James Westbrook, 2005)

——, and T. Fuller, *The Complete Illustrated Book of the Acoustic Guitar* (Wigston, Leics.: Lorenz Books, 2012)

White, J., *London in the Eighteenth Century: A Great and Monstrous Thing* (Bodley Head, 2012)

Williams, G., *A Dictionary of Sexual Language and Imagery in Shakespearean and Stuart Literature* (Athlone Press, 1994)

Winter, J., *London's Teeming Streets, 1830–1914* (Routledge, 1993)

Young, J. B., 'An Account of Printed Musick', *Fontes Artis Musicae*, 29 (1982), 93–113

Electronic Resources

17th and 18th Century Burney Newspapers Collection, at www.gale.com/intl/c/17th-and-18th-century-burney-newspapers-collection

19th Century UK Periodicals, at www.gale.com/intl/primary-sources/19th-century-uk-periodicals

Boye, G., *Chronological List of Tablatures from the 1700's*, at https://applications.library.appstate.edu/music/lute/C18/1700.html

British Library Newspapers, pt i, at www.gale.com/intl/c/british-library-newspapers-part-i

British Newspaper Archive, at www.britishnewspaperarchive.co.uk

Coldwell, R., *Giulianiad*, at www.digitalguitararchive.com/2012/02/giulianiad-contents

——, *Luigi Sagrini Works*, at www.digitalguitararchive.com/2013/02/sagrini-works

Consortium for Guitar Research at Sidney Sussex College, Cambridge, at https://guitarconsortium.wordpress.com/

Early English Books Online, at https://eebo.chadwyck.com

Eighteenth Century Collections Online, at www.gale.com/intl/primary-sources/eighteenth-century-collections-online

Fellowship of Makers and Restorers of Historical Instruments, Bulletins and Communications, at www.fomrhi.org

Hall, M., *Baroque Guitar Research*, at https://monicahall.co.uk

Jeffery, B., 'Sor, Teaching, and the Enlightenment', at https://tecla.com/fernando-sor/sor-and-the-enlightenment

Kloss, J., *The 'Guittar' in Britain, 1753–1800*, at www.justanothertune.com/html/guittarinbritain.html

Latcham, M., 'Harpsichord-piano', in *Oxford Music Online*, at www.oxfordmusiconline.com

Lexicons of Early Modern English, at http://leme.library.utoronto.ca

Manuscript of Emily Brontë's Gondal Poetry, at www.bl.uk/collection-items/manuscript-of-emily-bronts-gondal-poetry

Old Bailey, *The Proceedings of the Old Bailey: London's Central Criminal Court, 1674 to 1913*, at www.oldbaileyonline.org

Oxford Dictionary of National Biography, at www.oxforddnb.com

Oxford English Dictionary, at www.oed.com

Rasch. R., *Geschiedenis van de muziek in de Republiek der Zeven Verenigde Nederlanden, 1572–1795*, ch. 13: *Het concertwezen*, at www.let.uu.nl/~Rudolf.Rasch/personal/Republiek/Republiek13Concerten.pdf

——, *The Music Publishing House of Estienne Roger and Michel-Charles Le Cène, 1696–1743*, at http://docplayer.net/6666597-The-music-publishing-house-michel-charles-le-cene-1696-1743-of-estienne-roger-and-my-work-on-the-internet-volume-four-rudolf-rasch.html

Sparr, K., '*Journal des troubadours avec accompagnement de guitare ou lyre*, with its Unusual Dating Code and Ferdinando Carulli as Composer and Arranger', at www.tabulatura.com/Journal%20des%20Troubadours2.pdf

The Gipsey Prince, at https://romantic-circles.org/editions/gipsy_prince

The National Archives, at http://discovery.nationalarchives.gov.uk

Verrett, L., *The Early Romantic Guitar*, at www.earlyromanticguitar.com

Walpole, H., *Horace Walpole Correspondence*, at https://walpole.library.yale.edu/collections/digital-resources/horace-walpole-correspondence

Picture Credits

Index

Page numbers in *italic* refer to the illustrations and their captions; **bold** numbers refer to the musical examples.

Index
294

Index

Index